ON THE CAINS

Atlantic Salmon and Sea-Run Brook Trout on the Miramichi's Greatest Tributary

Brad Burns

STACKPOLE
BOOKS
Guilford, Connecticut

Published by Stackpole Books
An imprint of The Rowman & Littlefield Publishing Group, Inc.
4501 Forbes Blvd., Ste. 200
Lanham, MD 20706
www.rowman.com

Distributed by NATIONAL BOOK NETWORK

Maps and illustrations by John Rice

British Library Cataloguing in Publication Information available

Library of Congress Cataloging-in-Publication Data available

ISBN 978-0-8117-3813-2 (cloth : alk. paper)
ISBN 978-0-8117-6815-3 (electronic)

™ The paper used in this publication meets the minimum requirements of American National Standard for Information Sciences—Permanence of Paper for Printed Library Materials, ANSI/NISO Z39.48-1992.

Contents

Guide Jason Curtis poles his angler down the Cains River to fish a new pool on a rainy autumn day. For the past 100 years anglers have come to the Cains River for the chance to hook a big salmon in such a beautiful setting.

Acknowledgments

A heartfelt thank-you to the people whose help made this book possible. If I have forgotten to mention anyone here, I am genuinely very sorry. I received only the most generous and frank information from almost everyone that I approached, and I am truly grateful.

SPECIAL RECOGNITION

Ashley Hallihan, Miramichi Valley High School teacher, and one of his students, Alex Leslie, for the drone photographs of the Cains Rivers's pools and lodges.

Byron Coughlin of Country Haven Outfitters, Gray Rapids, New Brunswick, who knows everyone in New Brunswick, for his help in every possible way.

Charles B. Wood of Cambridge, Massachusetts, for providing a physical copy of one of the rarest of all privately printed books about the Cains River.

David Gaudet of Service New Brunswick in Moncton, New Brunswick, for the use of the province's software that allowed me to look up the Crown grants, deeds, and other public records that were important to this book.

Dr. Arne Youngberg of Cheshire, Connecticut, whose history of the Admiral Pool was very valuable.

Drs. David and Richard Wade, and Astrid Wade, David's wife, of Fredericton, New Brunswick, for the use of their family photos and memories of their father and grandfather, Herb and Charlie Wade, respectively, of Wade's Fishing Lodge.

Duane Mercer of Energy and Resource Development Fredericton, New Brunswick, who provided much of my information and historical documents on Cains River leases and mapping.

Emery Brophy of Blackville, New Brunswick, who provided a lot of information on all aspects of the Cains River.

Gary Colford of Blackville, New Brunswick, whose family, like Emery's, has been on the Cains since the beginning. A book or two could be written about what Gary and Emery know and have forgotten about Miramichi and Cains River salmon fishing.

Howard Moore of Fredericton, New Brunswick, who owned the famous Hopewell Lodge on the upper Cains for more than 30 years. He provided me with fascinating information about the old lodge and some of the people connected to it.

Jason Curtis and Darrell Warren of Blackville, New Brunswick, both guides at Campbell's and Keenan's. Prior to its disbanding, Jason had been the manager of Wade's Fishing Lodge. Both men helped greatly by calling for my benefit on their great local knowledge of the area and people of the Miramichi Valley, where they have lived their whole lives.

Jerry Doak of W. W. Doak, Doaktown, New Brunswick, for valuable information about the history and development of various Cains River flies, especially the Bomber and the Whiskers.

Keith Wilson of Wilsons Sporting Camps in McNamee, New Brunswick, for information on his family's long history on the Cains River as well as piloting me to the North Branch and taking me through the woods to the Duffy cabin.

Mark Hambrook, President of the Miramichi Salmon Association South Esk, New Brunswick, for his review of the Cains River salmon biology and other important information.

Morris Green of the Miramichi Salmon Museum in Doaktown, New Brunswick, who is a terrific, historical resource on the Miramichi and Cains Rivers and generously helped me procure many of the photos of Hopewell Lodge.

Nathan Wilbur of the Atlantic Salmon Federation Fredericton, New Brunswick, for various information and especially his summer spent examining the thermal buffering of the Cains River headwaters area.

Patrick and Deborah Ayres of Seiad Valley, California, who hosted me in their home and helped me to photograph the original Camp Stanton logbooks.

Ralph Vitale of Boxford, Massachusetts, who photographed all the flies for this book.

Rip Cunningham of Dover, Massachusetts, for so much information about the history of the Black Brook Salmon Club, Six Mile Brook camp, and the fishing on the club's waters.

Rolf and Judy Hofer of Pottstown, Pennsylvania, Carol Houser of Lehighton, Pennsylvania, and Lester Vickers of Blackville, New Brunswick, for their photographs and information on the Popples Camp and Herman Campbell's outfitting business.

Sarah Foster and James Woods of the American Museum of Fly Fishing in Manchester, Vermont, for providing digital copies of information and images on Cains River salmon fishing.

Tim Humes of Miramichi, New Brunswick, and Robert Doyle of Little Bartibog, New Brunswick, both officers of Canoe Kayak New Brunswick, for their information on the ancient aboriginal portage routes of the province.

Wayne Curtis of Blackville, New Brunswick, for sharing with me information and contacts that he has gained through a lifetime of living beside the Miramichi River.

William Utley of Harpswell, Maine, who gathered all the recipes and tied all the flies for the book.

FOR IMPORTANT CONTRIBUTIONS

Alex Mills of Halifax, NS
Al Gallagher Worcester, MA
Angus Curtis of Blackville, NB
Barrie Duffield of Fredericton, NB
Bill Hooper of Doaktown, NB
Cappi Thompson of SmugMug Mountain View, CA
Christine Lovelace of The University of New Brunswick, Fredericton, NB
Copley Fine Art Auctions LLC of Boston, MA, for the digital files of Ogden Pleissner's paintings of Camp Stanton and the Mouth of Sabbies River
Darrell Tucker Blackville, NB
Dawson Hovey of Fredericton, NB
Ernest Long of Wilsons Sporting Camps in McNamee, NB
Karl Wilson of Wilsons Sporting Camps in McNamee, NB
Harvey Wheeler of Cumberland, ME
James Marriner of Moncton, NB
Jason Burns my brother from Brunswick, ME for being my behind-the-scenes technology department
Jim Corrigan of Blackville, NB
John Cunningham of Boston, MA
Kevin Sabean of Fredericton, MA
Kris LeBlanc of Moncton, NB
Marc Poirier of Moncton, NB
Michael O'Donnell of Nelson Hollow, NB
Richard Seder of Worcester, MA
Sandra Ferris of Penniac, NB
The Black Brook Salmon Club members Blackville, NB
Tom McCaffrey, David Bent, and Joshua Green of the Provincial Archives in Fredericton, NB
Topher Browne of Pownal, ME
Vince Swazey of Boiestown, NB
Wesley Curtis of Blackville, NB
William "Willy" Bacso, late of Blackville, NB, whose stories about the Cains and introductions to its fishing helped create my interest in the river
Winston Curtis of Blackville, NB

Introduction

Some folks have wondered why I would write a book that features the Cains River, especially when it is simply a tributary of the world-famous New Brunswick Atlantic salmon river, the Miramichi. The answer is because the history of fishing on the Cains River and the Miramichi are inseparable, and the unique contributions and attributes of the Cains deserve their own opportunity to be recognized.

As Atlantic salmon rivers go, the Cains River is of medium size. It is the single largest tributary of the Southwest Miramichi system and almost identical in drainage area to the also important Renous and Dungarvon River complex. All these rivers and their various tributaries join the Southwest Miramichi in the village of Quarryville to form the great tidal pool that is said to have produced over 100 rod-caught salmon in a single day. The Cains River taken by itself is a far-above-average salmon river regarding both the number and the unusual size of the Atlantic salmon and brook trout that it produces. The fall-run, highly rain-dependent nature and relative remoteness of the Cains River can make it difficult for anglers to experience its best fishing—and this is in a sport that is famous for unpredictable results. However, the enticing potential rewards of really large Atlantic salmon and sea-run brookies, coming from a moderately sized and highly wadable river, which is contained in what is still essentially a wilderness area, makes the Cains River an unusually compelling fishing destination. For the anglers I know who have fished the Cains over the years, the attraction the river has for them is magnetic. From a lifetime of angling, the memories they have of fishing the fall salmon run against an unspoiled backdrop of dark green spruce and colorful hardwoods, or seeing 20-inch-plus brookies sipping the emerging insects from a headwaters pool in June, are among their most cherished. And for more than a few, these are memories that they shared with their fathers and even their grandfathers, who were also drawn to this place and fished with previous generations of men from the same families that are still guiding on the Cains River today.

For many years, the Survey Branch of the Department of Natural Resources in Fredericton, New Brunswick, produced a series of fishing guides. I have one for the Southwest Miramichi and another for the Cains River that were sold in 1969 for $1.00 each. The large-format booklet shows the full length of the Cains River divided into five map sections or plans. It separates the river into public and private fishing stretches and shows the names of many of the recognized fishing pools. In the back of the book is a page titled "Angling Statistics—N. B. Atlantic Salmon Rivers." I've reproduced that page here as an illustration, and it reveals some very interesting information about the New Brunswick salmon rivers for the years of 1967 and 1968. Bill Hooper, a retired salmon biologist for the Department of Fisheries and Oceans, said that 1967 was the last great run on the Miramichi. He felt that the total run that year of salmon and grilse was well over 500,000 fish, approximately five times the best numbers that we've experienced in my 15 recent years on the river.

In 1967, the rod catch on the Southwest Miramichi was calculated to be 34,280 bright salmon and grilse—as opposed to kelts from the spring fishery. To show the variability that exists in salmon fishing, the next year, it was only 11,536 fish. By comparison, in 1967, the mighty Restigouche, known for a run with a much higher percentage of really large salmon, had estimated landings of 1,619 bright fish. The Northwest Miramichi had 2,325, the Little Southwest Miramichi 3,675, the Renous and Dungarvon combined had 1,009, and the Cains had *6,480*! The Cains produced a rod catch four times as large as the Restigouche and roughly equal to all the other branches of the Miramichi—except the Southwest—combined. A rod catch of 6,480 is just an incredible number and stands as indisputable testimony to the fecundity of the river.

The next year, in 1968, which the guide calls a bad year—and it certainly was for the Cains—the Main Southwest had 11,356, the Little Southwest was up to 4,282, the Northwest dropped to 1,168, the Renous had 1,942, but the Cains had only 284! How did that happen? Remember, in both these good and bad years, we are talking about the rod catch and not the total size of the run. Deeper in this book, we will explain the fall-run tendency of the Cains River and how vital it is for the rod catch that a sufficient volume of water be present before the fishing season closes. We'll also look back on the comparative conditions for the fishing seasons of 1967 and 1968.

Beyond its fish-producing powers, there are other attractions to the Cains that lure fishermen. The greatest of these attractions is that, even compared to the relatively rural makeup of the Miramichi Valley, the Cains provides fishermen with a real feeling of wilderness. I hear the reverence in the voices of the local men when they speak of the Cains. "Where'd you get your moose, Johnny?" "Shot him at the end of that big woods road that goes nor'east on the way to Shinnickburn, over on Cains River." To those who know it, the words "Cains River" do not simply mean a river; they mean a piece of old New Brunswick, an area still largely untouched, where one can find beauty, quiet, and relative solitude.

In the 1905 *Bulletin of the Natural History Society of New Brunswick*, number 22 volume 5, part 2, University of New Brunswick professor and naturalist Joseph Whitman Bailey said that there were then three great wilderness areas left in New Brunswick: the Great New Brunswick Wilderness, running to the north of the Miramichi that extended off into Quebec, was the largest; the smaller of the three, called the Head of Canaan River, lies well to the southeast of the Miramichi; and sandwiched in between them is the second largest, called the Cains River Wilderness.

In 1905, the 1,500-square-mile Cains River Wilderness area reached to within two miles of the City of Fredericton. Bailey said that to achieve this wilderness designation the regions must have no railways, no roads—other than those used by lumbermen—and no permanent human habitations. Even today, most of the Cains River area still qualifies. Throughout its 70-odd miles of flowing river and an additional 15 miles of boggy headwaters, there is still no year-round human inhabitant. The 1905 map of the area showed the exclusion of a small tongue of land that started at the mouth of the Cains, ran narrowly along the river, and extended for barely a couple of miles beyond Muzzeroll Brook. It appears that the old Arbeau farm near the point of the Indian portage to the Gaspereau and Saint John—about 25 miles upriver from the mouth—was as far upriver as any

ANGLING STATISTICS - N. B. ATLANTIC SALMON RIVERS

These angling statistics have been prepared to better acquaint you with world famous New Brunswick salmon angling. Much of this information has been made available through CONSCIENTIOUS ANGLERS who submitted their angling reports on the reverse side of their fishing licences. You too can provide a valuable service to salmon conservation by reporting accurately your angling success on your licence's SALMON KILL RECORD. Your information provides a fundamental need in salmon management and research to determine Atlantic salmon catches and angler success. YOUR COOPERATION MEANS ATLANTIC SALMON CONSERVATION!

New Brunswick Atlantic Salmon Rivers	Popularity of the River: (Percent of Total Salmon Angling Trips Made)	1967-A Good Catch Year		1968-A Poor Catch Year*		Peak Angling Periods	
		Black Salmon	Bright Salmon	Black Salmon	Bright Salmon	Black Salmon	Bright Salmon
1. Southwest Miramichi	52%	10,422	34,280	9,228	11,356	April 15-May 7	July 5-August 7 September 8-September 30
2. Little Southwest Miramichi	8%	2,520	3,675	738	4,282	April 15-May 7	July 1-August 15 September 1-September 15
3. Restigouche	7%	0	1,619	0	1,025	No Angling	June 5-July 31
4. Cains	6%	480	6,480	660	284	April 15-May 7	September 20-October 15
5. Northwest Miramichi	6%	1,500	2,325	465	1,168	April 15-May 7	September 8-September 30
6. Big Salmon	6%	0	999	0	541	No Angling	July 1-October 15
7. Renous-Dungarvon	4%	617	1,009	340	1,942	April 15-May 7	July 1-July 31 Sept 15-Oct 15 (Renous only) Sept 5-Sept 15 (Dungarvon only)
8. Petitcodiac	2%	460	738	231	4	April 15-May 7	September 15-October 15
9. Nashwaak	2%	117	115	0	248	April 15-May 7	July 7-July 31 September 15-October 15
10. Alma	1%	0	211	0	363	No Angling	July 15-Sept 15
Other Salmon Rivers	6%						

* Very Low Water Conditions

This illustration from the fishing guide produced by the New Brunswick Department of Natural Resources reveals some amazing statistics for the 1967 and 1968 salmon catches in various New Brunswick rivers, including the Cains. Note the difference in catches between these famous rivers during each year depending on water conditions, as further explained in the text. The Cains can be not only the most productive Miramichi tributary, but by itself, it can produce more salmon than any of the famous Gaspe salmon rivers.

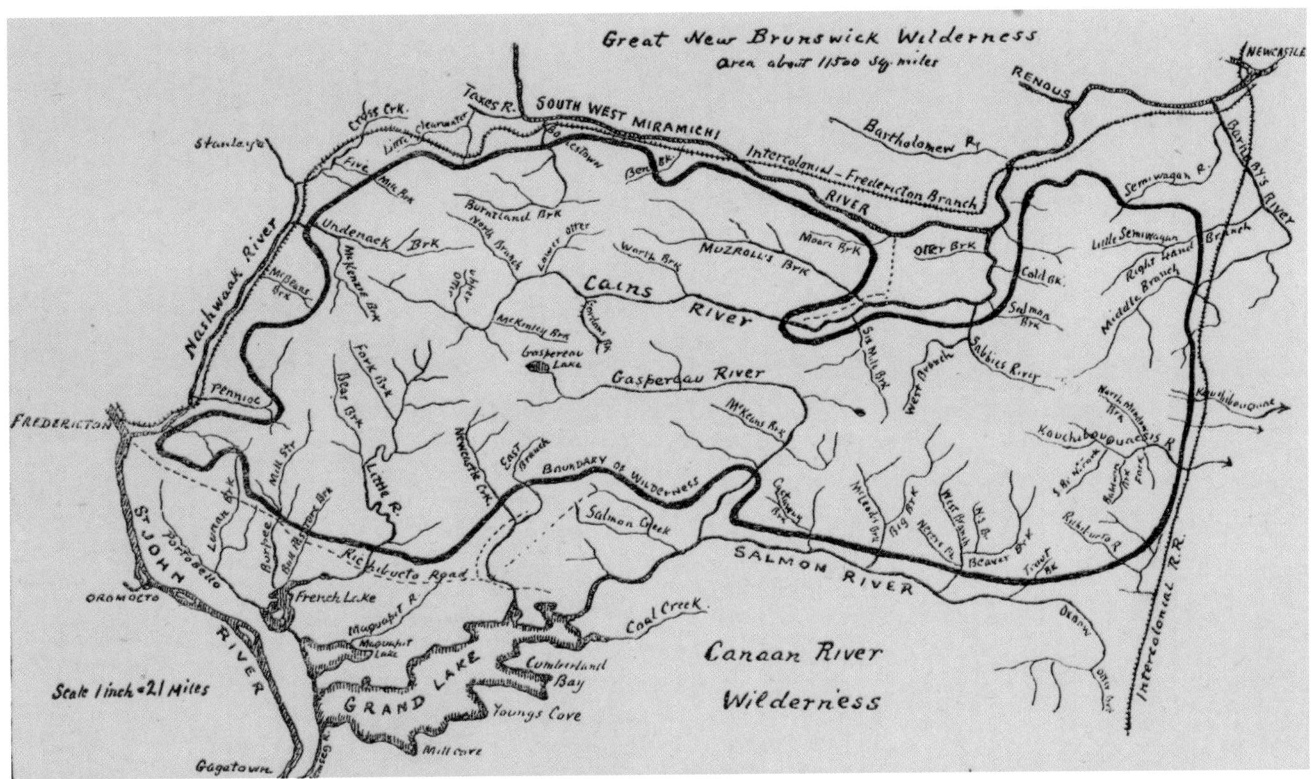

Cains River Wilderness Map 1905. In 1905, the Cains River area was designated as one of three areas within the Province of New Brunswick that met the fairly rigorous standard necessary to be labeled as wilderness. In 2019, very little has changed, and in some ways, the Cains today is even less settled—it does not have a single year-round inhabitant—than it was 115 years ago.

settlement ever got. Even that sliver of settlement is all gone now. Today, there is one railroad line that cuts across the headwaters through the Bantalor Wildlife Management Area, but there is no train stop; it is more or less just a 40-mile straight shot through the wilderness to get from McGivney to Chipman.

Even when Bailey's wilderness map was drawn, over a hundred years ago, almost all the old farms had fallen into disrepair and been abandoned. No one lives year-round in the Cains River valley anywhere, and in reality, the period when people endeavored to populate the Cains lasted not much more than 50 years. At a time of relative prosperity, when New Brunswick was being settled and roads and railroads built, the Cains was returning to the wild. The only Cains River town that ever existed was Shinnickburn with its one-room schoolhouse. The village was never serviced by electricity, had a maximum population of approximately 100 people, and was originally called the Horse Shoe Settlement, probably after the shape of the river in the vicinity of the town. The town was said to be named after the first postmaster, William Shinnick, who lived in the town from 1879–1907, and was doubtless descended from the original Crown grant Shinnick family. A burn is a name for a small stream in Ireland or Scotland, and my guess is that the town was named after a brook or stream that flowed through William Shinnick's property.

The government officially closed the town in the 1970s. According to Emery Brophy, whose family settled on the Cains in 1842, the last year-round resident was either Douglas Cashen or Horace Kervin. Cashen lived just a little downriver from where the Shinnickburn Road came across from

This photograph, probably from the 1940s, is of a man with salmon kelt taken on the Cains River at Shinnickburn. The old schoolhouse, visible across the river with an upstairs apartment for the teacher, is now gone, but the Schoolhouse Pool is still there and still produces salmon.

Great New
Charlie Wade
Harry Allen
Miramichi Uplands
George Allen
John Brophy
S.W. Miramichi
Southwest Miram
Town of Doaktown
Town of Boiestown
Taxis R.
Burntland Brook
Muzzeroll Brook
Muzzeroll Lake
Leighton Brk.
Wildcat Brk.
C.N. Railroad
Avery Portage
Lower Otter Brook
Crown Reserve
Cains
Mile 52
Pools
North Branch Cains R.
Duffy's Camp
Gordon Brook
Otter Brook
Caribou Barrens
Saint John River Via Nashwaak River
McKinley Brook
Mile 61
Bantalor Brook
Young's Brook
The Meadows
Bantalor Game Reserve
Landers
Railway Chipman
Zionville Portage
Cains R.

UNSWICK WILDERNESS
To: Miramichi Bay
Bartholomew R.
Town of Blackville
Wade's Fishing Lodge
Black Brook Salmon Club
Black Brook
To Barnaby River
Admiral Pool
Brophy Pool
Campbell's
The Popples
Layton's Pt.
Cold Brk.
Otter Brk.
Shinnickburn Rd.
Camp Stanton
Mile 8.7
Salmon Brk.
River
Cashens Cabins
hire of Blissfield
Sabbies R.
Oxbow Pool
Northumbrland Shore Drainage
Moore's Pool
Muzzeroll Brook
Bill Boyd Camp
Six Mile Camp
Mile 19
Arbeau Farm Pool
Stone Chimney Pool ?
Six Mile Brook
Deep Woods Camp
ke Rd. 123
Seabury Stanton
Elkins Pool ?
Meadow Brook
Wendell Allen
er
Ancient Indian Portage
To Saint John River via Gasperaux & Salmon Rivers
To: Grand Lake
N
NW
NE
W
E
SW
SE
S
To Chipman
Gasperaux River
Bay of Fundy Drainage
CAINS River
New Brunswick
Watershed
0 miles
5 miles
10 miles
15 miles
J. Rice

This January 2018 picture of the Shinnickburn Road was taken near Moore's Pool as it runs along the Cains River by camp owner Marc Poirier from Moncton. Marc had come in the eight miles or so from Route 8, the nearest plowed road, on an ATV with tracks to check out his camp. The Shinnickburn road and many like it are no longer maintained in any way by the Province of New Brunswick. They depend on a patchwork of repairs by property owners along the route and, in a larger sense, on timber harvesters who need to keep them fit enough to bring heavy equipment in and logs out. The Cains River had broken free during a warm spell a short while before Marc's visit, and the river had shoved huge ice cakes several feet thick up against and on top of the roadbed. There, the whole mess had frozen solid again and received more snow. PHOTO COURTESY MARC POIRIER.

Upper Blackville and reached the Cains River, and Horace lived with his brother Everett—whom he survived—in a small house beside the mouth of the Cains River's largest tributary, Muzzeroll Brook. By the early 2000s, everyone was gone, and the village of Shinnickburn was just a handful of old camps and memories.

In researching and writing this book, I could not find a map that showed the entire Cains River watershed and the names of various places along the river in any detail. The closest that I could come was a document supplied to me by the University of New Brunswick created in 1910 by William Francis Ganong titled "Map of Cains River and adjacent waters to illustrate their physiographic relations."

Using the physical map details supplied by Geo New Brunswick, artist John Rice created the illustrated map that you will find on pages ix and x. The illustrations include people central to the history and development of the Cains River fishing during its most formative years in the first half of the twentieth century, and it also shows some of the more iconic wildlife species: black bear, ruffed grouse, now-extinct woodland caribou, Atlantic salmon, brook trout, and the constant companion of man in the Cains River wilderness, the Canada jay, or "whiskey jack." The map also has an illustration of indigenous people spearing salmon from a birchbark canoe.

The text of the map shows the locations of many of the important places along the river that will be mentioned in the text of the book. The readers can enjoy looking up these locations as they come to them in the text and then finding these locations on the map. In many cases, it will help the reader understand the relevance that the physical location of a particular place has to that of other areas on the map and how that warrants its place in the history of the Cains River.

Up- or downriver from Shinnickburn there is either nothing or an occasional fishing camp—mostly nothing—as there are only about three dozen structures along the river's 60-mile-plus course, and in many sections, there are miles between them. Nothing is left to be seen of the couple of dozen farms and barns that once stood among cleared fields along the river, and the fields themselves, once cut from the forest by hand, have gone back to woods. From November until well into May, most of the Cains River is unreachable other than by driving up the frozen river by snowmobile.

The remoteness of the Cains even today is highlighted by the fact that during the late 1980s the Cains was one of the three candidate sites for a "Low-Level Air Defense Training Area," otherwise known as a bombing range. According to retired New Brunswick judge and lifelong sportsman Jim Marriner, the New Brunswick Wildlife Federation was very active in rallying public support against the idea of bombing the Cains. In an Environmental Impact Assessment dated May 15, 1990, it was stated that there would be some mortality on salmon and trout eggs since the training exercises would coincide with spawning activity. In the end, the Cains was dropped as a candidate site, and finally, the Canadian Forces Base in Chatham was closed entirely by the federal government; thankfully, this made the suitability of the Cains River watershed as a bombing range a moot point.

Guide Jason Curtis with a Cains River hookbill and angler Bill Utley with a big hen salmon. The hen came from the deep Mahoney Pool, while the cockfish was waiting beside a boulder in the narrow run in front of the camp.

Even though the attempts at settling the river eventually failed, there is a silver lining. Except for a very few sporting camps located on the handful of original Crown grants, the river is completely owned by the government, and well over 95 percent is public fishing water. There have been a handful of Crown leases made for the purpose of building camps, but even on these, a substantial setback from the river is required, and the public has complete access to the shoreland and fishing.

In my research for this book, I found many photographs of fishing and canoe travel along the Cains dating from the very early 1900s. When one passes down the Cains today, the views are essentially the same as then. There aren't many reasonably accessible places left today about which that can be said.

The author holds a large hen salmon caught in late September 2019 at Campbell's Pool on the Southwest Miramichi, two miles below the mouth of the Cains River. There are lots of eggs in this beauty. Will she bear right at Black Brook and continue up the Miramichi toward Juniper, or will she turn off to the left into the Cains, perhaps destined for the famous spawning grounds upstream of Grand Lake Road? PHOTO COURTESY OF DARRELL WARREN.

CHAPTER 1

The Source of the Cains River

In early May 2018, the photographer Alex Leslie, fishing outfitter Keith Wilson, and the author stood on the south bank of the Cains River a few yards upriver from its junction with the North Branch. At this point, we were approximately 53 miles up the Cains River from where it flows into the Miramichi. One could never get this far upriver under power except in the high flows of the spring freshet. Above and below here lies a marvelous, vast network of brooks and streams that, along with the main stem of the Cains itself, provides incredible spawning and nursery habitat for Atlantic Salmon and sea-run Brook Trout.

I've always been intrigued by the idea of the source or physical beginning of a river, the place far back in the upland where a mighty river first collects enough seeps and rivulets to be worthy of its name. In *Highland River*, Neil Gunn, a Scottish author, writing about his own life through a character named Kenn, walked for miles up his native Dunbeath River, past the private salmon waters of the estate near where he lived as a boy, and watched the river grow smaller as he went upstream. He continued up into the hill country and, eventually, came to a place where the small burn that the river had become actually flowed right out of the ground. Was this, though, the source? He walked farther up the hill and found where the stream again flowed along the surface, and then came again from out of the ground. This repeated itself several times, with each iteration of the stream being somewhat smaller, until finally, a short way from the top of the hill, from a little pocket in the rocky ground, the stream barely oozed to the surface even though the longest stick Kenn could find would not touch the bottom of the inky black hole from which the water emerged. No trace of the stream could be found above that point on the hill.

The Cains has captured the imagination of anglers from far and near for well over 100 years. Standing here on this spring day, my mind's eye can instantly travel back to the dawn of the twentieth century and see the Chestnut canoes of Harry Allen's outfitting business, loaded with provisions and wealthy sports gliding down the river in front of me. Strong, confident, young guides are poling the boats, anticipating encounters with big salmon or brook trout and perhaps the glimpse of a moose, caribou, or black bear. This book is the story of the Cains River: its fish, fishing pools, camps and lodges, and the men who spent their lives guiding and outfitting on its waters.

Nathan Wilbur works his canoe over a beaver dam in the Meadows stretch of the Cains River headwaters. Early explorers remarked about how these industrious animals created dams completely across many sections of the headwaters of all New Brunswick rivers, including the Cains, and it is still so today. In fact, with the decrease in fur values during modern times, there is far less trapping activity, and the number of beavers has increased dramatically from the early parts of the twentieth century. This is of mixed consequences for fish. Beaver dams can block salmon from accessing upriver spawning habitat in low-water years, and beaver dams can slow the flow of a stream, creating ponds that warm up during sunny summer weather. On the other hand, these impoundments are a desirable habitat for insects and juvenile fish during low-water periods. PHOTO COURTESY OF NATHAN WILBUR.

It is unlikely that I will ever stand on the ground exactly where the Cains begins, and perhaps it isn't even possible to say with any certainty exactly where that spot is. The far western reaches of the Cains River headwaters end only about five miles due west of the tiny community of Nashwaak Bridge where Route 8 moves away from the Nashwaak and heads across an ancient Indian portage route to Boiestown and the Miramichi—now Route 8. Using the Geo New Brunswick aerial photography software, we can see that in the headwaters area south of Boiestown the Cains River is fed by the North Branch, and that the branch to the south simply retains the name Cains River. This south branch, named the Cains River, flows from a network of brooks that drain a sizeable area of boggy land called "The Meadows" located at the western end of the Bantalor Game Refuge. In the late summer of 1910, W. F. Ganong, perhaps New Brunswick's most famous scientist and wanderer, together with his assistant, came through a short portage from Zionville to the Meadows and launched their canoe into the Cains. In good water, the river can be canoed from this point down to the mouth, though beavers have frequent dams in this area that stretch completely across the small river. Anyone venturing down this stretch of the Cains will need to get out from time to time and haul their boat over the tops of these beaver dams.

Using Geo New Brunswick's aerial and topo maps, I have traced the Cains River west from what appears to me to be the last point where it is distinctly visible as a defined stream. Tracing back to the west from that position for about five miles, an unnamed tributary stream flows toward our last known point on the Cains. This stream twists and turns through boggy ground running southeast from its indistinct origin separated by a distance of approximately 1,800 feet from the beginnings of an

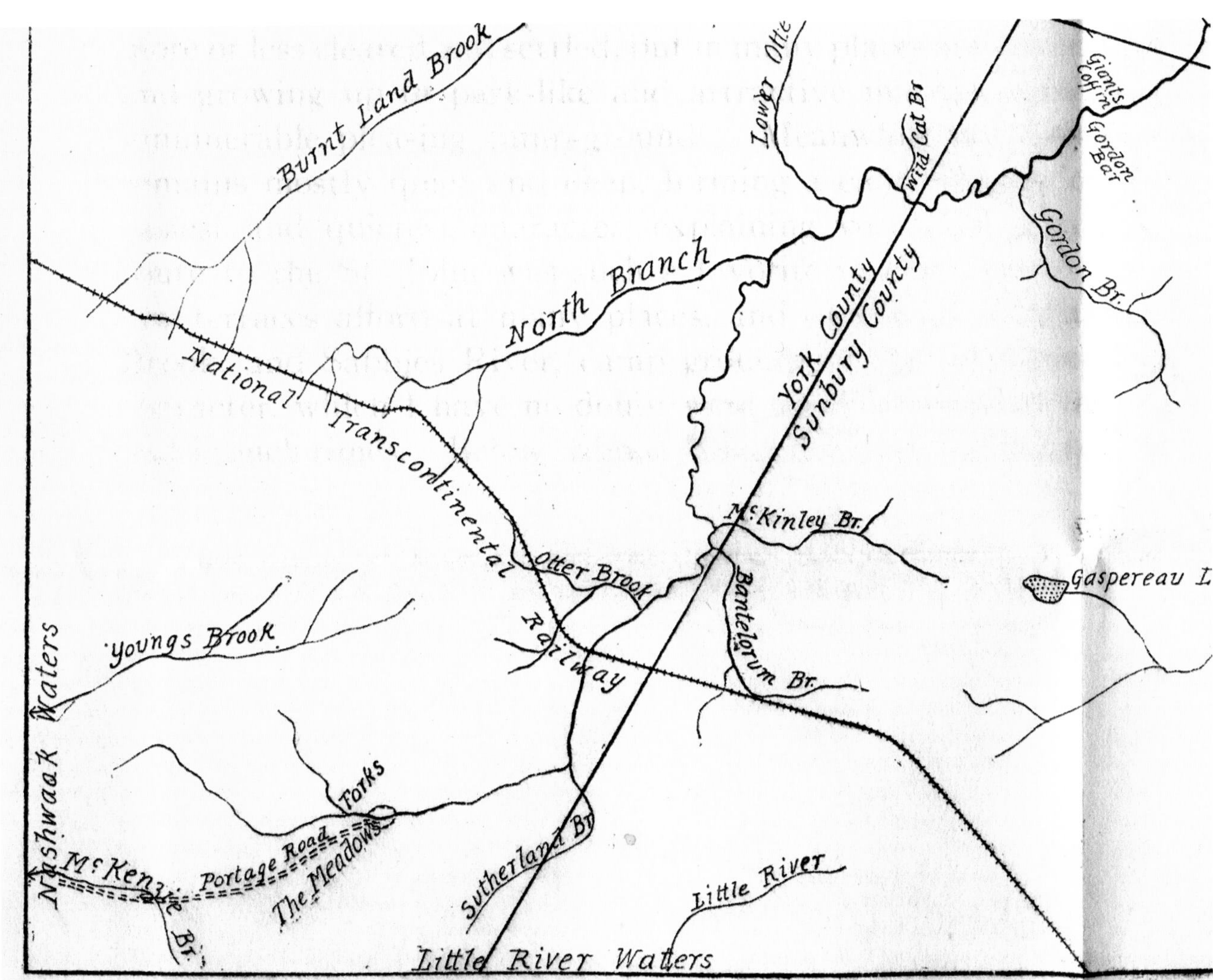

W. F. Ganong's map from 1910, cropped to show the Cains River headwaters and their proximity to the tributaries of the Nashwaak River and, thus, the Saint John River. As explained in the text of this chapter, the vast networks of brooks and streams that are the beginnings of all the rivers of New Brunswick interlock with each other in many locations. The exact point at which an area of ground changes the direction of its drainage from one watershed to another can be very indistinct, even though the final destination of each respective flow to the sea can be more than 100 miles apart. GANONG'S MAP SUPPLIED COURTESY OF THE UNIVERSITY OF NEW BRUNSWICK.

equally small tributary of Young's Brook that runs in the opposite direction. From the point where the two streams emerge and flow in opposite directions, it is about nine more miles to the west before Young's Brook empties into the Nashawaak River—a tributary of the mighty Saint John River. Within that 1,800-foot-wide no-man's-bog, it is a toss-up as to whether the ground belongs to the Saint John watershed or that of the Cains River and, therefore, the Miramichi.

Other nearby tributaries of the Cains are interlaced with still more brooks and bogs that feed instead into the Little and Gaspereau Rivers. These two rivers flow off in somewhat different directions, but eventually, they both turn south, emptying into Grand Lake, and via the Jemseg on into the Saint John River, eventually reaching the Bay of Fundy. The Cains, on the other hand, flows northeast, merges with the Miramichi, and ends up entering the Atlantic on New Brunswick's Northumberland Shore, more or less parallel with the northern tip of Prince Edward Island. Thus, raindrops falling within feet or even mere inches of each other eventually end up in the ocean on opposite sides of the province some 140 miles apart as the crow flies—approximately 690 miles by water, even using the Canso Canal shortcut to eliminate the log route out around Cape Breton.

The North Branch of the Cains doesn't make it quite as far west as the South Branch and begins its journey from a point about six miles north-northeast of the Cains River's source described in the last paragraph and eight miles from the town of McGivney located due north on Route 8. The North Branch's tentacles intermingle with those of West Burntland Brook, a branch that, eventually, becomes the lively Burntland Brook that fisherman headed for the Miramichi drive across when on Route 8 in Boiestown. Burntland Brook is often our first hint of what conditions will be like on the Miramichi, because if it is full, you will likely encounter rising water and, hopefully, a good run of fish on their way into the river.

The relatively flat, boggy, headwaters area, home of this labyrinth of brooks and bogs that the North Branch of the Cains River, as well as the Cains River itself, drains, is perhaps 15 miles in diameter—176 square miles, or 112,000 acres. To put this in perspective, the area is small compared to a river such as the Miramichi or the Restigouche, but it is by no means insignificant. By Scottish standards, 112,000 acres would be a very large estate, and the Cains headwaters can easily match those from some of Scotland's best-known salmon rivers. The Cains River is not just the Miramichi's largest tributary, it is a major salmon river in its own right. All told, the journey—not accounting for the myriad twists and turns along the way—is approximately 70 miles from the farthest point of the headwaters to where the Cains River enters the Miramichi at the great Black Brook salmon pool.

The condition of the water that slowly gathers in this large network of bogs and relatively flat headwaters landmass before draining into the Cains has a couple of notable effects on the river's fishing. First, it is the process of water steeping in the boggy ground that gives this river its signature tannic waters. After a summer of low water, the rains of fall can flush this potent tea from the grounds of the headwaters, and the river flows almost black. A yard-long salmon can hardly be seen to be netted until it breaks the surface at your feet. Also, the relative insulation of such ground causes the headwaters to run cooler than the shallow summer riffles downstream that are constantly exposed to warm summer air and hot sunlight. This cool, clean, brook water has long made the Cains a summertime favorite of brook trout, including some of the large Labrador proportions that spend a good part of their lives feeding in the Miramichi's bountiful estuary.

CAINS RIVER PHYSIOGRAPHY

The Cains River was first noted on a recognized map by De Meulles-Franquelin in 1686. It was referred to then as Ouelamouki River, which is phonetically the same as Welamook, the spelling of the Mi'kmaq name for the river. The

The clear water of Weasel Brook flows from a rocky hillside into the Cains River just a few miles above its mouth, and it contrasts dramatically with the tannic flow emanating from the boggy ground of the river's headwaters.

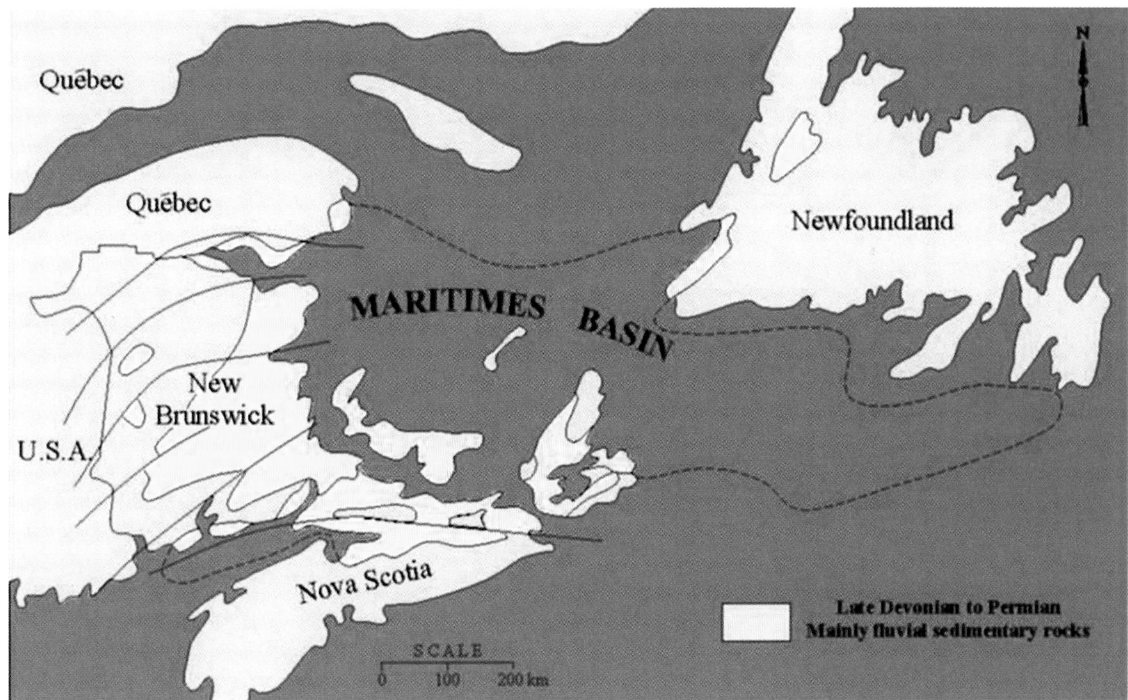

This map by the Canadian government depicts the Carboniferous Basin of Eastern Canada. Rivers within the basin are characterized by sandstone bases. While the sandstone is not nearly as tough as granite, many of the Cains River pools have areas of ledged sides and bottoms and, thus, are very stable in the short run of a human lifetime.

Cains is the longest New Brunswick river to lie completely within the Maritime Carboniferous Basin, a relatively low, gentle, easterly sloping area of largely sandstone rock base that is sandwiched between the Central Highlands to the north and the Caledonia Uplift or Terrace to the south.

The average headwaters elevation is approximately 460 feet, and it drops to about 40 feet at the mouth 60 miles away. This is an average drop of seven feet per mile over the entire distance. This will allow for good time to be made in a canoe heading downriver, but it would still be possible to paddle upstream against it as the Indians did when going places. The pitch, though, is only marginally uniform, and there are many places where the flow is quite lively, and other long, placid sections where the pace is so slack that a small outboard motor is a godsend—even if you are going downstream. Very few places in the whole river really warrant the term "rapids," and then only where there is an elevated height of water. Hell's Gate, less than a mile or so from where the Cains meets the Miramichi, is known as the strongest flow on the river, and except in times of unusually heavy rains or the spring freshet, it is no big deal and easily navigable by an experienced canoeist.

According to Ganong, who, in addition to all of his other various scientific accomplishments, was an expert on the derivation of the names of New Brunswick places, the Mi'kmaq Indians in 1908 were still calling the Cains by the name of Welamook. Rand's Mi'kmaq-English Dictionary translates Welamook to "handsome" or "beautiful" river. It was

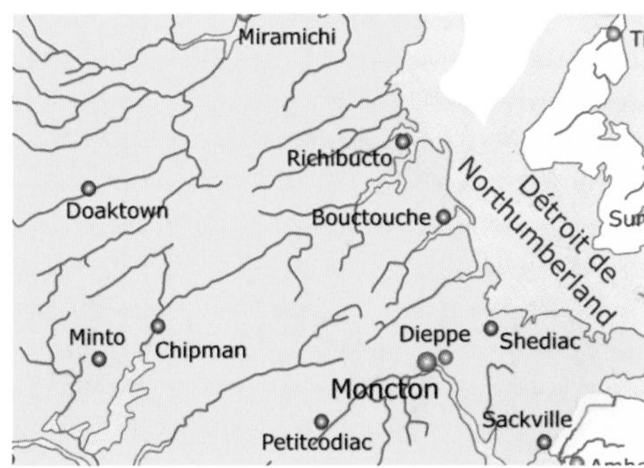

There is consistent northeast flow that describes to a large degree all the rivers that lie along the carboniferous plateau of New Brunswick.

Ganong's belief that they were not talking about the scenery—though the river is undeniably lovely to look at—but rather were describing how easily it could be canoed. The aboriginal people used the waterways of the province as one of their two chief means of transportation—walking was the other—and the Cains was the leading pathway from the upper Northumberland shore and points north across to the Saint John and the Fundy coast where the Mi'kmaq traded and sometimes fought with the Maliseet, since the Saint John Valley was Maliseet territory and the Miramichi was Mi'kmaq. The Cains River Valley is close to being right on the line.

The relatively deep, slow flow of the river interspersed with the occasional quick riffle defines the character of the salmon-fishing water on the Cains. Miramichi author Wayne

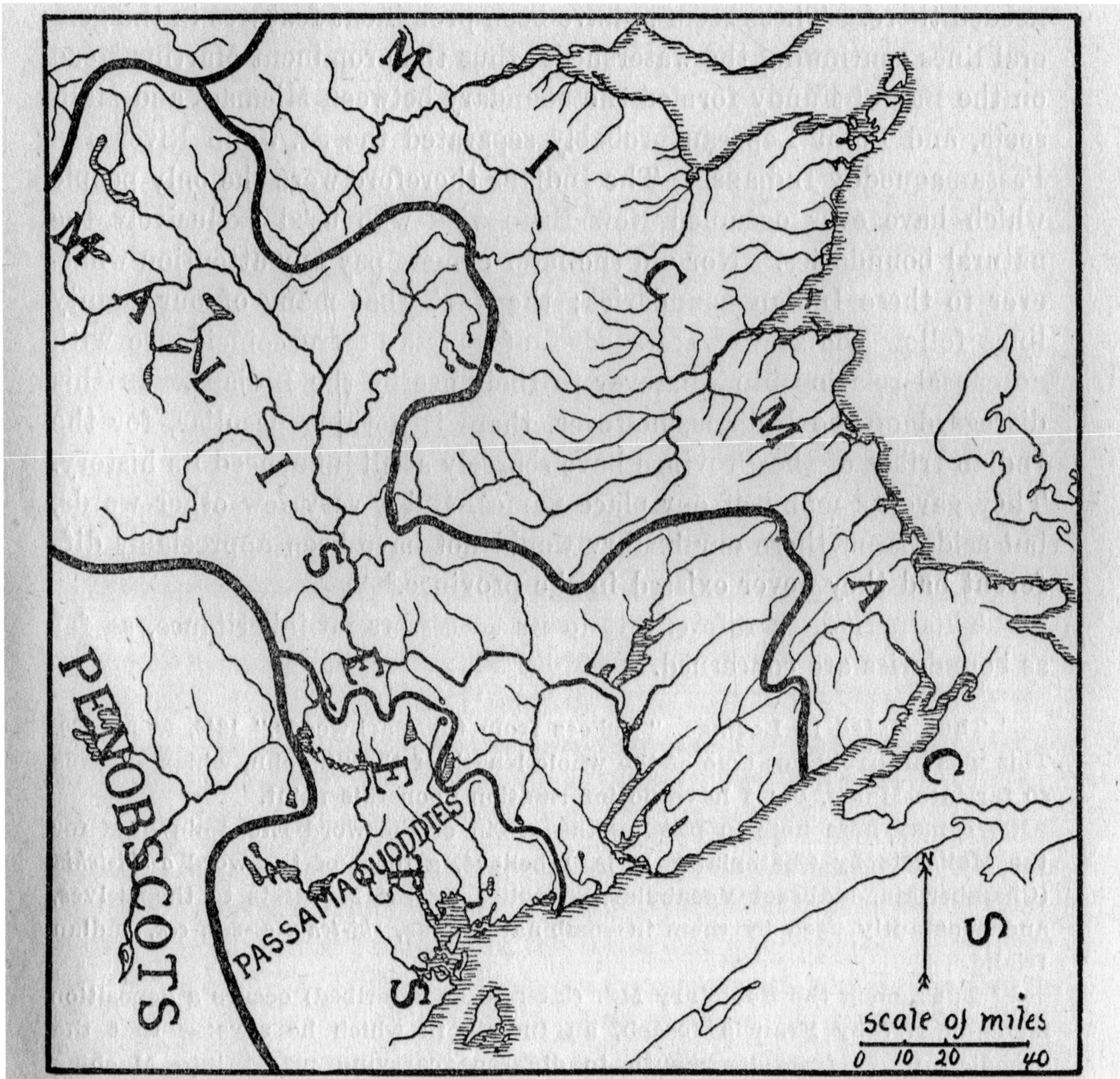

This map, based on work attributed to William Francis Ganong in 1899, shows the respective Mi'kmaq and Maliseet Indian territories. The Cains River was essentially on the line between the two tribes. The Maliseet lived largely along the Saint John River Valley and were more agricultural than the hunter/gatherer Mi'kmaq. The result may have been that neither group was particularly likely to have set up large, permanent encampments on the Cains River and none are known to have existed, though the river was used a great deal for transportation.

Curtis loves to quote his father, John Curtis, an outfitter on the Main Southwest Miramichi and the Cains Rivers during the 1960s: "The old Cains is the best we got come fall. You can catch a fish in just about every inch of that river." The fall salmon do love to stack up in those deep, slow pools but can be caught in the faster water too, especially when they are on the move.

Ganong also loved to speculate about the early geographic layout of the various rivers in the province. We don't often think, when looking at a sizeable river, that over its long life it may have flowed through entirely different valleys and in different directions than it takes today. Ganong noted that all the rivers in the general vicinity of the Cains have a "striking continuity of direction" flowing northeast toward the Northumberland Shore. Ganong felt that it was likely that instead of turning northwest at Salmon Brook to run toward its merger with the Miramichi as the Cains does now, it once ran straight down the valley of Salmon Brook—against the direction that Salmon Brook now flows in—and continued in the bed of the present Barnaby River to reach the coast.

CHAPTER 2

Cains River Biology, Atlantic Salmon, and Brook Trout

While the Cains River has very few areas that approach rapids status, it is also without the broad, slow areas found here and there in the lower portions of the Miramichi. In periods of low flow, some of the deeper pools do become slow, but even these pick up to a good fishing pace with a modest raise of water. On the other hand, the river quickly shrugs off all but the most extreme raises of water, clearing up and dropping to a reasonable flow level. In short, the Cains is a river of consistently moderate flows.

Since the Cains winds through an area of sandstone ledges, there are some pools found over the entire length of the river that are at least, in part, solid ledge bottomed. But still, the most common bottom for the Cains River is gravel. An actual mud or sand bottom is rare and usually just occurs in small pockets. Round pebbles or rocks up to one inch in diameter can handle about 0.75 meters per second in flow before becoming mobile, while coarse gravel with some cobblestone-sized pieces can withstand about 1.2 meters per second. Having had pool-enhancement work done on the Cains and the southwest Miramichi, I have found that very few places attain current speeds of over 1.2 meter per second except in spate conditions. This means that there are very few places along

A stretch of river located just downstream from the author's camp at Mahoney Brook on the Cains. I observed recently made redds and salmon spawning there in the fall of 2017. The basic bottom structure and pace of current flow in this area about four miles upriver of Shinnickburn is very similar to the area between Sabbies River and Salmon Brook where the Miramichi Salmon Association noted, in their 2007 research titled *Spawning Survey during the Season Extension—Mouth of Sabbies River to the mouth of Salmon Brook*, they reported locating approximately 100 redds during the spawning period that year.

A recently made salmon redd on the Cains River in early November 2017. The hen salmon moves upstream of the redd where she and male salmon had just spawned, and she uses her tail to dislodge gravel that drifts downstream to cover the eggs. The larger rocks drop more quickly through the water, and the smaller rocks and sands are therefore more visible on the top.

the Cains where the bottom substrate is consistently much larger than coarse gravel. According to M. Gordon Wolman of John Hopkins University, a loose, general rule is that salmon can spawn in gravel that has an average diameter of roughly 10 percent of their body length. Therefore, a grilse would enjoy gravel of about five centimeters, or two to two and a half inches. A meter-long salmon, though, might be more comfortable in the coarse gravel to cobblestone-sized mix in the four-inch size range, but there is considerable room for variances from these statistics in the material that I have read. According to Nathan Wilbur of the Atlantic Salmon Federation, the larger gravel sizes may be the case in faster-flowing rivers, where current speed would more easily move these large stones, but the Cains salmon would not require such large gravel. Furthermore, states Nathan, good spawning gravel for salmon is found in abundance for salmon throughout the entire Cains River.

In a report called *The Ecology of the Atlantic Salmon*, produced in England by K. Hendry and D. Gragg-Hine, it is stated that favorable locations for Atlantic salmon spawning are likely to occur in river gradients of 3 percent or less, current velocities of 25 to 90 centimeters per second, and water depths of between 17 to 76 centimeters. The average gradient for the Cains is 1.4 percent, though certainly in faster flowing or riffled areas, it would be steeper than that. The desirable current velocity of 25 to 90 centimeters per second presents quite a wide range, and suitable depths at these velocities are very easily found throughout the Cains. It was also stated in the article that transitional sites where the pools tail out into riffles are very desirable. This is because the hydraulics of the current being pushed over the bars at the tails of the pools forces oxygenated water to flow through redds made in these areas. The riverbed of the Cains is one of small hills and valleys all along its course, and the river drops continuously from pool to pool, providing many of these desirable tail-of-the-pool areas.

I saw fresh salmon redds made in the Cains River about 20 miles up from the mouth in early November 2017, and I saw other fish in the process of making them. The conditions where I saw the salmon spawning fit their preferred gradient and gravel size quite closely. Mark Hambrook, president of the Miramichi Salmon Association (MSA) and, in the past, a biologist for the Canadian Department of Fisheries and Oceans (DFO), told me that most of the spawning occurs at night and on the upstream edges of bars. Over on the Saint John River, about 80 miles to the west of the Cains, the biologists for the

New Brunswick DFO go out onto the bars at night during spawning season to net broodstock for the hatcheries. The fact that I was able to observe spawning activity during the day on the Cains probably meant that quite a lot of spawning was taking place in the area.

During the fall in 2006 and 2007, an experimental extended fishing season for the section of the Cains River lying downstream of the Route 123 bridge was trialed. The original idea was for a two-week extension to run until October 30 instead of the normal ending date of October 15. The trial was cut short by a year, and in the end, the season extension was not permanently adopted. Apparently, the overriding concern was that fishermen would be fishing at the same time the fish were actually in the act of spawning, and that would not be good either from the standpoint of hooking fish at the stage of spawning or of anglers wading through the new salmon redds.

The MSA did studies during this experimental season to help the DFO understand the timing of Atlantic spawning

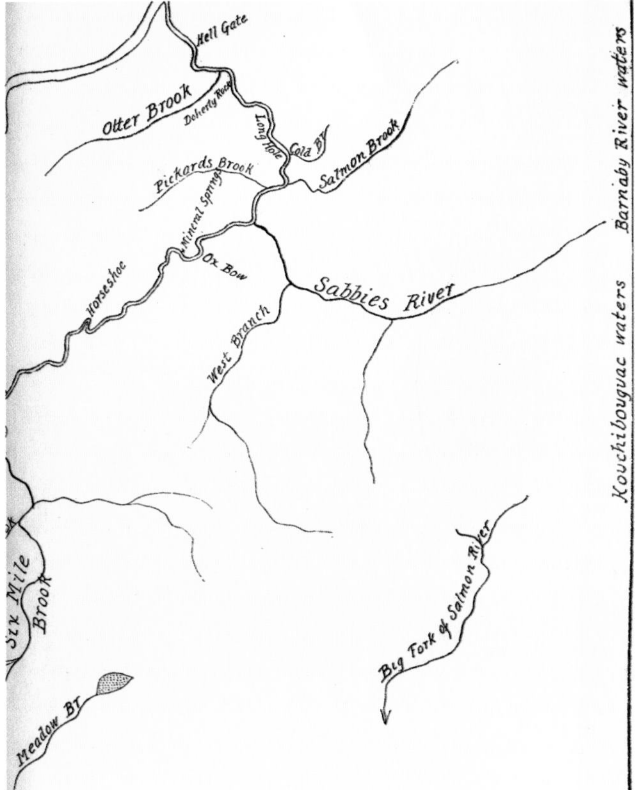

In this section of the William Francis Ganong map mentioned earlier, the Sabbies and Kouchibouguac Rivers headwaters are shown to intermingle. This is noteworthy because Northumberland Shore Rivers such as the Kouchibouguac are the latest spawning rivers in the province, with most spawning occurring in November. Similarly, the MSA reports that of the salmon from various branches of the Miramichi that they spawn in their hatchery, the last of the fish to become ripe are those from the Cains River. Spawning in the Cains often takes place well into November. MAP COURTESY OF THE UNIVERSITY OF NEW BRUNSWICK.

on the Cains River, so there was value to the experimental season extension. The reason that the experimental season was not tried above Route 123 is that mid to late October is the acknowledged time for brook trout spawning in this very important area for the species in the upper Cains, and there was fear that anglers would walk on the freshly laid brook trout eggs.

It turns out that the Cains River salmon spawn over a wide period of time, starting around October 18 and running well into November. Hambrook told me that they have captured pre-spawn salmon broodstock in the Sabbies River—a large tributary of the Cains that enters about nine miles upstream of the mouth—in mid-November, so this is certain. Hambrook also told me that the Cains River broodstock collected for hatchery spawning are the last group to spawn of any collected in the Miramichi system. While most Cains River fish spawn during the last week of October, the average timing for other Miramichi broodstock range from October 12 for the Northwest Miramichi fish, to the majority spawning from other tributaries around October 23.

In its spawning lateness, the Cains is really more similar to some of the rivers along the Northumberland Strait, which are known for their November spawning timetable. In rivers located there, such as the Kouchibouguac River, Hambrook said that the peak of the salmon spawning happens routinely during November. Interestingly, the headwaters of the Kouchibouguac and the Sabbies River tributary of the Cains both originate in more or less the same place near the town of Rogersville. The Kouchibouguac flows east out to the Northumberland shore a short distance south of Point Escuminac. The Sabbies generally flows west, entering the Cains about 8.7 miles upstream from the mouth. Certainly, much about that shared headwaters area is different than the higher elevation, colder region where the earlier-spawning Northwest Miramichi flows from. Like the Kouchibouguac, the other Northumberland Strait Rivers are also known for a late run of Atlantic salmon that spawn well into November.

REDD PRODUCTION

Another benefit of the MSA fieldwork during the extended season was the observation of the numbers of redds that could be seen in a particular area. Here is an excerpt from an MSA report of what was seen during the 2007 survey.

> *Spawning Survey during the Season Extension—Mouth of Sabbies River to the mouth of Salmon Brook*
>
> The first salmon redds were observed on this section on October 23, when two redds were observed. On October 26, the maximum number of redds (53) were observed during the survey. On November 3, 29 redds were observed in this section. The survey was conducted on November 14 and 26, but no redds were

observed. Observing possible redds on November 14 and 26 was made more difficult by the high water.

In 11 days from October 23 to November 3, 85 redds were seen in this 1.6-mile stretch of the Cains River. It is nearly certain that more were made than that, but high water after November 3 made it very hard to see. There is probably no good reason to assume that this stretch of river is better than average over the course of the Cains' length, but if we allow ourselves the exercise of rounding the 85 up to 100 to allow for later spawning that is known to take place and multiply this by 40 to get the entire 60-plus miles of river included, we come up with over 4,000 redds. My first thought when I read this is to think of the millions upon millions of dollars and pounds being spent in Europe and North America to rebuild nearly extinct salmon populations and how the conservation groups absolutely rejoice over finding even a tiny handful of redds, and here we have thousands of them. Do we realize how incredibly fortunate we are?

Beyond this observation, the Cains is a river that is fed by a great many small- and medium-sized streams that, in themselves, present important spawning habitat. There are three major tributaries to the lowest portion of the Cains: Otter Brook, which flows out into the Brophy Pool, is the smallest. The somewhat larger Salmon Brook and much larger Sabbies River are the other two. The Sabbies, in most flow conditions, is just a large stream as opposed to a river. Between Sabbies and the Route 123, aka Grand Lake Road, bridge, an additional 25 miles upstream, there are two more large tributaries—Muzzeroll Brook and Six Mile Brook. James Marriner told me once that he had been hunting in that area years ago and stopped by chance on the Muzzeroll Bridge for a look into the river. It was an early November morning, and Marriner told me that it "looked like Alaska" with the water simply black with salmon staging to spawn in the Muzzeroll. In a phone conversation with longtime Miramichi guide Lester Vickers, who has lived in sight of the mouth of Cains River his whole life, he related a very similar story to me. He and a friend were deer hunting, and when driving across the Muzzeroll Bridge on the Shinnickburn Road, they decided to stop for a look into the water in the same place as Marriner. It's something I've done many times myself, just never that late in the season. Fishermen just love to look off bridges into the water to see what fish are around. He said it was late in the fall, around the last of October or early November, and in the stream running down from the bridge there were many salmon finning as close together as smelts. Anecdotally, I've been told stories about all these streams hosting spawning salmon.

There are many other streams in the headwaters area above the Grand Lake Road bridge that are large enough to provide

Muzzeroll Brook during a period of strong spring flow. Muzzeroll and Sabbies Rivers are the two largest spawning and tributaries and parr nurseries of the Cains River. The 26 officially recognized salmon spawning tributaries on the Cains River collectively make up 24 percent of the river's total spawning habitat.

some very good salmon spawning habitat. These streams provide extra spawning potential that can only be utilized once the streams have swollen with the late fall rains. According to Barrie Duffield, owner of the Burntland Brook Pool on the Miramichi, and who for years ran canoe, camping, and fishing trips on various areas of the Cains, the salmon go very far up the Cains to spawn, certainly in both branches well beyond the confluence of the North Branch and the main river, approximately 80 percent of the way up the 100-kilometer-long Cains River. Lloyd Bartlett also told me that his old friend Buddy Randall, who had been a nuisance trapper for the railroad, keeping the culverts and bridges along the line from McGivney to Chipman clear of beaver dams, said that the biggest kind of hookbill salmon would push their way far up in to Bantalor during the late fall for spawning.

Wilson's Outfitting guide emeritus Ernest Long told me that when he was a boy the local men would take a team of horses and a wagon back into the Cains River headwaters and net fall salmon to salt down. As you stood in the river setting your net, the salmon would be going right by your legs on their way upstream to spawn. There were also salmon spawning in all the major brooks. According to Long, you could walk up Otter Brook for not too great a distance to where the river is blocked by a ledge; there would be salmon everywhere that had gathered to spawn.

The great number of large streams feeding into the Cains may very well be the secret to the river's potential fecundity. The Cains is prone to years when fall fishing is poor during the open season due to a lack of rain, but eventually, the rain does come, and the fish can then utilize this stream habitat. The potential benefit of the stream habitat is twofold: first, to find a place to lay their eggs, the salmon don't need to dig up the redds of salmon in the main river that had spawned earlier. Second, the streams often melt down without an ice run in the spring, and this easy ice-out does not disturb the gravel beds.

In 1983, the Halifax office of Fisheries and Oceans Canada used aerial surveys done between 1974 and 1978 along with maps and other information gathered from back to the late 1950s to measure the Atlantic salmon habitat for the Miramichi River system. The study by Peter G. Amiro was titled "Aerial Photographic Measurement of Atlantic Salmon Habitat of the Miramichi River, New Brunswick." The calculation itself is very complicated as to exactly what is or isn't included as salmon habitat. I'm making the following statements only to illustrate the importance of the brooks to the Cains salmon-producing system, and then the Cains to the overall Southwest Miramichi system of which it is a part.

The Cains River has a total salmon-producing area, according to the survey, of 46,515 times 100 square meters. Of this, there are 26 officially recognized salmon-producing tributaries to the Cains that collectively provide 11,336 square meters, or approximately 24 percent of the river's total salmon-producing area. The Cains itself amounts to 12.7 percent of the Southwest Miramichi's 366,581 by 100 square meters of total salmon producing habitat. It is the second-largest tributary system, with the largest being the combined Renous/Dungarvon complex having 58,207 and, thus, being 15.9 percent of the Southwest Miramichi salmon habitat.

Ice runs in the spring can be devastating to salmon redds. In the lower Miramichi room-sized, and two-to-three-foot-thick pieces of ice are propelled by the current, turning end over end and digging up the bottom to a very considerable degree as they proceed down the river to the sea. At my Campbell's Pool camp in Blackville, Jason Curtis witnessed a huge piece of ice wedge into a big boulder at the head of the pool and stand up on end high enough to touch the power lines that cross the river. To look at that same scene in the summer is to find it totally unbelievable. Standing in a canoe, you cannot reach anywhere near those lines with a 15-foot Spey rod. Salmon-fishing pools are routinely filled in, and new ones are excavated by the ice. The loss of fertilized, unhatched eggs can be catastrophic. The lower main stream of the Cains is itself subject to heavy ice runs, and every summer, we marvel at trees along the bank where ice has ripped off the bark at unbelievable distances above the summer surface of the water. Thankfully, during the spring freshet, the river is usually high enough so that river ice is not constantly connecting with the gravel bottom, but unfortunately, it does sometimes happen.

A couple of years back in late April, Jason Curtis and I were headed up to our Mahoney Brook camp for, among other things, our traditional season-opener hot dog cookout. As we motored through the Oxbow stretch a couple of miles below Shinnickburn, we saw the biggest mass of ice cakes I

On April 25, 2015, Jason Curtis and I were running up the Cains River near the Oxbow Pool when we encountered the remains of a huge ice jam that had pushed up onto the shore on both sides of the river for a distance of over a quarter of a mile. It would have been a frightening spectacle to have witnessed when it took place, but I'm certain that it was not seen by a living soul.

had ever seen. Some of these were more than three feet thick and twenty or thirty feet long. The cakes were laying all over a big grassy plain on one side of the river, here and there stacked up two and three deep, and on the other side where the banking came steeply down to the river, some were pushed right up into the trees. They must have simply smashed and broken their way into the forest. Jason said a big jam had been reported there during ice-out. The brooks, though, are not subjected to this sort of destruction, and redds made in their relatively gentle confines have an excellent chance of successfully producing young salmon.

SIZE AND TIMING OF THE CAINS RIVER RUN

One thing that I've heard asked many times is "What is the size of the Cains River salmon run?" I'm not aware of anyone trying to make an official estimate of this number, but we can make some reasonably intelligent guesses that should put us in the ballpark.

In a September 1997 article by Philip Lee written for the Competitive Enterprise Institute based in Washington, DC, William K. Hooper, then a senior biologist for the New Brunswick government, is quoted as saying this about the historical production of the Miramichi River system: "There were big years in the 1920s and 1930s. I wouldn't be surprised if the river was producing a million fish. . . . People have forgotten what fish abundance really was like." According to Hooper, the Miramichi experienced its last great run in 1967, and the total run was somewhere upward of 600,000 fish.

Let's look again at the 1967 salmon run, which had a rod catch for the entire Miramichi system of 47,769 salmon and grilse. The estimate for the Cains catch for that year was 6,480, or 13.6 percent of the catch for the total Miramichi River system. Now, admittedly, that was a barn-burner year, but if Hooper was correct, and the run was 600,000 or more fish, than the Cains River alone, with 13.6 percent of the fish caught, should logically have hosted 13.6 percent of the run, or 81,600 salmon and grilse—a mind-boggling number. Another good reality check of the 13.6 percent number is that the spawning habitat of the Cains River was calculated in that 1983 survey to be 12.7 percent of the entire Miramichi system. The numbers 13.6 and 12.7 are very similar values.

In 1968, the overall run was thought to be much smaller, and the total rod catch on the Miramichi slumped to an estimated 19,032. Of those 19,032, the Cains produced an unbelievably low 284 bright fish, or just 1.5 percent of the total for the system! How could this be? I'm going to compare the conditions during both 1967 and 1968 in detail later, but it is certain that at least a fair amount of fish came into the Cains to spawn with raises of water after the season had closed. It is also true that the Cains, just like the Miramichi itself, went into a decline during the late 1960s and early 1970s from which it has never fully recovered. Here are some statistics on the Cains River catch that were provided in a 1976 Angling Survey of the Cains River by New Brunswick Department of Fisheries and the Environment.

NUMBER OF BRIGHT SALMON CAUGHT			
Year	**Grilse**	**Large salmon**	**Totals**
1970	258	49	307
1971	1 no data available for 1971		
1972	1,135	425	1,560
1973	150	103	253
1974	246	162	408
1975	22	8	30
1976	101	124	225

No statistics were available for 1971. While the catch in none of these years approaches the 1967 catch, the extreme variability that we saw between 1967 and 1968 shows itself to be not all that unusual as illustrated by the rod catch of 1,560 salmon and grilse in 1972 and only 30 in 1975. Another table of statistics for the Cains River that I found continued until 1994 and averaged less than 500 rod-caught bright fish annually.

These days, the Miramichi system has a run of about 40,000 fish, though it is quite variable, and years like the 100,000 or so that came in 2011 are still possible. The first full season was in 2011, which was after I had acquired the Mahoney Brook camp. We caught 15 salmon and grilse there in the last week and a half of the season while learning the water, and I know that Black Brook landed more than a hundred fish on their Admiral Pool water. There were many more also caught at Brophy's, Buttermilk, Salmon Brook, Sabbies, Moore's Pool, Six Mile, and Doctor's Island. This says nothing about all the water along the river that is not as well known, and it also says nothing of those caught in the upper-river pools where most of the run is heading to spawn. I'm confident that the rod catch in 2011 was in excess of 1,500 fish and very likely well over 2,000.

If we look at 1967 and logically deduce that the Cains caught 13.6 percent of the run because 13.6 percent of the fish went up the Cains and then use 40,000 fish as the size of the current run, you get an estimated run of 5,440 salmon and grilse just in the Cains. The next year, 1.5 percent would only give us 600 fish. That might be accurate for the fish that came in during the season, but it is safe to assume that many more came in after the season had ended. Therefore, the run is probably somewhere near the larger of those two numbers. I've also heard others throw around a figure of 5,000 salmon before for the Cains, and while I don't know how others estimated it in the past, that number certainly sounds reasonable to me based on the evidence that I have just presented. Just to put that in perspective, 5,000 in the Cains compares to about the same sized run as typically found in the Gaspe Peninsula's very famous Cascapédia River.

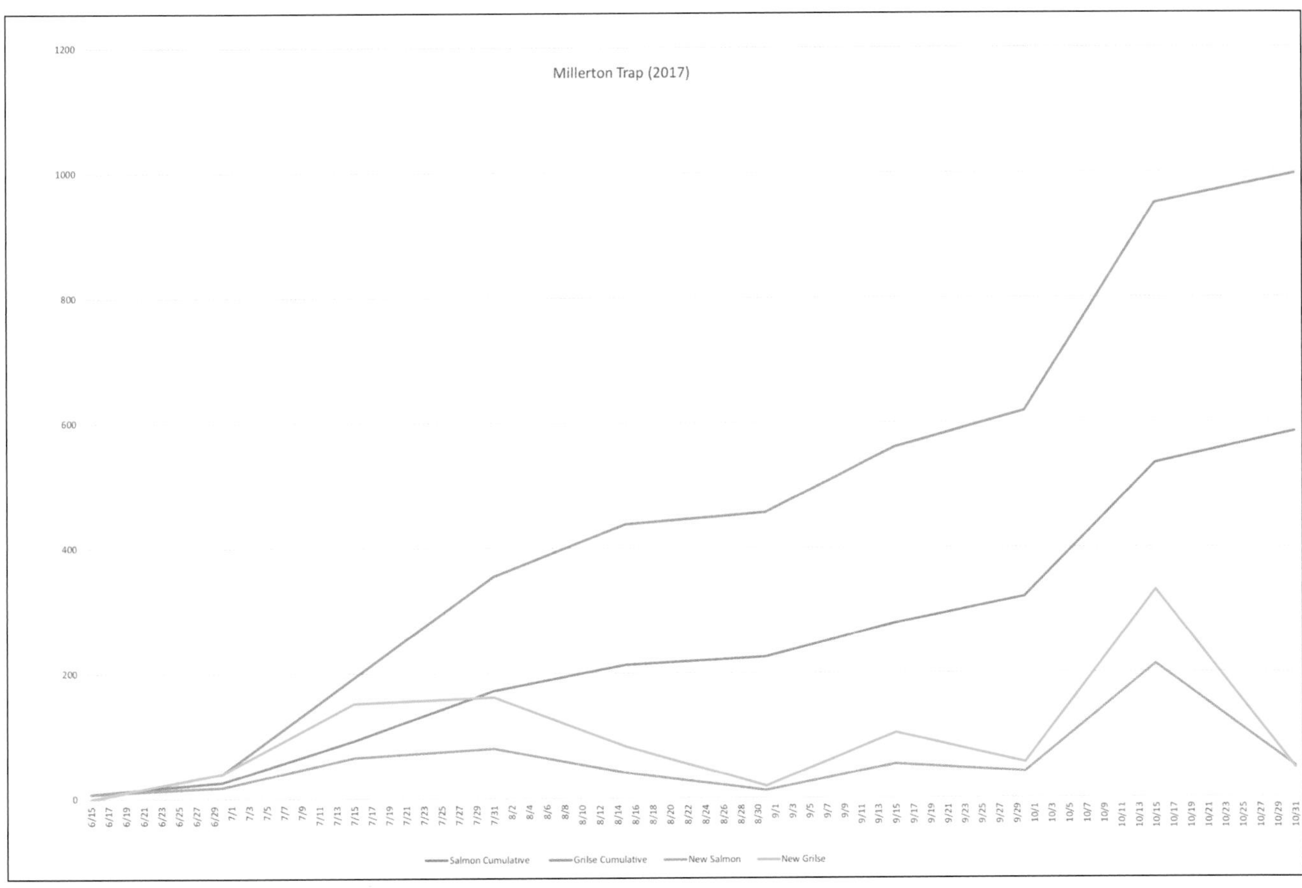

Salmon and grilse tagged at the Millerton trap in 2017. Note that roughly half of the 997 grilses and two-thirds of the 584 salmon were tagged at Millerton in the 45 days after September 1, 2017. With salmon, 305 of the 584 entered the trap after September 30. With grilse, it was 436 out of 997, a smaller percentage, but still, about 44 percent, arriving in the last two weeks of the fishing season. This result is almost a complete reversal from the apparent trend less than 10 years earlier toward a diminishing fall run and an increasing summer run entering the river during July. No one knows why the timing of these runs trends back and forth between early- and late-arriving fish.

It has been established that the Cains River run comes during what the salmon biologists historically called "the time of the late-running fish" from September 1 to the end of the season. These are fish that predominately come into the freshwater portions of the river after the early run—through July—has passed. Typically, unless there is an unusually large, cool rain, the period from late July to late August sees a relatively few fresh salmon enter the river. Before 1970, the records show that the late-season run into the river was a much larger number of fish than came during the early-season run. Since the early 1970s that has changed, and with a few recent exceptions, the early run is normally the larger of the two. It is also noted that these percentages can vary considerably even from just one season to the next. My personal observations from spending a lot of time in camp are that over the last three years—2015 through 2017—the percentage of fish coming in the late run has increased, and the government fish counting-trap numbers clearly show that during 2017 twice as many salmon entered the system during the late run as did during the early run.

DATE	SALMON CUMULATIVE	GRILSE CUMULATIVE	NEW SALMON	NEW GRILSE
6/15	8	0	8	0
6/30	26	41	18	41
7/15	92	193	66	152
7/31	172	355	80	162
8/15	213	438	41	83
8/31	225	457	12	19
9/15	279	561	54	104
9/30	321	618	42	57
10/15	534	950	213	332
10/31	584	997	50	47

Tag returns from tagging studies undertaken in the 1930s in Miramichi Gully—in the ocean off the entrances to Miramichi Bay—show that while most of the late-run fish are in the estuary by August, a significant number of these fish do spend additional feeding time in that general area compared to the early-run fish. This is very likely why the fall grilse are on average larger than the summer grilse. It can also mean that extra mortality from predators may be reducing the numbers of the late-run fish as they continue to actively feed in the ocean not too distant from the mouth of the Miramichi.

The Cains run can be prolific, and there have been quite a few occasions in recent years when I have witnessed firsthand the movements of large numbers of salmon and grilse toward the end of the fishing season in the Cains. During the last few days of the 2011 season, I was making daily trips to fish for a couple of hours in the morning at our Mahoney Brook camp. I knew that there were a good number of fish holding in the slow, deep section of the home pool, but they were very poor takers. As the week wore on, we had a couple of small rain events, and the river slowly rose a few inches. I was seeing more fish rolling on the surface farther up the pool toward the faster water, but my trips down through the run were only yielding a very occasional catch. It rained the night before the last day of the season, and my friends and I decided that, based on the fish I knew were holding on the Cains, we should invest our last day there. Even as we sat on the deck of the camp pulling on our waders, we could see fish jumping in the home pool. All that day we saw groups of fish working up the river. Sometimes you could see them in the water close enough to touch with a rod tip. Bill Utley, a biologist by education and a lifelong salmon fisher, was confident that we saw over a thousand salmon go by us that day—though, of course, there was no way for us to really count them. They certainly weren't very interested in flies, as fish moving on rising water often aren't. Ashley Hallihan, from Blackville, was fishing that same day near Buttermilk Pool some 14 miles downstream, and he had a similar experience. He told Jason that the fish were swimming right by his feet.

THE CAINS RIVER AS A PARR NURSERY

For parr, the Cains provides an excellent nursery. First, the dark waters of the Cains provide some natural measure of protection, as do the numerous brooks and brook mouths with overhanging foliage. The Cains also provides a lot of insect life to feed the parr.

During the mid-1950s there was heavy spraying of DDT by the forest products companies in conjunction with the federal government to control spruce budworm. This killed a lot of the salmon, both mature and immature, that were within the river, but it also killed a high percentage of aquatic insects. Those populations are thought to have recovered but to exactly what degree is uncertain. Articles I found online complained about an inadequate amount of research having been done on the aquatic insect populations of the main stem of the Miramichi River system, but some work has been done in the tributaries.

One report in 1996 by Donna Giberson and Heather Garnett came from studying Catamaran brook, a tributary of the Little Southwest Miramichi. It cited 25 genera of mayflies, 19 of caddisflies, and a vast number of midges and beetles, and stated that the greatest volume of all in their emergence traps were blackflies. I remember giving a talk years ago on a fishing trip that I took to Victoria Island in the Canadian Arctic. I told my audience that we saw few aquatic insects in that very cold water that featured icebergs grounded in the mouth of the river we were fishing in. It was a mystery to us what the great many large Arctic char and lake trout subsisted on. A female biologist in the audience spoke up and said that she had done a summer of research in the Arctic, and as incredible as it sounds, blackfly larvae are one of the most important food sources there for young char and salmonids. I was glad to hear that there is some good use for blackflies since they are the bane of human existence during much of June and July on the Cains River. For whatever reason, black flies seem far worse at my camp at Mahoney Brook on the Cains than they do on the Miramichi.

Additionally, the Catamaran Brook research revealed 31 species of stoneflies, of which eight were new discoveries for the Province of New Brunswick. In addition to the insects, small prey species, which include blacknose dace and slimey sculpins, are abundant. This forage supports a lot of brook trout and salmon. The famed Muddler Minnow fly was developed to fish for giant brook trout in the Nipigon River, where the world's record brook trout was caught in 1915. The fly was designed to imitate sculpins. A 1995 publication called *Rivers of North America* states that the volume of fish in the Miramichi River is quite remarkable, and that by biomass approximately 50 percent of these fish are Atlantic salmon—of all age-groups.

I can attest that there are very abundant hatches and often several at once going on throughout the season on the Miramichi and Cains Rivers, though certainly, the period from late May to the Fourth of July finds them being most common.

THERMAL REFUGE

I interviewed Nathan Wilbur, the New Brunswick Program Director of the Atlantic Salmon Federation (ASF), for information on thermal refuges. I first met Nathan when he was giving a presentation on his master's degree thesis paper, "Characterizing thermal refugia for brook trout (Salvelinus fontinalis) and Atlantic salmon (Salmo salar) in the Cains River, New Brunswick, Canada," to the Miramichi Salmon Association during the late winter of 2011.

Nathan and his assistants mounted a thermal infrared imaging camera to a helicopter and flew along the 30 or so miles of the Cains River above the Grand Lake Road bridge. They mapped the areas by water temperature, and then Nathan spent the summer living at Wilson's Wildcat Lodge and examining—including by skin diving—the various areas of the river that showed cooler water temperatures.

A Cains River parr holding on his "home stone." Salmon parr are considerably more tolerant of warm water than brook trout.

PHOTO COURTESY OF NATHAN WILBUR.

The goal of Nathan's experiment was to learn how the salmon parr and brook trout utilized the various thermal refuges in the upper sections of the Cains River—above Route 123—to survive the summer temperatures, which can briefly reach as high as 28°C and perhaps greater. This far exceeds their preferred temperature range and can be lethal if they do not seek out suitable thermal refuges. This work can now be utilized to physically enhance other sites along the Cains and other rivers where cold-water inputs exist to achieve similar temperature-buffering results. The work was done in 2010, at a time when the population of large trout was still apparently quite robust and during what was perhaps the warmest summer in living memory.

What Nathan found was that when the Cains River reached a temperature of 21°C the brook trout in the river had moved to a source of colder water, and they remained in the cold flow until the water cooled off to below that critical temperature. The Atlantic salmon parr, though, did not begin moving to a cold-water retreat until the temperature exceeded 25°C; instead, the parr remained out in the river at their "home stone."

Snorkeling through the areas identified by the infrared survey to be cool enough to qualify as a refuge, Nathan came across four areas that held significant numbers of large brook trout—between 15 and 24 inches—and a few smaller groups as well. Some aggregations had 100 or more trout in them, and the smaller ones were significantly fewer. All in all, in Nathan's estimation, 500 or less large, sea-run brook trout spend the summer in the stretch of river between the North Branch Pool and the Grand Lake Road. There are definitely some more summering a little farther down in the river, but just how many is unknown. The belief is that the vast majority of the Cains River sea-run brook trout are lying in a relatively few locations within this 30-mile stretch of river. The required conditions, according to Nathan, are a cool stream or spring flowing into the river and sufficient depth to keep most of the avian predators at bay. Springs, bubbling up cool water into the stream, contribute very cold water (5 to 15°C), and although it is a lower volume of cold-water input compared to stream inputs, these provide critical thermal refuges as well. Nathan found that there was an even split between large trout holding in the plumes of streams and springs.

Note this large, solitary salmon in the upper center holding amid this aggregation of bragging-size sea-run brookies at a cold-water source in the upper Cains River. The location of this pool is roughly 70 miles from the sea. Research by Nathan Wilbur showed quite conclusively that very few adult salmon move into the Cains River headwaters until after the warm summer season has ended. PHOTO COURTESY OF NATHAN WILBUR.

In all cases where the trout were holding, the infrared imagery identified a visible cold-water input flowing from the riverbank—spring or stream. The Cains is typically a fall-run Atlantic salmon river, but interestingly, among all these gigantic brook trout in midsummer was one, single, yard-long Atlantic salmon. Clearly, during 2010, which was a year with a relatively robust salmon run that took place at least in good part early in the season, there were essentially no salmon summering in the upper Cains River. To me, Nathan's findings are a clear indicator that there is no significant summer run of salmon to the upper Cains River. I can also state from personal observation that there was a good run of salmon into the upper Cains that fall. Why the trout don't remain in the estuary during the summer, and the more temperature-tolerant salmon run up and wait in the headwaters, is hard to understand. The trout are feeding, though, and the Cains River provides a reliable flow of insect food in the summer, so that might be the lure.

CHAPTER 3

Before Sportfishing, Aboriginal Fishers and Early Settlers—the Crown Grant System

Before the concepts of sportfishing came to the Cains River, the fish and game of the river valley, and, for that matter, the physical presence of the river itself, fulfilled many of the basic needs of the aboriginal peoples and then later the first European settlers. There were no major aboriginal villages recorded along the Cains as there were around the mouth of the Miramichi, which hosted the well-known Eel Ground and Burnt Church campgrounds. However, other villages existed farther out in the headwaters, such as a very large one at the confluence of Clearwater Brook and the Southwest Miramichi. Estimates of the Mi'kmaq population in their New Brunswick territory before European colonization were only in the vicinity of 3,000 individuals in total. The Maliseet numbers were greater, but the bulk of these was to the west of the Miramichi and Cains River watersheds along the comparatively fertile Saint John River Valley.

Still, though, the gentle flowing Cains, rich in salmon and trout as well as game of all kinds, was an attractive place that the natives apparently did visit with some regularity. Ganong says that without ascribing a source: "It is said, by the way, that the aboriginals had favorite camping places at the mouths of Six Mile and Muzeroll brooks, and Sabbies River." One night during the winter of 2018, I visited Angus Curtis of Blackville, New Brunswick. Angus and his father Ab guided during the 1970s at the Black Brook Salmon Club, including the club's property at Six Mile Brook on the Cains River. Angus is a person who has an interest in the historic aboriginal presence along the Cains, and while he was working up at Six Mile, he spent some of his free time looking around the mouth of Six Mile Brook for artifacts. Angus showed me a fine collection of arrowheads that he had picked up near the mouth of Six-Mile Brook and one very impressive spearhead.

According to the authority who examined the weapon, it is thought to be between 3,700 and 4,000 years old. Apparently, the shoreline of the Cains in that area has remained relatively stable for a long time so that these artifacts could still be found in the gravel by the stream mouth.

The aboriginal's traditional method of spearing salmon with a specialized spear they called a *naygog* caused a lot of angst within the early sportfishing community of New Brunswick. Dean Sage, in his 1888 book *The Restigouche and Its Salmon Fishing*, has a detailed description of going out on the Restigouche by torchlight. The sight of the stupefied salmon in the pools was more than the aboriginal guides could bear to witness without making a stab at them. The gist of the passage was that even though Sage was close to his guides, and they all seemed to have a good and mutually beneficial relationship, the sight of fish under torchlight rekindled their ancient passions. It is worth noting that on similar excursions at other salmon camps, even the sports couldn't get

A collection of Indian arrowheads gathered over several years by Black Brook Salmon Club guide Angus Curtis from the shoreline near the club's Six Mile Brook camp proves that Indians, in fact, spent a considerable amount of time at this location.

ARCHAEOLOGICAL COLLECTION FORM PAGE NO. 1

COLLECTOR Angus Murray Curtis COLLECTION NO. AMC

No.	Description	Location	Photo No.
1	Stemmed Projectile Point about 3700-4000 years old	mouth of six mile brook, Cains River	87B7:1-4

Aboriginal "stemmed projectile" gathered near Six Mile Brook on the Cains River believed by one authority to be between 3,700 and 4,000 years old.

enough of the spearing, so it was probably nothing specific to aboriginals.

It was around 1840 before any number of white settlers occupied the Cains River Valley. Whatever the aboriginals did in the way of a salmon harvest up on the Cains before that time seems to be completely unknown. By 1840, when the Cains started to become settled, the Indians had already been rubbing up against the European settlers around the province for over 100 years, and the Mi'kmaq population within New Brunswick was estimated to be down to only 900-odd souls. In any case, using the *naygog* effectively may have been difficult in the Cains. This is partly because the fish are only in the upper portions of the river for a short while during spawning season but mostly because the water from the Cains is normally terribly dark, making it hard to see the fish even in bright light. Additionally, the headwaters of the Cains River, where the most prolific spawning would be taking place, were right on the borderline between the Mi'kmaq and Maliseet tribes, and both may have preferred to do their fishing on waters that were more securely within their own respective territories.

THE ANCIENT PORTAGE ROUTES

The Cains was known to be a favorite pathway for Indian travel between the Miramichi and points north in the eastern half of the province as well as the Saint John watershed to the south and west. One of the most famous of the aboriginal portage routes that existed led from the Cains River across a relatively narrow strip of level if somewhat boggy ground down to the Gaspereau River, then on into Grand Lake and, eventually, the main stem of the Saint John River. There were other portages in the area too, such as the Avery Portage

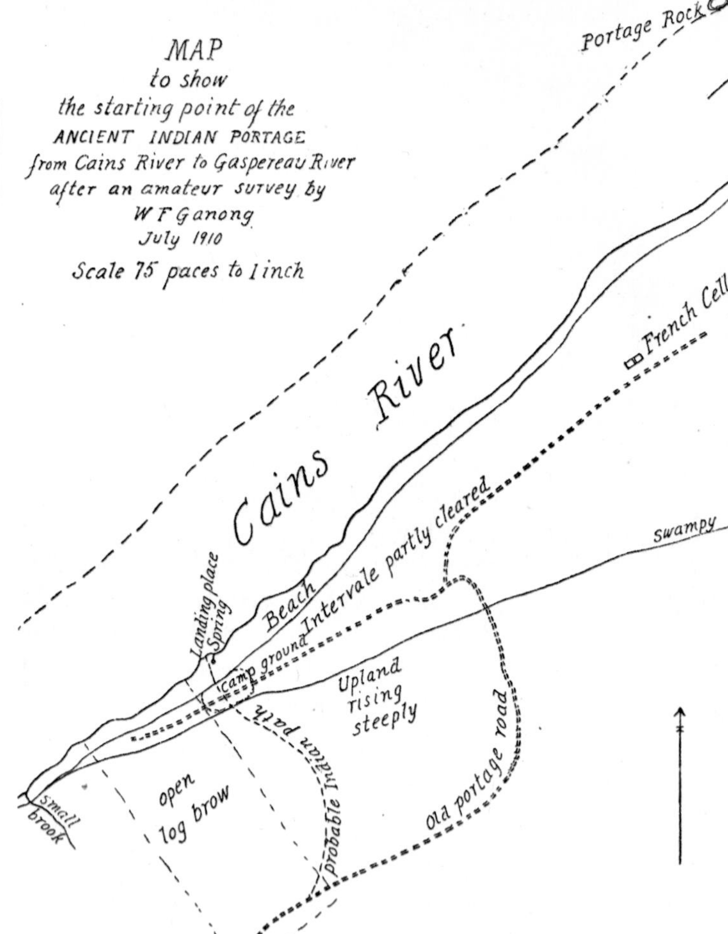

W. F. Ganong drew this map in 1910 of the site where he believed the ancient Indian portage from the Cains River to the Gaspereau River intersected the Cains. The map was published in the *Bulletin of the Natural History Society of New Brunswick*, no. 28. Modern GPS and LiDar mapping technologies have now verified exactly where this path ran, even though it is invisible to the eye and has not been used in more than 150 years.

Portage Rock signaled arrival at the point of the portage trail. Ganong said the aboriginals saw a crude face in the rock, and he surmised that it doubtless spawned many superstitious stories around the campfires. The big dark circle in the center of the rock could easily be a great, all-watching eye looking down over the sharp beak/nose combination of some mythical creature.

running between Cross Creek on the Nashawaak and Portage Island near Boiestown on the Miramichi.

On his 1909 trip down the Cains to search for the point where the Gaspereau portage left the Cains and headed south, Ganong used another old aboriginal route that, previous to European settlers' roads, ran up Young's Brook from the Nashawaak to just west of Zionville, where a short overland portage brought them to the headwaters of the Cains River.

To a fisherman, this location on the Cains—the Gaspereau/Cains portage route—has special significance because the place where the portage route is believed to have left the Cains is only a few hundred yards from the location of the Arbeau Pool. The Arbeau Pool is still fished today and will be discussed with the other known, important pools of the Cains later in this book.

According to Ganong, the aboriginals wanted several features to be found in the areas where the portages left or arrived on the rivers. First, before carrying cargo and canoes across these portages, the Indians apparently enjoyed a rest, or maybe they were rendezvousing there with other parties of aboriginals before continuing. Therefore, the Indians liked a vantage point near the river where they could see both up and down for some distance so that they did not get any nasty surprises. Second, they wanted this campground to have a relatively clear and level terrain for setting up their tents. Thirdly,

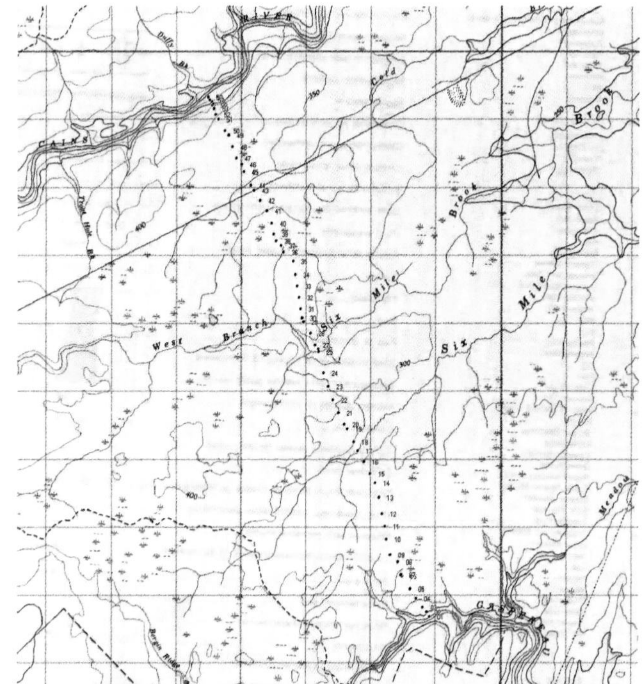

The computer-generated Cains-to-Gaspereau ancient portage trail supplied by the Canoe Kayak New Brunswick Ancient Portage Trail project. The trail is approximately five miles in length.

In the spring of 2018, red ribbons placed by Doyle and his volunteers marked the Cains River entrance to the ancient portage trail down to the Gaspereau River and, eventually, the Bay of Fundy.

Right: This circa 1926 photograph is said to be from near the Arbeau Pool. Could this open log brow be the same one mentioned in Ganong's 1910 drawing? It would make sense from the information that we have on the subject. PHOTOS COURTESY OF THE PROVINCIAL ARCHIVES OF NEW BRUNSWICK.

they did not want to carry much water with them because of the weight, so they wanted a nearby spring to get plenty of fresh, cool drinking water. The map by Ganong from his trip there in 1909 shows that all these things were available on the Cains at a point approximately 25 miles upriver from the mouth. There was even a large, conspicuous piece of sandstone ledge that had slipped down and lay at an angle next to the river. The ledge has long been known as Portage Rock and is said to have signaled to the aboriginals coming up the river that they had arrived at the Cains River end of the portage.

Robert Doyle, a New Brunswick man who has devoted much of his life to studying the ancient aboriginal portage trails connecting water routes around the Province of New Brunswick as well as to Maine, has studied this portage route exhaustively and has accumulated incredible documentation of its location. Beyond this, Doyle, Tim Humes, Kevin Silliker, and other members of a group called Canoe Kayak New Brunswick have spent a great deal of time marking out and clearing these trails, placing markers, and even laying down boardwalks over wet areas. By putting together all of the various clues, including locating an 1836 survey line drawn by a man named Sam Fairweather—a map that Ganong knew about but could not locate—Doyle and his friends, with the use of modern GPS equipment, believe that they have found exactly the locations where the portage trail left and arrived at the Cains and Gaspereau Rivers.

THE FRENCH INFLUENCE ON THE CAINS RIVER

The Cains itself was originally called the Etienne River by Europeans. The name Etienne instead of Cains appears on a Crown grant to John Cunard in 1830 for land on the west or south side of the Cains that is now part of the Black Brook Salmon Club's Admiral Pool property a short distance upriver from the mouth of the Cains. While the name Etienne has a French sound to it, Ganong, who did extensive research and wrote an entire book on the names of New Brunswick places, felt confident that Etienne was the name of an aboriginal chief. The word Etienne was then corrupted through several intermediate stages (i.e., Etienne, Ekienne, Kienne, Cains).

In the summer of 2019, New Brunswick canoeist Kevin Sabean was camping in essentially the same location noted by Ganong for "the French cellar," according to Kevin, 50 to 75 yards downstream of the now well-marked portage path location. He took this photograph of the remains. Kevin said that the outline of the foundation is still quite well defined.

French names did, however, replace aboriginal names for two of the important tributaries: Minooisak became Muzzeroll Brook, Namamgamkikac became Sabbies River—Sabbies itself a corruption of Savoy. According to Ganong, old records show that Muzroll and Savoy were names that commonly appeared in the records of the French settlement at the mouth of the Miramichi.

The defeat of the French fortress at Louisbourg in 1758 and the 1760 siege of Quebec City led to the 1763 Treaty of Paris, and the fate of French governance in New Brunswick was sealed. Many of the French, though, refused to pledge loyalty to the English sovereign. The Indians and the French continued a guerilla war against the English, and during the 1760s, the English expulsed the French in two waves from much of Atlantic Canada, reducing their population, by some estimates, to about 2,600 remaining individuals, most of whom had simply managed to avoid detection. This extraction included the French settlement at the mouth of Miramichi. For a period during and after the French and English wars, the French apparently used the Cains River as a place to live and means to travel—as the aboriginals had historically done—with comparatively little risk of contact with the English military.

On Ganong's 1910 map of the Cains River end of the Gaspereau portage route, there was also located a cellar called "the French cellar." Apparently, a house and chimney had been located there that was said to date back to the period in New Brunswick history after the American Revolution when the English were driving the French from all of Acadia—according to some sources derived from *L'Acadie*, a Mi'kmaq word meaning land of plenty. Naturally, many French were reluctant to leave and kept themselves just out of reach of the English. The Gaspereau portage route would have been very helpful in evacuating the French citizens from the Fundy coast inland to the north, and the French House may have been a point of shelter or gathering before or after the portage between the Cains and Gaspereau.

THE CROWN GRANT SYSTEM

After defeating the French, it was then necessary for the English to populate the area with their own subjects in order to develop the land's potential and defend it against future attacks. The first of these settlements was an enormous land and fishing grant that included the confluence of the Renous and main southwest Miramichi Rivers to William Davidson and John Cort in 1765. This grant was later forfeited because they were unable to attract enough settlers as was stipulated in the deal. Ironically, even though the Miramichi region was helped enormously by the American Revolution, which supplied some loyalist families to the area, it wasn't helpful to Davidson and Cort. This is because in the early stages of the war, the Mi'kmaq sided with the American revolutionaries, and the aboriginal hostilities are said to have driven Davidson to the safety of the Saint John Valley where there were already a lot of British Loyalists in residence. According to research by a Mr. Robert Doyle, Davidson's journey was reported in an 1897 article titled "Cains River, Past and Present—The Lesson of its Fate," by an R. Attridge. The article appeared in an old Chatham newspaper called the *Miramichi Advance*. The article reported that Davidson made this journey to the Saint John by poling up the Miramichi and then the Cains River, finally continuing through a branch of Six Mile Brook over to the Gaspereau via a portage of only two miles. The article goes on to claim it was the route of many Mi'kmaq war parties on their way to attack "Milecites" on the south side of the province. Doyle believes that this information is probably wrong and that Six Mile is small and twisted enough to make such a route impractical and definitely less attractive than the well-known Cains/Gaspereau track, which, though closer to five miles long, was very level and well-trodden. The same article, incidentally, states that the Cains River's original European name of Etienne comes from a family in France, one of whose members was an Acadian explorer and the source of information about the Six Mile Brook portage route. I suppose that definitive answers to some of these questions are simply lost to history. I personally have walked a fair distance up Six Mile Brook. Perhaps just after ice-out, when it is flush with the spring freshet, one could pole or paddle the several miles up it that would be required to reduce the portage to two miles, but it would not be as easy as it might sound. Six Mile Brook has a thickly overhanging canopy, it is very narrow in many places, and that is before it splits off into the branches you would have to navigate to reach the location where the portage would take off. I agree with Doyle that it seems highly unlikely that this was Davidson's route.

Lingering issues with the French and aboriginals, combined with the unexploited natural resources of the land, begged for a new population of European settlers loyal to the Crown of England. This need opened the door for an expanded Crown grant system that would conditionally deed property—and fishing rights—to settlers of suitable background who would clear the land for farming, build permanent homes, live on the land, and who were, above all else, loyal to the King of England. There were still no trains, cars, or even roads to speak of, and in the early 1800s, the network of aboriginal portage routes throughout the province continued to be an important route of transportation, even for the early settlers. When Ganong interviewed settlers along the Cains in 1908, there were still a few people who claimed to recall seeing people using the portage trail from the Cains to the Gaspereau, but it was said to have been out of use for over 50 years, and no one could show Ganong exactly where either end of the portage trail was located. The trail itself was grown up to the point of being totally obliterated.

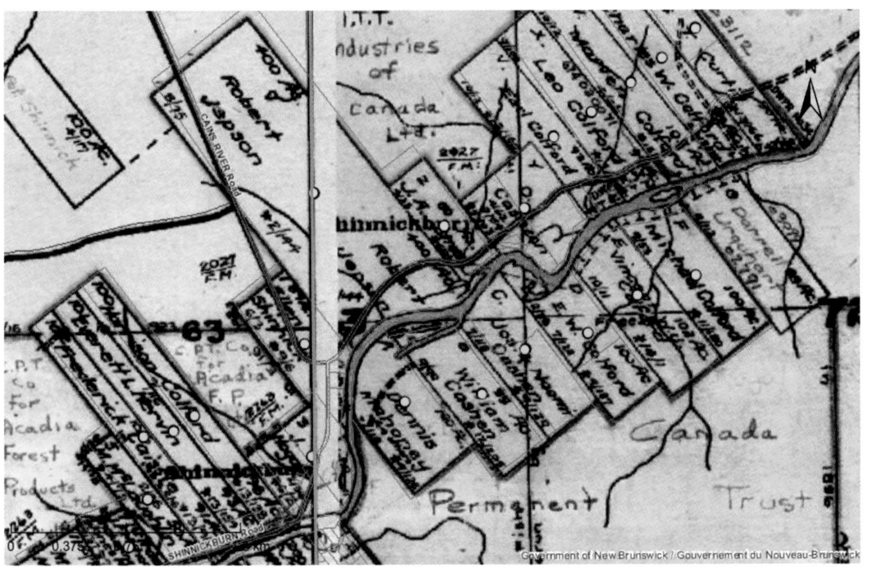

Page of original Provincial Government Crown Grant maps illustrating the Cains River village of Shinnickburn. Note that Irish names like Cashen, Colford, and Kervin were and still are prominent in the area. There was a grant to a person whose name appears to be Ellen Shinnick exactly where Shinnickburn Road now meets the Cains River. The Crown grants ended quite abruptly when you go up the Cains River a mile or so beyond Shinnickburn Village. ACCESS TO PLANET SOFTWARE PROVIDED BY SERVICE NEW BRUNSWICK.

While a fair number of loyalists to the English monarchy moved to the Saint John Valley during and after the American Revolution, the settlement of the Miramichi and Cains River Valleys was just in its infancy at the time. New Brunswick was part of Nova Scotia until 1784. Before that time and for a while later, the Miramichi and Cains River Valleys were wilderness outposts. The Crown grant system was designed to attract settlers to the fledgling province. You have to look at a lot of Crown grant records to find one along the Miramichi River system that was granted earlier than 1800. With very few exceptions, the grants began around 1830 or so. This is more than 60 years after the American Revolution, so the majority of these settlers were not displaced Loyalists, nor were they wealthy people. The Crown grants all offered more or less the same things: land, game, fishing rights, and freedom to carve out your own place. Successful grantees may have had some military service to the Crown, and some were adventurous people from upper-class backgrounds, but generally speaking, the settlers were working-class people from various locations around today's United Kingdom who would swear allegiance to the Crown and came to the New World for the land they couldn't hope to own in Europe. Applicants had to petition the land grant office, asking for the area of land that they wanted, and provide some evidence of good character and reasons why they would be successful as settlers. Coming from a farming family would certainly be a strong indicator that they would be successful at making a living from the resources of their new land.

The settlements of both the Cains and Miramichi Rivers by the Crown grant system took place at the same time. Service New Brunswick gave me temporary access to their online land registry system, and I looked at 18 Crown grants that are the locations of what I know to be some of the better fishing pools on the Cains River. The earliest of those grants was 1830—not all that long ago in the grand scheme of things. With no roads to speak of, and no railroads either; the rivers were still the major source of transportation. There were centers of civilization, and the towns of Chatham and Newcastle located near the mouth of the river—which, together with several smaller villages, became what is now Miramichi City—was one of those centers. If one looks at a map of the Miramichi watershed Crown grants, it is clear because they were chosen earliest that the most desirable locations were the ones closest to the mouth of the river. The onetime village of Shinnickburn, 16 miles or so up the Cains, is similar in distance by water from Miramichi City to Doaktown, and both areas were settled at around the same time in the 1820s. The Cains up to just beyond Muzzeroll Brook was settled as early as locations a comparable distance up the main stem of the Miramichi from the mouth—settlements spread up the river. There were only three or four grants made farther up the Cains River than Six Mile Brook. The decreasing size of the river made transportation difficult in low water, and that must have been an important factor. It is hard to say, though, why some locations were settled at certain times compared to others. In 1837, Michael McLaughlin received a Crown grant for land that borders what is now called the Moore Pool, just beyond Shinnickburn, some 17 miles up the Cains. A year later, in 1838, James Teedlan received the grant for the land surrounding the Teedlan Pool—which is one of the few pools on the river still known by the name of the original grantee. The Teedlan Pool is only 1.9 miles up the river, and so it is 15 miles closer to the mouth of the Miramichi than the Moore Pool, yet it was granted a year after. One would think that 15 miles would have been very important to someone who had to pole a dugout canoe or walk over rough trails to get back and forth from homestead to civilization. There was also a lot of excellent land available all along the Cains that was never granted to anyone; in fact, I would estimate that more than 95 percent of today's Cains River frontage is owned by the Province of New Brunswick and not private citizens.

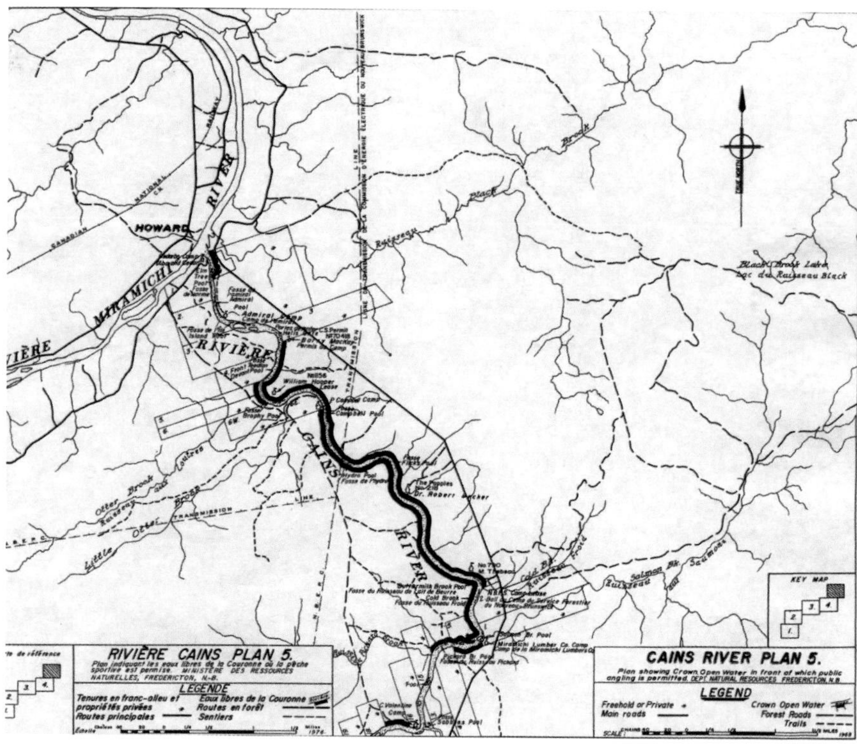

The dark black lines along the river shoreline indicate the open water or public fishing areas of the lower Cains River. The rectangular boxes are the areas of the Crown grants, and the river shoreline in front of them is private. The vast majority of the shoreline is public, and as you go farther upriver, the amount of public fishing water is even more pronounced. There are five of these maps that collectively comprise the entire Cains River, and in the upper three, the river is essentially 100 percent public.

I spend a fair amount of time on these rivers, and I'm constantly struck by how wild the Cains remains to this day. The idea of trying to clear acreage—a requirement of keeping your grant—with an axe; trying to grow and catch enough food to survive; cut, split, and dry enough firewood to stay warm in your drafty cabin; and do all the myriad tasks needed to get by must have been incredibly daunting. When you add that this strange new place has six months' worth of winter that is much more severe than anything experienced in the British Isles, it is no wonder that the conditions of many of these grants were never fulfilled. The people simply left for warmer climates and cities that offered jobs. Certainly, there was no time for sportfishing and money for things like rods and reels. If you were going to buy something with which to fish, it was going to be a net or fish spear so that you could put the salmon, trout, chubs, eels, Gaspereau, shad, or smelts that migrated up and down these rivers on the table to feed your family.

It is interesting to note what a relatively immediate and significant effect the European influence had on the salmon stocks of the Miramichi. Almost from the days of the first grant to Davidson and Cort, the population began to decline. There were many lamentations written about the utter disregard for any regulations.

A letter in 1849 from Alexander Davidson to the Fishery Commissioner Moses Perley Esquire recounted the sad state of the Miramichi fisheries at that time:

> From the foregoing information as to the Fisheries of the Miramichi, the following information can be drawn:
>
> 1st That although an Act of Assembly was passed in 1835 to regulate the Shad Fishery of Northumberland, yet there is now no such Fishery in the Miramichi, nothing being heard of shad.
>
> 2nd That the Gaspereau Fishery, formerly very productive, has almost ceased, and is now without value or importance.
>
> 3rd That the Basse Fishery is nearly, if not quite, destroyed.
>
> 4th That the Salmon Fishery has greatly decreased, and is in a fair way of being destroyed also."

According to Davidson and other's accounts of the day, it was not the lack of reasonable regulation that was the problem but rather a total disregard for the regulations and lack of enforcement that caused the overfishing.

Salmon were pursued from the time the fish arrived off the mouth of Miramichi Bay in May until they were on their spawning beds in the shallows of the far upriver reaches in October. In the ocean, it was drift nets and seines; in the estuary and river, it was set nets along the shores; and in the upper reaches, it was spearing. Spearing was blamed more vehemently than other forms of fishing, probably because it was the way in which the aboriginals harvested their salmon. It was said that upwards of 100 boats were fishing the headwaters areas with spears some nights in the autumn, and that catches of 80 salmon per boat were not uncommon. These were not all for food either; many of these were brought down river to Miramichi and sold.

Through much of the early twentieth century, a considerable fleet of small boats netted Miramichi Bay and the ocean just outside the Bay for salmon. During the 1920s and 1930s, these boats took approximately 300,000 salmon annually. There was still plenty of salmon to seed the spawning reaches. These photos show the large Atlantic salmon fleet docked in Escuminac during 1937 and a smaller one at Bay du Vin. Bay du Vin is considered by some to be a corruption of what is believed to be the original name of this French settlement Baie de Vents, which means "bay of winds." Note the double-ender construction of these boats. This made them much safer in a following sea when trying to navigate the channels between the barrier islands of Miramichi Bay. PHOTOS COURTESY OF THE PROVINCIAL ARCHIVES OF NEW BRUNSWICK.

Settlers all over the river set nets from their properties, and in large measure, they disregarded the regulations that required them to leave a substantial portion of the river open. Another letter to Perley from a James L. Price circa 1849 mentions two locations on the "South West Branch of the River" notorious for poaching: one at the property of a person named Astle near the confluence of the tide, and another at Arbo's just above Cains River. Price wrote that: "At both these places, it is the common practice to extend nets across the entire River, at every favourable opportunity; and in the latter place, to adopt besides, every other known method of unfair fishing, some of which are indeed peculiar to the parties. To these unfair practices. . . . doubtless to be attributed the fact that the annual catch of Salmon is less by more than nine-tenths, in the upper 80 miles of fishing ground, than it is in the corresponding distance below."

In Perley's report, only the slightest mention is made of sportfishing, where it says: "Above Boiestown, fly fishing is practiced to a considerable extent, by occasional visitors, but this method, from its uncertainty, and from the large portion of time consumed by it, cannot be pursued by the inhabitants generally." At least the uncertain outcome and use of large amounts of time part haven't changed all that much!

As the nineteenth century went on, regulations and the enforcement of those regulations did improve somewhat. Netting continued to be a problem for Miramichi salmon populations until the early 1980s when the netting of salmon was finally prohibited on the entire river system.

Compared to today, though, the percentage of salmon smolts leaving the Miramichi River that survived to return either as grilse, or multi sea winter adult fish, was extremely high, as much as five times or so what it has been in some recent years. The salmon populations had the ability to bounce back quickly, and educated calculations of the number of adult salmon returning to the river in the early 1900s ran to as many as a million grilse and salmon. That was the condition of the fishery when the next era dawned, the time of the early sport fishery for salmon on the Miramichi and Cains Rivers.

CHAPTER 4

Early Sportfishing through 1932

According to Peter Thomas in his book *Lost Land of Moses*, which was written about New Brunswick's first fishery commissioner Moses Perley, it was English military officers who brought sportfishing to New Brunswick. With relatively few exceptions there was very little salmonfishing activity, especially from central New Brunswick, until the middle of the nineteenth century. The preface to Thomas's book states the following: "When Sir James Alexander, a military surveyor, arrived in the Province in 1844, he declared that 'Neither in England nor in Canada was much known of New Brunswick: the general idea of it was, that it was an immense expanse of dark woods, over which hung everlasting mists, that a few fishermen inhabited the stormy coasts, which were bound up in ice for many months of the year, and that the interior was unfit for settlement.'"

That was one man's view, and while there was at least one much earlier reference made in the late 1700s to the Nashwaak River being "useful" for salmon angling, things on the

Outfitter Harry Allen and his guides took Lee Sturges of Chicago on a float trip down the Cains River in 1915. This map shows the areas that they canoed each day, where they camped and fished, and how long they stayed at each location. I was unable to pinpoint one of the named pools that they fished during their trip—the Stone Chimney Pool—but in this chapter, I've made some educated guesses.

salmon sportfishing front were just beginning to happen in 1844, and much of that early activity was generated by British military officers. A military career was the route that many well-born Englishmen took through life, and Thomas asserts that is was the younger sons of landed gentry who would be given assignments as adventurous as a post in the Canadian wilderness. Many of this class would have known about fly fishing for trout and salmon from their family estates in what was then the United Kingdom of Great Britain and Ireland. There are a few records of Canadian salmon angling by men such as Captain Richard Lewes Dashwood, whose fishing trips to North America from England in the 1860s classified as real adventures and not merely fishing trips. Most frequently, Quebec's Gaspe Rivers and the northern part of New Brunswick, including the Restigouche and the Nepisiguit, were the areas fished. The Miramichi was known for salmon fishing in its upper stretches, as was pointed out in the last chapter, but the lower river, with its large number of privately owned fishing nets festooning every pool, was not as highly thought of. However, in the early 1900s, that began to change.

THE FIRST CAINS RIVER SALMON OUTFITTER

There have always been some who can afford sportfishing. The cities of Canada and America had many citizens who could take time from their professions and had the disposable income to go on hunting and fishing trips. The wilds of New Brunswick were just the place to do this, with big game hunting targets such as moose, black bear, and woodland caribou. Most of the early hunting outfitters such as Thomas Pringle, W. Harry Allen, and Adam "Barn Door" Moore also did some fishing in the off-season.

By the 1870s, men like Alexander "Boss" Gibson of Marysville textile fame had brought the railroad to New Brunswick, so a relatively speedy means of transportation was in place, and the outfitting business had this necessary piece of infrastructure. W. Harry Allen was one of the founders of the New Brunswick Guides Association and its first president. Allen worked to bring things such as live moose and prefab log cabins to Boston and New York sportsmen's shows, and in fact, he traveled over a lot of the northeastern quadrant of America

In 1901, New Brunswick was still a wild promised land of fish and game. The province financed annual trips to sporting shows to promote the hunting and fishing outfitting industry. Pictured from left to right are William Chestnut of canoe fame; legendary hunting guides Adam "Barn Door" Moore and George Armstrong; W. Harry Allen, who will become the hero of our story; and the most famous New Brunswick hunter of all time, Henry Braithwaite, who knew all the central wilderness interior of New Brunswick like the back of his hand. They are pictured at the "Chicago show." PHOTO COURTESY OF THE PROVINCIAL ARCHIVES OF NEW BRUNSWICK.

Fishing and Hunting in New Brunswick

W. HARRY ALLEN

Guide and Hunter. Lessee of Cain's River. Unsurpassed Trout Fishing.

Special Attention given Boys and Young Men not enjoying best of health.

Write for full information

W. HARRY ALLEN

Penniac, N. B. - - Canada

Above: Magazine ad of W. Harry Allen in *Outing Magazine* from 1917. While he never married, Allen found time in his busy life to be a father to both George and Harriot Allen, the son and daughter of Harry's brother Charles, who died tragically as a young man during a log drive.

Left: W. Harry Allen in 1916 at the height of his career. Allen was a great promoter and traveled widely to major cities in the eastern half of America promoting his outfitting business by speaking at private clubs and sporting shows. Allen set the example that other successful outfitters followed throughout the twentieth century.

talking to sportsmen's clubs and advertising his business. He wrote many of his own advertisements and had a way of making his pitch quite personal. His ads often featured himself as a strapping woodsman with a rifle held by the muzzle and slung over his shoulder, or a big fish hanging from his hand as he stared you directly in the eye.

Other of Allen's ads showed a paternalistic side that kept revealing itself in Harry's actions throughout his life. The text of one ad from *Outing Magazine*, which shows up from time to time in searches, states: "Special attention given Boys and Young Men not enjoying the best of health." Perhaps a week with Allen on the Cains was just what they needed to put some glow back in their cheeks and a little muscle on their frames.

The extensive amount of Cains River frontage that was in public ownership shaped the beginnings of the sportfishing industry on that river. Allen, brought up on a farm in Penniac, not far from the Cains River headwaters, turned out to be the father of the fishery. As we shall see, the effects of Allen's energy, ambition, and talents were far-reaching. Allen is credited by some with *discovering* the Atlantic salmon fishery in the Cains River. In 1909, W. F. Ganong put considerable effort into exploring the Cains/Gaspereau Indian portage route, and he camped along the Cains near the Arbeau farm site—which is regarded today as one of the finest pools on the upper Cains River. Ganong said that he obtained a great deal of his information from an elderly Alexander Arbeau, who grew up on the farm, so clearly Arbeau had experience on the river going back into the mid-1800s. While the comment isn't attributed to Arbeau directly, Ganong said that the Cains River residents told him that the river was unsurpassed for brook trout but that the dark waters were no good for salmon. It seems like an incredible statement when you realize that at the same time Ganong was hearing this, Allen was building a very successful tourism fishing business for salmon on the very same river.

The big draw to the river was the Atlantic salmon, which, by the surviving accounts of Allen's trips, were available there in large numbers. The Arbeau Pool was one of the more important ones on the upper river, and in fact, in 1923, Allen himself purchased this property from Alexander Arbeau assumedly because of the fishing. This must be the same Alexander Arbeau who 13 years earlier told Ganong that the Cains was too dark to be any good for salmon. Allen sold the Arbeau Pool a year and a half later to a man from New York State—probably one of Allen's clients who saw the abandoned farm on a fishing trip with Allen. In this way, too, Allen was ahead of his time since this may well have been the first pool bought and sold on the Cains River simply to accommodate salmon fishing.

As unimaginable as it may seem today, Allen was able to secure an exclusive lease from the province for *all* of the public water on the Cains River. The Province of New Brunswick has always leased certain portions of its Crown Waters to the highest bidder for a period of years at a time. The earliest Cains Rivers Crown land lease that I could find was in 1890. An A. S. Murray of Fredericton leased the entire Cains River and Branches for $110—a respectable sum in 1890. Murray was probably interested in the trout fishing that the Cains was famous for. The province must have been pleased with the auction, which only had an upset price of $30.

The first Cains River lease to Allen that we could find evidence of in the Provincial Archives began in 1910, though I would believe Allen's Cains River fishing started a little earlier than that. The 1910 lease was a two-year lease and was jointly to W. H. "Harry" Allen and Allen Pringle, another famous hunting outfitter from the same area as Allen. Ganong's ink, reporting that the Cains River was unsuitable for salmon, was hardly dry!

Beginning in 1912, the leases became 10 years in duration, though they were paid annually. They also continued to

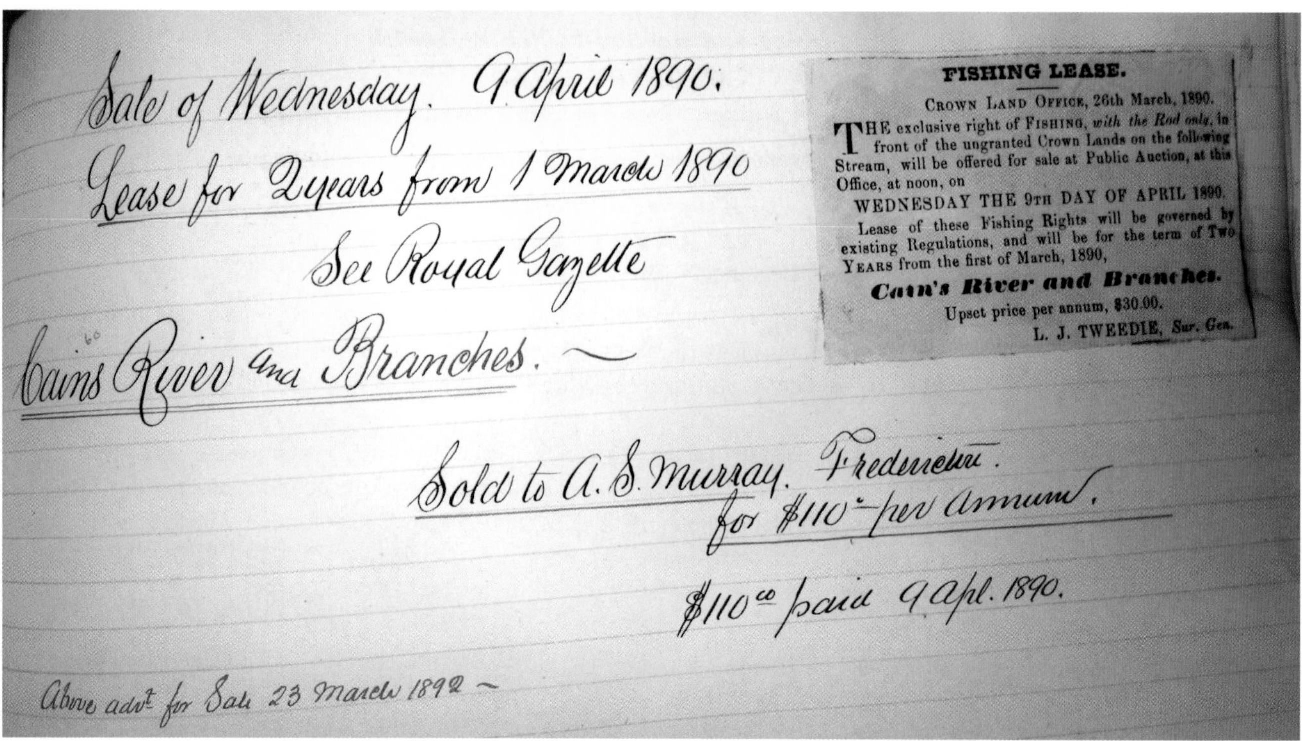

Sale of Wednesday. 9 April 1890.
Lease for 2 years from 1 March 1890
See Royal Gazette
Cains River and Branches. ~
Sold to A. S. Murray. Fredericton.
for $110.- per annum.
$110.00 paid 9 Apl. 1890.
Above advt for Sale 23 March 1892 ~

FISHING LEASE.

CROWN LAND OFFICE, 26th March, 1890.

THE exclusive right of FISHING, *with the Rod only*, in front of the ungranted Crown Lands on the following Stream, will be offered for sale at Public Auction, at this Office, at noon, on

WEDNESDAY THE 9TH DAY OF APRIL 1890.

Lease of these Fishing Rights will be governed by existing Regulations, and will be for the term of Two YEARS from the first of March, 1890,

Cain's River and Branches.

Upset price per annum, $30.00.

L. J. TWEEDIE, *Sur. Gen.*

This is the documentation from the Province of New Brunswick Crown Lands Office of the 1890 auction of the Cains River fishing rights—tributaries included. The entire river was leased for $110.00 per year to A. S. Murray of Fredericton. Who needs a computer with penmanship like that? The record shows that the price was properly advertised and paid in full.

Right: Documentation from the Province of Allen and Hopewell paying the first year's lease of $335 for Crown Lease number 33, which was for the entire Cains River and tributaries. An interesting note is that a few lines above Allen and Hopewell's signatures are those of the Miramichi Fish and Game Club, which operates and leases water on the NW Miramichi to this day.

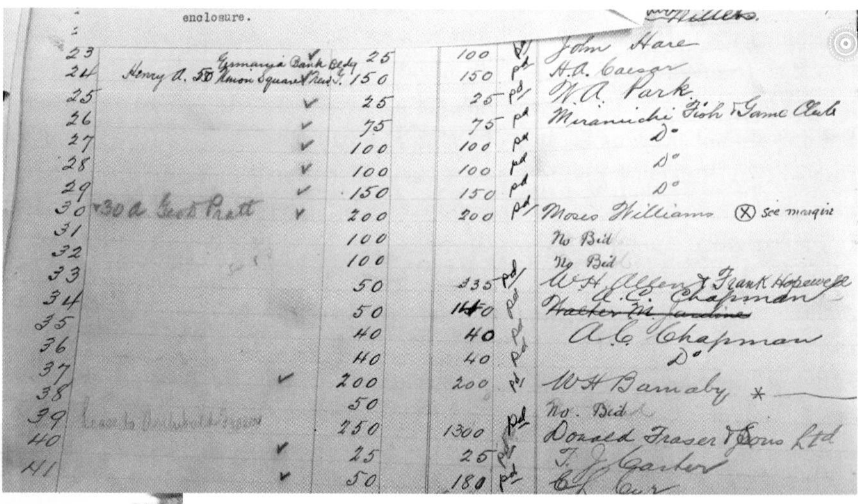

enclosure.

23		25	100 pd	John Hare
24	Henry A. 50 Union Square ... Germania Bank Bldg	150	150 pd	H.A. Caesar
25	✓	25	25 pd	W.A. Park
26	✓	75	75 pd	Miramichi Fish & Game Club
27	✓	100	100 pd	Do
28	✓	100	100 pd	Do
29	✓	150	150 pd	Do
30	30a Geo. Pratt ✓	200	200 pd	Moses Williams ⊗ see margin
31		100		No Bid
32		100		No Bid
33		50	335 pd	W.H. Allen & Frank Hopewell
34		50	1140 pd	A.C. Chapman ~~Walter M. Jardine~~
35		40	40 pd	A.C. Chapman
36		40	40 pd	Do
37	✓	200	200 pd	W.H. Barnaby *
38		50		No. Bid
39	Lease to Archibald Fraser	250	1300 pd	Donald Fraser & Sons Ltd
40	✓	25	25 pd	T. J. Carter
41	✓	50	180 pd	C. L. [illegible]

Left: This photo was in Dr. David Wade's family scrapbook, which had some photos that came from his grandfather, Charlie Wade. The man in the picture is unidentifiable, but the text on the back of the photo says "April 1929, Mile 36." Mile 36 is the approximate location of Hopewell Lodge. Men quite familiar with this stretch say that it appears to be slightly down and across the river from Hopewell. You can see the ground across the river rising on the left side of the photo on its way up to where the lodge might be situated. Charlie Wade, whose mother was Harry Allen's sister, began his salmon-fishing career guiding for Harry in the early 1900s. Charlie was destined to become the most famous person in the history of the Miramichi River Atlantic salmon fishery.

This is the front and back cover of the 1932 auction flyer and the "description of the angling stretch" that was included. The slogan "New Brunswick Land of Beauty and Royal Sport" dates to a time when Canada still very strongly identified with Great Britain. The handsome flyer also indicates strong support by the New Brunswick government for the commerce-generating outfitters association.

cover the entire river. These leases were named as trout leases, but it sounds as if Allen was able to keep his salmon fishery reserved for his clients. On this lease, as he had done on the 1910 lease, Allen took a partner. This time, it was in the form of Frank Hopewell, who owned the Hopewell Lodge, not far upriver from the Grand Lake Road. Hopewell Lodge was an incredible place, and we'll discuss it in much more detail later in the book. Assumedly splitting the lease lowered both of their costs, and there was no conflict, as Hopewell would have been interested in the upriver trout fishing while Allen wanted the spring salmon fishing that started a few miles downriver of Hopewell Lodge.

These leases brought, and still do bring, some revenue to the province, and they typically provided jobs for guardians, guides, cooks, and other personnel required to maintain a backwoods fishing camp. The province did its best to hype the auctions and produced quite an elegant brochure. In 1922, Allen signed Crown Fishing Lease #34 and again for $335 per annum. This was also for the entire Cains River and branches, and it would be his last 10-year lease. Allen passed away in the summer of 1932, and he was in declining health for some time before, but he lived to see the end of his own era in that the comprehensive leases he had enjoyed up to that point were ended in March of 1932. Instead, the Cains was divided up into four lease numbers—43, 44, 45, and 46—in the next auction. For #43, it ran from just above Muzzeroll Brook upriver to the Arbeau Farm; #44 was from Arbeau's up to the Murray camp—just below Route 123; #45 was from the Murray camp up to Otter Brook; and the final lease, #46, was from Otter Brook up to the Canadian Railway Bridge where Allen began his float trips. (Note: The province has historically also offered camp leases on Crown-owned land. These leases typically do not include angling rights but just the right to build and keep a camp on the site. The Murray Lease was such a camp lease.) The crown water below Muzzeroll became open public water, as it remains to this day. Interestingly, the two downriver sections—which would be more known for their salmon fishing—failed to reach the upset price that the government had raised to $500 for each section.

The upper stretches were leased out, undoubtedly to people who wanted to fish for the river's big sea-run brook trout. Apparently the government had a change of heart, because at the end of October 1934, there was a new auction for a slightly modified item #43, that was now for the Cains—without any tributaries—from Muzzeroll upstream all the way to the Canadian National Railway bridge from where Allen and his guides used to launch their trips. This lease was for eight years so that it would expire with the other 10-year leases in 1942. George Allen won the lease for $200 a year. The new terms were expanded considerably from the original 1932 lease that

Purchased by:- J. H. Whalen
Boiestown

43. Cains River, not including its branches, from a point ½ mile above the mouth of Muzroll Brook to the lower line of a clearing known as the Arbo Place 500.

Purchased by:-

44. Cains River, not including its branches from the lower line of a clearing known as the Arbo Place to a point ½ mile above Murray's Camp 500.

Purchased by:-

(continued) 150

Item No.	Description	Upset Price per Annum $	Sale Price per Annum $	Remarks
45	Cains River, not including its branches, from a point ½ mile above Murray's Camp to a point ¼ mile below mouth of Otter Brook.	500.	500	
	Purchased by:- Edward G. Parrot, 140 Federal St. Salem Mass			
46	Cains River, not including its branches, from a point ¼ mile below the mouth of Otter Brook to the Canadian National Railway	200.	200	
	Purchased by:- G. Stewart Neill for James S. Neill & Sons Ltd Fredericton			

This book from a 1932 auction shows that there were no winning bids made for items #43 or #44—the Cains River from Muzzeroll upstream to Arbeau Farm, and then from Arbeau's up to the Murray Camp, respectively. The second entries show that the lease from Murray Camp and then to Otter Brook brought a whopping $500 per year. The less desirable stretch from Otter Brook to the railroad bridge brought $200 annually. Two things are clear from this development. First, W. Harry Allen left big shoes to fill, and with his death, there was no one ready to aggressively pursue the salmon fishery as Harry had done it. Second, the relatively good prices for the upper river show that the brook trout fishery that could be carried out all season long was very desirable.

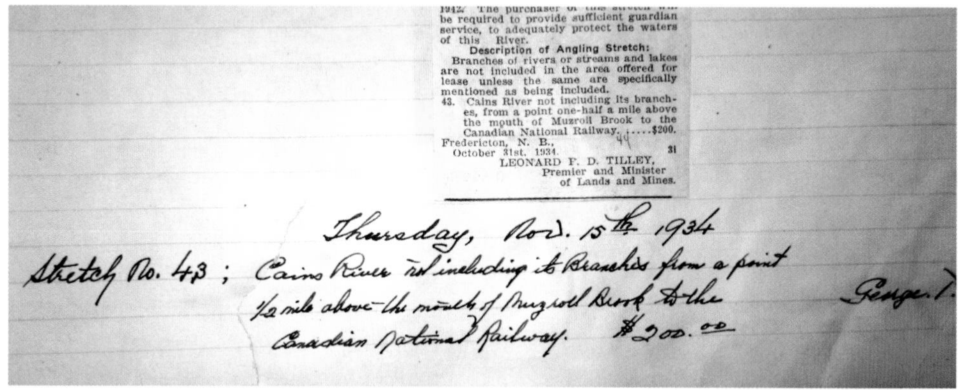
1942. The purchaser of this stretch will be required to provide sufficient guardian service, to adequately protect the waters of this River.

Description of Angling Stretch:

Branches of rivers or streams and lakes are not included in the area offered for lease unless the same are specifically mentioned as being included.

43. Cains River not including its branches, from a point one-half a mile above the mouth of Muzroll Brook to the Canadian National Railway. .....$200.

Fredericton, N. B.,
October 31st, 1934. 31

LEONARD P. D. TILLEY,
Premier and Minister
of Lands and Mines.

Thursday, Nov. 15th 1934

Stretch No. 43 ; Cains River not including its Branches from a point ½ mile above the mouth of Muzroll Brook to the Canadian National Railway. $200.00 George T.

This is a record of George Allen's winning bid in 1934 for item #43, presumably a special, new lease on the Cains River from Muzzeroll to the railroad bridge in Bantalor for salmon fishing.

had cut the area up into four pieces, but it was not as expansive as the 1922–1932 lease that covered the entire Cains River and tributaries. It appears from this that Allen's lease must have been created for salmon only since this stretch also included the two areas already leased in 1932, which were undoubtedly just for trout since that is how the original bids had been worded.

There are two extraordinarily important pieces of surviving information on the early days of Cains River salmon fishing with Harry Allen. Probably foremost among those is a story named *Salmon Fishing on Cain River New Brunswick*. It was printed in 1919 by a man named Lee Sturges from Chicago. Sturges was a businessman of considerable importance and also an artist. He was an accomplished fly-fisher and hunter who, before this trip, had hunted caribou and moose in New Brunswick.

The small book is pleasantly written and contains some rare observations of wildlife and human settlements as they existed at that time along the Cains River. Also, Sturges personally decorated his book with many first-class etchings of

SALMON FISHING ON CAIN RIVER

NEW BRUNSWICK

BY

LEE STURGES

PRIVATELY PRINTED
MCMXIX

Title page of Lee Sturges's privately printed book, *Salmon Fishing on the Cains River New Brunswick*. Sturges was an accomplished businessman and artist from Chicago. He was influential and was connected to other well-known fishermen of the day who continued to come out to New Brunswick to fish with Harry Allen. They all helped make the Miramichi and Cains Rivers a famous fly-fishing destination. PHOTOS OF STURGES BOOK COURTESY THE AMERICAN MUSEUM OF FLY FISHING.

The bidding was lively in this early 1900s fishing-lease auction held at the Legislative Assembly Chambers in Fredericton. In the picture with the balcony, the fourth man from the left in the front row, wearing glasses and a light-colored suit and tie—next to the woman—is Charlie Wade. Times have changed. Many of these men were rugged outdoorsmen, but they took this opportunity to come to the city and dress like Wall Street tycoons. PHOTOS COURTESY OF THE PROVINCIAL ARCHIVES OF NEW BRUNSWICK.

(A) This is the artwork for the title page of the film made in 1915 by the Canadian National Railway System to promote Atlantic salmon fishing on the Cains River in the Province of New Brunswick, specifically the Cains River. In his book, Lee Sturges quotes Harry Allen: "Fish are in the river. Be here Friday. Wire number in party. If no objections, Government will send a moving-picture outfit to photograph the salmon fishing." Allen was always promoting, and clearly, Sturges was seen as an influential fisherman. **(B)** In this segment of the film, the fishing party is now headed downriver to a new pool. Based on the film ending in the vicinity of Sabbies River, I believe this is somewhere between the Arbeau Pool and the Sabbies River. That is a distance of more than 15 miles, but there is really no way to pin it down more closely than that. **(C)** Outfitter W. Harry Allen and sportsman Lee Sturges are seen here selecting their flies for the upcoming day's fishing. This was before the Cains River streamers were developed, though the forerunner, the Allen Streamer, may have already been in existence. They were probably selecting from the traditional, English-designed, feather-wing salmon flies that Allen had instructed Sturges to purchase for the trip. **(D)** Guides are shown here gaffing salmon. Almost all the fish caught were kept and eaten on these trips, including kelts. The caption in the film says that this picture was taken at the Whirlpool between Shinnickburn and the Mouth of Sabbies River. **(E)** Harry Allen's group tented on this gravel bar in the mouth of the Sabbies River. This bar is still there today but in varying sizes year to year. It is always being swept away by ice and/or high water and then redeveloping. It seems like a very precarious choice for a place to camp, and possibly, it was just staged for this film. You can see a tall, slim guide poling hard *downstream* in the far, front canoe. This scene was probably also staged for the film. **(F)** George Allen, who was known for his cooking, is on the right cutting up salmon steaks and depositing them in the cast-iron skillet. These would be steaks from black salmon or kelts. No one would think of eating these today, but at one time, they were very commonly eaten, and according to accounts I have heard, they are quite delicious since they lacked the oily fat of fresh-run fish. **(G)** Lee Sturges and Harry Allen are left and right on the far side of the fire. I believe that George Allen is sitting next to the pole across the fire on the left side. I cannot identify the other guides present. ALL PHOTOS IN THIS GROUP ARE COURTESY OF THE AMERICAN MUSEUM OF FLY FISHING.

scenes that he encountered on that trip along the Cains. The book was said to be privately printed in a run of only 50 copies. Most of these were reportedly lost when Sturges's house burned, but one expert collector tells me that he knows of approximately 20 copies, so it is unclear how many actually survived.

The American Museum of Fly Fishing in Manchester, Vermont, was very helpful in providing me with scans of the Sturges book and a digitized copy of the promotional film made of that trip by photographers hired by the Canadian National Railway. In this early film, you can see Harry Allen and Sturges sitting together comparing salmon flies, men gaffing salmon at the famous Horseshoe Pool, George Allen frying black salmon steaks, camping tents set on the gravel bar at the mouth of the Sabbies River, and some terrific footage of the guides poling down the Cains with the outrageously long poles used for high-water travel as well as holding the canoes in position for fishing. The quality of the image has the limitations of such an old film that was first transferred to a VHS tape format, but it is still thrilling to see moving images of these early days of Atlantic salmon fishing on the Cains River.

A selection of pictures that we extracted from the film is shown on this page.

The other book, called *Fishing Memories*, is by Dorothy Noyes Arms. Arms and her famous husband, artist John Taylor Arms—he did those incredibly detailed, dark-gothic etchings of gloomy, medieval cathedrals with gargoyles perched over

These wonderful drawings are a selection of illustrations by William J. Schaldach from *Fishing Memories* by Dorothy Noyes Arms, which was published in 1938. Photographic equipment was very expensive and ponderous to carry around in the early 1900s. It was also very possible for the equipment to get wet and ruined on a Cains River canoe trip. Most sporting books of the day were illustrated with pen-and-ink drawings or etchings by artists such as Schaldach who were also sportsmen themselves. The first drawing, called "In the Tackle Room," shows a long, feather-wing streamer fly. This may be the only existing drawing of the Allen Streamer, a fly that was inspired when a backcast by one of Harry Allen's sports snagged a piece of long grass and sent it out into the pool where it was taken by a salmon.

ancient European streets—were a fishing couple who lived in New York City. While *Fishing Memories* was published in 1938, the book says that they had been coming to the Cains for many years, assumedly from back in the 1920s or before. They booked their first trip after they had heard Harry Allen speak at a meeting of the angling club they belonged to back in the city.

Sturges's 1915 trip was the only one for him that we know of. The two books provide two different perspectives on the fishery. Arms's writing is very lively, and she offers quite a different view of the events along the river than does Sturges. Arms's book was illustrated with drawings of Cains River scenes by William Joseph Schaldach, who was an important name in the sporting-art world for a solid 50 years during the middle of the twentieth century. He spent some years before the Second World War at *Forest and Stream*, then he came back to work there for many more years after the war when it had been renamed as *Field and Stream*. Between the two small but nicely detailed books, as well as my own time on the river, I'm left believing that I have a decent feel for what one of these early-1900s canoe trips down the Cains must have been like.

I've included a selection of my favorite half-dozen Schaldach illustrations from *Fishing Memories*. The one named "End of the Trail" is particularly interesting to anyone who is familiar with the Cains River today. It looks so different to me from the current view of the mouth of the Cains River that I thought perhaps Schaldach simply created it. First of all, the hillside leading down from the Howard Road and the Catholic Church is essentially cleared whereas it is heavily wooded today, in addition to several buildings on the right-hand side of the road, which are not there now, there are a very large house and quite-elegant-appearing house at the bottom of the hill that is also gone. In the drawing, the landscape on the right side of the river depicts a steep bank. Today, that shore is very gradual and flat. According to Emery Brophy—who grew up a couple of miles upriver at the Brophy farm—the missing house was a Colford property. Brophy also named every other building in the drawing. The shore on the right-hand side of the river mouth is now quite low and flat. Brophy says that while it was never as steep in his time as it is shown, it was much steeper in his youth than it is now, and it simply has been ground down by spring ice over the years to its current appearance.

Among Harry Allen's employees were four men who would all figure heavily in the history of the Miramichi and Cains River salmon outfitting industry with impacts that come all the way down to today's fishery. These men were George Allen, Wendell Allen—a different branch of the Allen family—Clarence Wade and his brother, Charlie Wade. Both Sturges and Arms spent some time in their books describing the guides they got to know quite well on these trips. Both writers spoke with respect and affection for Harry, which is probably in no small measure the reason why he was so successful. Sturges and Arms both noticed Harry giving things such as food, tobacco, and sweets to the people they met along the river, including children. Sturges saw a man and grown boy driving a handful of logs down the river but who were having a hard time of it in a heavy rain. Seeing their difficulty, Harry and his men jumped into their canoes and helped them round up their logs, gave a hot meal to the wet river drivers, and watched them head home down the Cains in the sunset. Sturges called him "big hearted Harry."

Arms dug into the characters a little further: "They are a closely-knit group, bound to each other by the most complicated ties of marriage, which we sort out with utmost difficulty, and by long friendship." It is certainly true, as Harry, who never married, brought up as his own George Allen, whose father—Harry's own brother Charles—was lost in a log drive, and Harry's sister Minnie was Charlie and Clarence Wade's mother.

Harry Allen's death certificate said that he passed away from myocarditis with a contributing factor of arteriosclerosis in June of 1933 at 72 years of age. That means that Harry was 54 at the time of the Sturges trip. Arms said that while Harry was strong and active to the end, he had gained a lot of weight. No doubt the weight, along with the high cholesterol and salt diet of the day, plus the fact that Arms reports Harry as a heavy smoker, did not help his heart and arteries. Harry's death and the proceeds of his estate put all the younger men into the outfitting business for themselves. I was able to find Harry's will, and while his estate did not contain a lot of money, Harry clearly loved good fishing and hunting properties, and he had camps and land at strategic locations on the Cains and the Miramichi River as well as back near his home in Penniac. Harry was truly the father of what we can call the Cains River branch of the Miramichi outfitters.

Harry Allen's lease on the Cains River included all the water in front of the crown property from the government of New Brunswick—which is the great majority of the river. Harry also made other arrangements for fishing the privately owned pools of choice, too. In a couple of books written about trips with Harry, the authors noted his gifts of salmon, food items, and treats to people where they stopped to fish or camp here and there along the river. He also purchased produce from the farmers, and Arms notes a farmer named Porter bringing chickens and eggs to their camp near the mouth of Sabbies River. Harry knew how to get along with people.

Harry and his guides took their parties down the Cains River from the headwaters to the mouth. These fishing trips could last for up to two weeks, and while Harry did have the occasional use of a camp, most of the time, they all stayed in large, outfitter-style canvas tents. It was a real outdoor adventure. In the railroad film, you can see the tents perched on the gravel bar mentioned earlier at the mouth of the Sabbies River. This seems to me incredible from several standpoints. First, that gravel bar is today well underwater during virtually all of the spring fishing. It is a testament to how much further into the spring Allen Outfitters fished the Cains than we do today—since the river height typically drops greatly between the beginning of spring salmon fishing in mid-April and the end of May when it is clear Allen was still fishing. Even if the bar was out, a good rain could raise the water up enough to submerge that bar within a few hours. It just seems incredibly risky, but I am sure that Allen and his guides had the situation well in hand, or as I suggested earlier, the location was actually just staged for the film. If they did camp on the bar, they certainly didn't have to walk far for their fishing.

The Sturges book begins with him being informed by a telegraph from Harry that "fish were in the river." Herein begins what was for me originally the great mystery of this trip. There is no way in the writing or illustrations to tell definitively what time of the year this trip took place. I used to believe that it was in the fall. This was because the fall fishing for late-run bright salmon is the sport that the river is now famous for. It is hard for me to imagine someone coming out from Chicago and getting completely outfitted to fish for kelts, but I now believe that is what Sturges and hundreds of other customers of Harry did. There are various clues as we go through the story, and while some seem to be contradictory, after thinking about this a great deal and discussing it with others who have studied the Sturges story, I think the preponderance of the evidence says they were kelt fishing, and that the time of this trip was at least mid-May and very possibly a little later. This is extremely late by modern standards for kelts to still be holding in the Cains River.

The Sturges etchings depict trees without leaves and somewhat bleak scenes. This could possibly be artistic license, but it could also be either spring or fall. During the last week of Cains River fall fishing in many seasons, the trees are largely bare, and they certainly are in April and May when kelts might still be present in the river. Sturges mentions the "gray-green budding foliage of the birch and poplar." However, the fish do not *arrive* in the river during the spring, and trees are not budding in the fall—statements from the book that seem to contradict each other. Some fish are still there after spawning the previous fall, but these are kelts, not fish that fight by leaping into the air and fighting like tigers for 20 or 30 minutes, as Sturges describes them.

The Arms book, though, is unquestionably about kelt fishing, though she does mention the odd bright fish, as we will discuss later. Arms states the following: "We first went to New Brunswick in May. The spring freshet had passed and the stream was rapidly approaching its summer level." A little later, she writes, "Since then we have gone in April when the melting snow, lying drifted through the woods, makes a boiling torrent of the river." She also writes about long, extended fights with the larger fish that they caught, as well as the fish making many jumps clearing the water and landing with a resounding splash. Arms also talks about seeing the swirls of the fish chasing her fly and fish rushing after it with open mouths. All of this certainly seems unusual for kelts, but they could also be just a bit of exaggeration.

There are subtle keys to the timing in the Sturges book. Near the end of the story, Sturges states that: "Good salmon fishing during a short season; fine brook trout fishing later." I assume that "later" means the late May or early June run of larger, sea-run brookies—historically up to seven or more pounds—that the river is also famous for, and we'll discuss that later in the book. This certainly points to a spring trip and perhaps one made earlier rather than later in May. The timing of both trips and the kind of fishing described seems confusing and hard to reconcile with what we know about the fishing today.

Another difference in the fishing compared to modern times appears to be the average size of the fish. Both authors talk about some large specimens. Sturges was not a longtime salmon fisherman, and he didn't have much of a frame of reference. Arms and her husband, J.T., though, were veterans at salmon fishing. Many spring fishermen today, me for one, just see it as a chance to get out on the river and be in the New Brunswick countryside early in the season. It is fun to catch a few kelts, especially if you get a large one. I know, however, that these fish are only a shadow of what they were when they entered the river and what, with luck, they will be again after a little feeding in the ocean. The Armses fished in the ocean and out west for trout. They were sophisticated fisherfolk. They chose kelt fishing over bright salmon fishing because she very honestly states that she and her husband simply didn't have the patience to fish for the more elusive bright fish. Arms also went on to say that they thought that fishing for the fall run was unsporting. She admitted to never having witnessed it but had been told that during the fall run, "The salmon lie so close to each other that sides touch sides, and their fins rise above the surface of the water like a vast fleet of tiny black sails." She reported that the fish were so thick, "Even if none rose to a fly, one could hardly fail to snag any number among the

Above left: In this etching from Sturges's book, you can see the large size of the reel and the use of a two-handed rod. Before coming on the trip, Sturges agreed to: ". . . set about securing the necessary two-handed fly rod; large salmon reel, the 150 yards of suitable line." Later American-style single-handed fly rods became the custom, and by the 1950s, two-handed rods had virtually disappeared from the scene. *Above right:* A heavy two-handed rod stands next to a large catch of salmon.

hordes." If there is any truth to that, the fall run up the Cains must have been something in 1920! Arms kept detailed track of the catches by herself and her husband and their sizes. She talks about many very large salmon: "a great dark form lay inert in the net and I was so exhausted that only the sight of the scales registering twenty-two pounds revived me." A few pages later, she talks about a 25-pound hen fish, and then finally a 45-inch, 28-pound male. There are many more references to kelts that weighed upward of 20 pounds and some lost—of course—that were even larger. One of the old glass photos that I purchased has written in the margins that it is of a 31-pound Cains River salmon. The fish in the picture is of a very long kelt. These fish were mostly kept and eaten in those days and were probably weighed by scales. Just how accurate the weights given in a fishing book are is never certain, but a 28-pound kelt would weigh approximately 40 pounds as a bright-run fish. The large average size combined with the great fights, jumps, and surface strikes that both authors described creates quite a different image of spring salmon fishing then we generally think of today.

My conclusion is that the fish caught by Sturges and Arms were very well mended kelts. We do find kelts occasionally putting up fights like this in the lower Miramichi late into the spring fishing season. It seems very likely that there were simply so many more fish in the run 100 years ago that the small percentage of kelts left in the lower Cains River were still enough to provide some great fishing. These fish, now nourished by insect larvae and small forage fish, were far enough along the scale of rebuilding that they put up an excellent account of themselves.

Before leaving for Fredericton from his home in Chicago, Allen sent Sturges off to buy a large, double-handed salmon rod and reel. Undoubtedly, the two-handed rod was left over from the British military influence of salmon fishing in Canada during the nineteenth century. The two-handed rods were thought necessary to cast the heavy lines that carried the big, air-resistant streamer flies of the day and to muscle in big salmon. The dominant culture on the Miramichi, and for that matter all New Brunswick salmon rivers, is still that of single-handed rods, even though currently European Spey-casting techniques have started to become more popular on Canadian rivers. Arms says in her book that: "When we first ran the river, two-handed rods were still in use there, and I remember our surprise when we saw the flailing technique necessitated

The angler in the bow of this canoe is fast to a big fish using a single-handed rod. The rifle in the boat, and the fact that it is obviously a big fish, indicates to me that this was taken during the fall hunting season and this was a salmon on its spawning run up the Cains. The timing of this photo is thought to be circa 1936. PHOTO COURTESY OF THE PROVINCIAL ARCHIVES OF NEW BRUNSWICK.

At McGivney Station loading a canoe for the train ride over to the drop-off point at Landers in the Cains headwaters. Note the protective skids on the canoe to keep the rocks from scraping through the canoe canvass. Arms's book mentions that some years there were times when the upper river was so shallow that it was necessary for the guides to drag the canoes through some of the shallow areas. Aboriginal travelers pioneered this technology on their birch bark canoes long before European arrivals. PHOTO COURTESY OF THE PROVINCIAL ARCHIVES OF NEW BRUNSWICK.

by them. They have long since dropped out of the picture, and the lighter and more graceful tackle is the order of the day." I would assume that this must have been between 1925 and 1930. That period of time may be the point when the original British military influence on salmon-fishing equipment began to die off and very likely American fishing tourists converted the fishery over to the single-handed equipment they were used to back home.

In addition to the rod and reel, Sturges was told to purchase a number of flies. These included popular English featherwing patterns such as the Durham Ranger, Wilkinsons, and Silver Doctors. No mention is made of "the Allen Streamer," which was named after W. Harry Allen, who invented it. The original Allen Streamer was said to be no more than a few long chicken hackles tied to a hook. Again, just a few years later, Arms talks about a move away from the traditional British flies to a new streamer design. Arms states that their annual trips to the Cains lapsed for several years, and when they returned, the Cains River streamer fly had been invented, and at least three guides took credit for the invention. Arms describes the exact act: "All honor to who honor is due." The mythical "he"—meaning the guide who actually invented the Cains River streamer fly—was guiding a sportsman fishing with a standard pattern when his backcast caught up a bit of grass. Before anything could be said and the hook freed, the "sport" had cast again, and the fly, complete with a long, wiggling piece of grass, was sent out into the river. At once, a salmon struck this unintentional invention. Although the pool was visibly full of fish, and many had previously rolled up without taking, this was the first strike of the day, and it made the guide wonder. Procuring a long feather, he tied it on, thus creating the first "Cains River Streamer" and immediately, the luck turned. Ever since then, these long and gay flies have been the "accepted takers" on the Cains and Miramichi Rivers in the spring. We'll further trace the history of the Cains River Streamers in a later chapter devoted to flies and tackle.

Sturges finally arrived in Fredericton, where he met up with Allen. The next day, leaving before light, Allen and his guides took Sturges and a photographer supplied by the Canadian National Railway to film the expedition, up to McGivney Station some 30 miles NNE of Fredericton. They then took another railroad car down through the marshy

This is a picture of the guides unloading the canoes and supplies at Landers, where the train tracks cross the Cains River to begin their trip downriver. Upon reaching the Miramichi at the end of their trip, they brought their canoes up the hill to the train station at Howards for the trip back to Fredericton. Years ago, this sort of transportation to and from remote fishing and hunting locations was commonly utilized all over Canada. PHOTO COURTESY OF THE PROVINCIAL ARCHIVES OF NEW BRUNSWICK.

A fishing party having lunch before heading down the river. Note the sport on the left wearing breeks and knee socks. The English sporting influence was still very strong in Canada during the first half of the twentieth century. PHOTO COURTESY OF THE PROVINCIAL ARCHIVES OF NEW BRUNSWICK.

plateau that contains the headwaters of the Cains River to a drop-off called Landers at a railroad bridge that crosses the river in the heart of the Bantalor Wildlife Refuge. This point in the journey was used for many years by anglers taking this

Sturges's etching of the group starting out. COURTESY AMERICAN MUSEUM OF FLY FISHING.

Right: Sturges's etching of a bull and cow moose wading in the Cains River. The last few caribou left in New Brunswick were being shot around the years of Sturges's trip. COURTESY AMERICAN MUSEUM OF FLY FISHING.

As we can see by the small width of the Cains River in this photograph, this is the very beginning of the journey. Look at the loads that these canoes are carrying! Their capacity was considerable, but they are sitting very deep in the water. No wonder that they needed the protective skids. PHOTO COURTESY OF THE PROVINCIAL ARCHIVES OF NEW BRUNSWICK.

trip, and there have been many photographs of it published. Dorothy Noyes Arms describes the scene at Landers like this: "Upon a high embankment lay a huge and conglomerate heap in which were all the things we should use for two weeks, and beside it stood the men on whose skill our very live lives would depend, and with whom we should pass the days in that strange, close intimacy of camping. At our feet the Cains River foamed on its headlong onward course. To its rushing current we were about to entrust ourselves, and from beneath its inscrutable surface we hoped to tempt the Atlantic salmon we had come to seek."

The canoes were slid down a steep bank, and the journey began.

At this point, the Cains is just a stream perhaps 30 feet across. Sturges says that it was shallow, and care was needed to keep the canoes from scraping the bottom. I suppose it is possible that even in spring one could find these conditions, but it would have to be at least a fair while after ice-out. Kelts have somewhat particular overwintering requirements. They like places where there is some depth to the water and respite from flow velocities. Allen's guides had to go a long way downriver from Landers to find suitable habitat for kelts to be holding.

It is known from tagging work that many kelts in the Main Southwest Miramichi drop all the way down to the estuary after spawning to overwinter in deep, relatively ice-free pools. We are not talking here strictly about surface ice. Winters along the Miramichi and Cains get cold enough so that ice forms on the sides and bottoms of the rivers too, and this can considerably restrict the flow of water, causing velocity to increase and forcing the kelts to drop back. There is very little black salmon fishing done today on the main river above Boiestown, and to my knowledge, there is none done in the upper two-thirds of the Cains. According to Mark Hambrook, this is because even though the Miramichi and Cains River headwaters are the scene of the greatest spawning activity, the salmon leave there for the deeper, slower lower river after sowing their seeds in the gravel beds. Even though he has experienced quite good kelt fishing in the bottom four or five miles of the Cains, and fishes it every year, guide Jason Curtis has seldom found any kelts farther upriver than the mouth of the Sabbies River, and there are not many of them at that. In early May 2017, we did catch a kelt grilse and lost another at the bottom of our home pool at Mahoney Brook, but for us, it was a first, and we try every year. The Mahoney Brook pool is only one-third of the way up the river, and it is still five or

The river in these photographs is much larger than the Cains, and I expect that they were taken on the Southwest Miramichi in the vicinity of Black Brook where the Cains flows in. The sports are unknown. I acquired these photos together with the next group, and I assume that they were all taken on the same fishing trip.

six miles downriver from where Allen's guides began fishing for kelts at the Elkins and Arbeau pools.

If Sturges left Chicago for Fredericton after getting the word to come from Allen, a minimum of two weeks must have passed before Sturges was on the river. This is precious time in the spring salmon fishery. These days, the good fishing is definitely over by May 15 and a good deal earlier in some years. This is especially true on the Cains, which, judging by our experience, is best during the last two weeks of April. It appears, though, that at least in some years during the early 1900s things were a lot different. Undoubtedly the larger runs of those years were the biggest factor, but also, the upriver pools might have been deeper, and from the combination, the fishing simply held on later.

In December 2017, on eBay, I was able to acquire glass-negative photographs of two men fishing for trout and salmon on the Cains River. The photos were taken by a Eugene S. Jones, who was the official photographer for the Boston and Maine Railroad and author of "Maine, The Sportsman's Paradise," a 1922 short story and picture review of hunting and fishing in Maine. When I looked at the pictures on eBay, I recognized a large rock that sits in the mouth of the Sabbies River junction pool with the Cains. This is the pool where Camp Stanton now stands. Even though a large cleared field visible just up the river is now forest, I was fortunate enough to be able to recognize the entire scene from personal experience. Curtis, head guide at Campbell's Pool camp, who grew up fishing these places, confirmed it, saying that he had stood many pleasant hours trout fishing on that exact rock.

There are two older men pictured reeling in Atlantic salmon and carrying a good-sized brook trout. There is also a much younger man, I would say in his twenties, who appears to be a guide, as well as another older man who I believe was also guiding. Neither of these men has any fishing equipment, and they are pictured holding up the catches of the men for photographs. The fish being held up are unquestionably kelts, one of them exceedingly long. The frame of one photograph reads, "31 pounds Cains River Atlantic salmon." It might have been true when the fish was fresh off the tide seven or eight months before, but the weight seems exaggerated when you look at the picture—which shows that not all that much has changed with fishermen.

This group of photographs was taken at the mouth of Sabbies Pool on the Cains River. The center photo is especially unmistakable, in that the large rock off the bow of the canoe is still there, and in fact, the author stood upon it almost 100 years after the photographs were taken, casting into the seam where the Sabbies and Cains Rivers meet. The young guide in the top and bottom photos is none other than Charlie Wade, who would follow his uncle W. Harry Allen as the most important name in Cains River and Miramichi salmon fishing for more than 40 years after Harry's death in 1932.

This is what the Duffy Camp looked like in May 2018. You can see the foundation outline in the ground and the remains of an old stove and icebox in the corner. Sturges described the brook as: "A beautiful little stream racing over the rocks and full of miniature water-falls supplied pure, ice-cold water." It is still traveling its ancient route down the hillside and onward into the Cains.

Given Harry Allen's exclusive lease of the entire river, one must assume that this was one of Harry's guided parties working its way down the river. I also recognized by the lines of his mouth and general stature that the young guide was Charlie Wade, the founder of Wade's Fishing Lodge. I sent the pictures to Charlie's grandsons—Herb Wade's boys—Drs. David and Richard Wade of Fredericton, who immediately confirmed that the picture was, in fact, their grandfather.

It is interesting to look closely at the pictures and see the conditions that they were fishing in. They were not dressed like Eskimos, as we often or usually are when kelt fishing. The clothes worn by the guides are very European, showing the close ties the New Brunswick culture still held to the United Kingdom at the beginning of the twentieth century. The men wore tweed breeks with the accompanying knee-length, woolen stockings, woolen flat caps, and full-buttoned cardigan sweaters. The water level is down quite far with lots of beach all around, and there are no ice cakes anywhere to be seen. Also, the aforementioned rock is out of the water as it would be at a normal fall fishing height. Almost certainly this means that we are talking about at least mid-May before the river would settle to that height. Mid-May in 2017 means that the kelts are gone, more or less, from everywhere along the Miramichi except for a few down in the Rapids section of the river just above tidewater. By our experience in recent years, there would be no kelts at all in the Cains by the time spring had advanced to the point in those photographs. The whole fishing situation is very different than what one would expect in modern times.

After canoeing from the railroad bridge for about 12 miles down the upper reaches of the Cains River, the Sturges party stopped for the first night at a friend's cabin, called "Duffy's," to which Harry had access. They got their water from a cold spring beside the camp. Duffy's camp went on to have a further place in Cains River fishing history. On a spring trip to the upper Cains in 2018, Keith Wilson took me to the site of the old Duffy camp where his grandfather had housed sports as late as the 1950s. Keith and his brother had spent a nervous night in the then fallen-down Duffy's camp after getting lost in the nearby woods while hunting in the 1960s. What Sturges described as a commodious camp in 1915 was now just a few scattered items, including the remains of an icebox and woodstove and the outline of a foundation in the ground.

The following morning, the Sturges party continued on downriver and noted passing the Hopewell Lodge, which will be covered thoroughly in another section of this book. On

hunting camp, "Duffy's," about twelve miles below the railway. This was a commodious and well-furnished camp. Harry had the key, so we made ourselves at home and cooked our trout and slept on spring beds. A beautiful little stream, racing over the rocks and full of many miniature water-falls, supplied pure, ice-cold water.

"Duffy's"

This Sturges etching is of the Duffy Camp circa 1915. Dorothy Arms also mentions staying at this camp on trips with Harry Allen. The Wilsons later used this camp to house sports up until at least the 1950s.

the way, though, they would have passed this very prominent sandstone ledge area where the remains of a big lumber camp called "Heather" still stood on top overlooking the river. Wilson immediately recognized this spot, though, as Ganong pointed out there are many areas of such ledges along the Cains River, though few as prominent as this one.

The Sturges party didn't fish until the afternoon of the second day when they were a couple of miles above the old Arbeau farm—which, in 1919, was already long abandoned and rotting into the ground. Harry pointed out to Sturges that the area was very impoverished. It hadn't taken much more than 50 years for the earliest settlers to strip the watershed of the great stands of white pine that had covered the area around the Cains, and there was very little economic opportunity to keep people on the land.

A good quarter or more of the trip was used up in getting to the first salmon-fishing hole. Between Duffy's and Route 123, they passed through some of the most important spawning areas on the Cains for Atlantic salmon, but the kelts had gone downriver to find deeper water after spawning. They caught plenty of fish later in the trip, and I think that in the more leisurely style of the times sightseeing and a good dose of the Canadian wilderness were as important as the fishing to Harry's clientele of largely affluent urban dwellers. Besides that, the train bridge over the Cains in Bantalor was the only place that you could unload a canoe

painter. The rich, dark
spruce and hemlock; the
lines of the trunks and
gray-green buddir
birch and poplar;
earth and weathe

The Deserted 'Arbeau' Farm.

This etching by Lee Sturges is the only likeness I have ever seen of the Arbeau farm that was deserted in 1919. When W. Harry Allen purchased the farm in 1932, the deed did include the farm buildings, but doubtless, they were too far gone to be of any value.

The "Heather" lumber camp about five miles below "Duffy's camp" was perched on a large shale cliff overlooking the river. It made a dry and relatively pleasant location for the camp. PHOTO COURTESY OF THE PROVINCIAL ARCHIVES OF NEW BRUNSWICK.

The former site of the Heather lumber camp. Note the same rock in midstream, though more submerged in the higher water of this May 2018 photo. After 100 years, the site is less developed now than then. Keith Wilson knew the river so well that when he saw the 1920s photograph, he took me directly to the location though all traces of the old camp visible from the river are now gone.

The Elkins Pool was one of the first pools that the Allens stopped at on their way downriver to fish for salmon. I have not found anyone who knows where this once-famous pool is, but I believe it to be just slightly upriver of the Arbeau Pool. PHOTO COURTESY OF THE PROVINCIAL ARCHIVES OF NEW BRUNSWICK.

from a train track directly into the Cains River. Instead of trailering their canoes out from Fredericton behind a pickup truck loaded with their provisions, they left town on the train. That was their transportation. We assume that the vehicles, boat trailers, and, perhaps most important, woods roads of the day would have been unsuitable for reaching the headwaters of the Cains at that time of the year.

When they arrived at a pool in the general vicinity of Upper Trout Hole Pool about three miles downriver from the current Grand Lake Road Bridge, they described the scene as follows: "About five o'clock that afternoon we came upon the first salmon pool, and saw a salmon leap from the water and fall back with a mighty splash. It was an inspiring sight." They caught nothing but trout at this pool, however. Note that this may have been the Elkins Pool also mentioned by Arms. I can find no mention of that name on any charts or maps nor by any of the people that I interviewed for this book. The party then proceeded downriver another mile or two to the site of the Arbeau farmstead where they planned to fish and spend the night. The pool where the old Arbeau farm was located is still well known to many anglers today who either fish it by canoeing down the river and stop at likely spots, much as Harry Allen and Sturges did, or also by driving down woods roads and hiking in to do some fishing.

At the Arbeau Pool, they fished for a short while the evening that they arrived, and both Sturges and Allen managed to catch a couple of fish. They spent the entire next day there and landed seven salmon. The party camped on the shore beside the pool for two nights, not far from the ground that the Aboriginals before them had used for many hundreds of years to rest up before tackling the portage over to the Gaspereau River.

The next morning, the Sturges party loaded the canoes and headed downriver, stopping after a while at an unnamed pool where Sturges caught another nice salmon that he wrote rushed both up current and down, leaping clear of the water five or six times and requiring 30 minutes to land. After leaving this pool, Sturges also reported that they caught two nice trout, one of which was a sea trout "with very red flesh." You do not hear of a sea trout being caught up in the Cains much before the end of May or first of June.

In what Sturges writes was a short while, they reached a large, deep pool called the "Stone Chimney Pool," since the house attached to it had long since burned and been reclaimed by the ground. At that time, only a pile of rocks from the chimney was left. Sturges found the fishing slow there, but they had lunch and didn't stay for long. It is hard to say where these two pools that came after the Arbeau Pool are actually located. After Arbeau, there are only two Crown grants before you get to the well-known Six Mile Pool. These are the Murray Pool and the Mahoney Pool. Both are fished by me quite a bit since I have a camp at the Mahoney Pool. The distance between all these pools is just not that far. In fact, Emery Brophy, whose father John guided for Harry Allen's outfit and then for many years at Wades Fishing Lodge, told me that Dr. Joe Scherer, one of the original members of the Black Brook Salmon Club, and a person who lived and fished well into his nineties, used to walk up from Six Mile Brook to fish the Murray Pool. The distance is less than two miles, but walking along the shoreline in and out of the water over slippery rocks, it would seem triple that long.

The Stone Chimney Pool could have been either the Murray Pool or the Mahoney Pool, but I have no way of knowing if either of these were the pools that Sturges referred to. One could assume that the house with the stone chimney had been built on a Crown grant—which increases the likeliness that it was Murray or Mahoney; otherwise, the homeowner would simply be squatting on government land, but I have read that squatting was commonly done. I did some research on the Arbeau Pool, and it is clear that there never was a Crown grant for that farm, nor was there ever a deed that we could find. People who were unhappy with their Crown grant sometimes simply built a new home on some other nearby piece of vacant land that they liked. With so much of the Cains outside of the area around Shinnickburn being vacant—and the long arm of the law probably being quite scarce along the Cains in those days—there probably was not a lot at risk in simply squatting. In any case, the first Crown grant headed downriver from the Arbeau farm would have been the Murray Grant. The Murray Grant's Pool is relatively narrow and fast, at least at the top, and it is not the kind of place one would think of for kelt fishing, but since it probably was well into May, the somewhat rejuvenated kelts might prefer the livelier water. We do know that there was a cabin located there on the inside of the bend that was reportedly used by outfitters for overnighting many years ago. Neither Arms nor Sturges mentions a cabin at the Stone Chimney Pool.

The Cains is well known for its slow pools, and in the fall, the bright fish will stack up in these, but I think that is largely because, in the relatively small and shallow Cains, deeper water and faster water are hard to find at the same time. Pools that do have both of these characteristics are the exception and tend to be the best pools on the river. Moore's Pool, Mouth of Sabbies River and Doctor's Island's Muzzeroll Pool are all good examples of Cains River pools that are both fairly deep and relatively fast. Once the kelts start to recondition and the water warms up a bit, they are sometimes caught on lies that are similar to those preferred by bright fish, but again, in modern times, the kelts have left the Cains long before this time.

Another candidate for the Stone Chimney Pool is the Mahoney Pool. I have a fishing camp on this property, so I know it quite well. The Mahoney Pool is fairly long and deep as Sturges claims the Stone Chimney Pool was, and the water offers quite a slow swing speed, which would be good for kelts. Additionally, William Kervin, who grew up in Shinnickburn during the 1950s, told me that a pile of stones exists on the Mahoney property that he claims are the remains of the chimney from the old house there. He says that some of the stones have writing on them. This may very well have been the pile of stones that Sturges refers to in his book.

We have fished the Mahoney Pool for kelts several times in seemingly good conditions, but so far have landed just one grilse kelt, and that one was caught around the first of May. The water was running deep and cold, and there was still ice stacked here and there on the shore.

After leaving the Stone Chimney Pool, the party stopped at Six Mile Brook to see a settler named "old Davey"—Davey O'Connell. I found that this property was granted to an Edmund O'Connell in 1861. This could be the same man, or perhaps his son. O'Connell, though, had died that winter. According to Sturges, there was no good fishing pool at Six Mile Brook, which certainly surprised me because that stretch is known today as some of the better fishing on that part of the Cains. I have fished a little at Six Mile for kelts in the springtime and have never caught one, but the large clear brook feeding into the deep, slow pool there seems to be ideal according to what I know about kelt fishing.

From Six Mile Brook, the party dropped down to the area just below Muzzeroll Brook. They met John Kerwin and Mr. Mahoney; both men undoubtedly descended from the original Crown grantees with the same family names who had settled there some 80 years before. This was very near the community of Shinnickburn, and Sturges found it to be in tough shape. The tall stands of white pine were gone, the ground was too poor for good crops, the train route had bypassed the area, and there was no local industry for employment. So few people remained even 100 years ago that, according to Sturges, the school had been closed and made into a church. It must have reopened for a while, though, because there was a school and tiny year-round population there up through the 1960s. Allen gave some of the salmon they had caught to the locals, who told them that they had no means to catch these large fish. Eating kelts or "black salmon" was commonly done by the early residents of the Miramichi and Cains River Valleys. There was no report of Sturges fishing in this vicinity even though I know there are several good pools, including the mouth of Muzzeroll Brook and the Schoolhouse Pool.

Note in these period photographs that rather than anchoring, the party is fishing for a short while in various spots as they work their way downriver by "holding on the pole." The guide plants his pole in the bottom and finds a comfortable angle—often under his arm to use the upper arm, shoulder, and back muscles to hold the canoe back against the current while the angler fishes. Poles used in this type of canoe work were much longer than the canoe poles used strictly for upriver pushing that are found today on the Miramichi and Cains. I can assure anyone who cares to try it that this forgotten skill is exceedingly difficult to master. Emery Brophy said that his father John, who guided for Harry Allen, could hold the canoe with one arm on the pole and cast with the other doing a single-handed retrieve with his fingertips! PHOTOS COURTESY OF THE PROVINCIAL ARCHIVES OF NEW BRUNSWICK.

Lee Sturges portrait of old John Kerwin. Kerwin's descendants were among the very last people to give up year-round residence on the Cains River.

The party now dropped downriver about seven miles to a famous pool called the Oxbow. The Oxbow is still a well-known fall, bright salmon pool with a relatively strong flow of current, but again, it is not the kind of place we associate with modern-day kelt fishing. They caught several salmon and trout here and camped for the night. It was reported that it was very cold that night and that a half-inch of ice was at the bottom of the water bucket in the morning. There is footage in the Canadian National Railroad film of men fishing and gaffing salmon at the Oxbow—see the page of snippets from the film presented earlier in this chapter.

The next morning, the party dropped down through a pool called the Whirlpool that bears the same name today. No fishing was reported, and they then carried on another two and a half miles to the Mouth of Sabbies, their last camping and fishing spot on the trip. This is true even though all of the pools where we normally have our best spring salmon fishing for kelts are located in the remaining seven miles downriver from the Mouth of Sabbies. Arms does talk in her book about some fishing at pools farther toward the mouth.

While the guides were still setting up the tents, Sturges walked down to the river and hooked a big salmon. Sturges wrote that, "The pool being large and the fish full of fight I could see at once that I was in for quite a battle. His first run took all the enameled line off the reel, and a considerable piece below the splice. . . . Time after time he would leap far out of the water and fall back with a mighty splash." Sturges went on to say that he simply couldn't land the fish without a gaff, and he just slugged it out with the creature until the guide came by with a long-handled gaff and put an end to the struggle. Sturges characterized the Mouth of Sabbies Pool as one of the finest on the river. Some of the pictures that I mentioned earlier of young Charlie Wade, the other man I assume to be the senior guide, and their sports were also taken from this same spot.

Both Sturges and Arms report that they spent quite a bit of time fishing the Mouth of Sabbies. While the old photographs

This Sturges etching of Sabbies Pool is taken from an angle as if you were standing in the mouth of the Sabbies River. Judging by where the tent was placed on the bar in the film snippets, that may be exactly where Sturges sat and made his drawing. From that spot, he was looking back up the Cains River in the direction of Shinnickburn. Twenty-five years later, industrialist Seabury Stanton would build his impressive lodge almost directly across the river from this spot.

The stern anchor pulley was a very simple setup. You just dropped your anchor and slipped the anchor line around the front of the pulley. When things came tight, you just put your anchor line around the big wooden jam cleat that was mounted to the inner rail. To pick up the anchor, you didn't have to turn around, you just pulled up and back on the anchor line against the pulley.

I have show the anglers fishing from the shore, I know this to be a large pool, and it is especially wide just above the Sabbies where many of the kelts would come from. In Arms's book, they write of fishing this pool from the canoes, and in higher water, early in the season, it would assuredly have been done in that way quite often. This brings up one of the big changes in Atlantic salmon-fishing technique that has taken place since Harry Allen's day. This change has to do with the anchoring of the canoes. If you were a guide paddling down the Cains River, especially without an outboard motor, as was the case up through the 1930s, you would want to simply slow down your descent with the paddle or pole and then just slip the anchor over the transom. The double-ended canoes, or those with narrow transoms like the Chestnut Ogilvies, will hang in the current nicely even when anchored by the stern. This sure beat turning around and then trying to paddle or pole back up into the spring runoff currents, which you would need to do to anchor the canoe from a bow pulpit anchor system as is done today. However, the stern anchoring technique presented its own problems.

Lester Vickers, who guided 20 seasons of spring salmon fishing during the 1970s and 1980s for Charlie Valentine at this same pool, said that the Chestnuts equipped with the stern anchor were dangerous in several ways. First, once anchored, you could only see back upstream by turning around from time to time. That alone is quite difficult in the very narrow sterns of the old Ogilvy Chestnut canoes. Room-sized ice cakes, floating in good part below the surface of the water that could ride up an anchor line and suck a canoe beneath the surface, are not uncommon for the first couple weeks of the spring season. Anchoring by the bow allows the guide to constantly have an eye on what is coming down the river. Also, when a salmon was hooked, especially a large one, it was very difficult for the angler sitting in the front half of the canoe to pull the fish far enough upstream to be netted. Often, the guide had to put both hands on the opposite sides of the canoe and crawl over and around the angler to get far enough forward to net the fish. This was very dangerous from the standpoint of a possible upset throwing both men into the freezing river. Today Lester Vickers guides for the Houser family, who own the Popples Camps farther down the Cains. It was not until the late Dr. Ben Houser purchased two Sharpe canoes with the bow pulpit anchoring system that Vickers got away from the old setup, but he was very glad that he did. Even at 26 feet in length, an eight-horsepower outboard can quietly and quickly move a canoe of this size up against the current to position it for fishing.

While Arms was talking about fishing and camping at the Mouth of Sabbies, she wrote that "old Pete Porter" showed up to watch her land a fish and comment on how it would have weighed 35 pounds during the fall run. The nearby Porter place was one of the last farms in the area to fall back into the ground and be reclaimed by the Cains forests. While they were camped by the Sabbies, Porter brought over a couple of hens and a bag of eggs to provide some variety to the Arms party's menu. This pool was all in private ownership, but clearly, Harry Allen had built a relationship with the owner that allowed them to camp and fish there.

After their stay at the Mouth of Sabbies Pool, the Sturges party then went the rest of the way down the river, slept in the Keenan Siding railroad station overnight, and loaded everything aboard for the trip back to Fredericton the next morning. Arms mentions a final night of camping at the mouth of the Cains River before heading back to Fredericton the next day. She also mentions seeing the old Catholic church on the Howard Road that is clearly visible in Shaldach's illustration at the top of the cleared hillside across the Southwest Miramichi from where the Cains enters. Today, even the tip of the church's spire is invisible from the river.

It was impossible for an innovative guy like Harry Allen to have missed the potential that existed at the mouth of the

This is a 22-foot Chestnut Ogilvy canoe that is very similar to the ones used by Allen Outfitting. I bought two of these canoes from the Wades Fishing Club and rebuilt them under the help and guidance of my brother, Jason Burns. The canoes both originally had stern anchor pulleys that we removed, and, instead, we added the much safer bow pulpit assembly seen in the picture.

A Sturges etching of one of Harry Allen's tent camps. Judging by the large amount of cleared land and where these pictures are located in the book, these tents are probably pitched on the old Arbeau Farm property.

Cains River. The spring fishing ground in the very mouth of the Cains, and along the shore from Black Brook itself down to where Wade's Fishing Lodge is located, is one of the premier areas for kelt fishing in this section of the river. For many years Wade's made a substantial portion of its annual revenue from guests coming to fish for kelts. In those years when Allen and his sports squeezed the kelt season to last until toward the end of May, they very likely saw bright silver salmon jumping near Black Brook as they still do today. In those years of million-fish runs, though, their numbers would be amplified, and Harry, George, and Wade would have grasped the potential for bringing sports to fish here at stationary lodges rather than, or at least in addition to, the labor-intensive canoe trips that also required guides per angler rather than anglers per guide.

Changes were in the wind, and while Harry Allen didn't live to see them, the industry that he had begun on the Cains was about to move into a new era, and the men he had trained would be at its forefront.

CHAPTER 5

The Outfitters' Heyday: 1933 through the Mid-1990s

W. "Harry" Allen's death in 1933 marked the end of one era but also the dawn of a new one, made possible in no small part by his leadership in guiding, customer service, and marketing. In Harry's time, he essentially was the sole proprietor of the Cains. His operation was successful, and it spawned the beginnings of rod and line salmon fishing on not only the Cains River but at its junction with the Miramichi. In 1930, three years before his death, 70-year-old Harry Allen had acquired from Lorenzo Savage—who had, in turn, acquired it in 1924 from Joseph Porter, about whom we will hear more later—the property that would soon become Charlie Wade's famous fishing lodge and George Allen's outfitting operation that would later become the Black Brook Salmon Club. Doubtless many other of the Miramichi outfitters that flourished over the next 60 or more years were inspired by Harry Allen's example and by the fact that he had done much to make the Miramichi and Cains River region a famous destination for Atlantic salmon fishing.

This was the golden age of Miramichi salmon fishing. Not for the fish, of course; their golden age ended in the late 1700s when Davidson and Cort, along with the beginning of the Western European immigration, moved to the Miramichi Valley. Before that time, the evidence suggests that the Miramichi River system had a run in excess of a million salmon. The Aboriginals speared quite a few, but with the number required to fully seed the rivers being substantially lower than a million fish, as well as the ocean survival being much higher than today, the fish the Aboriginals harvested hardly mattered at all. It really is amazing just how early in the history of European settlement we succeeded in drastically reducing the runs of fish into the river. Between the various forms of netting that took place all up and down the river plus at sea, and the very liberal bag limits of the era—if anyone even paid attention to the bag limits—the Miramichi gave up a harvest of salmon that for many years was many times greater than the entire run is today.

Over the roughly 200 years that spanned the time between robust European settlement and the present day, the salmon endured a lot. In numerous writings going back to the beginning of the 1800s, there are frequent references to the many different forms of netting, as well as torching/spearing activities, which greatly reduced the size of the salmon runs. The salmon even had to endure the Great Miramichi Fire in 1825. The exact origin of this fire is unknown, but most speculation leads to the hand of man. It came on October 7, when most of the year's spawning run would have been in the river if not on the spawning grounds. The intense heat of the fire brought the water temperatures up to such a degree as to kill most of the salmon in the river. This is not just adults but fry and parr, including the next spring's smolts. It may have also wiped out a lot of the aquatic insect life and other forage that the parr depended on. It is estimated that the river took more than 25 years to recover, but it did recover, and large runs returned to the river.

In October 1949, the Atlantic Salmon Association in Montreal produced "Document Number 9," which was written by Percy Knobbs, an important man in Atlantic salmon conservation of that day. The document was titled *The Miramichi Fisheries*, and it amounts to Knobbs's assessment of the Miramichi as a salmon river and includes some of his thoughts on directions that should be taken in its management. Knobbs makes the following statements about the Miramichi system: "Thus we have in the Miramichi basin over 500 miles of accessible rivers great and small and, above and beyond that, over 300 miles of the small upper waters, and the brooks, so important for breeding purposes." At the bottom of the same page, he adds: "For practical purposes we may say there are no obstacles in 525 miles of salmon water. In this the Miramichi and its tributaries are unique, among Canadian rivers frequented by Atlantic salmon." On the next page, Knobbs went on to comment on the Miramichi's spawning potential: "Another strikingly satisfactory characteristic of the Miramichi rivers—referring here to the entire system overall—is the immense area of suitable spawning gravels. It is the area of such gravels that in many cases determines the limits of salmon production on a river. On many a 40-mile salmon river this may represent only a few acres and sometimes only a fraction of an acre. A rough computation of the Miramichi Rivers—meaning all branches—would give us 60 miles of gravel beds averaging 40 feet wide, or say half a square mile or 320 acres. That would mean an average of over 20 acres of prime spawning gravel for each of the 14 rivers of the system. For practical

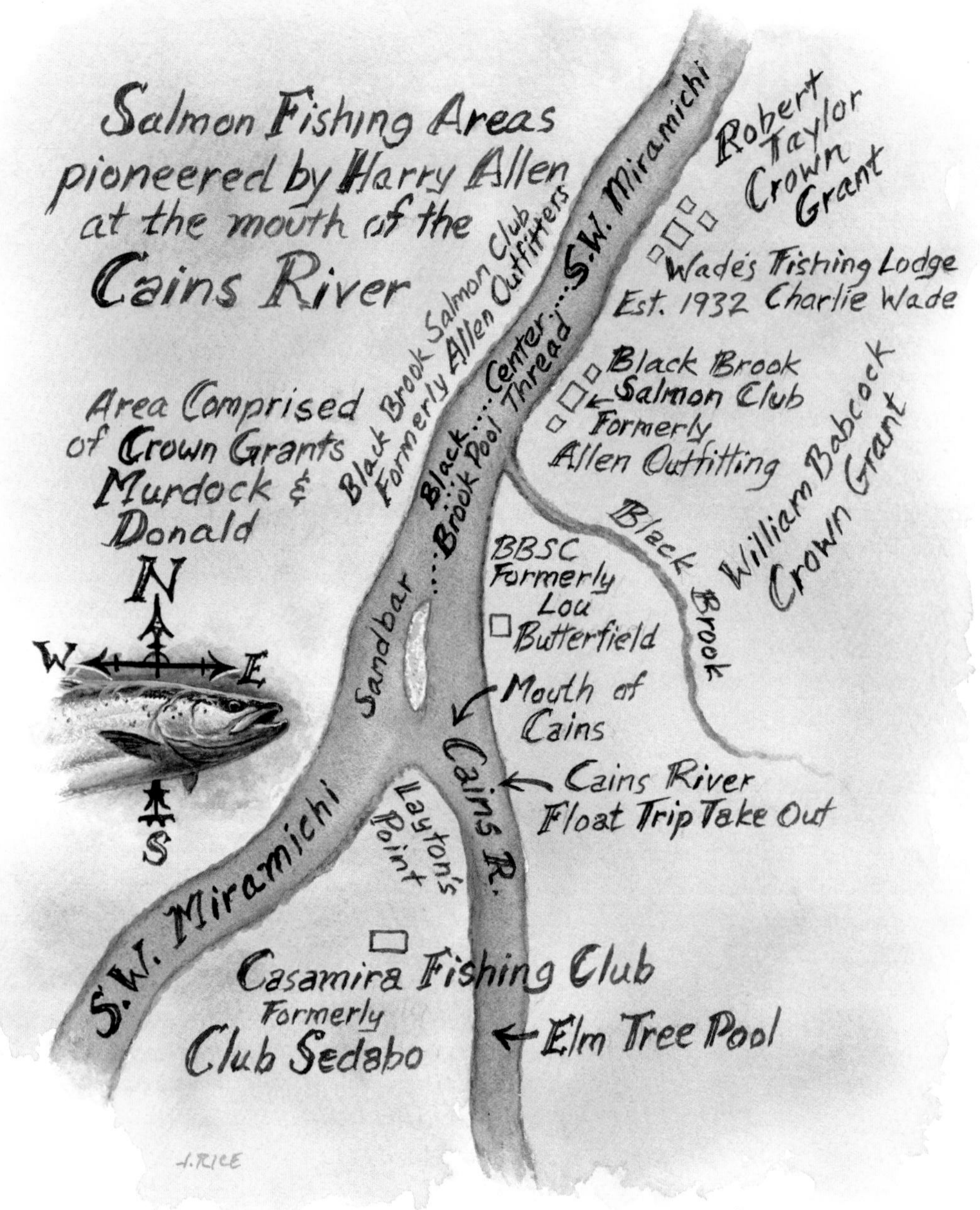

Salmon-fishing areas pioneered by W. Harry Allen at the mouth of the Cains River. This map shows the layout of the area where the Cains River flows into the Southwest Miramichi. It is arguably the most important salmon-fishing water on the lower Miramichi River, and it was W. "Harry" Allen in the early 1900s who recognized its potential. George Allen's outfitting business, the Black Brook Salmon Club, and Charles Wade's fishing lodge, all iconic Miramichi and Cains River organizations of their day, owed their beginnings to Harry's foresight.

purposes the spawning area of the Miramichi is thus unlimited: also, do to the gentle gradient of the river, the spawning areas are virtually all readily accessible to the fish." Therefore, in his comments, Knobbs defined the Miramichi as Canada's finest natural production facility for wild Atlantic salmon. That is what the outfitters had to work with during the twentieth century. It hasn't changed much today either; what has changed the most is survival in the ocean.

The Southwest Miramichi and the Cains go hand in hand. Before I became captivated by Atlantic salmon, I spent many years of my life as a serious striped bass fisherman. The pinnacle of that was my time in Falmouth, Massachusetts, which is on the south side of Cape Cod. When telling friends that I was going striper fishing and identifying where, I'd just say that I'd been fishing the Cape and Islands. That is even what the road sign in Buzzards Bay reads as you turn onto the bridge that crosses the Cape Cod Canal. On any given day, I could have been fishing at Cuttyhunk's Sow and Pigs Reef, on the Vineyard along the beach at Menemsha, back on the Cape in Wood's Hole, or any of dozens of fishy locations. I was just fishing the Cape and Islands and moved around between fishing spots as the weather and fish dictated.

To a degree, fishing on the Miramichi is similar. You have the Rapids down in the lower Miramichi where the later run fish tend to stack up in lower water. You have the headwaters section 100 miles away where some fish arrive on early raises of water, and then hold in deep, cool pools providing summer fishing when the rest of the river is too warm. And in between, there is a huge amount of diverse habitat that can all produce excellent fishing with the right temperatures and raises in water. It is true that you can't just fish anywhere you want, and anytime that you want, like you can in saltwater, but mixed private and public fishing ownership has its benefits. Each section of the Miramichi offers a great amount of purely public water, and this is especially true of the Cains. For residents of the province, most of the public water doesn't require any sort of advance registration or any sort of fee beyond the annual license. They can just walk down to the river and fish. I have come to regard the Cains as an integral part of the whole Miramichi system, and when in camp, we look for the conditions and time of the season when the Cains will generate good fishing. Sports arrive full of hope at outfitting camps along the river, and their guides look to provide a positive experience so that their clients will come back again. It is a true blessing for devotees of the Miramichi—and the outfitters who serve them—to have the beautiful and intimate Cains River as part of that system.

Arriving with hope was how it was for us in early September 2002 when George Watson and I stayed and fished at Wade's Fishing Lodge on the Miramichi. Jason Curtis was the camp manager, and because we were there to view the property as potential buyers, he was assigned to us as our guide. At lunchtime during our second day in camp, Jason said to me that he knew where he would be fishing this evening if he were going out on his own—"The Cains," said Jason. I didn't know very much about the Cains. My entire experience with the river had been a beautiful but fishless canoe trip through the lower five miles or so during some hot weather back on the Fourth of July during that same year while fishing at the Black Brook Salmon Club. "Why is that,

During the outfitters' heyday, the Miramichi region was a big draw for traveling sportsmen from the United States and Canadian cities. This group of fishermen and their gear is on its way to an unknown fishing destination on the Miramichi or Cains Rivers. PHOTO COURTESY OF THE PROVINCIAL ARCHIVES OF NEW BRUNSWICK.

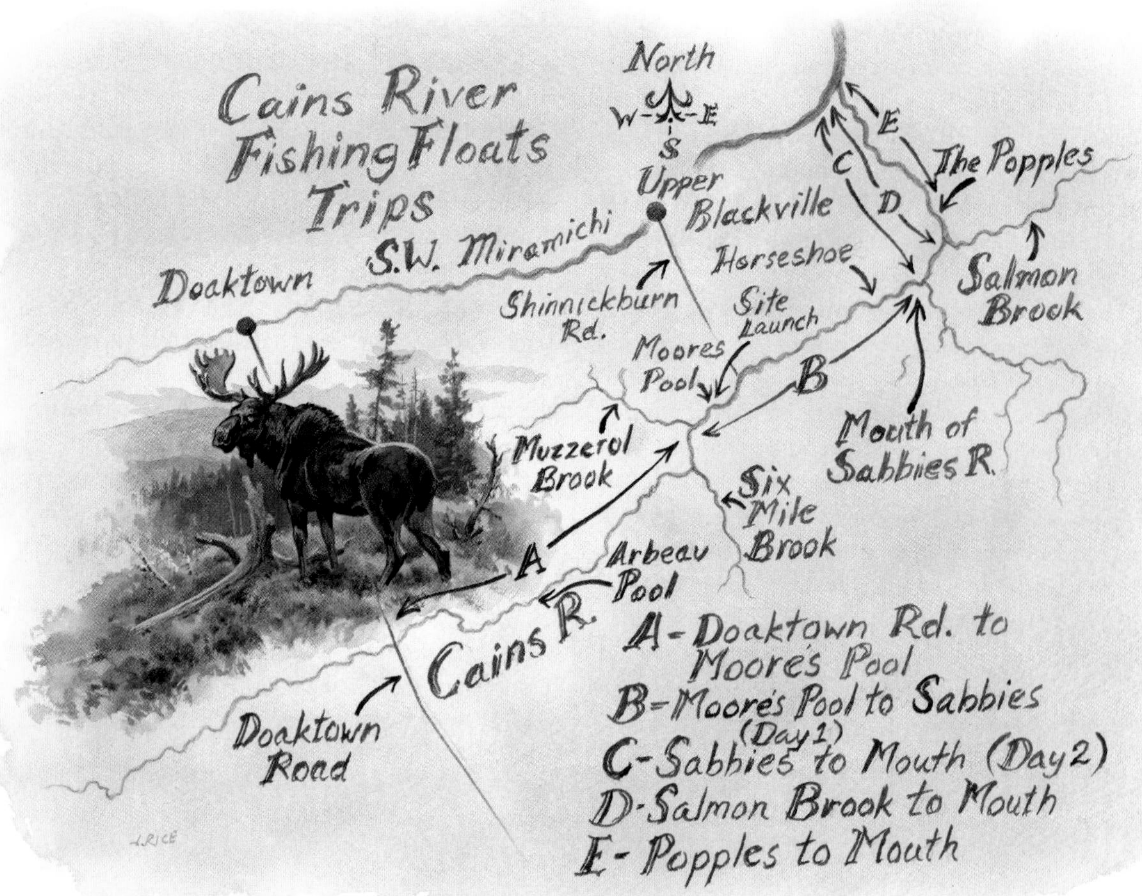

Cains River Float Trips. Depending on the time of the season, height of the water, and, therefore, the areas in the Cains where the majority of the salmon run is then located, the outfitting lodges and clubs offered float trips "sailing the Cains." Usually, a guide would accompany two anglers in a canoe. The legend in the illustration lays out four of the most popular trips—one being a two-day trip. The two-day trips seem to have disappeared around the same time as the end of Wade's Fishing Lodge. Black Brook Salmon Club and Wade's took out at their own camps. Other outfitters visiting the river took out at the landing at the mouth of the Cains River. These trips were very popular with visiting sports. Trip A, which was from the Doaktown Road to Shinnickburn, was also a popular late May and early June trip to intercept the sea-run brook trout migration up the Cains.

Jason?" I asked him. "Oh, the Cains is just really nice to fish. It's a smaller river, and it's really pretty. Conditions are just right there now too," he said. That evening, we drove up to fish the public side of Teedlan Pool. The private side across the river had once been owned by Ted Williams, who had the channel deepened by a bulldozer so the salmon would be more likely to hold in it. I did enjoy the fishing, though we neither saw nor caught anything.

On many occasions during my 15 years of owning Campbell's and Keenan's Pools on the Miramichi, I have been lucky enough to be in camp on many occasions when we had a good raise of water that boosted the river enough to send a pulse of fish into the lower Cains. I was also lucky enough to have guides Willy Bacso and then Jason Curtis, both of who loved the Cains and were always looking for chances to fish it. Early on, by driving and then walking in, and later on by jet canoe, we would fish public pools such as Buttermilk Brook, Hooper's, and Campbell's, all located within a couple of miles of the point where the Cains enters the Miramichi. My guests always loved these excursions, and when the conditions were right, the effort paid off, and we caught fish.

Then again, there were fall seasons on the Miramichi when we received one rain after another. The Miramichi was simply flooded out. It ran heavily silted for days. At my Campbell's Pool camp on the main river, we fished while standing up against the alders on the riverbanks, or from canoes anchored just off the shore and casting in. Occasionally, we got lucky, but mostly, we just cast. It was the only option that we had. I saw later, though, on the fishing blog river reports from guides like Rodney Colford, who had access to some pools farther up the Cains River than I had ever been, pictures of some great salmon catches. This is how the guides and outfitters in the know utilized the Cains for the benefit of their sports. We'll discuss that later in this book, but suffice it to say that there are times when it is hard to catch a fish on the main river, but a trip up the Cains can really pay off. Beyond this, the entire Miramichi River was at one time closed to salmon angling as of September 30, but the Cains was open until October 15. This gave the outfitters two full weeks of good fishing and income to continue their businesses into the fall.

Wayne Curtis, son of a Miramichi outfitter, guide, and author of many books about the Miramichi region, told me one time that every outfitter in the greater Blackville area—meaning from Doaktown downriver to the mouth—had access to the Cains River for the fall fishing. Some, like the Doctor's Island Club, had a great camp on one of the finest private pools on the river just below the mouth of Muzeroll Brook. The Black Brook Salmon Club had a similar setup with their ownership of Six Mile Brook. Wade's Fishing Lodge was located just downriver of Black Brook and specialized in taking clients up the Cains by motorized canoe and making a day of it—motoring up and then fishing back down, stopping at this pool and that on their way back to the lodge. Many others simply brought canoes up the river to some put in location and then dropped down the river fishing the public pools until they reached the mouth. Another truck would have been left at a predetermined take out for them to put the canoes on and head back to camp.

There are some traditional put-in and take-out locations for these trips, and some other outfitters customized the trips based on the season. One traditional launching or put in site is at the Grand Lake Road—aka Route 123—and the take out is where the river comes right to the road at Moore's Pool in Shinnickburn. This makes a fairly long day where you cover 16 miles of river. This run wouldn't normally be made for salmon until the second week of October so that the salmon would be likely to have reached these upriver pools. This is also a trip that Barrie Duffield of Burntland Brook Lodge did many times for brook trout in late May or very early June. The second common trip is to start from Moore's Pool in Shinnickburn and run on down to the mouth. There are many good pools on this 17-mile stretch, and generally, it was done in two days, stopping at the Mouth of Sabbies overnight. Byron Coughlin of Country Haven told me that they sometimes made this trip in one day and used a small outboard motor to save time between fishing pools.

My old friend and guide at Campbell's, Willy Bacso, ran the Shinnickburn to mouth trip for years at Wade's. He really enjoyed it and said that they caught more fish on the main river, but the guests loved the Cains. Some folks asked for it every year when they came, but some years, there just wasn't enough water to run down with the canoes. For one thing, the dark, tannic waters of the Cains make it almost impossible to see rocks that are more than a couple of inches below the surface. It is very easy, especially with a relatively inexperienced person on the paddle in the front of the canoe, to hit a rock and turn the canoe over in the current potentially.

The third trip, and the one that usually offers the most fish in the earlier parts of the fall season, is to put in at Salmon Brook and take out at the mouth. Salmon Brook is just a stone's throw from Willy's overnight spot at Sabbies, and the approximately seven-mile run makes for an easy day trip on the river. According to Wesley Curtis, who began guiding on the Cains River in 1967, they had a variation on this trip whereby they put in where the South Cains River Road crosses the Sabbies River, and they fished down to Buttermilk Pool, where they would take out. This trip featured the Sabbies River Pool, Pickett Brook, Salmon Brook, Cold Brook, and Buttermilk Brook and was designed to intercept fish holding in this area of cool brooks just before the fall rains brought the fish farther upriver. Many folks who live in the Cains River area call these trips "sailing" the Cains. The Salmon Brook to the mouth of Cains day trip is certainly the most commonly done of all these, and it can produce good fishing from midsummer on if conditions are right.

The Miramichi system has long been known for its autumn, or, as they call it in Scotland, back-end runs of salmon and grilse. Historically, the percentage of salmon to come during the back end versus the early season is quite variable. We have seen stretches of years in the past when something close to 40 percent of the entire Miramichi system season run, and actually higher than that when talking about large, MSW salmon as opposed to grilse, come after September 15. It is during these years, especially, that the Cains River provides excellent salmon fishing, sometimes better during that period than offered by the pools on the main river. During the most recent really good salmon year of 2011, the Black Brook Salmon Club was said to have caught about the same number of fish on its Admiral Pool camp water on the Cains as they did from their famous junction pool on the main river. With the majority of the Cains water, including some of the best pools, being publicly owned, it is easy to see why almost all of the outfitters counted on the Cains for not only productive fall fishing but for variety in making the fishing experience as valuable for their customer as possible.

From the years 1935 through 1995, here is a roundup of the outfitters that were known to fish the Cains River with regularity:

ALLEN OUTFITTING

After Harry's death in 1933, George Allen and Clarence Wade continued Harry's Cains River outfitting business. According to George Johnson, who had guided for Harry since 1923, George Allen essentially had been running the business for the last few years as Harry's health was failing. If anyone was the heir to Harry's throne, it was George Allen.

This guide is netting a fish on the Allen Outfitting water on the Howard's side of the Southwest Miramichi across from Black Brook, owned at the time by Lou Butterfield. The photograph is thought to be from the late 1940s. PHOTO COURTESY OF THE PROVINCIAL ARCHIVES OF NEW BRUNSWICK.

In addition to operating the Cains River float trips, George purchased land and fishing rights on the Howard Road side of the river across from Black Brook. He also inherited the old farmhouse property next to Black Brook from Harry. Wendell Allen began to build the facilities there that housed the sports at Black Brook right up until 2016 or so. George soon bought Wade's interest in the business. Keith and Neil, George's sons, also worked with him in the business.

Up until 1943, Allen Outfitting and Wade's Fishing Lodge fished the same Miramichi water on the Black Brook side of the river that the Black Brook Salmon Club does today. They didn't own it all, though. While George Allen owned the Howard Road side, George Porter owned the Black Brook side upstream of the brook. On that side, the pool extends up into the mouth of the Cains River, and it is by far the prime fishing water on that side of the river.

Both Allen's and Charlie Wade's sports leased this water on a per diem basis from Porter for $2 per day. In the 1930s, it must have been an excellent source of income for Porter. Porter also had a guest fishing the water named Lou Butterfield. In the mid-1930s, Butterfield married Lorna Colford, who was George's daughter from a previous marriage. Butterfield was an inventor who had made some money back in Maine, and he made a loan to Porter and his son to start a business in Miramichi that went bust. The loan was secured by Porter's real estate. Butterfield let the loan slide for several years, but when wealthy Seabury Stanton objected to Butterfield fishing alongside the paying fishermen and tried to get George Allen to throw Butterfield out of the pool, things changed. The next year, Butterfield foreclosed, and his friends were the only people allowed to fish the pool. It caused quite a stink.

Allen Outfitter's continued to do just fine. They had excellent fishing on the Howard side, they had the Cains River at their doorstep, and salmon runs were huge compared to current levels. It did crowd things a bit down at the mouth of the Cains, though, and the Stantons were not happy about it.

Stanton hired talented builder Wendell Allen to build him a camp called the Popples just under five miles up the Cains, and shortly after that, he started on another one up at Salmon Brook. The Allens managed these properties for Stanton. The Stantons' relationship with the Allens lasted for the rest of George and Wendell's lives, which was a period of nearly 30 more years.

That some parts of Harry Allen's business model legacy held on with George for quite a while is noted in a short book by Charles E. Willis titled *The Three Must Get Theirs*. Charles B. Wood III of Boston owns the only copy of the book that I know of. This very small, privately printed book, like the Arms and Sturges books, is about three men, including the author, who lived near the Attleboro, Massachusetts, area. They were guided by George Allen—at that time 59 years old—and some of his staff on the Bantalor to Black Brook canoe trip that his uncle Harry Allen made famous. What is different about this trip is that it is not a spring trip for kelts but was made for bright fish during the first week in October of 1943, 10 years after Harry's death, and at a time when the Allens did not have exclusive use of the Cains River. Also, the trip was a cast and blast, in which they shot bear, deer, ducks, and partridge as well as fished for salmon and trout.

Wood included a brief synopsis of the book in his *Bibliotheca Salmon Salar*, published in 2017 by David R. Godine of Boston. In his synopsis, Wood says that the Willis party put in at Landers, fished and stayed overnight at the Wildcat Brook Camp, fished for trout at Blue Rock and Leighton Brook, fished for salmon at Arebeau Farm, Stone Chimney, Six Mile, Sabbies River, Pickett Brook, Salmon Brook, and Mouth of the Cains. I suppose it is true that you simply can't stop at every good pool, but I do think it is worth noting that these are the same pools that George and Harry fished nearly 40 years before this trip. Certainly, though, these pools are all still highly regarded today, and with the fishing that probably existed in 1943, there may have been no reason to start trying new pools. The catches on this particular trip, though, were not great, with only a salmon and grilse or two taken here and there along the way.

One of the most interesting things about *The Three Must Get Theirs* is the window that it provides into the friendly relationships that existed between the Willis party of New Englanders—who the text clearly indicates are regulars on the Miramichi fishing scene—and a number of outfitting personalities of the day, including George Allen, Tom Boyd, and Doaktown flytier D'Arcy O'Donnell. The vehicle trip from Attleboro, Massachusetts, to McGivney Station and back is also a vintage adventure in that it took two days each way with around-the-clock drivers. Willis admits to feeling guilty about the 1,100-mile round trip made despite World War II gas rationing. After stopping earlier in the evening at the famous L.L.Bean store in Freeport, Maine, they pulled into the old Bangor House hotel in the middle of the night, slept a couple of hours, and hit the road again at 6 a.m., arriving in Fredericton at 4 p.m.. Given the time difference, that is nine hours of travel, whereas today, it would take approximately three and a half! After buying their fishing licenses for the trip, and a few extra flies at Neil's Sports Outfitters, they all went over to Landen's Restaurant and enjoyed a "substantial" roast beef dinner for $1.20 a head.

Much about the salmon fraternity falls into the small world department, and another case of that emerges here. *The Three Must Get Theirs* book mentions that John Taylor Arms—noted artist and husband of Dorothy Noyes Arms, author of *Fishing Memories* discussed at length in the Early Outfitters chapter, built the camp at Six Mile Brook, probably picking up the property from the heirs of Old Davie. As mentioned earlier, Kingsbury "Crib" Browne later bought that camp and sold it to the Black Brook Salmon Club, of which he was one of the founding members. Just as one generation of guides or camp owners passes their experience on the river on to the next, so do the fishermen. Willis says the word was that the Armses built the camp and only spent one night there before deciding that they preferred to spend their time on the river in Allen's tents. Arms does not mention owning or planning to own a camp at Six Mile Brook in her 1938 book. I would guess then that Six Mile Brook camp must have been built in the 1939 to 1941 time frame. The Willis party stopped at Six Mile and cooked "hot biscuits and home-made doughnuts." Given his long relationship with the Armses, whom he had guided many times for Harry Allen, George doubtless had a key that allowed him to use the camp.

George died of a heart attack in 1953 on his way to promote the province's sporting businesses at a show in Boston. This thrust George's son, Neil, into the position of running the business, which he did with his brother-in-law, Wendell Allen, for many years. Neil had a lot of interests outside of fishing, and in 1969, he left the outfitting business, selling his interests to Wendell and his wife Doris—who was also George Allen's daughter. Stanton financed Wendell's purchase of Allen Outfitting and, at the same time, conveyed the Popples Camp to Wendell.

At that point, Wendell had a great opportunity. He had fishing for his sports on the Miramichi and the Cains, and he was comfortably tied in with the wealthy industrialist Stanton. Unfortunately, the next winter, Wendell suffered a heart attack and died a couple of weeks later. Neil was forced to come back in and help his sister Doris run the operation. It turns out that the best solution was for them to sell the property to a group of Allen's regular clients who had purchased Lou Butterfield's water in 1961 and formed the Black Brook Salmon Club. After a nearly 70-year run, this development effectively removed the name of Allen from the Miramichi outfitting business.

BLACK BROOK SALMON CLUB (BBSC)

The BBSC has fished the Cains River as much as or more than any of the commercial outfitters since they began their existence in 1961 by purchasing the famous pool at the meeting of the Cains and Miramichi Rivers from Lou Butterfield. Butterfield retained his house on the property overlooking the pool, and he also continued to have a life tenancy to fish there. This turned out to be quite a bargain for Butterfield and a surprise to the members, since Butterfield, 71 at the time of the sale to the BBSC members, had a health scare the winter before in Florida, and that was what precipitated the sale. He went on, though, to live and fish hard for another 20 years, and he was known as a complex and irascible personality; he was accomplished at ballroom dancing and inventor of the whiskers fly, but he hated to share the prime lies with anyone. His refusal to rotate through the lies often infuriated other anglers sharing the beat.

Since the original members of the club included Crib Browne, who owned the camp at Six Mile Brook, the members originally stayed there. They finally bought the camp from him in 1963. From 1963 up until 2002, the Six Mile Brook camp was also the location of the BBSC's Cains River fishing water. While Six Mile was an excellent, late-season salmon-fishing spot in years when there was decent water, it was a hike back and forth to Black Brook. Therefore, when it became available in 1971, the BBSC purchased Doris Allen's property, both the private fishing water on the Howard Road side of the river, and the camps and water on the Black Brook side. These properties remain their fishing waters on the Miramichi to this day.

In 2002, the club purchased the Admiral Pool property from the disbanding Wade's Fishing Lodge Club, and they fish that property daily when conditions are good. The club then sold the property at Six Mile Brook.

With few exceptions, the Black Brook Salmon Club fishes at least eight anglers on their Miramichi and Cains River junction pool water on a daily basis from the middle of June to the end of the season. If the fishing is particularly good, they can stretch that to 12 rods fishing another four on their Admiral Pool water. A vacant rod is unusual at the Black Brook Salmon Club, even in the warmer parts of the season when most of the lodges have slow attendance. Only one or two of the commercial outfitters can accommodate more rods at any one time than the Black Brook Salmon Club.

The Admiral Pool is, though, by no means the extent of Black Brook's relationship with the Cains River. The upstream end of Black Brook's pool on the east side of the river is, in reality, as much or more a Cains River pool as it

This is the farmhouse as it appeared in 2009 that served for many years first as Allen Outfitter's lodge and then the Black Brook Salmon Club. You can see to the left of the farmhouse one of the cabins built by Wendell Allen and on the right side the new style, one of which has since replaced the last of the older ones that Wendell built.

Black Brook Salmon Club as it appeared in 2018, with the new lodge and cabins. Black Brook stream itself is on the right side of the photograph.

Pete Howell and guide with a nice, late-season salmon along with the slim fly that caught it at Black Brook in October 2017. In the fall, low-water fish destined for the Cains River—as well as the Miramichi headwaters—hold up in the Black Brook home pool waiting for a raise to head upstream on their spawning run. PHOTO COURTESY OF PETE HOWELL.

is a Miramichi one. The largest holding area on the Cains River is undoubtedly Black Brook, something that I am certain Harry Allen understood quite clearly when he moved to secure his place at the mouth of the Cains River almost 100 years ago.

BURNTLAND BROOK LODGE

Moncton-born Barrie Duffield, now in his mid-eighties, has been a hard fisherman and hunter all his life. Unusually, after a career in business, Duffield retired into the outfitting business. He bought a lodge where Burntland Brook enters the Miramichi in Boiestown, and he began taking sports fishing. Twenty-five years later, he is just winding things down. When I began researching this book, Kevin Sabean, an avid fisherman and canoeist from Fredericton whom I met on the Cains, told me that: "You should contact Barrie, he knows more about the Cains from the Grand Lake Road to Shinnickburn than anyone."

I've met men like Duffield before. He just has this innate understanding of the way things work in the natural world, and he has an intense passion that makes him a great hunter and fisherman. After our interview, Duffield gave me an old map book of the Cains where he had colored in the locations of a few of the pools. "I never paid much attention to the names of the pools, or where they were located on the maps," he said. "I just read the water and figured it out on my own." His specialty from late May into early July was Cains River brook trout, which he largely fished for in three-day trips, putting in at the Grand Lake Road Bridge and taking out in Shinnickburn. I asked him where he normally camped at night. "Wherever the fishing dictated," was his answer. "Sometimes we hardly moved for two and a half days and had to hurry downstream to get to Shinnickburn by the end of the last day, and sometimes we fished nearly every pool in the stretch. Where the run of sea trout will be at any point in time is hard to predict."

Virtually all of Duffield's brook trout fishing is done with a floating line and dry flies. Occasionally, he said he would use a wet fly, but this was very rare. Cains River sea trout generally like even bigger dry flies and bombers than salmon, said Duffield. Perhaps the most often used of these was the Burdock, which looked like a shaggy bomber variant, with a long, thin, mayfly-like tail.

Duffield also did a lot of salmon fishing on the upper Cains, keeping a trailer for the last two weeks of the season at the Acadia Bridge Pool not far above Hopewell Lodge. From that base, Duffield and his sports fished all of better pools on the upper Cains for salmon.

CAINS RIVER ENTERPRISES

Cains River Enterprises was the only commercial outfitter that I have run across that was actually home-based on the Cains River. Bob Brown owned an industrial supply company in Moncton with large contracts for cleaning supplies with institutional and industrial customers. His son-in-law, Ralph Thompson, was one of the guides and managed the properties.

For many years beginning in the early 1970s, John Brophy was the head guide for Cains River Enterprises, and his wife, Mary, was the cook. They had a large camp on a hill overlooking the Cains near the Schoolhouse Pool in Shinnickburn, another camp located just above the Oxbow, and a small camp located up at Mahoney Brook two miles above the Muzzeroll Bridge.

Emery Brophy, John Brophy's son, told me that his father frequently took parties from the upper camp at Shinnickburn, downriver to the Oxbow camp fishing pools as they would go, then spend a couple of days around the Oxbow, Whirlpool, and Wangytang Pools area.

In the late 1950s, Barrie Duffield stayed at camps in Shinnickburn to fish for fall salmon. The first picture shows Duffield poling his son in one of the flat-bottomed river skiffs that are still used on the Miramichi and Cains. The second is of his wife, Joan, holding a nice Cains River male—hookbill—salmon with the river in the background. The third is Joan standing on the deck of the camp rented from Doug Cashen in Shinnickburn. PHOTOS COURTESY OF BARRIE DUFFIELD.

Certainly, his employment with Cains River Enterprises was on familiar water for John Brophy, who had grown up on a Cains River farm down at Brophy Meadows and had learned to pole a canoe and fish for salmon as soon as he could walk.

John's reputation as a guide and a human being was second to none. This little poem survives him:

King of the Cains by Clayton Harris

Now here's to a man called Brophy
Born on the flats of the Cains.
Loggers the people before him,
Irish the blood in his veins.
Well over six feet was his stature,
Weathered and wrinkled his hide,
And he knew from early childhood
His life's work was a fishing guide.
And never a man was better
At anything he cared to do,
But the Lord singled out John Brophy
For someone to pole his canoe.
Am many American sportsmen,
Surely, they thought him daft
When swiftly, through turbulent waters
Safely, he guided his craft.
For fifty full years on the river,
This man worked at his chosen trade,
And a good many sports owe their lives today
To decisions John Brophy made!
And any of the guides you will meet today
Will really never come near,
To the uncrowned king of Cains River
A champion of yesteryear.
As in many the time through this life of ours
In this world of dollars and cents,
No matter how much the danger,
They'll give you no recompense.
So the best can hope for John Brophy,
Is that God wants to ride his canoe
And when he comes to the pearly gates,
The Big Fisherman lets him pole through.

Brown passed away in the late 1970s, and the business was dissolved.

CAMP STANTON/VALENTINE'S

We have dealt extensively with Camp Stanton under Seabury Stanton's ownership in other parts of this book. It is important to note that with the Stantons and their friends, and then Charlie Valentine and his friends, that this camp was one of the most vibrant fishing organizations on the Cains River from 1945 right up through modern times.

Some years after Charlie Valentine's death in 2007, a fisherman who came to Byron Coughlin's Country Haven outfitters every year from Europe bought Camp Stanton. The name was

The Mouth of Sabbies Pool and Camp Stanton/Valentines where the Sabbies River enters the larger Cains River. In the autumn, hundreds of salmon can lay in this pool, and spawning takes place all over the area, including far up into both branches of the Sabbies River.

changed back from Valentine's to Camp Stanton, and James McKervill—former owner of Smoker Brook Lodge on the Northwest Miramichi—was put in charge. The intention was to operate as a full-service fishing lodge, but the short season on the Cains made it impractical. Country Haven fished it intensively each fall up until it sold again in 2016. "Some years," said Coughlin, the owner of Country Haven, "we caught over a hundred salmon and grilse there."

CASAMIRA FISHING CLUB

Located across the Cains from Black Brook, a group of home- and landowners collectively hold the peninsula of land on the south side of the Cains that divides it from the Miramichi. They have fishing shared by the various owners on both rivers. The private fishing is supported by an original 100-acre Crown grant to a Michael Scott from 1830.

For many years, this property was also known as Layton Point, and the Layton family not only had a large farm there, but they operated a livery stable for the stagecoach on its way from Fredericton to Newcastle. In summer water flows, the coach was said to simply ford across the Cains River.

In the early 1970s, the property was sold to two men: the late George Abordeely Jr. and Richard Seder from Worcester, Massachusetts. These friends had previously fished out of Wade's Fishing Lodge just downriver. Seder told me that when they bought the property, there were no buildings still standing on it. At closing, the new owners actually received a copy of Scott's original Crown grant, complete with a big, blue seal.

What was very unusual about Seder's ownership was that he was only about 30 years old. Most men buying a fishing camp 400 miles away in another country are well beyond their thirties, and they are at a point in their careers where they are beginning to have the time and extra money to afford the commitment. Seder and Abordeely were full of desire and energy and had the enviable experience of making this move while they were young enough to get the very most out of the experience.

After buying the property, they hired Ivan Vickers to build them a private fishing lodge on the property that they named "Club Sedabo," a combination of their last names. Seder told me that, in the process of building, they found the foundation of the old house at Layton Point. After a few altercations with some local residents regarding the private fishing rights on the property, the house mysteriously burned during the winter season. Seder again hired Vickers to rebuild the camp, which he finally sold in the mid-1980s.

Seder and his partner owned the property for just 12 years, and in addition to fishing their own water on the Cains and Southwest Miramichi, Vickers guided them on occasional fall canoe trips down the Cains from Shinnickburn, taking out at

The point of land across the Cains River from Black Brook where the Casamira Fishing Club is headquartered. Junction pools are often some of the best water on any salmon river because fish tend to accumulate in them if the timing is not right for the fish to run up one of the branches. This area has not only the junction of the Cains and Southwest Miramichi Rivers going for it, but the cooling waters of Black Brook lie just below the junction.

This picture is of Layton Point in the late 1930s. According to Emery Brophy, he believes that the stagecoach used to stop at the larger of the two buildings under the old elm trees on the left side of the picture. The photo is of anglers and guides spring fishing out of Allen Outfitters. Brophy believes that Joe Colford, who was the head guide, is probably at the tiller of the outboard driving this raft of canoes upriver where they will split up and fish their way down individually. PHOTO COURTESY OF THE PROVINCIAL ARCHIVES OF NEW BRUNSWICK.

Far left: Richard Seder holding up a grilse in front of his new camp built by Ivan Vickers on the junction of the Cains and Miramichi Rivers. PHOTO COURTESY OF RICHARD SEDER.

Left: Young Richard Seder in 1972 with a pair of lovely salmon that could be kept in those years. What an adventure it was for a man in his early thirties to have been able to own one of the great salmon pools on the junction of the Southwest Miramichi and Cains Rivers. PHOTO COURTESY OF RICHARD SEDER.

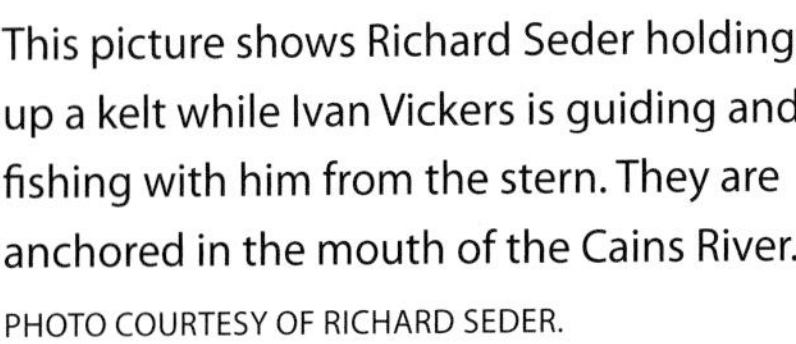

This picture shows Richard Seder holding up a kelt while Ivan Vickers is guiding and fishing with him from the stern. They are anchored in the mouth of the Cains River. PHOTO COURTESY OF RICHARD SEDER.

This view from Camp Sedabo/Layton Point, is the far less often seen view of the mouth of Cains with Black Brook on the far-right bank. PHOTO COURTESY OF RICHARD SEDER.

their own camp. When Seder began coming to the Miramichi, Wendell Allen was still alive and running Allen's Outfitting. Seder was a client of Wades Fishing Lodge before building Club Sedabo, and he remembered meeting Allen. Seder also remembered watching Lou Butterfield fishing over at Black Brook.

The waters of Casamira Fishing Club are very actively fished today, both the Miramichi and the Elm Tree Pool on the Cains.

CURTIS FISHING CAMPS

John Curtis—grandfather of my friend and guide, Jason Curtis—operated from camps that he built in 1962 along the shore of the Miramichi in Blackville, on land that was part of his family farm and with logs cut on the family woodlot in the late 1950s. Today, these same cabins, along with some additional houses—which are just across and slightly upriver of my Campbell's Pool property—are the homes and cottages of two generations of the Curtis family. Locally, we refer to the area as Curtisville.

The sports were served their meals in the dining room of the large Curtis farmhouse, and they slept and drank down in the riverfront cabins. Farming had declined along the river, and the price of wood was low, and many local families took a crack at the outfitting business during the 1950s and 1960s.

All the camps prized their better sports, and Curtis Fishing Camps attracted Dr. Niles Perkins from Bowdoinham as well as Evans Page from Bangor. Both men had their own group of salmon-fishing friends that often ended up coming along with them to the Miramichi. According to John Curtis's son, the Miramichi author Wayne Curtis, the camp's first sports were Tom Ritchie and Al Beternicy from Connecticut. These men literally started coming even before the camps were really finished, and they kept on coming every year. When you start digging into the history of these outfitters and the sports who supported them, you find many cases of this sort of loyalty. There is a great romance with being on a Canadian salmon river like the Miramichi or the Cains, and people can become very attached to their link with something that they love so much.

Wayne Curtis also told me that three men from Lincoln, Maine, used to come to the camps. The cabins were full, and they stayed in a tent that was erected where Wayne's own camp stands now. Wayne said that he was too young to have been guiding, but the men paid him $6 a day plus a pack of Camel cigarettes. Business was booming in those days, and it wasn't unusual to even fit extra people on bunks in the storeroom. Mrs. Curtis cooked for as many as 18 some nights at dinner. The salmon fishing was good, and everyone wanted to be on the Miramichi.

Among the men who came through the camp was noted fly-fisherman Art Flick. It was quite a thrill for a young Wayne to guide the famous American fly-fisher, but really, the thrill was Art's. He was fishing on the famous Miramichi.

According to Wayne, in his book *River Guides of the Miramichi*, his father had guided for Tom Boyd, Doctor's Island, and Wades Fishing Lodge before opening his own outfitting business. All of John's sons—Winston, Wayne, Gary, and Herb—did some guiding in the family business. Winston said that in addition to the extended float trips from Shinnickburn—which they did quite a few of—that they generally fished the lower Cains River from the Popples down as far as the Brophy Pool. According to Winston, it was great fishing most years during the 1960s, and the king of the flies was a #6 or a #4 Cosseboom that they modified by using either red, yellow, or green hackles.

After John's retirement, Gary and his wife Penny continued the business in a smaller way, keeping sports at his big house on the river just a couple of hundred yards upstream from where John's camps were located. Gary still has the occasional sport and guides them in his backyard on the family's Miramichi River pool.

The Curtis family has roots out around Shinnickburn on the Cains where the name T. Curtis appears on an original Crown grant, and Mrs. Curtis was a Porter whose lineage goes back to a Crown grant made to an Andrew Porter that ran from the downstream edge of Salmon Brook to Cold Brook on the north or east side of the river. Wayne's grandfather, Tom Curtis, had a cabin on the top of the big hill overlooking Buttermilk Brook. John Curtis was staying in that camp when he was a teenager, and in the morning, he looked down on the river to see a string of caribou walking up the river ice. They are said to be the last of the caribou seen on the Cains River, which once supported a good wintering population in the barren lands up in the headwaters area.

THE DOCTOR'S ISLAND CLUB

The Doctor's Island Club pool and camp just below Muzzeroll Brook on the Cains River along with the club's headquarters on Doctor's Island in Blackville were both acquired in 1966 from Paul O'Haire, who ran a commercial outfitting business from those locations during the late 1930s through the early 1960s. O'Haire had left Madison Avenue advertising for a simpler life in New Brunswick. He was known to be quite a chef, and dinners at Doctor's Island in O'Haire's day were apparently excellent. The original members of the club were a group of friends from New York and Chicago that included Royal Victor and Marshall Field V. Victor's son David told me that he assumed his parents' membership in the club during the 1990s and finally relinquished his own membership in 2012 after making an annual September fishing trip from his home in New Mexico for many years. His parents came in September because it was the Cains River fishing that they loved so much. They always kept a canoe up at the Muzzeroll camp and fished here and there up and down the river as conditions dictated.

The uniquely designed, long, slim log camp was said to be built by Max Vickers, first O'Haire's head guide and then the manager of the Doctor's Island Club. His son, Brent Vickers, who succeeded Max as the manager of the club, told me that when he was a guide under his father he stayed in the camp for nearly a month at the end of each fishing season, and the camp was always filled with club members.

Wesley's father, Roy Curtis, also used to guide for O'Haire, and it was at O'Haire's operation that he met Ted Williams, who later asked him to come to work for him full time as his caretaker and guide.

A photo album given to the Doctor's Island Club in 1999 shows Darryl Tucker guiding club member Archie Douglas and guest John Douglas on a canoe trip down the Cains. The album was put together by John. The title is on a label on the front cover of the album, and it reads, "Sailing the Cains 10/13/99 Archie Douglas," and under that "1919 Lee Sturges," so I took this to be at least inspired by Sturges journey discussed in detail elsewhere in this book. The Doctor's Island Club even had a pair of 22-foot Chestnut canoes that they used especially for Cains River trips.

I interviewed Darryl Tucker, who started guiding at the Doctor's Island Club when he was 19 years old and was one of the Douglas parties guides in the trip documented in the album. Tucker insists that the 1999 date on the album may be the date the album was presented to the club but that the

John Curtis's grandson Jason Curtis prepares to take Stephen and Audrey Prucnal from Campbell's Pool on the Miramichi up into the lower Cains River by jet canoe for a session of fishing. This trip requires a fair raise of water to get through the rocky shoals even in the jet boat. The camps on the water across the river in this photograph were originally built to house sports for the Curtis Fishing Camps.

Facing: These photos depict a canoe trip believed to have been taken in 1983 showing Doctor's Island Club guide Darryl Tucker, who is still guiding today, but for Country Haven outfitters, shepherding club members Archie Douglas and his guest John Douglas down the Cains River in the late part of the salmon season. The leaves on the trees would place this trip as taking place during the first two weeks of October. The photos were taken by unknown guides and sports piloting a second canoe from the Doctor's Island Club. The second photo in the sequence shows Deep Wood's Lodge high on the hill on the left side of the river. I believe that the next few photos are taken in the vicinity of the Trout Holes and the Arbeau Pool as the party progressed down the river.

Right column: In the first of these photos, the party is having their lunch in the stretch not too far upriver of Six Mile Brook, and then running down to the Doctor's Island camp at the mouth of Muzzeroll Brook. The bottom photo is of two canoes from the Ledges Inn in Doaktown passing by the Doctor's Island camp on their way down the Cains on a cast-and-blast trip. The guide poling the rear canoe is Shelly Betts, with dog handler Tom Randall in front. The front canoe is poled by Bill Hooper, a retired salmon biologist for DFO who guided in his spare time, with dog handler Christopher Clarke in front. An unknown sport is in the middle.

trip was taken in 1983 not long after he began guiding at the club. Darryl told me that the club members historically took many fishing and cast-and-blast trips down the Cains. It was traditional to put in at the Grande Lake Road and fish down to the Club's camp at Muzzeroll Brook on the first day. On some trips, the fishermen were so eager to get going that they left camp before light and stopped after getting on the river for a shore breakfast. Darryl recalled that the fishing was usually quiet in the upper stretches in most years, and they started to run into good fishing in the vicinity of Six Mile Brook. On day two, the party would fish down to Salmon Brook, where they generally took out the canoes and drove back to their lodge. The same members insisted on the trip year after year.

HERMAN CAMPBELL CAMPS

In 1958, 24-year-old Rolf "Bud" Hofer made his first trip to the Miramichi and Cains Rivers with two of his fellow Bucks County, Pennsylvania, residents Dick Clark and Chip Stauffer. Both men were noted Pennsylvania trout fishermen and fly tiers. Stauffer was known for breeding chickens specifically for their fly-tying hackles, and Dick Clark invented the "Dick Clark spinning block," which is a slotted block of wood that allows the angler to trap fuzzy spinning materials between two layers of normally frustrating silk floss. In the 1940s and 1950s, the Miramichi became an important destination for many of the East Coast trout-fishing elite who wanted to fish for large, wild fish such as the Cains and Miramichi brook trout and Atlantic salmon. Clark and Stauffer had become clients and friends of Herman Campbell. Stauffer had encouraged Campbell to expand his operation, and when they went up, they stayed in the camp right next to Campbell's house. However, he didn't fish the Cains on that trip, and he would not be back again for nearly 30 years, until he and friend Ben Houser came up to fish at the Popples on the Cains in 1987 at the invitation of its owner, Dr. Becker. Ben bought the camps the next year, and Bud and his wife Judy have visited and fished with the Hofers every year since.

Bud said that for the average seasoned salmon fishermen at Campbell's catching three or four salmon each day was standard and more or less expected. Herm, Bud said, while very much loved by his regular guests, had little tolerance for high-maintenance fishermen. One day, the famous Preston Jennings, a noted fly tier and author of the era, was fishing at Campbell's camps and was unhappy with the beat to which he had been assigned. Jennings came in at lunch and complained quite stridently to Campbell about his dissatisfaction. Campbell said that if Jennings didn't like the way things were done there, he'd make his bill up right now, and Jennings could pay it and leave—which Jennings did.

From Herman Campbell's Cains River water, guides could take people downriver to Hooper's or Tedlin's and upriver as far as Buttermilk in a relatively short length of time. Campbell

Herman Campbell Camps in 1958. The camps were built right next to his house, and the row expanded as his business grew. The camps are still there, and the facility has been renamed Salar Haven. The units were sold off individually, with each owner having access to the property's fishing pool. PHOTOS REGARDING HERMAN CAMPBELL CAMPS COURTESY ROLF "BUD" HOFER.

Young Bud Hofer on his first trip to the Miramichi in 1958. In 2019, he is still coming back each year to the Miramichi and Cains Rivers.

The woman holding court is Maxine Atherton, author of *The Fly Fisher and the River*, which has some incredible stories of her fishing exploits. She was a very adventurous woman, doing things such as taking the iceberg-dodging coastal steamer to the wilds of Labrador alone to fish the Adlatok River in the days before outfitters arranged every detail.

Three salmon-fishing friends from around Philadelphia reunited at Herman Campbell's for some fishing. Note the long-standing colors of the blue-and-yellow Pennsylvania license plate. The man in the blue suit sitting in the middle is the famous artist and fly tier Charles DeFeo. He is also present in the photo with Maxine Atherton.

Chip Stauffer, also of Pennsylvania, with a nice salmon, probably a Miramichi River photo. The colors of the fish and other hints indicate that this is a mid-September fish.

also had arrangements for fishing the Brophy Pool either before Coleman Moore's ownership or even perhaps during it when Moore was fishing his upriver property known as Moore's Pool. In the picture with Campbell, sitting on his camp deck smoking a pipe, you will note a big boulder in the middle of the Cains River in the background. That is a small spot, but when a good run of fish was underway, the area around it may very well have provided Campbell's guests with some continuously good fishing.

MOUNTAIN CHANNEL

Mountain Channel, formerly Camp Thomas, formerly Uncle Tom's Cabin—Vince Swazey worked for the Pittston Company, an energy company from America that had corporate salmon-fishing retreats on the Bonaventure and the Miramichi. In 1980, Swazey helped Pittston acquire Uncle Tom's Cabin, formed by Tom Boyd, where a cool brook coming out of property owned by the Mountain family flowed into the Rapids section of the Miramichi. Swazey then managed the property for Pittston until they sold to Ingersoll Rand in 1987 and continued on with them until 1995. Wesley Curtis, formerly a part-time guide, began guiding full time for the Mountain Channel in 1988 when he was hired by Swazey.

When Curtis came to work there, the camps also had a small facility on the east side of the Cains River just above the mouth of Muzzeroll Brook. This lodge appears on the New Brunswick Natural Resources (NBNR) map of 1967 as the Tom Boyd camp, and it is located on the inside of a sharp bend in the river with good depth and current flow. The bend is known locally as Hannah's Bend—Curtis says that Boyd had it built. It is correctly spelled Hannan, which is the name of the family who originally had a Crown grant there. This was the primary way that Mountain Channel clients accessed the Cains River fishing. Curtis said that they enjoyed good fishing in years when sufficient water allowed the run to reach them within the season. Under Swazey, who personally has a long history as a canoe man from his Boiestown area home waters, also ran canoe trips at Mountain Channel, down not only the Cains River but also down the Dungarvon and the Renous. Swazey says that the Cains was everyone's favorite, though. They loved the gentle but remote nature of the river. Swazey said that guests could have a week's excellent fishing at Mountain Channel but would write him personal notes of thanks mentioning nothing but the great experience they had on the Cains River trips, even if nothing was caught.

Wesley Curtis, a guide at Mountain Channel Lodge, being inducted into the Atlantic Salmon Museum Hall of Fame, Doaktown, New Brunswick, October 2016. He is the brother of George Curtis, longtime proprietor of the Black Rapids Fishing Lodge on the Miramichi, and both are sons of Roy Curtis, Ted Williams's personal guide, camp caretaker, and close companion when Williams was on the Miramichi.

Curtis remembers taking a client from New York on a three-day trip, putting in at the Grand Lake Road on October 3, 1991. They fished their way down to their camp above Muzzeroll, catching and seeing no fish. Just before dinner at the end of the day, they lost a big salmon in front of the camp. The next day, they fished around the camp, dropping down to fish the public water across from Doctor's Island and another pool closer to Shinnickburn before poling back to the camp for the night. That day produced three nice salmon, so things were looking up. On the third day, they caught fish right off the bat at the Mouth of Muzzeroll Pool before heading downriver to try different spots on their way to Buttermilk, where they were being picked up at the end of the day. It was raining that day, and fishing was excellent, hooking salmon and grilse and seeing fish at most of the pools where they stopped along the way. Curtis felt that they had simply run into the run that was making its way up the river.

Mountain Channel, now part of a three-lodge combination that also owns The Ledges and Harris Ledge, still accesses the Cains through this same lodge above Muzzeroll Brook, though the camp and water have now been sold to Terry Buggie.

RIVER VIEW HAVEN AND OLD RIVER LODGE

River View Haven was the name of a salmon-fishing lodge in Blissfield owned by Atlantic Salmon Museum Hall of Famer William Arlington "Arle" Bamford. In 1972, Coleman Moore decided to consolidate his Cains River properties and sold the Brophy Pool land and water to Bamford and two of his sports, Bill Thomas and Sy Ritchie. Like Coleman, both men were from Pennsylvania. There was no camp then at the site, and River View Haven used the property for its Cains River fishing until 1976 when Bamford sold River View Haven to young attorney Alex Mills. Mills was later instrumental in his work on behalf of the New Brunswick Outfitters Association to end the net fisheries for salmon in the Miramichi.

Mills renamed River View Haven as Old River Lodge, and he began his own outfitting career, which ended with his sale of Old River Lodge in 2003. Mills did not purchase the Brophy Pool, and Bamford, Thomas, and Ritchie continued to own the property until 1982, when it was sold to Tom

Truelove and Alan Small. Old River Lodge did take sports to the Brophy Pool for a couple of years before the sale.

Mills is a bird hunter and dog man, and under his ownership, Old River Lodge became known for its Cains River cast-and-blast float trips. On these trips, Mills loaded two Old Town Tripper XL canoes with two hunter/fishers, a dog, guide, and hunting and fishing equipment for the day, and a third canoe—a 26-foot Miller—was manned by a camp man. This canoe carried all the camping gear and provisions needed for a three-day float trip down the river. It was a great way to get all the best that the Cains River has to offer in the fall. Mills had two great stories about memorable trips that he told me.

The day of Old River Lodge's very first cast-and-blast trip arrived, and it was cold, dark, and rainy—perfect for fishing—and typical, late-season Cains River weather. Having a decent height of water, they put in two big Old Town canoes in at the Grand Lake Road Bridge and headed downriver. The camp man was to paddle down later in the day, pass by the other canoes that would be either hunting or fishing, and prepare the camp near Duffy Brook about six miles downriver for the first night's stay. Note that this is not the Duffy Brook/Camp that Harry Allen stayed at 25 miles farther upriver. The Duffy Brook we are speaking of here is located about six miles down from the Grand Lake Road and more or less across from the old Arbeau farm site. The camp man had fresh, dry sleeping bags, food, and whatever else was needed for each of the two nights they would be out on the river.

At the end of the day, everyone was really looking forward to arriving at the warm camp with a roaring fire and enjoying that first cocktail. Unfortunately, when they got there, the camp was dark and closed up. The camp man had mistakenly gone right by the place and ended up several miles farther downriver at the tent campsite where they were to spend the second night out.

With no other course of action, Mills took off downriver in the gloaming and caught up with the camp man. After the urge to kill subsided, said Mills, they loaded everything back into the two canoes. Mills rigged a Coleman lantern on the end of a pole tied out over the bow of his canoe, and the two started poling back up the river in the dark. They arrived—by the grace of God—at Duffy Brook just around midnight. Mills said that the sports took it all in stride.

The second story from Mills was about a trip on which Mills and Herb Curtis—brother to author Wayne Curtis—guided well-known writer Charles Gaines—of *Pumping Iron* fame—and a "fancy photographer" from New York City, on a cast-and-blast overnighting at Millet Underhill's camp halfway between Shinnickburn and the Sabbies River.

The Cains, downriver of Millet's lodge, flows through an area where there are many sandy islands in the river, and the channel twists and turns, or "braids," through the islands. I can attest that this is a great section of the river to hit bottom unexpectedly when running through in a motorized canoe. These channels, though, create little holes and fingers of current that, with a good eye for reading the water, can produce some decent salmon fishing. At just such a spot, Herb—a lifelong guide and well-known Miramichi author—was guiding along with Mills. Part of guiding on a trip like this is to try and get a fish on the line for the photographer. Herb hooked and landed what Mills said was one of the most memorable salmon of his life. The fish, according to Mills, "Was probably about 12 pounds and fought like a banshee, and when he got it close enough to see, it was a burnished, blue-silver female that I never forgot. The lodge got a great article out of it all in *Men's Journal*." With the help of Black Brook Salmon Club member Rip Cunningham, I contacted Gaines, but none of us were successful in getting a reprint of the story or copies of any of the photographs. This was only in the 1980s; how quickly time can bury this sort of information.

MILLETT UNDERHILL'S

The Underhill family has a long history on the Cains River, with Crown grants encompassing several hundred acres running to both sides of the Cains in the area of the Sabbies River, the west side of the Cains bordering the Salmon Brook Pool, and another smaller grant that became the location of some small camps built by Millet Underhill. He also built a larger log building on a Crown land campsite across the river from the cabins, and he also fished the Miramichi from family property down in the Rapids section of the Miramichi. Their Cains River fishing was done at pools located from upriver of the Oxbow on down to Pigeon Ledge and the Sand Hole. According to Underhill's eldest son Richard, the family outfitting business began in 1958 and ceased operations in 1981, though the camps were still leased out as self-catering into the early 2000s.

Note the cable across the river connecting the main lodge and the cabins. Jason Curtis is pictured running the canoe.

Millett Underhill's defunct lodge "Milletts," barely visible through the grown-up trees in the spring of 2018.

WADE'S FISHING LODGE

For many years, the most famous establishment on the Miramichi River was one founded by Charlie Wade, who had guided for his uncle W. "Harry" Allen. By the late 1920s, Wade's position with Allen had grown to overseeing his own fishing parties.

Near the time of Allen's death in 1932, Wade started his own lodge, again on land that his uncle had had the foresight to acquire from Lorenzo Savage. While there are several men who had great influence over the history of Miramichi and Cains River salmon fishing, none had more than Charlie Wade. Wade perpetuated Allen's dedication to the comfort and safety of his clients. In a 1983 interview for the *Nashwaak Bicentennial*, George Johnson stated that he had gone to work in 1922 for Allen and had been assigned to work with Wade right away. Wade, he said, was a disciple of Allen, and Johnson practiced Wade's and Allen's philosophy of customer service first. Charlie's brother Edgar was a cook for Allen, and Johnson made many Cains River runs with Wade as skipper and Edgar doing the food. In the off-season, Wade found time to be a professional hockey player, and then he was a coach and a referee. He was also an authority on skeet shooting, an expert canoe man, and tied flies professionally for the Weber Like Fly Company that first made the Cains River streamers commercially available. There wasn't much the man didn't do well. When MGM produced a movie called *Johnny's First Moose*, Wade was the moose caller.

In 1938, Charlie's son Herb came into the fishing lodge business with his father. After a wartime hiatus, Herb returned to the business and worked alongside his father for many years until Wade's gradual retirement in the early 1960s. Herb was a renowned fisherman and fly caster, regularly winning the annual competition in Fredericton. One year, not only did Herb win it, but so did his wife, Dorothy, and one of his twin sons, David Wade, won the junior division.

One of the young guides who worked for Wade at Allen's was John Brophy. Brophy was 11 years Wade's junior, and it was to be a long and mutually beneficial association. Brophy was the head guide at Charlie Wade's Fishing Lodge from the time it started in 1932 until the early 1970s, when it was sold to Atlantic Richfield. Brophy wasn't much for big companies, and he left to take a position with Cains River Enterprises.

Wade's Fishing Lodge was located just downstream of George Allen's camp at Black Brook. As of this writing, the property has gone through a few ownership changes since Herb Wade retired and sold to some longtime clients, who formed a club in the 1990s. Herb had profitably bought the

The New Brunswick contingent was a very convivial and well-dressed group at the Boston Sportsmen's Show in 1941. Charlie Wade is on the far left, and George Allen is third from the right with glasses. The booths at the sporting shows could be quite fancy, with prefab cabins, game being cooked, and live big-game animals on display.

lodge back from Richfield when they moved their headquarters to the West Coast. The buildings are still there, but all of the fishing water they once owned has been sold except for the home pool.

In reality, Wade's Fishing Lodge and Black Brook share the same pool, though they are very different parts, with Black Brook having the far more productive—especially in low water—upper end and junction with the Cains River. Starting at the brook, the water becomes deep and slow, and that continues downstream to near the bottom of Wade's property, where it tails out into a comparatively shallow, rocky area with a decent flow that provides some good fishing in sufficient water heights. Jason Curtis says that this area contained 9 O'clock Rock, which I have waded up against in low water. It was so named because often after seeing all the sports off to a morning's fishing—usually around 9 o'clock—Herb Wade would make a couple of casts over this very dependable, fish-holding structure and catch a salmon.

On the way downriver, the cool flow of Black Brook diffuses into the river along the shoreline with some of the cooling effect making it down as far as the middle of Wade's property. This water is generally too slow for good fishing, but

A 1962 newspaper cartoon paying tribute to the many skills of Charlie Wade from his grandson Dr. David Wade's scrapbook.

ARTWORK COURTESY OF DR. DAVID AND ASTRID WADE.

Herb Wade teaching a young boy how to fly cast. As a teenager, a friend of the author's, Dr. George Babikian, was taught about fly casting by Herb Wade. Dr. Babikian stated the following: "Herb Wade was a magician with a fly rod, and that it was he who first showed me what a fly rod could do." PHOTO COURTESY OF DR. DAVID AND ASTRID WADE.

The most upriver camp at Wade's Fishing Lodge was one of the earliest constructed. The man is unknown. PHOTO COURTESY OF DR. DAVID AND ASTRID WADE.

Dorothy Wade makes a terrific advertisement for Cains River salmon fishing in the early 1940s. It was truly a fishing family. PHOTO COURTESY OF DR. DAVID AND ASTRID WADE.

John Brophy on left and Charlie Wade on right with a mess of nice brook trout from the Dungarvon River. Brophy's son, Emery, said that after the black salmon season ended on May 15, Wade brought guides and sports to these leased camps on the Dungarvon to fish for early-run salmon and sea-run brook trout that were always there in good numbers. PHOTO COURTESY OF DR. DAVID AND ASTRID WADE.

Wade's Fishing Lodge as it appeared in April 2018. The buildings and home pool were for sale at that time. The lodge and dining area can be seen just to the right of center with a row of windows facing the river.

at times, fish do hold throughout the area. According to the guides at Wade's, during warm weather when Black Brook was full of salmon looking for a cold-water refuge, some fish would drop back down during the night through Wade's water and be throughout the pool early in the morning. As the day warmed, the fish would again crowd with their noses to the cool brook water.

This combination of Black Brook Salmon Club's water, starting in the mouth of the Cains River and ending down a short way below Black Brook itself, and then that of Wade's—essentially the lower half and tail of the pool—is about 2,800 feet, or a little over a half mile in length. That is quite a long stretch of Atlantic salmon-fishing water by almost any standard.

With a couple of immensely experienced Cains River men such as John Brophy and Charlie Wade himself in charge of Wade's Fishing Lodge, the Cains continued to be a very important part of their fishing offerings. John's son Emery, whose family is the namesake of the Brophy Pool, told me that Wade's did take sports on the overnight float trips down the Cains, much as Harry Allen had done. Later, though, they accessed the lower sections of the Cains by driving motorized canoes up the river about as far as the Oxbow and fishing their way back downriver through the many public pools and private pools to which they had access. These trips were made in Wade's fleet of 20-foot and 22-foot Chestnut Ogilvie fishing canoes powered with five and a half horsepower, short-shaft outboards. Each sport had his own guide who knew the river well enough to navigate safely through the many shoal spots along the river, as long as the water wasn't unusually low. Shore lunches of a split grilse cooked over an open fire were a standard part of the daily fare. The sports loved it, and a lunch provided by the river was good for Wade's budget too.

My original caretaker at the Campbell's Pool, Willy Bacso, ran Cains River float trips for many years at Wade's Fishing Lodge during Herb Wade's ownership. Willy used to tell me about the two-day trips from Shinnickburn to Sabbies, and then from Sabbies to the mouth, and about the one-day trips that started at Salmon Brook. The run from Salmon Brook on down, on a hot July day in 2002, was my first look at the Cains River.

The Colford name also goes back to the 1930s at the Wades' and Allens' fishing organizations. Gary Colford, whose uncle, Bill Colford, guided Seabury Stanton on his first trip to George Allen's camps in 1938, met Willy Bacso while fishing the public water across from Black Brook. They became friends, and Colford recruited him as a fellow guide at Wade's. Colford

John Brophy in an outboard-powered Chestnut canoe, with guide Jim Vickers on the outside and Mel Brophy on shore, prepares to take the ingeniously rafted canoes upriver for spring salmon fishing. This photo was taken at the shoreline in front of Wade's Lodge. Though the mouth of the Cains River is only about 1,500 feet upriver from here, the lift against the spring currents was much appreciated. The non-motorized canoes could then fish their way back down current to the lodge. PHOTO COURTESY OF THE PROVINCIAL ARCHIVES OF NEW BRUNSWICK.

Charlie Wade and grandson—even David and Richard couldn't tell themselves apart from this early 1950s photo—with a nice salmon from the lower end of the home pool at Wade's Fishing Lodge. PHOTO COURTESY OF DR. DAVID AND ASTRID WADE.

Charlie Wade in another early photo with a trophy hookbill salmon. PHOTO COURTESY OF DR. DAVID AND ASTRID WADE.

told me that Wade's frequently took anglers on even shorter Cains float trips to hit just the bottom pools of the river. The put in places besides Salmon Brook were sometimes a little farther down at Buttermilk Brook or even the Popples. There were many pools that they fished along this stretch: Slide Pool, Hydro Pool, Campbell's Pool, and the public side of Brophy's and Hooper's. I got to fish them all with Bacso, as well as later with Jason Curtis via our jet canoe—though that required higher water.

In addition to the float trips, Wade was the longtime caretaker of the Admiral Pool Camp, and the Wades used the property more or less as their own through most of the season as Ferguson only really used the camp for spring fishing. Colford remembers, while guiding at Wade's, that they fished the entire stretch of Admiral Camp water from Hell's Gate down to a pool called The Ledges—just a few hundred yards up from the Elm Tree Pool near the mouth. A very short while after Herb Wade sold the business to the newly formed club, the Admiral Camp property was offered to them for sale, and they acquired it. This Admiral Camp property, along with a piece of shoreline across from Black Brook that Wade's owned called the Brophy Run, was sold to the Black Brook Salmon Club in 2002 when the Wade's club dissolved.

The original Wade's Fishing Lodge letterhead proudly states, in big letters, "Miramichi and Cains Rivers." Of all the outfitters along the river, Wade's was probably the most synonymous with Cains River salmon fishing.

Someone with a good brush hand recorded the catches on the walls of the Admiral Pool Camp. These are entries from 1947. In addition to salmon and grilse, there are several grouse and woodcock, plus one skunk killed under the camp by the cook.

Salmon and text on Wade's letterhead feature both the Miramichi and Cains Rivers. The year 1932 was the year before Harry Allen's death and the beginning of Charlie Wade's reign as the top figure in New Brunswick salmon fishing.

Herb Wade's twin sons, Richard, left, and David, with his wife, Astrid, at their home overlooking the Saint John River. David, in particular, idolized his grandfather and made a scrapbook about him.

WILSON'S SPORTING CAMPS

While Wade's Fishing Lodge was the premier commercial fishing lodge to service the lower Cains River, Wilson was and still is the undisputed name in Cains headwaters fishing. I would broadly define headwaters to mean above the Route 123 or Grand Lake Road Bridge. This amounts to about 25 miles of seasonally premier salmon and brook trout water.

The Wilsons began their Miramichi sporting history not long after immigrating from Scotland to Bloomfield Ridge—upriver of Boiestown—around 1850 when they started taking in sports. In 1862, Robert Barnwell Roosevelt, uncle of Theodore "Teddy" Roosevelt, fished out of Wilson's for trout and salmon. The journey was well recorded in his book *Game Fish of the Northern States and British Provinces*, one of the

Wildcat Brook camp and pool in May 2018. The Wilsons have taken parties in to fish the upper Cains River for nearly 100 years.

Amherst, N.S.

20. Cains River, not including its branches, from the ford, approximately one half mile above Hopewell Lodge, to but not including the pool at the mouth of Lower Otter Brook.	$2650.00	$2650.00

Purchased by: Wilsons Sporting Camps Ltd.
Karl Wilson
McNamee, N.B.
EOC 1P0

This is a copy of the receipt for Wilson's last lease on what is now the Upper and Lower Daily Live Release Crown Reserve section of the river. The combined sections were leased for $2,650 annually by Karl Wilson in the 1970s.

most important references on early fishing in North America ever written. In the 1920s, Wilson's moved downriver to their current location in McNamee, and Willard Wilson began running the Miramichi and Cains River salmon- and trout-fishing lodge that has evolved into today's high-caliber operation. The sports paid $8 a day, and the guides received $2 of it. The other $6 provided sleeping quarters, mountains of hearty food, paid for all the infrastructure, and, hopefully, left something for the Wilson family. Clearly, people liked it. Keith Wilson showed me the gold ring with a salmon pressed into it given to him by a man from New Jersey who had fished at Wilson's every year for 50 years.

Fishing trips by canoe were always part of the Wilson formula, and in the early days, they ran these trips down many of the area's rivers, including the Tabusintac, Northwest, and Dungarvon as well as their home Miramichi and Cains Rivers. They waded and fished from canoes on their Miramichi home waters and accessed the Cains by taking horses in the woods roads and staying at camps at Otter and Leighton Brooks. Later, they built their signature Cains River camp at Wildcat Brook.

Willard was followed by Murray Wilson, then Karl. Karl died a young man in 1983, and his son, Keith, then only 21, stepped into his shoes. Keith is now in his mid-fifties and still holding the reins. Keith's son Karl is now guiding and assuming some of the management duties. Of all the outfitters on the Cains and Miramichi Rivers, only the Wilsons' has survived the ups and downs of not only the fish but also the challenges of multigenerational succession.

The Cains is a perfect size river for intimate salmon angling. Here an angler wades and casts into the narrow channel along this long, grassy island while his guide waits for a hookup in the canoe a safe distance upstream.

CHAPTER 6

Cains River Camps and Pools

While it is true that the Cains River is largely made up of public fishing water, there are some pools and/or camps existing today that come down from the original Crown grants and, therefore, provide private fishing. Many of these private pools, as well as many of the public ones, all along the river are regarded highly enough to be named on the maps originally made up by the New Brunswick Natural Resources Department. There are five of these maps named Plan 1 through Plan 5. Plan 1 begins in the Cains River headwaters, and Plan 5 ends where the Cains enters the Southwest Miramichi. Virtually all of the important fishing locations are Plans 2 through 5. With a little googling, the individual detailed plan/maps are available on several internet sites.

Each map covers about 11 miles of river. Some of the pools are famous and storied in the world of Atlantic salmon angling. In this chapter, we are going to go downstream from

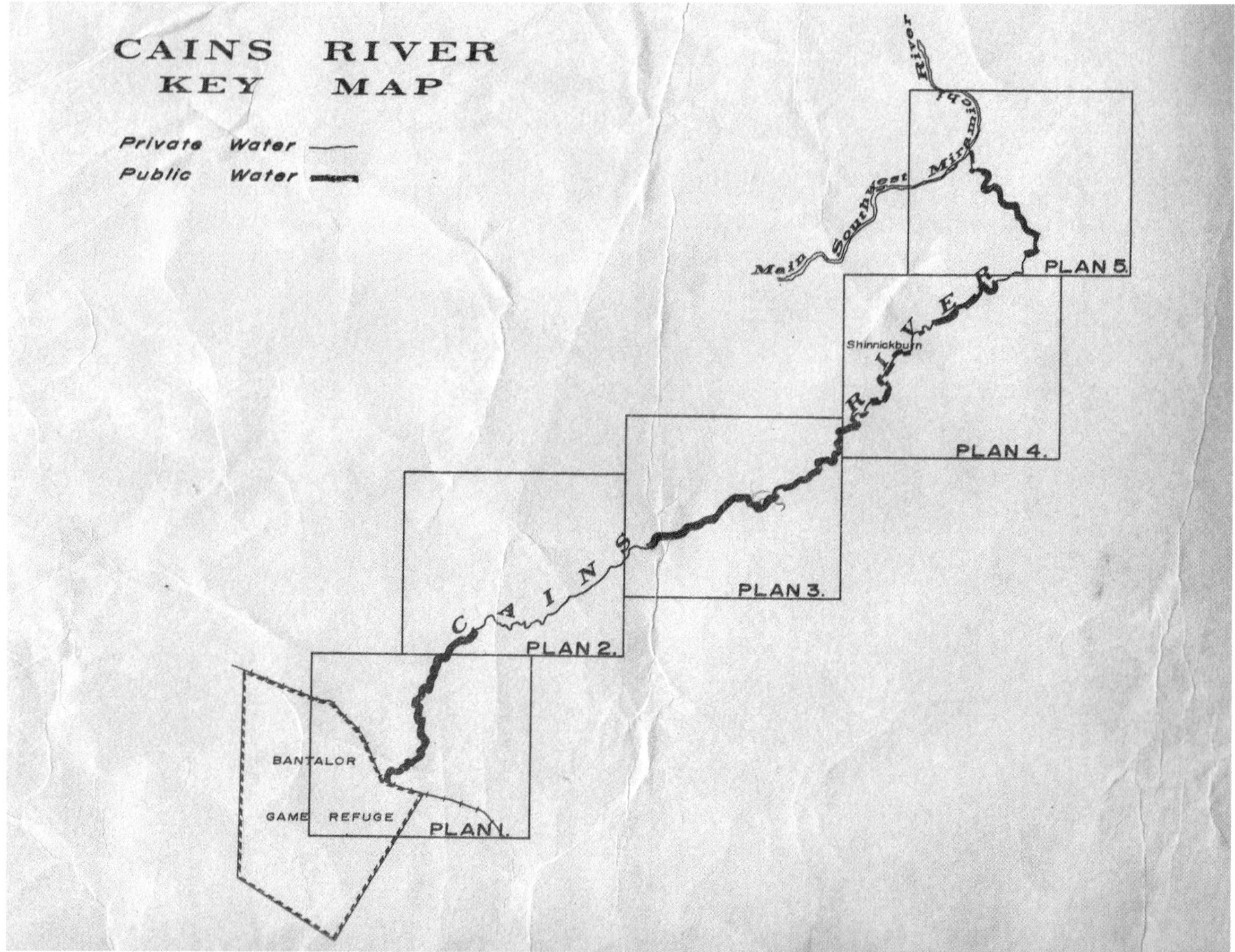

This map series shows the course of the Cains River main stem from Bantalor Game Reserve down to the junction with the Southwest Miramichi. If you look at the individual maps, you will see in some places a thick black line along the shore of the riverbank. These lines designate Crown or public fishing water. If you are not a resident of the province, though, you do need a guide. Areas of riverfront without the thick black line indicate private ownership. In general, these areas are open to the fishing public regardless of residence. You can see a thin line in most of Plan 2 and a little of Plan 3. That is the daily live release section, and it is available by advance reservation only to residents of the Province of New Brunswick. This map series is readily available on the internet.

the headwaters of the river and note and discuss the pools that are recognized as the most important in the Cains River fishery. On some of these named pools, the government has granted camp leases, and there are camps built at these locations even though the fishing water is still legally accessible to the public. The accepted custom at these locations is that if the camp owners are fishing the pool other anglers that come by just move on. If no one is in camp, then it is fine to fish the pool.

These named pools by no means represent the only waters on the Cains wherein you can catch Atlantic salmon. There are many other pools or even unrecorded pockets of attractive water that will produce salmon and trout. Wayne Curtis told me that his father, John Curtis, an outfitter on the Miramichi and the Cains beginning in the 1950s, used to say, "Come fall, the old Cains is the best we've got. You can catch fish in just about every inch of her." Over time, though, the pools listed in this chapter have shown a consistent ability to produce fish—realizing that we use the word consistent in the context of salmon fishing!

NORTH BRANCH POOL, AKA THE FORKS POOL

This is the farthest upriver recognized pool of significance on the Cains River. It is located toward the upstream end of Plan 2, of the five Cains River maps created by the Department of Natural Resources in Fredericton, New Brunswick. Located approximately 52 miles from the Mouth the Cains Rivers, this is where the North Branch of the Cains and the south branch—which is simply called the Cains River—meet. According to Nathan Wilbur's thermal buffering research, this pool provides a large flow of cool water, but the pool

Keith Wilson ran us up to the North Branch in the jet-powered canoe he uses to ferry sports to headwaters salmon fishing on the Cains. Even in this relatively high, seasonal flow, we scrubbed the tops of gravel bars in several locations and couldn't have gotten there in a propeller-driven craft.

Still flush with a fading spring runoff, the North Branch flows aggressively into the Cains River at the junction pool in May 2018.

Otter Brook Pool is one of the most highly regarded on the upper Cains River. It is the upstream end of the Daily Crown Reserve section and was the favorite pool of Wilson's famous longtime guide Ernest Long.

is shallow and does not offer a lot of cover for fish to hold there. This is a public pool and is upstream of the daily Crown Reserve section.

Note that the upper portion of the live release, the Crown Daily Reserve section of the Cains River, is defined as follows: from the mouth of Lower Otter Brook, downstream to O'Donnell's camp. The lower stretch is defined as being from O'Donnell's camp downstream to the river ford located approximately three-quarters of a kilometer above Hopewell Lodge. The upper stretch is about six miles long, and the lower stretch is approximately five.

Both stretches are known for high-quality brook trout fishing. The Crown Reserve catch-and-release-only season runs from June 1 through September 15. Fishing after that for fall-run salmon is not subject to Crown Reserve usage regulations. Only residents of the Province of New Brunswick can fish inside the Crown Reserve during the June 1 to September 15 period.

OTTER BROOK POOL

Located 50.5 miles from the mouth, Otter Brook is a deep, slow pool that holds trout and salmon in season. This is the favorite pool of Wilson's famous guide, Ernest Long. Otter Brook Pool is inside the Crown Reserve, as are all the pools listed below until we reach Hopewell Pool.

OGILVIE POOL

Located 50 miles from the mouth, this is a deep, slow pool with a brook that holds trout, but according to Keith Wilson, it is known mostly as a salmon pool.

WILDCAT, WILSON, AND BIG ROCK POOLS

Within a half mile of each other, and located 48 miles from the mouth, this water is all brook and spring-fed, and it is excellent water for both salmon and trout. These three pools were historically serviced by Wildcat Lodge, which was built by the Wilsons in 1967.

During the days of the Crown Lease that began in the early 1950s, and that Wilson's gave up in 1987, a standard Cains River trip to fish the Crown Waters consisted of putting in at the Bantalor Crossing and fishing down to Wildcat Lodge. The guides and sports would fish down to Wildcat on the first day, spend that night at Wildcat, and spend day two fishing the pools located near the camp. They would then spend the second night at Wildcat, and on the third day, they would fish down to the take out by the Grand Lake Road Bridge.

BIRCH LANDING POOL

Located 47 miles from the mouth, Birch is a deep pool located on a sharp bend in the river.

Ogilvie Pool is one of the quintessential upper Cains River pools with a private campsite owned by Jack Fitzpatrick from Fredericton.

Then graduate student Nathan Wilbur—now with the Atlantic Salmon Federation—camped out at Wildcat Lodge for a summer of research into aspects of cold-water buffering on the upper Cains River. PHOTO COURTESY OF NATHAN WILBUR.

Here is the view inside the old Wildcat Lodge. The author spent a night at Wildcat in early June 2018. It was 27°F on the deck when I woke up in the morning.

Nice trout taken by unknown anglers at Wildcat in 1939. The upper Cains still has sea-run brook trout of this size, though the numbers have not been great in recent years. PHOTO COURTESY OF THE PROVINCIAL ARCHIVES OF NEW BRUNSWICK.

GORDON BROOK POOL

Forty-five miles upriver from the mouth, the water below this brook is good for trout and salmon.

O'DONNELL POOL

At 42 miles from the mouth, this is a classic ledged pool with a brook good for both salmon and trout. Clarke O'Donnell, the current camp co-leaseholder, is the latest in several generations of O'Donnells to be at this location.

ACADIA BRIDGE POOL

Located 41.5 miles from the mouth, Acadia is a deep, spring-fed pool. A bridge was put in during 1969 but washed out the same year.

LEIGHTON BROOK

Leighton is 39 miles from the mouth, has a large brook, and is an excellent salmon pool.

Gordon Brook is one of the largest brooks entering the upper Cains River, and it is an important cold-water source for brook trout survival during the warm summer months.

The O'Donnell Pool is a classic ledged Cains River pool—deep, on the bend, and fed by an ice-cold brook.

There are three signs on the old Acadia bridge abutment. One is a government sign that just tells what pool it is; another one marks this as part of the special Crown Daily Reserve section; and the other faded one in the upper right corner goes back to the days of the Wilson fishing lease from the 1950s through 1980s.

The Leighton Brook pool has a deep, moderately paced upper end and a fast, ledged lower end sweetened by a large brook. The road along the river fords the brook. The pool has accounted for many large fall salmon. This camp lease is owned by Keith Wilson.

Gartley Clarke on the left, and Wallace O'Donnell on the right. Clarke was a famous fisherman in his day, and he is holding a pair of fine Cains River brook trout. The photograph was hanging inside of Wildcat Camp.

HOPEWELL LODGE AND POOL

Located 36 miles from the Mouth of the Cains but only a short distance above the Doaktown Road, this water is fast at the top and has a deep slot running along a ledged side. This is an excellent trout and salmon pool. Hopewell is the first notable pool downstream of the daily Crown Reserve Section, and it is shown near the upstream end of Plan 3 of the Cains River maps.

Howard Moore, whose great-uncle was the famous hunting guide "Barn Door" Adam Moore, owned Hopewell Lodge between 1969 and 2001 before retiring and selling to members of the famous New Brunswick Irving family. Moore's New Brunswick wildlife heritage also included a grandfather named William Moore who was one of the province's most important taxidermists.

Moore said that Hopewell Lodge and accompanying Camp Caribou were originally built by Frank Hopewell in 1887 for the then whopping sum of $10,000. A lease for the site of one of Harry Allen's camps was Crown Campsite Lease #1, and Hopewell Lodge and one of its nearby satellite camps called Camp Caribou were leases 2 and 3.

The great years for Hopewell Lodge ended with the caribou in the early 1920s, as did the Hopewell family's ownership. In 1923, the five-acre campsite lease for Hopewell Lodge was made out to James Clemens and Ruby and W. L. Van Wagenen of Boston. From there, it went to people with the last names

The photo is of the fishing pool at Hopewell Lodge looking upriver. The upper right just before the start of the bend to the left is a deep pool with a good flow and a succession of small brooks and seeps coming from the ledged hillside. You can see Irving's new lodge that replaced historic Hopewell in the trees on the right in the photograph.

Here is a simple advertising piece used during the 1960s by Hopewell Lodge. You can't count the steps up or down to the water, but it is too far for many of us! The stairs and the old lodge are long gone now. PHOTO COURTESY OF HOWARD MOORE.

of Perault, Judson, and Dean. It transferred to a church for a while and then to the town manager of Waterville, Maine, and back to New Brunswick to a Donny Long of Doaktown. Howard Moore acquired the property from Donny Long for $1,000, and by then, it was a shadow of its former rustic elegance. Sadly, but perhaps inevitably, Irving tore down the old Hopewell Lodge and built a new structure called Red Pine Lodge on the property almost immediately after buying it.

A ton of history goes along with Hopewell Lodge, and we still have the romance of that grand old place to dream about. The lodge itself was a massive structure, especially to have been built so far back into the woods. It was said to have been built by two of the sons of William Russell, known as "Chief,"

Metal tags to be affixed to the camps located on the leased land. Howard pulled these off the old Camp Caribou and Hopewell Lodge. With numbers of 2 and 3, Hopewell's leases were clearly among the very first ones handed out by the Provincial Government.

A guest hunter dressed in safety orange on the lawn of Hopewell Lodge in the 1960s. PHOTO COURTESY OF HOWARD MOORE.

In the early twentieth century, New Brunswick was still thought of as a big-game-filled wilderness. After the 1928 Baseball World Series, Mickey Cochrane, the American League's MVP, took off for the Miramichi with five of his sports friends to fish salmon and then hunt moose at Hopewell Lodge. Two of them, including Cochrane, were successful. There are many records of American sports celebrities hunting and fishing on the Cains and Miramichi Rivers.

Russell was one of the famous early outfitters in the area. Hopewell Lodge was set on a towering bluff overlooking the Cains River Valley. The Cains River wilderness stretched off to the south, east, and west. The veranda that offered this majestic view was 85 feet long. Hopewell was a well-known hunting destination, and it had six smaller camps set around the area. Foremost among those was Camp Caribou, which was a 16-by-24-foot structure built as a hunting camp. The other camps were simply converted lumber camps and were really a shelter if caught out with approaching nightfall.

It is said that early in the twentieth century when the effects of the great Miramichi fire were still visible, sitting on the veranda at night, one could see the lights of Camp Caribou, more than five miles away on the barren grounds where a herd of New Brunswick caribou wintered.

Howard spent several years at Hopewell before he finally found the remains of the old Camp Caribou. The location was due south of Hopewell, and Howard told me that on early attempts to find the old hunting camp they had underestimated the distances involved and didn't walk far enough to reach it. A huge spruce tree had fallen down through Camp Caribou and destroyed it. The big wooden door that people had traditionally used to carve hunting records into was still intact. Howard made a trip back into the camp the next year to retrieve the door, but someone had burned it down over the winter. The previous year when Howard had read the entries carved in the door, he saw that it had last been occupied during 1957.

Howard told me that there were three barrens located in hunting range of the camps. These were Ginny Barren, Blue Rock Barren, and Dry Barren. Camp Caribou was located closest to Dry Barren, which had lots of the big deer's favorite

CAMP TO CAMP GORDON VIA BARRENS

First Dry Barren	2-1/4 Miles
End Dry Barren	3 "
Blue Rock Lake	6 "
Large Barren	7 1/2 "
End Large Barren	8-1/2 "
Jinny Barren	9 "
Never Barren	9 1/2 "
O'Donnell Road	10-1/2 "
Camp Gordon	13-1/2 "

LODGE TO GORDON BROOK CROSSING

Morris Trail	2-1/2 "
(End of Morris Trail)	3-1/2 "
Gordon Brook Crossing	3 "

GORDON BROOK CROSSING TO CAMP GORDON

Plains and Wothen Brook	2-1/2 "
Wet Swamp	4 "
Camp Gordon	5-1/2 "

This aged print hung in a simple black frame in Hopewell Lodge. The document instructed the guests on how far from the lodge the various camps and caribou barrens were located.

Camp Caribou. Note the great width of the boards used to make the building. Howard Moore found the old camp in the 1970s, and it was burned that winter. It was last used in 1957. PHOTO COURTESY OF MICHAEL O'DONNELL.

Looking up the beautiful Cains River from the heights of Hopewell. This photograph was taken by Howard Moore in the 1970s. The old lookout is still there.

winter food: caribou moss. It is still there, and Howard said that you can feel it crunch under your feet when you walk on it in the late fall. Howard also said that the caribou were known to have used a very large circular trail that went from the barrens up to Muzzeroll Lake, then over to Otter Brook and back down to the barrens. The trail was so well worn and ancient that even in the last years of Howard's ownership the trail could still be seen early in the year before the new vegetation came in. Howard went on to say that during the early 1990s a friend of his who had grown up in Newfoundland—and was infinitely familiar with caribou—was adamant that he had seen one drinking in the river below Hopewell. There have been other claimed sightings too. Howard says that it is difficult to believe, but we can hope that perhaps there is truth to it. Some of the recent winters that have been so hard on whitetail deer would be right up the caribou's alley.

While Hopewell is famous for its hunting, it also has a great fishing pool. The shore in front of the lodge was accessed by an enormous set of stairs that cascaded down over the steep bank in several sections. According to Howard, the salmon began to show up in October, and many spawned near the lodge late in the month and into November. From the heights of the bluff above the water where Hopewell is situated, you could see the salmon spawning and hear them jumping all night long.

The early photographs of Hopewell Lodge, the nearby river, and the countryside in this section were provided by the American Salmon Museum in Doaktown and Michael O'Donnell of Nelson Hollow, New Brunswick, from a collection given to him by Robert Hopewell, a descendent of Frank B. Hopewell.

A bedroom at Hopewell Lodge. Note the early pinups on the wall to help the sports feel more comfortable in the wilderness.

Sport and guide with a late-season salmon at Hopewell. Note that the leaves are gone, but the shore grass is still standing up. In spring, it would have been flattened by winter ice.

A nice catch of trout at Hopewell Lodge decorated with spruce boughs.

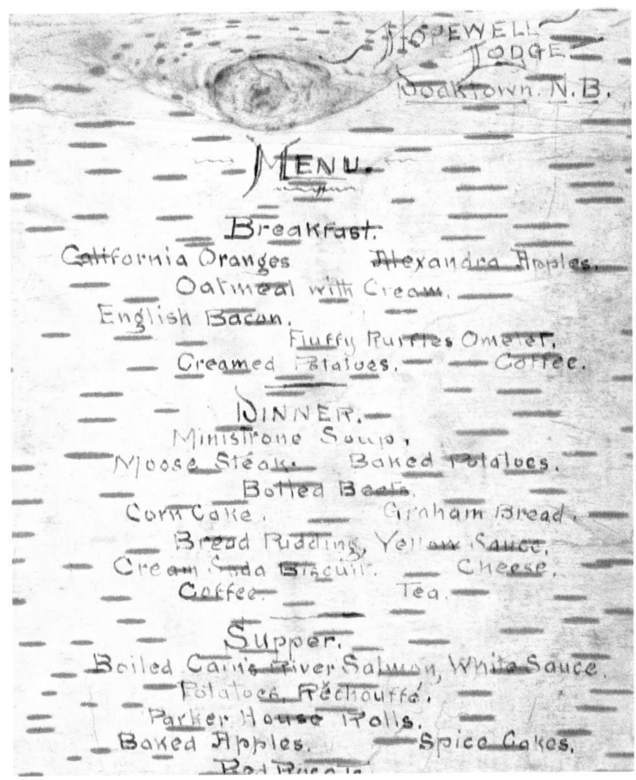

Hopewell Lodge
Doaktown. N.B.

Menu.

Breakfast.
California Oranges Alexandra Apples.
Oatmeal with Cream.
English Bacon.
Fluffy Ruffles Omelet.
Creamed Potatoes. Coffee.

Dinner.
Ministrone Soup,
Moose Steak. Baked Potatoes.
Botted Beets.
Corn Cake. Graham Bread.
Bread Pudding, Yellow Sauce,
Cream Soda Biscuit. Cheese.
Coffee. Tea.

Supper.
Boiled Cain's River Salmon, White Sauce.
Potatoes Réchauffé.
Parker House Rolls.
Baked Apples. Spice Cakes.

The menu at Hopewell Lodge was printed on birch bark and featured upscale foods such as California orange juice and English bacon.

An angler fishing the Cains River in front of Hopewell Lodge.

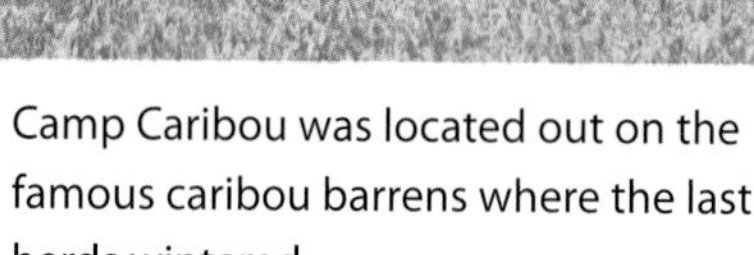

Camp Caribou was located out on the famous caribou barrens where the last herds wintered.

Left: Some of the staff hamming it up on the back deck of Hopewell Lodge. The chef, nicknamed "Pops," had his shotgun at hand so he could add the odd grouse that flew by to the menu.

CAMP TO CAMP GORDON VIA BARRENS

First Dry Barren	2-1/4 Miles
End Dry Barren	3 "
Blue Rock Lake	6 "
Large Barron	7-1/2 "
End Large Barren	8-1/2 "
Jimmy Barren	9 "
Never Barren	9-1/2 "
O'Donnell Road	10-1/2 "
Camp Gordon	13-1/2 "

LODGE TO GORDON BROOK CROSSING

Morris Trail	1-1/2 "
(End of Morris Trail)	3-1/2 "
Gordon Brook Crossing	3 "

GORDON BROOK CROSSING TO CAMP GORDON

Plains and Wothen Brook	2-1/2 "
Wet Swamp	4 "
Camp Gordon	5-1/2 "

Copy of an old document that hung in Hopewell Lodge that showed directions and distances to various hunting grounds.

A guide poles a guest up the Cains River.

Henry C. Hopewell at left in the doorway of Camp Caribou.

Top right: The Hopewell Lodge veranda was 85 feet long and had one of the greatest views in the province. *Left:* The new lodge built by Irving on the site of old Hopewell Lodge.

A moose crossing the river at Hopewell Ford seen from the "lookout" just upriver of the lodge.

Some of the province's last caribou were shot on the Cains River barrens. The man pictured is Henry C. Hopewell, nephew of the original proprietor Frank B. Hopewell.

The view upriver from the lookout is pretty much the same in 2018 as it was in 1912. The pond in the interval on the left is a little larger, but it is also springtime.

The giant stairway down to the river in 1912. Note the two women standing at the top.

The top landing of the stairway. Henry C. Hopewell is the second man from the far right.

Left: The little-used trail down as it existed in the spring of 2018 that has replaced the stairs.

RUSSELL POOL AND HIGH LANDING POOLS

These pools are located approximately 34.5 miles up from the mouth of the Cains River.

Bev Russell's camp sits on the north bank of the Cains just downriver from Hopewell Lodge. The camp location straddles the Russell and High Landing Pools. These pools are located about one mile above the Route 123 Bridge.

TEN MILE POOL

Ten Mile Pool is 33 miles from the Mouth of Cains, and like Reid Pool just a mile farther downstream, both of these pools are located where substantial brooks—Ten Mile and Mahoney respectively—enter the Cains River. Both pools are a relatively short distance from the Grand Lake Road Bridge, and consequently, they are fairly heavily angled.

DEEPWOODS LODGE AND POOL

Deepwoods is located two miles below the Ten Mile Pool and is therefore 31 miles from the mouth. Deepwood's camp is located on a high pool on the north side of the river. The pool is public and just downstream of the camp. This long section of good fishing water is home ground to the well-known fishing couple of Lloyd and Cheryl Bartlett. The Bartletts are now the senior members of a group of fishers who have, in some cases, been coming to the Cains since the 1970s.

In the general area of Deepwoods, and for a mile or two downstream, the Bartletts have learned every rock, bar, eddy, and bit of streamy water that might hold a salmon. They tent on Crown land and religiously spend the last couple of weeks of every salmon-fishing season at this location on the Cains. Lloyd's words echoed the comments of old outfitter John Curtis when he said of the Cains that you could catch a salmon

Deepwoods Lodge in 1939 looking out across the Cains River valley. PHOTO COURTESY OF THE PROVINCIAL ARCHIVES OF NEW BRUNSWICK.

in every inch of her. The Deepwoods stretch is quick water laced liberally with boulders that provide comfortable lies for the salmon.

In 2015, we had what amounted to a flood on the last day of September. About four inches of rain fell in a little over a day all over the Miramichi and Cains River watersheds. The Bartletts were sleeping in their tent the night of the flood. No one expected the water to come up quite as far and as fast as it did. Cheryl rolled over in the bed, and her hand dangled into the rising water. It was fire drill time, and while wading through knee-deep water, they loaded their gear into their truck and made it to high ground by the skin of their teeth.

The writings about the Cains right up through the 1940s consistently mention the Elkins Pool. In the Provincial archives, I found a picture of a guide and a canoe said to be in the Elkins Pool taken during the 1930s. I'm quite confident that it is in the vicinity of the Deepwood's Pool, whether slightly up- or downriver I have not been able to find out.

UPPER TROUT HOLE

This pool is located 30 miles from the Mouth of Cains. Upper Trout Hole is the quintessential deep, horseshoe bend in the river pool with the best flow close to the south or east bank.

LOWER TROUT HOLE

Lower Trout Hole is located about 28 miles upriver from the mouth of the Cains. It is located on the site of the most upriver of the Crown grants that were made. A small brook comes out near the pool, and as the name suggests, it is known more for trout than salmon. A large, new camp and outbuildings have been built here in recent times.

THE ARBEAU OR ARBO POOL

The much-written-about Arbeau Pool is located approximately 27 miles upriver from the mouth. This pool is not listed on the New Brunswick Natural Resources (NBNR) map of the Cains, but the location of the pool is on a bend in the river between Lower Trout Hole and the Indian portage path. Before the early 1900s, Arbeaus lived and farmed here, but there was never a Crown grant, and the pool is public.

Even though I have already said it is not totally inclusive, the fact that this pool is not named on the NBNR map is a bit surprising. It was one of the pools fished by the Sturges party on their 1915 trip with Harry Allen. It was also mentioned by Dorothy Noye Arms's book, and it shows up here and there in almost everything written about this part of the river. In 1932, Harry Allen actually purchased the Arbeau Pool and farm from Alexander Arbeau, later reselling it to a man from Geneva, New York, named Leuan Harris who we would expect to have been a sport of Harry's who had seen the abandoned farm on a trip with Harry, perhaps experienced some good fishing there, and became interested in owning it. This may very well be the first pool on the Cains River to have been purchased primarily for salmon-fishing purposes.

Deepwoods Lodge as it appeared in May 2018.

Angler James Gallagher guided by Lyman Gilks with two grilse taken from the Arbeau Pool during the late 1980s. PHOTO COURTESY OF AL GALLAGHER.

This LIDAR technology map supplied by the New Brunswick Department of Natural Resources uses reflected light to show otherwise invisible changes in the topography. You can clearly see the depth of the streambed and of a trail leading down from the hill on the left of the stream to the interval below. This could have led to the farm or could have been the trail that Emery Brophy used 60 years ago to lead horses down over the hill to drink from the river while they were lumbering. This is the area of the old Arbeau farm.

It is one that I know is regularly fished today by local folks who know the river. Additionally, it is the only pool that I am going to list in this section of the book that is not recognized by the NBNR map.

A search of legal records showed no sale of the property by Leuan Harris, yet it is owned today by a lumber company. Like many of the old Cains River properties, it may simply have been abandoned by Harris or more likely his heirs. There was never a Crown grant for this land, and it would be available to the public for fishing in any case.

AN UNNAMED POOL

Not all the pools along the Cains are named. The photo at the top of page 100 shows a good one that lies between the Arbeau and the Murray Pools that has no name that I know of. The person who showed it to me called it Lower Trout Hole, but it is several miles downriver of that one.

THE MURRAY POOL

Located approximately 21 miles upriver from the mouth, the Murray Pool is indicated at the very upstream end of Plan 4. The heart of the pool is a relatively quick and moderately narrow boulder-filled run, and it tails off into a broader, shallower

This pool is incorrectly called Lower Trout Hole Pool by some, but it is a good pool nonetheless. A great little stream comes out of a ledge and cascades down into the pool. I've only fished it a handful of times, but I have caught some nice trout and lost a salmon here one day.

flow with a ledged bottom. The Murray Grant is owned today by Fornebu Lumber, and the north or opposite side of the pool is public.

THE MAHONEY POOL

Located approximately 20 miles upriver from the mouth, the Mahoney Pool is listed near the upstream end of Plan 4, about a mile below the Murray Pool. The pool has two portions: one is a narrow and quick run at the top, and the other is a deep, relatively slow-moving section below the brook at the bottom. The Mahoney Pool stems from 1847 Crown grants to a Denis Mahoney on the west side of the river and Jeremiah Mahoney on the east. These pools were owned and fished during the 1960s by an outfitter called Cains River Enterprises owned by a Bob Brown out of Moncton. In addition to fall salmon, they fished in late May for sea-run brook trout near the mouth of Mahoney Brook.

Cains River Enterprises had a camp overlooking the pool located very close to the site where the current lodge now stands. The pools and camp are owned today by Brad Burns, the author of this book.

SIX MILE BROOK

Located approximately 19 miles upriver from the mouth, Six Mile Brook is one of the most famous locations on the Cains

Guide Darrell Warren holds a typical fall hen salmon at the Murray Pool on a great fall fishing day with moderate overcast and light winds.

Photograph of the Mahoney Brook camp on a rainy last day of the 2010 season. The Mahoney Pool is in the foreground, and the narrow run in front of the camp is the home pool.

Jason Curtis stocking salmon fry into Mahoney Brook during late June 2017. This work is done by the Miramichi Salmon Association. I love the organization's hands-on, roll-up-your-sleeves approach. PHOTO COURTESY OF THE MIRAMICHI SALMON ASSOCIATION.

River. The pool is listed on Plan 2 of the New Brunswick Natural Resources maps. Six Mile has a fast, relatively deep run starting above Six Mile Brook and ends with a deep, slow-holding pool at the bottom. The fishing water on the west or northside is private, stemming from an 1846 Crown grant on the west to Andrew McCormick and an 1861 Crown grant to Edmund O'Connell on the east. The map indicates that the run upstream of Six Mile Brook on the south side of the Cains River is public. The rest of the water around the camp and the northside of the run are private.

Some salmon ascend Six Mile Brook to spawn. One time while spring salmon fishing with Donald Colford, a longtime guide for the Black Brook Salmon Club, he told me that he had seen salmon spawning in Six Mile Brook and had also seen salmon caught up inside the brook during high water. Angus Curtis—who guided for the Black Brook Salmon Club, and whose father Ab Curtis guided for Kingsbury Browne at Six Mile Brook and then for the Black Brook Salmon Club who purchased the property from Kingsbury—told me that late one fall after the fishing season he had walked out on the camp road for quite a distance to a point where it ran right beside Six Mile Brook and saw several large salmon laying in the brook. Angus said the pool was quite deep, and the water was very dark. The fish were enormous, and at first, he thought they were just logs lying on the bottom, but he caught little glimpses of white as they moved their gills to breathe.

The Six Mile Brook property has had a private sporting lodge on the site since at least the early 1940s. According to Charles Willis, author of a book about a fishing trip on the Cains River called *The Three Must Get Theirs*, which was privately printed in 1943, the lodge was originally built by John Taylor Arms, a famous artist of the era, and his author-wife,

Six Mile Brook camp and pool. From the late 1940s into the early 1960s, Six Mile was owned by Black Brook Salmon Club member Kingsbury "Crib" Browne, the great-uncle of Spey casting expert Topher Browne, author of *Salmon Magic*.

Salmon ascend Six Mile Brook in the late fall to spawn.

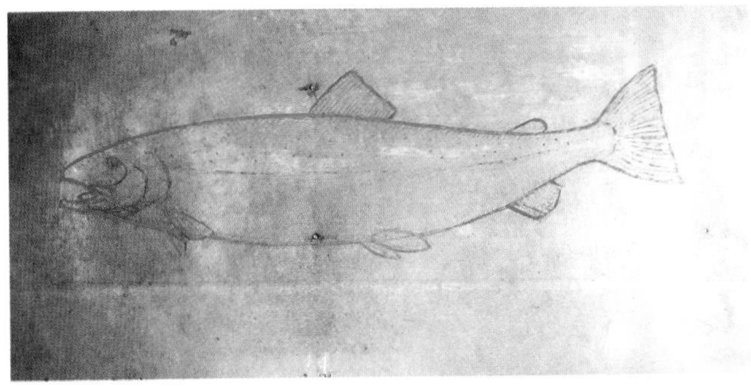

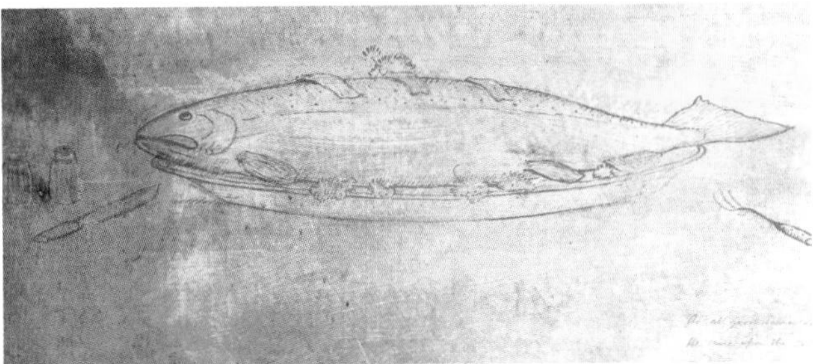

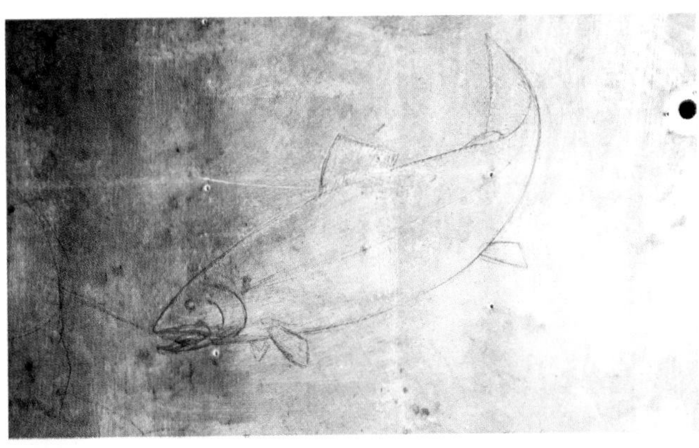

PHOTOGRAPHS COURTESY OF RIP CUNNINGHAM.

ALR SALMON VERSE

The laughing salmon smirks below
And vows he'll never take it
But if you change and try and change again
The chances are you'll make it
The laughing salmon got well hooked
And decided he would break it
He did a fancy flip flop
But found he could not shake it
The salmon now was pretty mad
And down he went and around a rock
The leader broke and that was sad
But what the fisherman said on the bank
Was very very bad
So now he laughs there down below
And vows he'll take no more
Fishermen may be nice perhaps
But I think they're an awful bore
As all good salmon do of course
He came upon the table
But not to hold a requiem grim
Or is that just a fable

Salmon and very bad verse by A. Lassell Ripley

Dorothy Noyes Arms. I could find no one today who remembered the Armses or their legacy on the river, but George Johnson recalled in a 1983 interview for Nashwaak Bicentennial Association that he "went guiding" for Harry Allen in 1922 and that he had guided the Arms couple during his early years. He said that they had ended up building a camp over in Shinnicksburn, further evidence that they were the builders of Six Mile Camp. Kingsbury "Crib" Browne, who ended up owning the camp, is the great-uncle of Spey casting expert and writer Topher Browne. Crib sold the property to the Black Brook Salmon Club in 1964. In 2005, Black Brook Salmon Club, in turn, sold it to the Six Mile Fishing Club, which is a subset of members from the Hershey Club located a mile and a half below Black Brook on the main Southwest Miramichi.

One characteristic of the Six Mile Brook camp is that the whole complex sits on the outside of the bend and does not have a great elevation above the water. It is prone to flooding and being hit by ice during the spring freshet. That has happened a number of times over the years, as it also has to other low-lying camps. Angus Curtis talks about one of the buildings, nicknamed the "Honeymoon Camp," being taken out by the flood of 1972. After that flood, Angus and others helped place the main camp back on its foundations.

Six Mile has also been known historically for its brook trout fishing. Horace Kervin, who Emery Brophy says was one of the last year-round residents of Shinnickburn village, would take his horses and a wagon over to Six Mile Brook and take Kingsbury Browne up to a smaller hunting camp that was located seven miles up the brook at a place they called Seven Mile Brook. Apparently, in the 1950s, the brook trout fishing there was nothing short of spectacular.

Browne was a Boston-area man, as were many of the original Black Brook Salmon Club members. One of the guests was the famous artist, hunter, and fisherman Aiden Lassell Ripley, who also hailed from Boston. Ripley painted some hunting and fishing murals on the interior of the lodge, and they were acquired from the Black Brook Salmon Club by club member Colin "Rip" Cunningham. The six murals are of a salmon in the river who anglers are trying to seduce with their flies despite the fish's determination not to end up on a platter.

These six murals were painted by famous sporting artist Aiden Lassell Ripley during one of his visits to the camp. He also wrote a little verse to accompany them about a salmon who was hooked after some difficulty but temporarily escaped the fate of ending up as dinner.

Here also is a painting by Ripley that shows a party comprised of a man and woman fishing at the mouth of Six Mile Brook. Their guide is Curtis, and he is about to net the salmon that is on the woman's line. The woman and the man in the painting were identified by Rip, a current member of the Black Brook Salmon Club, as his aunt and uncle, Jack and Jill Cunningham, who were founding members of the club. Jack commissioned the painting from Ripley circa 1960. His son, John H. Cunningham III, gave me permission to photograph the painting as well as this black-and-white image from around 10 years later of his father playing a salmon in the lovely run at the upstream end of Six Mile Brook's property.

Ripley painting of members of the Cunningham family fishing at Six Mile Brook with guide Ab Curtis preparing to net a salmon. John Cunningham, son of the couple in the picture, kindly allowed me to photograph this painting.

Jack Cunningham playing a salmon in the run above the Six Mile Brook water circa 1970. PHOTO COURTESY OF JOHN CUNNINGHAM.

ELIASON CAMP

Located just two-tenths of a miles downriver of Six Mile Brook is a camp with the gable end facing the river. This was called the L. R. Eliason Camp, and according to Emery Brophy, he believed that it started its existence as an old lumber camp. The story goes that Clarence Wade's son—Clarence was Charlie Wade's brother and also worked with Harry Allen—was a dentist who moved to Machias, Maine. The dentist told Linny Eliason about the camp. Eliason bought it and hired George Amos as his guide and caretaker. Brophy said that Eliason used to arrive in Blackville in an Edsel. It was the only one of those notoriously unsuccessful cars that Brophy ever saw.

This camp is not located on a Crown grant, but the water near and below the camp is both deep and fast, and it provides some of the best salmon angling habitat in the area. The camp is now owned by Kevin Anthony of Maine.

HANNAN'S BEND

Bordering the L. R. Eliason Pool, on the same side of the river and just downstream, is an original 99-acre grant to a Michael Hannan. The water here, like the L. R. Eliason Pool, is relatively deep, fast, and well structured.

TOM BOYD CAMP

The Tom Boyd Pool is located 18.6 miles upriver from the mouth of Cains River. A 1969 copy of the *Fishing Guide for the Cains River* produced by New Brunswick Natural Resources shows the pool as the Tom Boyd Pool. Tom Boyd and his son Bill were the owners of Uncle Tom's Cabin, a famous Miramichi fishing camp down in the Rapids that later was owned by a couple of large corporations before being sold to a local syndicate that included the owners of the Ledge's Inn salmon lodge in Doaktown. Like many Miramichi lodges, Boyd wanted a Cains River operation, and the Tom Boyd Pool was theirs. The water rights ownership was conveyed by a Crown grant to a William O'Brien in 1866. Recently, the property has been sold to a William Buggie of

The Eliason Camp, owned by Kevin Anthony from Maine. For years, the camp was looked after by Atlantic Salmon Museum Hall of Fame guide George Amos.

The Tom Boyd Camp is less than a half mile above the mouth of Muzzerroll Brook and on the south or east side of the river across from Hannan's Bend.

The pool where Muzzeroll Brook flows into the Cains River is just the head of the Doctor's Island Pool. It is, though, a separate piece of private property owned by the Roman Catholic Church. The outline of the old Kervin homestead can be seen at the back of the field looking up the brook. This is may be where Harry Allen and Lee Sturges stopped in 1915 to give some salmon to the residents of the area.

New Brunswick. See also the information about Mountain Channel listed in the previous chapter.

THE CHURCH POOL, AKA MOUTH OF MUZZEROLL BROOK POOL

The water right at the mouth of Muzzeroll Brook and leading downriver a short distance before reaching the Doctor's Island property is owned by the Roman Catholic Church. The Church Pool is actually a 1905 Crown grant to the Roman Catholic Church.

Country Haven Outfitters currently leases this pool from the church. The top of this pool is where the flow of the Cains River and Muzzeroll come together, and the bottom configuration can be a bit unstable year to year because of this. When it is good, there is a narrow area of fast flow near the top, and it can be a good producer. Some years, a gravel bar can develop there that hinders fishing.

The opposite side of the river from where Muzzeroll enters the Cains is open public water. Like a lot of Cains River pools, especially on the east side of the river, it is not a very easy pool to get to, but it is a very good stretch of water.

DOCTOR'S ISLAND

The Cains River property located a short distance downriver from the mouth of Muzzeroll Brook was originally a Crown grant to Michael McLaughlin in 1909. The pool is located 18 miles up the Cains River from the mouth. The Doctor's Island Pool and the Church Pool collectively comprise what is often called the Mouth of Muzzeroll Pool. Muzzerroll Brook itself, which comes in from the north or west side of the Cains River, is the second largest tributary of the Cains, accounting for nearly 7 percent of the Cains River's total salmon habitat, according to a Department of Fisheries and Oceans study mentioned earlier in the biology chapter. In good years, parr can be found up Muzzeroll Brook all the way to and beyond where the Grand Lake Road passes over it.

Junction pools of all types are often excellent places for fish since the conflicting currents provide changes in water speed, and they have bottoms that have been sculpted out of the pools by the cross turbulence and provide good holding water. The Doctor's Island Club water is just downriver a short distance from the Mouth of Muzzeroll.

The water here is relatively deep, well-structured with large rocks, and quite fast flowing. According to Wesley Curtis,

These are a group of pictures from October 2007 of fishing at the Doctor's Island Cains River camp just below the mouth of Muzzeroll Brook. That's angler Niels Jensen hooked up to all the big salmon. THE PHOTOS ARE COURTESY OF HARVEY WHEELER.

In this drone photograph of Doctor's Island Pool and camp, one can see that the pool has great center depth and flow, plus plenty of nice rocky structure. The best water is clearly located on the Doctor's Island side of the center thread of the pool.

who guided there during the fall fishery in 1984 through 1986, this is finest pool on the Cains River, and it holds fish in its bottom end during even lower water heights. Low water pools are the very scarcest of commodities on the Cains. The Club side of the pool is a bit deeper than the public side—but both sides are often productive—and can produce some very good fall fishing.

MOORE POOL

The Moore pool is only about seven-tenths of a mile downstream from Doctor's Island's Pool. Coleman B. Moore from Pennsylvania purchased the Moore Pool in 1953 from Charles Kervin. The Kervins were early settlers around the Muzzeroll area of Shinnickburn, and they were the last family to live year-round in the now defunct town. For 11 years, Moore owned both this pool and the Brophy Pool down toward the mouth of the river. Moore sold the Brophy Pool in 1972, assumedly to consolidate his holdings. Later, Bill Moore inherited his father's interest in the Moore Pool property. Bill recently passed away in very early 2017. The Moore family still owns the pool, camp, and land. The Moore Pool property stems from an original Crown grant to Michael McLaughlin in 1837. This individual grant was unusually large and included 150 acres running to both sides of the river.

This property, for several reasons, is one of the best-known—and best-producing—pools on the river. The Cains River here runs right up to within a few feet of the road on the west, or Shinnickburn village, side of the river. A nice lodge sits in the woods just across the road from the river. People park along the road in this area when launching canoes headed down the river, or to take out arrivals from upriver locations.

Gary Colford—one of the Miramichi's most famous guides, now with Country Haven Outfitters, and previously for many years at Wade's Fishing Lodge—has been the caretaker of Moore's Pool since the late 1970s. In that position, he followed his uncle Basil Colford, who was Mr. Moore's guide and caretaker from 1959 until Coleman passed away in 1977. Before Basil, Gary's grandfather, Willam G. Colford, held the position.

For me, this is an important and exciting piece of information. It is very difficult in 2018 to find a living person who has a clear memory of the chain of people that go back to Harry Allen's time and, essentially, the beginnings of Cains River salmon fishing. I interviewed Gary regarding his Cains River history on January 4, 2018. His memory was very sharp; it took him only seconds to recall names that he has probably gone years without uttering, remembering very accurately as other research work verified the timing of property purchases,

This photo of the Moore Pool is taken looking up toward Doctor's Island. The anglers are fishing at the top of the pool. The farthest upriver point visible is the Doctor's Island Pool. The late Bill Moore told me that his father greatly enhanced the pool by bulldozer, a common practice to deepen pools years ago. This is one of the most dependable pools on the Cains River.

Here is a bird's-eye view of the Moore Pool taken in fairly low water. The defunct village of Shinnickburn is just down around the bend to the left. Moore's camp is just out of sight across the road to the left of the foreground. The road seen here is the same road and location seen covered with snow and ice in the picture on page xii.

employment, camps being built or torn down, and so on. Gary said that Coleman Moore was a client of Harry Allen and took the weeklong canoe trips with Harry's staff down the Cains River. William Colford, Gary's grandfather, guided and cooked on these trips, and he met Coleman Moore that way. In Seabury Stanton's camp log, it says that, in 1938, on their first trip to George Allen's camps, Bill Colford was one of their guides. He must have stayed on with George after Harry's death in 1932. Clearly, Coleman became enchanted with the Cains, and William Colford helped him to find a property of his own to purchase on the river.

Moore usually brought several friends up for kelt fishing, and Gary began guiding there while he was still a teenager in the late 1950s. Gary says that spring fishing opened on April 1 in those years, and the Cains often iced out earlier than the Miramichi, and some years they fished in areas of open water between still frozen stretches of the river. When the river iced out completely, the guides would take Moore and his guests as far upriver as the Arbeau Pool and follow the kelt migration back down the Cains. There were many more fish in the run those days, and Gary said that there were always fish on the line, and he would often spend all day long unhooking salmon.

In those years, a shore lunch was cooked every day by the guides, and it often was Gary's duty. Some days, Gary would cook for as many as a dozen men. The meals were usually steak and fish, and the fish were kelts. Gary said that kelts had always been eaten by people along the river, and that he preferred them to bright salmon since they were not as oily or overly rich as fresh-run salmon can sometimes be.

A mammoth fall hen fish from the Moore Pool. Note the holding box for the Miramichi Salmon Association stocking program. The salmon was transported to the hatchery, where virtually all of the eggs would be successfully hatched for stocking the next spring as fry in areas where parr counts have shown a less than optimal population level. After spawning, the salmon are released back into the wild. PHOTO COURTESY OF COUNTRY HAVEN LODGE.

The Moore Pool, with its depth and good flow, is one of the most important pools on the Cains. There is an old saying that salmon run up the Miramichi and crawl up the Cains. This means that salmon are routinely in the Rocky Brook pools some 78 miles above the head of tide by the first of June, as early as anywhere in Main Southwest Miramichi. However, even in good years, it is late August before fishable numbers of salmon appear at the Moore Pool only 30 miles above the head of tide. By standards of the upper Cains, though, the Moore Pool is relatively early. Frequently, when we are still looking for our first fish up at Mahoney Brook in late September, I roll down the window when passing the Moore Pool and get the word from Gary, who is guiding at Moore's. They are usually seeing and catching fish daily a couple of weeks or more before we are just three miles or so upriver.

In 2016, I sat with Bill Moore and a couple of his old fishing buddies during the October 2016 Atlantic Salmon Museum induction ceremonies for new Hall of Fame members. Gary Colford was inducted that year, and Bill and I had both sent in letters of support for his nomination. Bill told me that as a boy he had witnessed the Moore Pool being built. In a few sentences, he described how a man—he thought named Underhill—who Moore claimed had built other pools along the river, had first made a gravel dam at the top of the pool during very low water in the driest part of summer, then gouged out a deep channel through the center of quite a long run. He ended the pool with a gravel and stone wing on each side of the lower end of the pool, then went back to the top. With water washing across the tracks of his bulldozer, at a level nearly up to his seat, the operator ran across the top of the pool and removed the dam that he had begun his work by creating. Voilà! The Moore Pool was made. Bill then looked at me and said that to his knowledge many pools on the Cains had been made just that way. I also heard that Ted Williams had this done down at the Teedlan Pool as late as the 1980s, and that was confirmed by lifelong area resident Lester Vickers. In Camp Stanton's log, Mrs. Stanton wrote that they got a permit to have the bar at the mouth of the Sabbies River removed by a bulldozer. I had heard about bulldozers being used to deepen the river before, but I had no idea it was at one time a common practice.

This pool work that government officials would have a stroke over today sure doesn't seem to have hurt anything. The Moore Pool is one of the most dependable salmon holding pools on the entire Cains River. Certainly, the potential is there to fill back in, but to this day the Moore Pool has both a good flow of water and adequate depth to hold fish in lower water, something that is somewhat rare on the Cains.

I know that it is trite to talk about time not standing still and all that, but I can never help marveling at it. Digging through the ownership history of these properties, you read statistics:

Country Haven's guide, Jeremy Vickers, is holding this great example of a classic Cains River hookbill. What a fish! Thirty months earlier, this fish was likely a scrawny grilse kelt. PHOTO COURTESY OF COUNTRY HAVEN LODGE.

births, deaths, fishing seasons, purchase and sale dates, and so on. What those never relate, though, are all the far more interesting human thoughts and actions that surrounded each of these events. Unlike the well-documented public information files, most of this information only exists as a brief note in some obscure journal, or a memory that will likely die along with the person who holds it. All those fishing trips from Coleman Moore's early times on the river are gone. Also gone are his remembrances of the beautiful sky-blue days on the river, the great fish that they caught, the changes to the riverbank caused by ice over the winter, and the floats down the Cains with maybe Harry Allen or young Charlie Wade pointing out a moose or a bear. A trip down the Cains River is great for dreaming about the past, and when I close my eyes, I can see those old scenes and hear the excited voices of people playing big trout and salmon.

I pulled into the yard of Moore's camp on the Cains in the fall of 2017, around the time that, for many years, Bill and his friends had made their annual fall fishing trip. Parked in the driveway, looking at the camp, my mind drifted back to Atlantic Salmon Hall of Fame the autumn before, at which I was seated next to Bill Moore.

Bill told me at dinner that he was dealing with some health issues, and I could see the worry in his eyes. Nonetheless, he had been asked to speak that evening, and he did a very good job with a short but witty story about his times on the river. He died over the winter, and the camp had gone the entire season without any use. I could see the porch where Bill and his friends sat over cocktails after what was hopefully a successful day on the river and the doorway through which they carried in all the baggage, food, and equipment for their annual trip. The steps were covered with pine pitch and needles, and one stair tread was rotted through. It doesn't take long for the New Brunswick weather to start to reclaim the ground. After I soaked it in for a minute or so, there was nothing to do but leave and take my own last look—thankfully for just the season—at the Moore Pool flowing on down to meet the Miramichi just as it did when the only boats passing through were the occasional aboriginal canoes.

A convivial table at the 2016 induction of Gary Colford into the Atlantic Salmon Hall of Fame. Bill Moore is closest to the camera on the right side of the table.

SCHOOLHOUSE POOL

The Schoolhouse Pool is located on the south or east side of the Cains River adjacent to the downstream end of Moore's Pool. The old schoolhouse building in the picture is gone now, but you can see the upstairs that Wayne Curtis tells me was an apartment for the teacher to live in.

G. REID POOL

This camp and pool are noted on Plan 2 of the 1976 New Brunswick Natural Resources (NBNR) map of the Cains. The pool is located 13.2 miles upriver from the mouth. The pool is public.

FINN BROOK POOL

The Finn Brook Pool is located opposite the mouth of Finn Brook at 12.4 miles up from the mouth. On the 1967 map, a camp across the river was owned by an E. S. Buckley, and on the 1976 map, it was owned by Beverley O'Donnell. According to Emery Brophy, O'Donnell brought some trout fishermen in during the spring and the occasional salmon fisherman during the fall, but largely, it was operated as a private camp. The pool is public.

HORSESHOE, OXBOW, WHIRL POOL, PEPPER POT, AND WANGY TANG POOL

Lee Sturges and Dorothy Noyes Arms both mention these pools from their fishing trips with Harry Allen, and the

A man with a nice salmon from near Shinnickburn on the Cains caught during the 1960s. PHOTO COURTESY OF WAYNE CURTIS.

selection of snippets from the railroad film displayed in this book show the Sturges party gaffing salmon at the Horseshoe Pool. The pools are located about two-thirds of the way from Shinnickburn down toward the Sabbies River. The Wangy Tang is very deep, and Sturges was told that many large brook trout held in the cool depths later during the summer. This whole stretch is all public water.

There are five named pools located here. In a row, starting from upriver, they are the Horseshoe, Oxbow, Whirl Pool, Pepper Pot, and the Wangy Tang. These are all located in a very pronounced S-bend in the river that produces a fast-running current along a rugged, partially ledged shoreline. This whole section of the river is public, but access is quite remote from either side of the river. It can be accessed nicely by canoe, but the next good take out going downriver from Shinnickburn is Salmon Brook. Putting in at Shinnickburn and taking out at Salmon Brook is only seven miles by the river but 28 miles by car, driving much of it over dirt roads. It requires a lot of logistical work to put in at Shinnickburn and then take out at Salmon Brook. There are many easier and equally productive alternatives for a day of fishing. The result is that this area does not see a lot of fishing pressure. This group of pools is about 11 miles up from the mouth of the Cains River.

Cains River Enterprises operated out of this camp during their years in business. It was then purchased by William Hooper, retired DFO fishery biologist and fishing guide. The nearby water is all public, but there is great fishing water on all sides. This is one of the most difficult areas of the Cains to access by any method. Roads don't really come near it, and it is a long way by water from any of the normal put in locations.

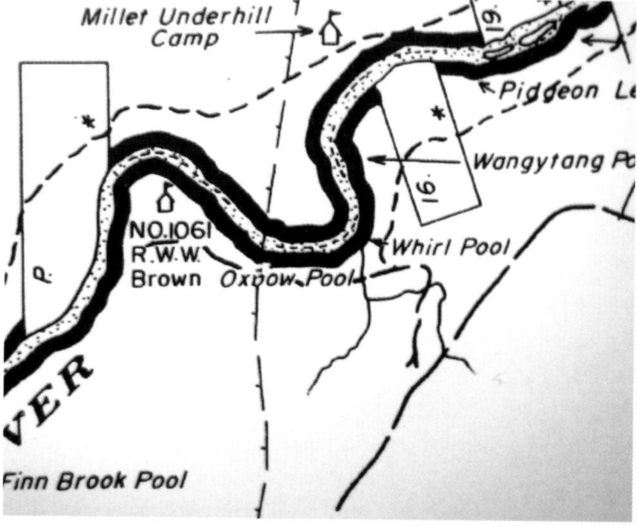

This snippet from the New Brunswick Natural Resources map of the Cains River shows the Oxbow, Pepper Pot, and Wangy Tang Pools. The big bend in the river before you get to the Oxbow—river runs left to right in this picture—was apparently called the Horseshoe Pool in some other old maps. Certainly, this entire stretch is rich in good fishing pools. You can see the campsite number 1061 to R. W. W. Brown—the Cains River Enterprises camp just pictured—located right inside the horseshoe bend. You can also see the location of Millet Underhill's camp and Pigeon Ledge Pool downriver to the right.

The Oxbow Camp, according to Emery Brophy, son of head guide John Brophy, was not the kind of lodge that people would check into for a week's fishing. Cains River Enterprises would fish their way down the Cains from Moore's Pool or Shinnickburn and spend a couple of nights at the Oxbow camp fishing the group of pools in that area. Emery said that during the 1960s the area offered terrific fall fishing for salmon.

PIGEON LEDGE POOL

Pigeon Ledge Pool is located about one mile downriver of the Wangy Tang Pool. Here one of the sandstone ledges that we run into along the Cains has caused the river to sculpt out a deep stable edge, which can provide good fishing.

Millet Underhill operated from a lodge on one side and camps on the other. The shore in front of the lodge is public fishing, but the small camps across the river that were part of the Underhill operation are on an 1847 Crown grant to Thomas Underhill. This may be the only Crown grant on the Cains River that is still owned by the same family that received the grant. The camps and the lodge were connected by a heavy wire strung overhead. The wire is still there.

An angler staying at Millett Undherhill's camps fishes from Pigeon Ledge. Flat, sandstone ledges like this are here and there all along the Cains River Valley.

MOUTH OF SABBIES POOL, AKA CAMP STANTON, AKA VALENTINES

The Mouth of Sabbies Pool is located 8.7 miles upriver from where the Cains branches off the Miramichi. I think of this as an important dividing point. From my observations, a fair number of salmon—I have no idea what percentage of the total run, but almost 100 percent of the summer portion—enter the Cains and hold in the lower few miles before heading upriver in the fall. The upper end of this summer holding section seems to be the junction with the Sabbies River. Even at that, the number of fish holding as far up as Sabbies in the average August seems very few, and it is probably not one of the better choices of fishing venue on the Miramichi system at that time—but consistently, there are some there. Despite the fishing at the Sabbies Pool not really getting going until September, this is one of the best holding pools on the river. It was an important stop for Harry Allen in his day, and it remains one today. The Sabbies Pool is deep and very slow above the point where the Sabbies River enters, and it can be a major holding area for salmon waiting to either spawn in the Sabbies—which they definitely do—or to further ascend the Cains. Sturges remarked that he walked a half mile up the Sabbies River and found that every inch of it was constantly on the move. I've walked up there myself, and the river is really quite shallow, and there is no deep, holding water for salmon in it at all. The Sabbies does not normally provide good salmon fishing, although in the log of Camp Stanton there is a brief passage about poling up the Sabbies for a distance and raising four salmon to the fly. The Sabbies does have a good stretch of aerated spawning gravel. Darrell Warren, a well-known local trapper and summer guide at my camp, told me that while trapping in the late fall he had come across the remains of a partially eaten eight-pound salmon. There were also scales from other salmon killed nearby. The fish were clearly killed by otters while in the process of spawning. The sad scene was located about one kilometer up inside the West Branch of the Sabbies River. The Sabbies branches out into the east and west branches two miles from the point at which it enters the Cains. Collectively, the Sabbies River, including both branches, amounts to 3,250 by 100 square meters of salmon habitat, making it about 10 percent larger than Muzzeroll Brook and the single largest spawning tributary of the Cains.

The majority of shoreline around the Sabbies pool is private fishing. This stems from several Crown grants, but the operative one was to Thomas W. Underhill

Millet Underhill's camps on the Cains located just downriver from the Oxbow complex of pools. PHOTOS OF MILLET'S COURTESY OF CAPPI THOMPSON OF SMUGMUG.

Camp Stanton, built by Wendell Allen for Seabury Stanton in 1945, photographed in the spring of 2015. This is the grand salmon lodge of the Cains River.

for 370 acres in 1830. This is assumedly the same Underhill who received the grant that founded Millet Underhill's camps. The shoreline, though, opposite the camp is public property. In 1996, the Avenor Paper company transferred their ownership in the small pieces of property on the east side of the river—these pieces have shoreline both above and below the Mouth of Sabbies River—to the New Brunswick Department of Natural Resources, so the fishing on the east side for some distance above and below the Sabbies River is open to the public. In reality, the public had fished this land for years courtesy of the paper companies, though many years ago, they did lease out the private fishing on their property to Seabury Stanton. Forest products companies are the source of other access points used by the public all along the Cains River, as well as on other rivers throughout the Miramichi system.

I think it is fair to say that the Mouth of Sabbies Pool is the most storied salmon pool on the Cains River and that is has long held that title. In 1945, Stanton, a wealthy, Harvard-educated industrialist from Massachusetts became interested in the property.

Stanton is famous for trying to outfox Warren Buffet in the takeover of Berkshire Hathaway. Stanton was chairman of Berkshire and its largest stockholder. He had reportedly run the company as if it was his personal property. Things weren't going well for Berkshire, which was involved in the declining textile manufacturing business, and his personal finances were intermingled with that of the company. According to Buffet, Stanton agreed to go along with a tender offer for the outstanding shares at a certain price, but when the time came, Stanton held up the works for a small amount more. At that point, Buffet pursued a tougher, hostile stance and eventually forced Stanton and Stanton's son Jack out of the business in May of 1965. I have no idea how that left Stanton financially, but we assume just fine, and we do know that he continued to own and fish Camp Stanton—as his lodge at the Mouth of Sabbies River pool was called—until his death in 1971. This is extensively covered in the chapter devoted to the Camp Stanton logbooks.

While Stanton may have been hard-nosed in business, he was very friendly to the extended W. Harry Allen fishing family. Seabury and his son Jack were frequent guests of George Allen's fishing camp at Black Brook before it became the Black Brook Salmon Club. In fact, it appears from searching the public records that Stanton had much to do with financing George and Wendell Allen's fishing operations on the Cains, as well as on the Southwest Miramichi, including fronting the money for George Allen's Cains River lease to be paid back at the rate of $1.00 per sport that booked with the Allens. In the deeds, it reveals that Stanton built one of the lodges at George Allen's camps so that he could use it himself. The deal was that Allen could house other anglers there if Seabury was not in camp. The agreement stipulated that Allen only bring in clients of a suitable caliber and that Stanton could have the building removed from the property at any time he desired. This is all in the public record.

Seabury started acquiring the land for his new lodge in 1944. The plan for the original location was down at Salmon Brook, but then Charlie Wade offered to sell Seabury the land where Camp Stanton is now located, and Stanton snapped it up. Stanton went on to acquire various pieces right through 1949. These included not only the Sabbies River Pool, but also the Mouth of Pickard Brook, the pool at Salmon Brook opposite the entrance of the brook, and more land farther upriver from the camp. Wendell Allen—who had built the aforementioned lodge for Seabury at George Allen's Camp, the Popples Camp located just under five miles up the Cains from the mouth, and who later bought George Allen's son Neil's interest in the family outfitting business—was hired by Stanton to build the new lodge at the Mouth of Sabbies River Pool. The lodge was completed in 1945, and it's a real classic. Still today it is one of the very finest structures on the river.

After Seabury's death in 1971, Stanton's estate sold the property to Valentine Tool and Stamping Company of Norton, Massachusetts, in May 1972. Charles Valentine, the president, was another Massachusetts businessman, though not of so rarified or colorful a background as Stanton. Valentine was a graduate of Norton High School and was simply a smart local boy who made good. You can imagine the pride and excitement in the Valentine family that summer as they explored their new property and prepared for their first fall season. While it was a sideline and not his main business, Valentine manufactured a line of single-action fly reels plus unique planetary gear, multiplying retrieve models that were designed by Charlie Valentine himself. This line of reels was quite popular in the fly-fishing business for years, and the planetary gear models are still made.

Lester Vickers, who has lived beside the mouth of the Cains River for 65 years, guided for Valentine beginning in 1972. Most of Vickers's guiding was spring fishing, but occasionally, he did a fall stretch, and on one of those outings in the 1970s, he guided an old guest of Charlie's to the biggest salmon that either of them had ever seen. The water was up a bit, Lester told me, and the fish were running. Lester's sport was an older man who had trouble wading, and when the man hooked this fish, Lester knew right away that is was a good one. It headed downriver, and the fishermen had to follow. The old sport couldn't get around a boat that tied up to the shore, so Vickers took him by the arm very carefully across a relatively slow portion of the pool. The fish took them well downriver and threatened to empty the reel a couple of times. Finally, they landed what Vickers claims was a cock salmon that weighed a minimum of 40 pounds, and Vickers is a very sober man who has handled many large salmon in his 50-plus years of guiding on the Cains.

My own time in salmon fishing the Miramichi slightly overlapped that of Valentine, but I never met him. Valentine attended the Miramichi Salmon Association Boston dinner in the winter of 2007, but he died on June 29 of that year. The next year, the property went up for sale, and it has had a somewhat bizarre history since that time. As I recall, the family built a website for the property and put it on the market for $450,000, a price that—considering the property had three good salmon pools, a particularly nice lodge, and several hundred acres of land—seemed realistic. It did not sell for two years, and the price was reduced to $345,000. The biggest reasons for the poor performance were simply that it was in a very remote location only accessible seasonally by woods roads, very roughly maintained by lumber companies, and the fact that the whole salmon season there is really just over a month in duration. Really, there is no season at all if the water is too low, and finally, one whole side of the very best part of the pool is public on the opposite shore from the lodge. What makes this bad is that the river there is narrow enough that a good caster can cover it bank to bank. Most fishermen have no problem rubbing elbows with their fellow brothers of the angle—or at least some of them—but you don't really want to invest a half-million dollars and pay plenty of taxes to put yourself in a position of likely conflict.

As a minor point, while there may have been good spring fishing there in 1920, there isn't today. I don't know if the kelts have changed the way they stay in the river, or if there were just a lot more kelts around 100 years ago, but I do know that Valentine couldn't catch many kelts there either even 20 or 30 years ago. They used to hire boats and guides who stayed nights up at the guides' camp but ran down to the Miramichi every day to do their fishing.

While the property was up for sale, the Valentine family leased the fishing rights to an outfitter in Blackville. During the high-water July of 2008, an Eastern European businessman named Viktor Ruzicka fished the pool and caught a 20-plus-pound silver bullet of a salmon. He heard that the property was for sale and was approached by Realtor James McKervill, who had made a deal to be protected as a broker if he could find a customer for the owners. When Ruzicka asked how much the property was, he was reportedly told $750,000. To Ruzicka—and I think to most wealthy people looking at the high-quality lodge and stunning waterfront property through the eyes of a normal consumer—the price made sense. You couldn't build everything that was there for less than that, and the 400 or so acres had to be worth a lot of money, right?

Ruzicka bought the property with the idea of making it a top-end fishing and hunting lodge in its own right. What he didn't know, and what every successful Miramichi outfitter must know, is the true, daily fishing—and/or hunting—potential of his property throughout the entire season. The reality is very different than Ruzicka experienced on that one-in-a-hundred July day when he caught that big, silver salmon in the home pool. Anyway, it didn't work out, even though Ruzicka spent many thousands on needless upgrades and overbuilding of the infrastructure. The property went back for sale through top-end, international sporting lodge brokers, and after a couple of years of inaction, the word went out that he wanted to sell, and $450,000 USD would take it. As incredible a deal as it was, it sat available for six months while party after party who could easily afford to buy it rejected the idea. It needed another Seabury Stanton or Charlie Valentine. It needed someone who could love the fishing there for what it is, despite its fickleness, tromp the grounds for a little late season grouse shooting, and be happy with their retreat in the New Brunswick bush.

The property was finally purchased by a Quebec corporation with a long number for a name. One day in the late summer of 2016, I received an email through my website from Michel Cadrin, the businessman behind the company. He had bought and read my book *Closing the Season* and wanted to meet. One of the guides at Campell's Pool, Darrell Warren, knew his way from his years of forestry work through the maze of lumber roads necessary to reach Camp Stanton by car, or more sensibly, a four-wheel-drive truck. Cadrin has no issues with the drive since he flies into camp in a helicopter—sold by one of the several businesses with which he is involved.

Warren and I arrived at Camp Stanton for lunch on one of those fall afternoons that salmon fishermen live for. It was a dark and damp but not terribly cold and with only enough breeze to slightly ruffle the surface of the home pool. It was only a week or so before the end of the season, and the only negative was that the water was low—a common autumn malady on the Cains.

The Cadrins turned out to be gracious hosts, and they had kindly invited us into a gathering of their extended family, which included two very handsome and friendly younger couples from the northern part of New Brunswick. We got a tour of the elegant facility, and then, before lunch, we all sat near the huge stone fireplace that is a central feature of the main lodge room. We talked about salmon, salmon flies, and salmon fishing in a river-view room filled with various memorabilia of Seabury Stanton's years at this place. It was really quite a treat.

After lunch, we went to the river, and I was invited to take a pass down through the home pool. This was a body of water with which I was quite familiar but from fishing either by wading or canoe from the far—public—side of the river. I had never fished the pool with the water this low, and from the unfamiliar side in lower water, it had a very different look. I'm used to thinking of the water up above the Mouth of Sabbies

This sign now hangs from the fireplace in Camp Stanton, a reminder of the day when Seabury unknowingly enforced private fishing that he didn't own along with some that he did.

as a sort of broad, slow pond that will bring the fly around—but barely. I remember, though, from other successful fishes here that it can hold a lot of salmon. In fact, during 2008, the second year of the two-year experiment to have a two-week season extension between the Route 123 bridge and the mouth of the river, I fished this pool on the next-to-last day of the extension and released a limit of four nice salmon. From time to time, fish seemed to surface everywhere in the pool.

This day, with the reduced water height, there was quite a clearly defined channel through the pool, and the current actually seemed quicker than I had remembered it. Also, I was now fishing from the inside of the bend, casting out into the wider sweep of the outside shoreline, which might have explained the faster swing. I looked at the surface of the pool, and the mirrored colors of the changing leaves were so vivid that it was difficult to tell as you looked up where water ended and the trees actually began. They were dulled somewhat by the gray day, but the kaleidoscope of autumn colors was all there. I thought back to earlier fish I'd caught on this pool and to anglers who had fished it in the plush days of Seabury Stanton's era—and even before that when Harry Allen and Lee Sturges camped on the far shore and caught large kelts and trout. A small cockfish leapt clear of the water down below me, just above the famous rock off the Mouth of the Sabbies River. It was a perfectly magical scene. I did not, however, turn a fish in my pass through the pool.

PICKARD BROOK POOL

The brook itself is part of the Camp Stanton holdings, and it is located just above Salmon Brook on the south or west side of the Cains River. The public water extends up the Cains River right to the mouth of Pickard Brook. The brook is a relatively small with a modest impact on the main Cains River, and I have not fished it since the extended season almost 10 years ago. During warm weather in the late summer, I'm sure that some fish can often be found holding off the mouth of this brook in warm weather.

SALMON BROOK POOL

The Salmon Brook Pool comprises both sides of the Cains River and is public water.

As with the Sabbies Pool property just a short distance up the river, the land along the opposite side from Seabury Stanton's holding was owned by the Avenor Paper Company. In 1996—for whatever reasons—they decided to give the land bordering the river to the New Brunswick Department of Natural Resources. This officially created what is one of the best public fishing pools on the Cains River. Fishing from an anchored canoe with a sink-tip line in very high water during October 2009, I landed a hen salmon approaching 30 pounds just off the mouth of the brook. It was one of the largest and best-conditioned salmon I've ever caught in the Cains. The cooling effects of the brook make the pool a summer run holding spot, and the crosscurrents of the entering brook have helped sculpt out a deep channel for the pool that makes it an all-around excellent holding pool. Adding to its summer fishing appeal, the pool is only seven miles upriver from the mouth. The brook itself is a departure from other large brooks like Six Mile and Sabbies River in that up, until recently, it was shallow, broad, and alder choked. The Miramichi Salmon Association, as part of its cold-water refuge enhancement program, cleared out and deepened the channel for some distance back from the Cains River. This allows the cold water from the brook to enter the deeper parts of the pool with minimum exposure to warm air and sunshine. Salmon Brook is very popular, and it is accessed from the South Cains River Road by a relatively short walk down along the brook. One can seldom go to Salmon Brook and expect to fish alone, and Salmon Brook is one of the most popular points for putting in canoes for day trips down the last few miles of the river.

BUTTERMILK POOL

Buttermilk Brook lies only six miles up from the mouth of the Cains, and it is probably the most-accessed salmon pool on the Cains River.

The river narrows up here, creating a quick little run down through a nicely structured rocky channel. If there are any fish in the lower Cains, there are always a few to be found here. A short distance above the quick run a substantial spring that is the namesake of the pool simply bubbles like buttermilk out of the bushes on the riverbank. The strength of the flow, especially after a rain, is surprising, and clearly, it holds fish looking for cooler water. This pool is just off the South Cains River Road, and it even has some parking in the woods.

Salmon Brook is one of the best cold-water holding pools on the lower Cains River. The largely obstructed mouth of this brook was recently deepened and stabilized by the Miramichi Salmon Association to help provide enhanced cool water flow into the pool.

Buttermilk Brook features a small brook that burst out of the hillside with such velocity during some parts of the season to create this buttermilk-appearing stream of bubbles down the river. At other times, all that can be seen is the thin line of rocks leading down over the bank—visible here in the lower-right-center of the photo. The pool is a nicely structured, rocky pool with good flow, and it has produced many excellent salmon catches over the years.

THE POPPLES CAMP

The Popples is downriver 1.2 miles from Buttermilk. This camp is unusual in that it is a fairly large structure, yet it is not located on any private fishing water, and the public water that it is located on, while reasonably productive for kelt fishing in the spring, produces only a very few salmon from a narrow channel along the shore at the very bottom of the home pool. Exactly why Seabury Stanton picked this location to build the camp is unknown, but he must have felt that he would have good kelt fishing in the spring and that they would be close enough to reach good salmon fishing in the fall of the year. Lester Vickers, caretaker of The Popples since the late 1960s, remembers that The Popples was leased for a month every fall to a Massachusetts man named Elbridge Bollong who fished the Salmon Brook Pool every day. The Popples location does allow relatively easy access to several pools up and down the river, but it is only convenient if the water is high enough to do that by boat.

Wendell was clearly a great builder, as The Popples, Camp Stanton, and the early Black Brook Camps—which have only recently been replaced—were all built by him and were quintessential northern river sporting camps with great eye appeal.

The Popples was built by Wendell Allen for Seabury Stanton. This is how it appeared in the late 1940s. PHOTO COURTESY OF THE PROVINCIAL ARCHIVES OF NEW BRUNSWICK.

The Popples is now owned by the family of the late Dr. Ben Houser. Here is how it looked in the spring of 2016.

Doctor Robert and Mrs. Becker with their caretaker and guide Lester Vickers. These were a couple of lovely, vintage Chestnut canoes—one double-ender, and one v-stern for an outboard motor—rigged in the old style for the angler to fish from the bow while anchored from the stern. PHOTO COURTESY OF LESTER VICKERS.

Vickers pilots the Beckers down the Cains River past anglers fishing in the Brophy Pool. Vickers probably took the canoe out in front of his home at the mouth of the Cains River another mile and half distant and trailered it back up to the Popples, otherwise he would have had a very long upstream pole with no motor and a relatively full canoe. PHOTO COURTESY OF LESTER VICKERS.

The original Black Brook camps have been replaced with new buildings, but the Popples and Camp Stanton are still straight and handsome today.

When Neil Allen decided to take a different line of work, Wendell bought out his main Miramichi holdings at Black Brook, but he then died of a heart attack while trapping the next winter. That same winter, the Popples was pushed off its foundations by ice. The government helped to move the camps back to a higher level, and the next year, the property was purchased by a Dr. Becker, who owned it for nearly 20 years until the late Dr. Ben Houser of Pennsylvania bought the property from Becker in 1989. Dr. Houser passed away in 2013. His wife, Carol, and family still own the property.

In 1970, the year that Wendell Allen died, there was a terrific flood in February. The raising, ice-filled waters jumped over the banks of the Cains. Large trees were mowed down in many places, and ice knocked The Popples off its foundations. That level of flooding has not been equaled since. This group of photographs shows some scenes from around the Popples, as well as the extensive damage due to the February flood in 1970.

Lester Vickers grew up beside the mouth of the Cains, and at one time or another, he has helped with the guiding for every camp along the lower Cains. These include Wade's Fishing Lodge, The A. D. Merrill Camp, Wendell Allen, and 20 years at Camp Stanton after its purchase by Charlie Valentine. Vickers began with Wendell as guide and caretaker at the Popples in 1966, and after Wendell's passing, he continued to maintain the property for Dr. Becker, Dr. Ben Houser, and now Dr. Houser's family. Vickers is still there today doing the guiding and caretaking of the property. Fifty-three years must be one of the longest unbroken stints on the river.

In addition to spring and fall fishing on the property, the camp provides excellent access to several good nearby pools by road or boat.

HYDRO POOL

The hydro in Hydro Pool refers to the large, overhead electrical lines that pass over this public pool located about 3.8 miles up from the mouth. There is no road here, but ambitious anglers who aren't canoeing the river hike down the power

These photos all show the terrific damage to the Popples Camp done by the big ice run of 1970. With enough rain, the river rises up and widens out to the point where the ice pack can float off down the river. When a wide spot in the ice hits a narrow spot in the river, it backs up, and the ice all has to go somewhere. It can stack up unbelievably high and be pushed out sideways into any open areas such as the clearing the Popples was constructed in. Note that in the last photograph the main cabin was simply pushed backward off its blocking. I'm told that the whole building was relocated farther back from the river after that event. THESE PHOTOS ARE COURTESY OF LESTER VICKERS.

Lester Vickers and angler Judy Hofer with a nice Cains River, fall-run hen salmon. Bud and Judy Hofer are very close, longtime friends of the Housers. PHOTO COURTESY OF BUD HOFER.

line and fish here. The pool is not particularly deep, but it has a great flow through its well-structured, rocky course.

THE CAMPBELL POOL, AKA BULL RUN

The Campbell Pool is located just three miles upriver from the mouth.

This was the famous fisherman and outfitter Herman Campbell's camp on the Cains River. Campbell's camps on the Southwest Miramichi were very well known, and today, they are the basis for Salar Haven Fishing Club.

The Campbell Pool property on the Cains was originally split off from the Brophy Pool property, which included both the Crown grants of James Dougherty and Cavan Brophy from 1842 and 1840, respectively. The camp land is all on the south side of the river, and fourth tenths of a mile upstream from the Brophy Pool fishing water. The camp side of the river is private, but the opposite shore is public but is not easily accessible by foot. The Campbell Pool is largely comprised of a narrow run along the north shore that, according to Emery Brophy, was nicknamed Bull Run. Bull Run is not

Herman Campbell's fishing camp on the Cains River as it appeared in the spring of 2016. Like many of the Miramichi outfitters, Herman had his own place on the Cains for the fall fishing.

Here is a picture from 70 years later of the Cains River rock appearing over Herman's left shoulder in the previous picture. In fact, the rock has long been a landmark, in that in Ganong's complete Cains River map from 1910, he noted the location of Doherty Rock. This must be the same James Dougherty—Ganong just spelled it differently—who received the original Crown grant that included this property. PHOTO COURTESY OF BUD HOFER.

Looking upriver toward the Campbell Pool/Bull Run from the Campbell camp. PHOTO COURTESY OF BUD HOFER.

A 2015 picture of Campbell Pool/Bull Run by Nathan Wilbur. Not much has changed in either direction in 70 years.

Students from Miramichi High School fishing club working Bull Run/Campbell Pool. PHOTO COURTESY OF ASHLEY HALLIHAN.

Herman Campbell sitting on the deck of his Campbell's Pool property on the Cains River in the 1950s. PHOTO COURTESY OF BUD HOFER.

usually a big volume producer but dependably has a few fish holding in the run. Like many Cains River pools, the run tails out into a fairly deep, slow pool. In good years of decent water, it is not unusual to find a lot of salmon holding in the slow water after the run but getting them to take is a real challenge.

The water along the shore in front of the camp is fairly deep in pockets with some nice structure like the big boulder in the photograph with Herman Campbell. That boulder was

Charles "CE" Hofer, father of Bud Hofer, in a 1958 photo standing on the Cains shoreline above Otter Brook with a salmon and a grilse. This appears to be a September photo as the trees show some color but are not yet in full October brilliance. PHOTO COURTESY OF BUD HOFER.

once referred to as Dougherty Rock after the original Crown grantee James Dougherty, and on W. F. Ganong's 1910 map of the Cains River, it is one of the few landmarks mentioned in the whole lower river. Today, though, I don't believe a living soul knows it by that name. When there is a good flow of water coming down the Cains and salmon are ascending the river, these small pools can be quite productive. In addition to Bull Run and the waters around the camp, Herman's guests frequently fished at the Brophy Pool.

Herman Campbell's camp and land are today a private camp owned by Herman's granddaughter.

BROPHY POOL

Brophy Pool is located 2.6 miles upstream from the mouth of the Cains River and is supported by the aforementioned Crown leases of Cavan Brophy and James Dougherty. This property was purchased from the Brophy family by Coleman Moore in 1961.

According to Gary Colford, whose grandfather William was Moore's caretaker, he and his grandfather took down the old house and barns the same year that Coleman bought the property.

Danny Coughlin, guide at Country Haven Lodge with an early fall salmon from the Brophy Pool, Cains River. PHOTO COURTESY OF COUNTRY HAVEN FISHING LODGE.

Brophy Pool with Otter Brook visible entering the pool on the lower left-hand side of this photo.

Old Brophy homestead, photographed sometime in the 1950s.

Gary said that the house had not been lived in for a long time, windows were missing, and the place was generally derelict. The original house and barns were located up on the hill near the site of the current camp. Coleman bought the property in large part because it was known for bird hunting, and Coleman was an upland gunner. The Moores put up a tent on the knoll upstream of the mouth of Otter Brook, and they occasionally camped there in the summer.

The Moores decided to sell the Brophy Pool in 1972. It was purchased by Arle Bamford, then the proprietor of Old River Lodge in Blissfield. In 1982, the Brophy Pool property was purchased by Tom Truelove and Alan Small. Truelove and Small hired Ivan Vickers to build a camp for them on the property, and that is the one still there today overlooking the pool. The Brophy Pool is currently owned by Jed Alger, Bob Bianchi, and Brad Burns, the author of this book.

The Brophy Pool benefits from the cooling waters of Otter Brook, as well as some substantial springs entering farther down on both sides of the pool. Brophy, Campbell's, Buttermilk, Salmon, and Pickard Brooks are all brook- and/or stream-fed pools, and they combine to hold a substantial portion of the salmon entering the Cains during the warm months.

HOOPER'S POOL

Hooper's is a nicely structured quick run of water located in front of the biologist William Hooper's campsite on the north side of the Cains River just 2.1 miles up from the mouth.

This section is all public water, and there is access by a long path in from the South Cains River Road. It is unusual in decent conditions, especially on a weekend, to not find people fishing at Hooper's. The reason is that it is quite productive. Hooper's is not a classic, deep, moderately slow pool as many of the Cains holding pools are, but the fish definitely do hang in the rocks down through the run, and it is one of the more dependable spots on the lower end of the river. The fishing

Otter Brook is not large, but it is big enough so that Emery Brophy, whose father John grew up on the farm and where Emery himself spent 10 years of his youth, says that salmon do go up into the brook to spawn.

Hooper's Pool is a moderately swift, rocky run that is lively to fish.

Stephen Tonning of the Miramichi Salmon Association and Country Haven guide Danny Coughlin with a nice fall salmon from the Cains River. PHOTO COURTESY OF STEPHEN TONNING.

stretch begins up around the corner from Hooper's camp, and it runs about 500 feet down to the bottom of the pool. It is all potentially productive water unless it is so high that the current velocity is prohibitive.

The Hooper's Pool is called the Magalloway Pool in the 1968 New Brunswick Natural Resources (NBNR) Cains River Plan 1 map. By the time of the 1976 version, the name had been dropped. If there was ever any reference to Maine's Magalloway River—and there probably was—it is now lost to history.

TEEDLAN POOL

Teedlan Pool is located just downriver about a quarter mile from Hooper's with the public side on the same side of the river—north—as the Hooper's Camp. Walking down there along the shore or on the edge of the river from Hooper's, difficult as it might be, may be the only reasonable way to access this water other than in a boat during high water.

At one time, Ted Williams owned this pool. The ownership succession from the original grant is now quite chopped up, and there was some commercial forestry ownership too. The complexities of following the title got the best of me, and I decided those details weren't all that important anyway. The important part is that the fishing on the south side of the river is privately owned. The pool has some nice quick water with a bunch of large rocks to break up the current. The pool is deep, and as with the Moore Pool, this is attributed to the fact that Ted Williams hired a bulldozer to scrape out the pocket.

Like the Brophy Pool, the Teedlan Pool is one of the few pools on the river that is still known by the last name of the original Crown grantee, Joseph Teedlan.

THE ADMIRAL POOL AND CAMP

On all the Cains, the Admiral Pool property is matched only by Camp Stanton concerning the magnitude of the private

Motoring through the Teedlan Pool in spring high water on the way upriver to fish for kelts. This pool was owned by Ted Williams and was deepened by bulldozer.

fishing water holdings that it possesses. The Admiral Pool is not limited to the home pool below the island. There are at least five and upward of six distinct pools located on the 1.3 miles or so of mostly double-bank fishing that it owns. It is 100 percent private water, and I believe it is the largest length of uninterrupted, double-bank fishing water privately owned on the Cains.

During the 2007 extended Cains season, I spent three days on this property, and we found fish the last week in October here and there from the top to the bottom. I remember that there were fish spawning in the gravel upstream from the large island that splits the river just above the camp. I thought it was like Alaska. The only noise was the wind in the tall pines and the water pouring over the rocks and gravel bars. You could see the wakes and occasional fins of the salmon as they worked on their redds. Every now and then an explosion of several 12-inch brook trout would break the water's surface and you could see the shoulders and wakes of big salmon chasing the trout away from the intended site of their redd.

The land along the west or south bank of the Cains, as well as the upper side of the north bank toward Hell's Gate, was a Crown grant to John Cunard in 1836. It was an unusually large, 510-acre grant. Another section on the north shore of the river and running downstream from Cunard's line was also a large, 501-acre section granted to Edward Miller but not until 1876.

An unidentified bather preparing to take a dip in the home pool of the Admiral Pool Camp in 1957. You can see in this picture that the breezeway sealed off in the first photo was still open, and that the screen room built onto the right-hand end had yet to be built. The pool directly in front of the camp is deep and slow and makes both a good swimming hole on a warm summer afternoon and a great holding pool when the fall run is on. PHOTO COURTESY OF DR. DAVID AND ASTRID WADE.

An autumn 2007 picture of the Admiral Pool Camp, owned by the Black Brook Salmon Club.

Emery Brophy identified this photo as being the shorefront in front of the Ferguson Camp. It was well known that Ferguson often brought up a group of his friends for spring salmon fishing, which is clearly the time of the year this photo is taken. PHOTO COURTESY OF THE PROVINCIAL ARCHIVES OF NEW BRUNSWICK.

Black Brook Salmon Club owns this property, and one of their members, Dr. Arne Youngberg, has pulled together various materials to create an interesting history of the property. A man named Homer L. Ferguson, who was first in his class at the US Naval Academy and had a very impressive business career in shipbuilding, bought this property in a deal similar to others that I saw a number of times while researching some of the property transfer and ownership records along the rivers. Charlie Wade bought the property from a man named Gutman on November 5, 1941, and then Wade sold it to Ferguson on November 22, 1941. I'm guessing that men like Harry Allen and Charlie Wade became used to dealing with sophisticated city businesspeople and would act as a sort of go-between so that local folks would feel comfortable with the transaction. In return for their services, the local outfitters—like Allen and Wade—got to use the private water when the owners were away.

Ferguson owned all the property and the Admiral Pool camp that the Black Brook Salmon Club has now. Merrill's camp, which was called the Hell's Gate Camp, was located a little farther down the river, and unfortunately, it was on somewhat lower ground. It was taken away by the flood of 1970 that also took out the Lou Butterfield camp just above Black Brook.

Ferguson fished mostly in the spring for kelts and then again for the Cains fall run as well as doing some bird hunting. Ferguson's career had spanned both world wars at the Newport News Shipyard, and he had acquired some high-powered military friends, including Admiral Tip Merrill. Merrill distinguished himself in battle against the Japanese, being the first

This is another shot of what I think is also the Admiral Pool shoreline—looking just a few feet to the right or downriver from the previous photo—and part of the same angling group. Not only does the shoreline match perfectly, but the sports had to be coming in or out of a camp because of the city dress. The canoe on the left is a 22-foot Chestnut Ogilvy with one of the 5.5-horsepower outboards that Wade's customarily used. This was set up to transport three anglers and a guide. That is far too many for any kind of fishing in this light craft, so clearly, they were just transporting the sports, probably from Wade's lodge up to the Admiral Pool camp. The Chestnut hull would be very tender with that load and caution would be needed not to end up with everyone floating in water that was just above freezing in temperature. PHOTO COURTESY OF THE PROVINCIAL ARCHIVES OF NEW BRUNSWICK.

to use radar-directed fire to sink enemy craft that were beyond the line of sight. Ferguson allowed Merrill to build a camp of his own on the property, which is the one now standing that the Black Brook Salmon Club owns, but Merrill never owned the land nor had any legal fishing rights—just a handshake between friends. Nonetheless, the pool became known as the Admiral Pool.

The Wades were always the Ferguson and Merrill caretakers, and as part of the deal, they fished the water when they weren't in camp. Homer left his property to his son Bill in 1953. Bill came to fish occasionally, and Admiral Merrill died in 1961. Bill finally sold the property to George Holmes of the Wades Fishing Club in 1990. It was purchased by the Black Brook Salmon Club upon the Wades Fishing Club's dissolution in 2002. Black Brook then sold their Six Mile Brook property since the Admiral Pool Camp provided Cains River fishing that was virtually contiguous with their water on the Miramichi. In fact, there is only a gap of about 1,700 feet of public shoreline between the two properties.

ELM TREE POOL

The Elm Tree Pool, according to the 1968 Cains River Plan 1 map of NBNR, is at the very downstream edge of the Admiral Pool property, continuing into the public water on the north or east side of the river. The fishing in the pool on the south or west side of the Cains River is now owned by Casamira Fishing Lodges Inc. Exactly where the Elm Tree Pool is, or even if it exists in similar enough fashion to 50 years ago to be called the same pool, is difficult to say—especially since the elm tree that marked it has been dead and gone for many years. Mobile gravel has shallowed parts of the Cains from below the Ledges Pool—the last small pool completely on Admiral Pool property—to where the river combines its flow with the Miramichi at the Black Brook Salmon Club junction pool about 3,000 feet downriver. There is a very pronounced gravel bar just below the top of the public water. Just above this bar the water is relatively deep and has a good flow. In my trips through here by canoe I have seen it frequently fished by the Casimara members.

BLACK BROOK SALMON CLUB

The property that is now the Black Brook Salmon Club stems from a Crown grant on the east side of the river from an early and large 410-acre Crown grant to a William Babcock Jr. in 1808. On the west side the fishing comes from Crown grants to George Donald in 1813, downstream of that from George Murdock in 1865.

Black Brook Salmon Club's annual catch of between 400 and 1,000 salmon and grilse is rivaled only by the Rocky Brook Fishing Camp on the Miramichi headwaters owned by International Paper. There are a lot of factors that go into making a great pool—actually with about 1,600 feet of fishing water on each side of the Miramichi the Black Brook waters would more properly be called a stretch of river rather than simply a pool. One of these factors is undoubtedly the junction of the Miramichi and the Cains River.

The gravel-filled shallows that begin at the bar just below the Elm Tree Pool continue on down through the public water and gradually deepen as the flow of the Cains merges with the Miramichi. From being almost exclusively Cains flow to the point where you are undoubtedly standing on the banks of the Miramichi is a distance of about 600 feet, though certainly the unique scent of the Cains must be strong in the melded flow of the two rivers all the way down to, and well past, Black Brook itself. One could argue that the east or north side of Black Brook's best fishing water is as much or more a Cains River pool as it is a Miramichi one. The reluctance of fish to enter the Cains in very low water flows causes them to stack up in the deep, comfortable flow of the Black Brook water. Only the Quarryville Pool at the junction of the Main Southwest Miramichi and the Renous Rivers offers as clearly defined a holding point for fish waiting to enter one of the Miramichi systems largest tributaries. The Renous, though, is an early-run river, and many of the fish run up the Renous during June and early July when the water level is still likely to be moderately high.

The Cains River is a fall-run river, and the fish do not like to run very far up the river without a decent raise of water. Since the season's lowest water typically happens at the same time as the fall run of Cains River salmon, a perfect storm is in the making. The substantial run of large, Cains River salmon tends to hold up in the mouth of Black Brook's pool. The water is nice and cool, and therefore, conditions are right for fish to take. Due to possessing good flow, depth, and the cooling influence of Black Brook, the pool offers good fishing throughout the season in various water heights, but the way that the east side of Black Brook's upper pool is situated to hold fish destined to spawn in the Cains produces the most impressive catches.

In 2017, a year of almost unprecedented low water, it provided one of those seasons where the fish destined for the Cains River were holding at Black Brook right up to the close in the season. Downriver a couple of miles from Black Brook

In 2016, Black Brook Salmon Club guest Pete Howell enjoys the comfort of the Black Brook Salmon Club's handsome new lodge.

This aerial photo shows the intricacies of the junction of the Cains and the Southwest Miramichi that in large part make Black Brook the great pool that it is. It is clear in this photo that the Cains flow pushes out into the Miramichi, shielded in large part by the big bar between the rivers, so that the Cains influences both sides of the Black Brook Pool. The cooling waters of Black Brook itself enter in the lower left of the photo into the slower, deeper part of the pool that is an important refuge for salmon during summer heat. The Catholic church that Mary Brophy poled her canoe back and forth to from the Brophy farm to attend Sunday services, and that appears in the William Schaldach illustration of the river mouth from *Fishing Memories*, can be seen in the clearing at the upper-right-hand corner of the picture.

at Campbell's and Keenan's Pools we were looking at shoreline that had never been above the surface of the water in my 15 years of ownership. The water was so low that it made the pool almost unrecognizable. Except for a small pocket or two, the upper half of the pool was too shallow to hold fish. The bottom of the pool, which is typically deep, broad, and slow, was now of reasonable fishing depth, quite a bit more narrow than normal, and instead of being dead water, there was actually a modest flow down through the center. The newly defined channel hooked over toward the Campbell side of the river whereas in normal flow Anderson's Point pushed the water back toward the Keenan side. This was because the area surrounding Papa's Rock and the large rocks out in front of it had become a shoal that was too shallow for salmon. The actual channel of the river—what I call the river within the river—was probably no more than 50 feet wide, and at the head of the pool, it disappeared altogether, and you could walk across the river at that point in water that was only slightly above your knees.

Every evening would see a trickle of fish moving up the river. There would be a handful of arrivals in the pool toward dusk that would mix with the old fish holding there, and a few fish would run through the pool and head upriver. Enough casting would eventually find one or two of these fish to take a fly, and so we picked at them. Most of the takers we caught were the more aggressive grilse, though we saw some monsters and hooked a precious few of them. At Black Brook, though, these fish, many of which were assumedly destined for the Cains River, stacked up on the east or Cains River side of Black Brook's water on the Miramichi. During the day, the fish hung down in the deeper water and played hard to get. In the evening, though, the restless fish were apparently testing the water depths and moved up into the faster-moving shallow water at the mouth of the Cains. The fishing wasn't an outright bonanza, unless you compare it to what most other camps were catching. The size of some of the fish was eye-popping. A number of mid and high 30-pound fish were captured as was one of approximately 40 pounds.

Here are four pictures from the Black Brook Salmon Club water in the years when it was owned by Allen Outfitters:

In this spring fishing scene, the guide is holding the canoe by the pole on the edge of the current. You can see dozens of canoes pulled up on the shore as far as you can see. Probably canoes from Allen's Outfitters are merged with others from Wades that abutted Allen's on the downstream side. PHOTOS COURTESY OF THE PROVINCIAL ARCHIVES OF NEW BRUNSWICK.

These anglers are fishing on Allen Outfitters water, on the Howard's side of what is now the water of the Black Brook Salmon Club. Butterfield's Rock, which is still visible today, is the right side of the first angler. Across the river you can see the guide's seasonal shelter and Lou Butterfield's cottage that was taken by a flood. The photo is looking across and up the Miramichi River. You can make out where the Cains flows in.

This angler is netting his own fish. The angler in the last photo on page 133 was also playing a fish and had a net leaning at ready up against himself. Catching fish may have been common enough in those days that guides couldn't be expected to cover them all, so netting your own if you were able was apparently common.

Wendell Allen is pictured on the shore near Black Brook with a young Ted Williams. This picture was probably taken in the late 1940s.

CHAPTER 7

The Camp Stanton Logbook

In my research for this book, I was lucky enough to come by several extraordinary documents pertaining to the Cains. Of these, the original, handwritten logbook for Camp Stanton rates at the top. In January 2018, I visited antique sporting book dealer Patrick Ayres, who lives on a family ranch on the banks of the Klamath River in California. I spent three great days enjoying the terrific hospitality of Pat and his wife, Deb, and, we carefully photographed each of 175 pages that comprise the two volumes of the logbooks.

I'm a veteran of reading salmon camp logs from a fair number of trips over the years to various locations in Canada and Scotland. The average log will have the date, name of angler, size of the salmon, weight, beat or pool fished, fly pattern, often the size of the fly, and water temperature. And so it goes: statistics, page after page, and in some old lodges, volume after volume. However, the ones from Camp Stanton are different. Certainly they list the fish caught and the size, and for this book, it was good information to have, but more importantly, Jean Kellog Stanton's writing offers a perspective on the Stantons' time on the river that is not limited to the number and size of fish caught.

You do hear about the fishing but also the weather, the travels, the trials and tribulations of building and managing your own lodge in a place with no electricity or real road, and their friendships and experiences with local people. There is talk about the local people, including who guided them, cooked for them, and drove them back and forth to the Brophy meadows, or the airport. Jean wrote about birthday parties and picnics, trips to town, and even Seabury Stanton's financial involvement with the Allens in helping them to buy and sell lodges and pools as members of the family moved in or out of the business.

The Stantons were very wealthy people by most standards. Seabury's father and grandfather were both whaling captains from New Bedford, so Seabury came naturally by his love of fishing. When Seabury was born in 1892, whaling was in its last throes, but 50 years previous, in his grandfather's day, New Bedford had the highest per capita income of any

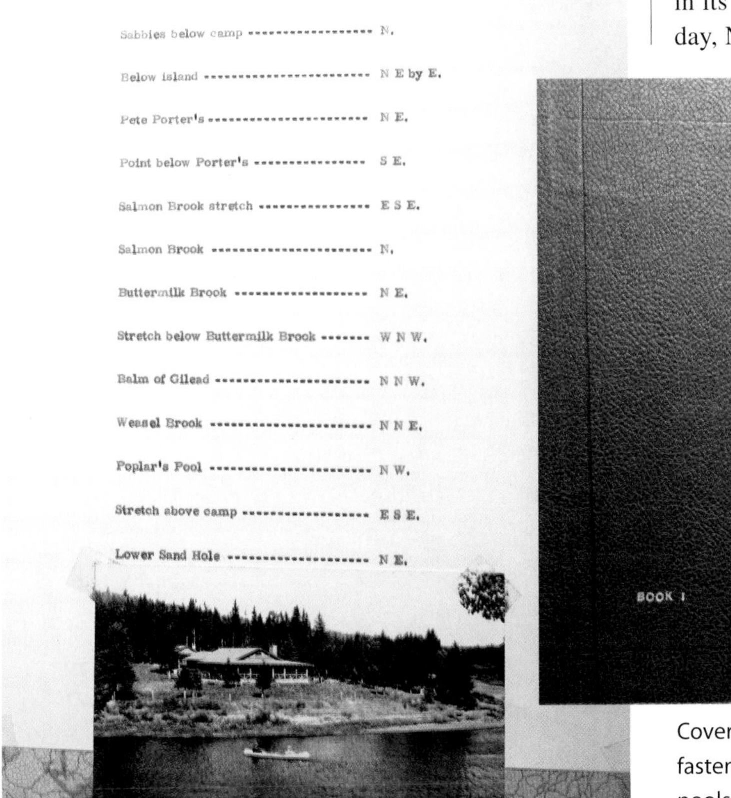

COPY....

Sabbies below camp ------------------ N.
Below island ------------------------ N E by E.
Pete Porter's ----------------------- N E.
Point below Porter's ---------------- S E.
Salmon Brook stretch ---------------- E S E.
Salmon Brook ------------------------ N.
Buttermilk Brook -------------------- N E.
Stretch below Buttermilk Brook ------- W N W.
Balm of Gilead ---------------------- N N W.
Weasel Brook ------------------------ N N E.
Poplar's Pool ----------------------- N W.
Stretch above camp ------------------ E S E.
Lower Sand Hole --------------------- N E.

Cover of the first of two Camp Stanton logbooks and note fastened inside the cover that describes the directions to various pools on the camp's property with an old photograph of the camp taken from a nearby hilltop.

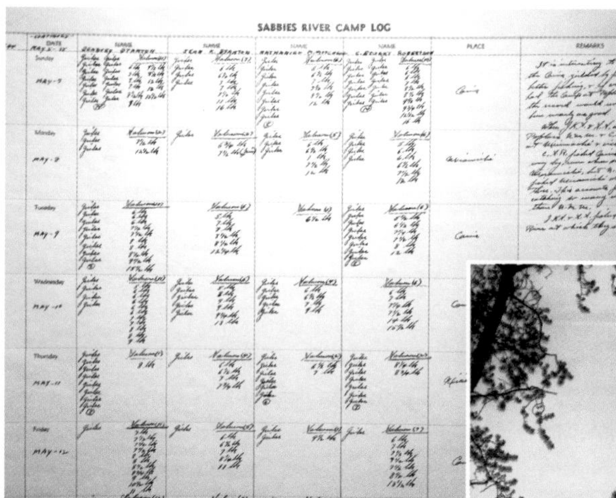

SABBIES RIVER CAMP LOG

DATE	NAME	NAME	NAME	NAME	NAME	PLACE	REMARKS
Sunday May-7							
Monday May-8							
Tuesday May-9							
Wednesday May-10							
Thursday May-11							
Friday May-12							
Saturday May-13							

Here is a page from 1944 showing a large spring catch in early to mid-May recorded by columns for Jean's catch, Seabury's, and their guests on this trip. Jean's notes in the right-hand column gloat over the superior fishing on the Cains where they had already begun to invest in salmon water.

These photos are of Wendell Allen's newly finished masterpiece, Camp Stanton. Camp Stanton was certainly, in its day, the grandest personal lodge to be built on the Miramichi or Cains Rivers. Wendell is seen sitting on the porch looking out in the direction of the home pool. PHOTO COURTESY OF THE PROVINCIAL ARCHIVES OF NEW BRUNSWICK.

city in America. The money came from whaling, which in the mid- to late 1800s was a fabulously profitable undertaking, and New Bedford, Massachusetts, was the undisputed home of the industry. With the decline of the whaling industry, the money flowed into cotton and woolen mills, and New Bedford was again the center of that undertaking, with huge stone mill buildings that are still the finest industrial structures in the town. That was Seabury's path in life. After getting an education at Harvard, he spent 50 years in the textile industry before resigning when Warren Buffet took over control of his company, Berkshire Hathaway—the company that Seabury Stanton had built by acquiring and piecing together the remains of his failing competitors. The Stantons, though, as the log reveals, despite the disparity in their circumstances, became fast and close friends with the Allen family, especially to Wendell and Doris.

I've gone through the logs and saved out bits of information that I hope will provide an interesting look into the Stanton family's time on the Cains River, which ran from 1938 until Seabury's death in 1971.

1938 Spring—This is the first page, and whether Seabury had fished the river in years before is not revealed. It is possible that Seabury had been a client of Harry's before his death in 1932 and that he continued to take those combination camping and fishing trips by canoe down the Cains with George and Clarence. The first writings in the log, though, are from 1938. Stanton was 46 years old in 1938, and it is likely that he did not have a long previous history, if any, on the river.

Seabury, Jean Kellog Stanton, and Jean Stanton—a child, the last name only appears twice in the logbook over 33 years—and a friend named Helen Cook came up to fish on May 8 at George Allen's camp where the Black Brook Salmon Club lodge is now located. The entry notes that the camps at that time had no bathrooms. In addition to the Allen family, the guides and staff included Bill Colford and Jim Vickers.

This group of pictures features Seabury Stanton, the wealthy sportsman, enjoying his time hunting and fishing at his camp in the wilds of New Brunswick. Stanton was the chairman of the Berkshire Hathaway company, finally losing control to Warren Buffet. He is guided by Wendell Allen, a man who was his friend and outdoor companion for 30 very special years. The fishing is being done in the home pool at the confluence of the Sabbies and Cains Rivers. You can see the gravel bar in the mouth of the Sabbies River where Harry Allen set his tent camp, recorded in the photo snippets from the old film presented earlier, and also the same shoreline where young Charlie Wade was photographed holding up the large kelts. I believe that in the top right photograph the man netting the fish is probably George Allen and not Wendell. George also provided services for Seabury from time to time at Camp Stanton. THIS GROUP OF PHOTOS IS COURTESY OF THE PROVINCIAL ARCHIVES OF NEW BRUNSWICK.

These surnames are still common today along the Howard Road across the river from the camps. The catch for the four anglers was 34 grilse and 44 salmon, of which the largest was 19 pounds. Fishing was done on the Miramichi and the Cains Rivers. Kelts were killed and eaten in those days, and so the weight was certain. The largest would undoubtedly have been a 30-pound fish when it entered the river. The fishing took place over six days, so the average catch was just over three per day each. That is not remarkable for spring salmon fishing, even today, but the women were not hard fishermen, and the second week in May is well beyond the prime fishing.

The log says that they "arrived by Pontiac." Much of that ride would have been over dirt roads.

1939 Spring—Clearly, the Stantons liked the experience because the next year they were back on May 14. It was noted that the camps now had the comforts of electric lights and running water.

1942 Spring—The Stantons were also in camp in the springs of 1940 and 1941, but there was nothing special to note. In 1942, though, they were without Bill Colford because he joined the army. For the first time, Wendell Allen was guiding. From that point on, Seabury and Wendell always seemed to be together.

Plans were made for the Stantons to build their own camp on George Allen's property just northeast or downriver of the main building. The Stantons would stay there when they came up fishing, but George could use it for his sports the rest of the time. Wendell built a good camp, and the Black Brook

REMARKS

First trip for J.K.S. J.S. + H.C.
Drove by Automobile. (Pontiac)
Stayed at George T. Allen's Camps
on Miramichi at Mouth of Cains.
Fished in Miramichi + lower
part of Cains River.
Allen's Camps had no bathrooms
at this time, + cabins south of
Main Camp had just been built.

Guides
Bill Colford (J.S.)
Jim Scott (J.K.S.)
Keith Allen (J.S.)
Jim Vickers (H.C)

This quote is excerpted from the first log entry in the book that includes the "drove by Pontiac" quote. Apparently, in 1938, it was still a real adventure to get to the Miramichi by car, and it required a great one like a Pontiac!

Salmon later acquired this property. The club's members and guests stayed in that building until October 2007, 36 years after Stanton's death in 1971. The camps were built in the style of many of the Restigouche camps, large and airy, with a deep front porch looking out on the river.

1942 Fall—This was the first fall trip for the Stantons, and the couple came up alone. I see this trip as important and signaling the beginning of the transition to fishing for bright fish as the dominant fishing culture on the Cains. We see later on in the logs that the Stantons began to miss some spring seasons, but after 1942, they never failed to come in the fall and fish for the fresh-run fish.

During the summer of 1942, Wendell built the Stantons' cabin on George Allen's property, and they stayed in it that fall Allen could use the facility for other guests when the Stantons were not in camp. Jean landed the biggest salmon of the year from George Allen's camps, a whopping 25.5-pounder. The couple landed 37 salmon and grilse between them in 7 days, a very good record for bright fish by modern fishing standards.

1943 Spring—Lou Butterfield of Kittery, Maine, bought the fishing water from Black Brook up to the mouth of the Cains River from the Porter family. George Allen is apoplectic over the development since his sports had fished this water along with the other side that he owns. He felt that he should have been given the first crack at it, but according to Jean K. Stanton, the speculation was that the Butterfields had a mortgage of some kind. Now the Butterfields fish this preferred section while all of Allen's and Wade's sports must fish together on the other side. It causes quite an uproar. Butterfield is an interesting character who started in chicken farming but invented a very successful egg-sorting machine, a toy car, and a machine to reset bowling pins automatically. His inventive nature also extended to fishing, and he is credited with inventing the Whiskers style of low-floating dry fly. Orvis had a poster in some of their stores of Lou Butterfield holding a salmon with some testimony about his wonderful Orvis rod. According to those who saw him fish, he was neither a great caster nor fisher, but his salmon catch was incredible. Then again, he was fishing in what some consider to be the best part of the best Atlantic salmon pool in North America.

The Black Brook Salmon Club history spells out exactly what happened in a bit more detail. Lou had been coming to the Miramichi area hunting and fishing since the 1920s, and he married one of George Porter's daughters. He also had lent money to members of the Porter family to start a musical instrument store in Miramichi. The mortgage was secured by a lien on George Porter's salmon pool at Black Brook. The store failed, and Butterfield let the mortgage slide for a few years. George Porter leased fishing by the day to George Allen's guests, and Lou Butterfield frequently fished there too, appearing as Porter's guest. Seabury Stanton, fishing at

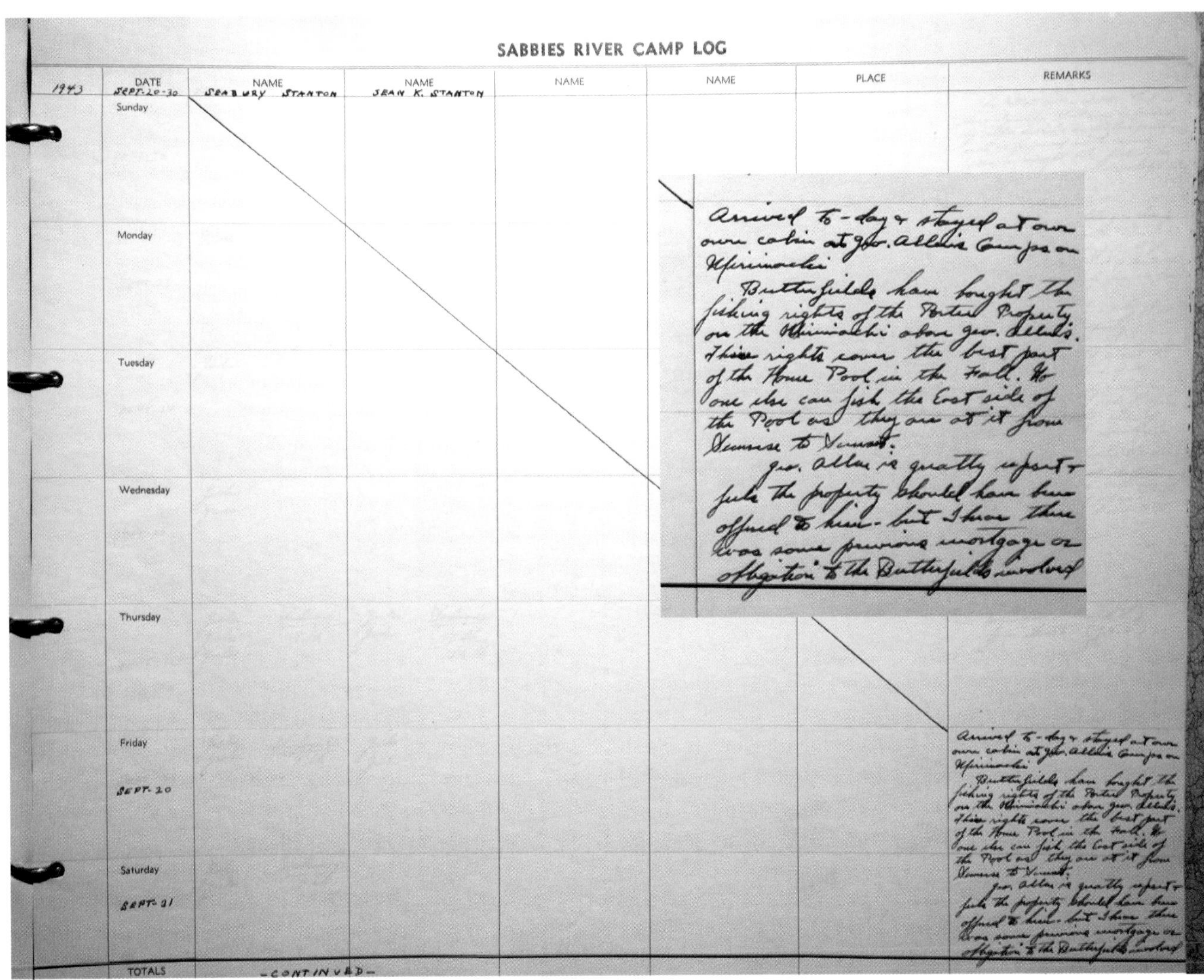

SABBIES RIVER CAMP LOG

1943 | DATE SEPT-20-30 | NAME SEABURY STANTON | NAME JEAN K. STANTON | NAME | NAME | PLACE | REMARKS

Sunday

Monday

Tuesday

Wednesday

Thursday

Friday

SEPT-20

Saturday

SEPT-21

Arrived to-day & stayed at our own cabin at Geo. Allen's Camps on Miramichi.

Butterfields have bought the fishing rights of the Porter Property on the Miramichi above Geo. Allen's. These rights cover the best part of the Home Pool in the Fall. No one else can fish the East side of the Pool as they are at it from Sunrise to Sunset.

Geo. Allen is greatly upset & feels the property should have been offered to him - but I hear there was some previous mortgage or obligation to the Butterfields involved

TOTALS -CONTINUED-

George Allen expresses his dismay at Butterfield's purchase of the Porter water at Black Brook. While both sides of this pool can be very good, there is no question that day in and day out the eastern side that leads up into the Cains River is the superior water. Allen knew that his customers would now have to watch other people catching and seeing more fish than they did on a daily basis.

George Allen's, took exception to Butterfield's presence as a nonpaying guest and demanded that Allen throw him off the pool. This angered Butterfield, who told Allen that next season he would not be able to fish that pool at all. Over the winter, Butterfield foreclosed on the mortgage and ended up owning George Porter's pool.

As a result of his unhappiness with the Butterfield developments, Seabury decided to have Wendell Allen build him a new lodge a few miles up the Cains River on the Popples Pool, and he hired attorneys to get a building lease from the province. He also bought the south side of the Salmon Brook pool and got George Allen to lease the other side—owned by a paper company—to secure private fishing. No more is said about this, but he must have been successful because the Stantons fished the water as their private property for the rest of their time on the river. Additionally, Stanton secured a right of first refusal from Charlie Wade on his property on the Sabbies River pool.

It turns out that many years down the road it was discovered that a strip of Crown land lay along the west shore of Salmon Brook Pool from a defaulted Crown grant and that Stanton never did own the private fishing there, though he managed it as his private property for over 20 years.

1945 Fall—Stanton had begun building his new lodge on the Salmon Brook Pool but immediately stopped work and switched all efforts to the final location across from Sabbies River because Charlie Wade decided to sell the land to him on which the camp now stands.

The Stantons arrived a week late on October 7 because Seabury was held up in Boston negotiating a big labor contract with the union. The couple slept the next week in the cookhouse but used the bathroom in the unheated, under-construction main camp building, hiding behind a makeshift wall of packing crates and a tarpaulin. Wendell was busy building the main lodge, Doris came up and cooked for them, and George did the guiding. Both Seabury and Jean caught

From left to right are Lou Butterfield, his brother, and his son. This photo was courtesy of the Orvis Corporation to which Lou had sent a letter extolling the virtues of the "Impregnated" 8.5-foot, 5-ounce fly rod. Lou said that he had caught 1,300 salmon on his Orvis rod, not to mention the ones that he lost.

several salmon each day, and both had fish in the 20-pound range. Wendell poled Seabury up the Sabbies, where they raised four fish landing one. Wendell said he had never heard of a salmon being caught in the Sabbies—and I never have either. The Sabbies is too shallow to provide fishing habitat for salmon, and if the water is up enough to provide depth, it flows extremely hard from bank to bank.

The Stantons headed home by canoe on the morning of October 16. Jean observed that the river was full of salmon, but the season had closed the day before. The Stantons must have been nearly overwhelmed by their good fortune.

1946 Fall—Jean stated that, "There must be 150 salmon lying in the slack water in upper part of the pool. There is no current at all, and they are lying in water about four-feet deep, and they will not take." There had been no rain for two months, and Wendell Allen is said to have remarked that it was the worst season he had ever seen—and so it ended.

1947 Spring—On April 25, the Stantons chartered a Widgeon airplane from New Brunswick Aviation. It picked them up in Boston, and after refueling in Old Town, they got lost in heavy fog and rain. They finally picked up the radio beacon from Moncton and landed there in 26°F weather among piles of snow and ice. Had it not been for a good pilot, said Jean, they might not have made it.

1947 Fall—At the end of the season, Jean wrote that they had hired Frank Saunders to stay in the camp and watch over the salmon in the pool until the end of November. The year before after the season both Salmon Brook and Sabbies River pools had been netted clean by poachers. George Allen reported that Frank stopped 32 people from attempting to net the pool and that a heavy run of salmon continued up the river during October and into November. The Stantons expected good kelt fishing the next spring because of this conservation, but there is really no reason to expect that would be the case. Areas of spawning activity and those preferred by wintering kelts have quite different properties.

1948 Fall—The Stantons drove into the Brophy Place, sometimes referred to in the log as Brophy Meadows because of the fields cleared around the farm. They visited with Mary C. Brophy and signed a purchase and sale agreement for two lots that she owned—numbers 18 and 19—upriver of Camp Stanton. Tom Washburn then drove them into Camp Stanton with his big truck.

Water temperature was 52°F at the end of the season—very warm by my experience. Jean Stanton reports that "a heavy run of salmon was coming up the river all day long and the fishing was excellent."

A great horned owl spied a grilse left in shallow water secured by a landing net and dragged it out onto the shore at Sabbies. The owl was eating the grilse when discovered, and the guides shot at it but missed.

A common tradition was to celebrate Seabury Stanton's birthday on October 9 while in camp. They had a supper party that night that included all the Allens, the Stantons, and Tom and Dot Washburn. Seabury got a cigarette box and a mount of his 6-pound trout from the previous year. They all played bagatelle, pin the tail on the donkey, and bingo. It was a delightful 56th birthday for Seabury.

They all left for home in the Washburns' truck. Driving by car to Brophy's, and then taking a large four-wheel-drive truck into camp had become the most common way for the Stantons to access their lodge. People lived along the Brophy Road up as far as Otter Brook, but after that, there were no year-round dwellings, and the roads were just for loggers.

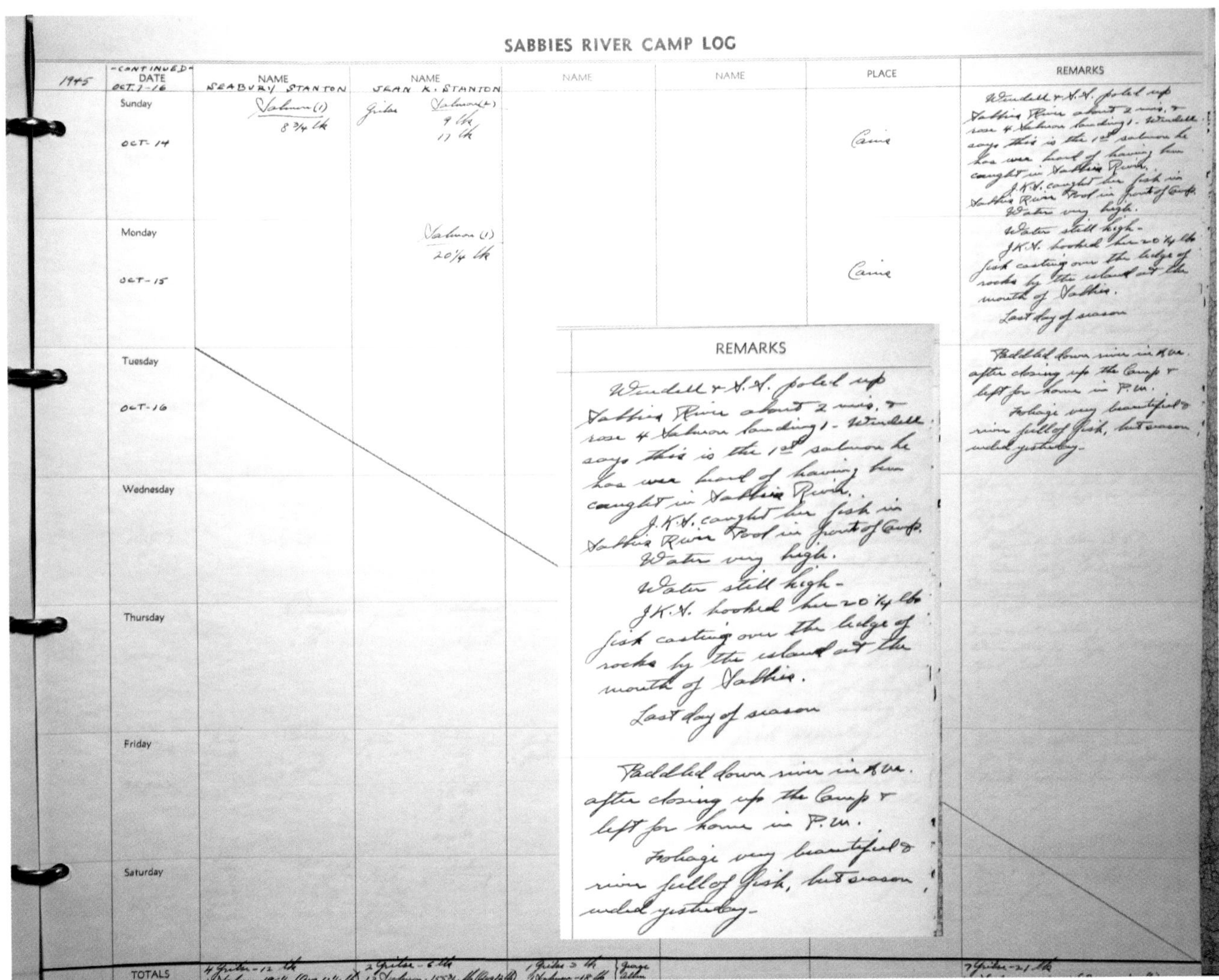

SABBIES RIVER CAMP LOG

1945 -CONTINUED- DATE OCT. 7-16	NAME SEABURY STANTON	NAME JEAN K. STANTON	NAME	NAME	PLACE	REMARKS
Sunday OCT-14	Salmon (1) 8 3/4 lb	Grilse Salmon (2) 9 lb 17 lb			Camp	Wendell & S.S. poled up Sabbies River about 2 mi. & rose 4 salmon landing 1 - Wendell says this is the 1st salmon he has ever heard of having been caught in Sabbies River. J.K.S. caught her fish in Sabbies River Pool in front of Camp. Water very high.
Monday OCT-15		Salmon (1) 20 1/4 lb			Camp	Water still high - J.K.S. hooked her 20 1/4 lb fish casting over the ledge of rocks by the island at the mouth of Sabbies. Last day of season
Tuesday OCT-16						Paddled down river in A.M. after closing up the Camp & left for home in P.M. Foliage very beautiful & river full of fish, but season ended yesterday.
Wednesday						
Thursday						
Friday						
Saturday						
TOTALS						

The diary here reveals that the Stantons are having the time of their life, catching salmon in their new pool at the mouth of the Sabbies River and camping like kids in the cookhouse of the incredible camp that the talented Wendell Allen was building for them. They enjoyed it all immensely for the next 25 years.

1949 Spring—A new law this year requires that you keep only five fish per day. "But," says Jean, "the guides have a license that allows them to keep 10 per boat per day. Barbless hooks are also required, and in spite of rain and snow all day, the wardens are out in force enforcing the law."

There was good luck one day above the elms, just upriver from Salmon Brook on the old Porter Pool.

The Stantons heard that the Sabbies and Salmon Brook Pools were again netted clean by poachers after the end of the previous falls fishing. It isn't said whether the pool warden failed at his job or none was hired that year.

1949 Fall—On October 3, Admiral Merrill visited the Stantons and caught a salmon in their pool. Fishing was good, and the next day, Seabury landed seven salmon; the smallest was 10 pounds, and the largest was 15.5.

Beautiful northern lights observed the evening of October 7.

The famous artist Ogden Pleissner was in camp for five days and landed six grilse and 12 salmon. The catch for the camp in the final three weeks of the season was 30 grilse and 63 salmon. There were between two and four anglers there all the time. That is a rough average of 1.5 fish per rod per day during the period. The fact that two-thirds of the fish were salmon instead of the majority being grilse was common in those years.

1950 Fall—Fishing is slow. Wendell Allen says the water has been high all fall, and many fish have already gone up. Also, the log says that in the big water there has been a lot of driftnet poaching in the pools. It then says "Larry Burke" but don't know whether he is reporting this or was accused of being the poacher.

The weather is very hazy due to large forest fires in British Columbia. The smoke goes all the way across the ocean to England.

The fall catch was 57 grilse and 64 salmon for three weeks and three rods. That is an average of nearly two fish per angler, per day. Seabury's personal catch was 36 grilse and

SABBIES RIVER CAMP LOG

DATE (-CONTINUED- 1947 APR. 23 – MAY 13)	NAME: SEABURY STANTON	NAME: JEAN K. STANTON	NAME: HELEN COOK	NAME: MORRIS K. BROWNE	PLACE	REMARKS
Sunday MAY-4	Grilse; Salmon (6) 6 lb, 6 lb, 6½ lb, 7 lb, 8 lb, 13½ lb			Salmon (2) 7 lb, 10½ lb	Cains	Temp 68° – No Wind – Raining. Best fishing so far. Understand all salmon in Sabbies River Pool & Salmon Brook were netted out last fall after we left. This fact together with the low water last fall, probably accounts for the poor fishing this spring.
Monday MAY-5	Salmon (3) 5 lb, 7 lb, 9 lb	Salmon (2) 8 lb, 13 lb		Grilse, Grilse; Salmon (2) 7 lb, 8 lb	Cains	Temp 58/52° – no wind – fog & rain – River rising.
Tuesday MAY-6					Cains	Temp. 58/49° Rain – River very high & dirty – No fish taken in AM. Did not fish in PM. No fish rolling.
Wednesday MAY-7					Cains	Temp 55/60° Wind W. River still falling but dirty. J.K.S. & S.S. did not fish.
Thursday MAY-8					Cains	Temp 54/44° Strong W. Wind. River high & dirty. Did not fish in PM. [illegible]
Friday MAY-9	Grilse, Grilse; Salmon (1) 8 lb				Cains	Temp 35/44° Strong W. Wind. River falling but still dirty. No fish rolling on morning, & there are obviously very few [illegible]
Saturday MAY-10	Grilse		Salmon (1) 12 lb		Cains	Temp 28/53° Sunny – N.W. Wind. River falling & water clearing up.

REMARKS

Temp 68° – No Wind – Raining. Best fishing so far. Understand all salmon in Sabbies River Pool & Salmon Brook were netted out last fall after we left. This fact together with the low water last fall, probably accounts for the poor fishing this spring.

Temp 58/52° – no wind – fog & rain – River rising.

The Stantons were dismayed to hear that Salmon Brook and the Mouth of Sabbies Pools were both netted clean of salmon by poachers the previous fall.

33 salmon. That is an average for him of nearly four per day for a three-week period—an outstanding record.

On October 14, Seabury landed three grilse and eight salmon from nine to 19 pounds. On the following day, Jean K. Stanton landed a 24-pound salmon, and Seabury caught another seven fish. Quite a couple of days, and quite a fall season! The conditions are cool and rainy with the water level constantly moderately high but flowing clear. The fish just keep coming!

The Stantons left camp on the morning of the October 16, and Doris Allen had a party for Jean K. Stanton at the Allens' home in Penniac. The Stantons drove to the party, then on down to Harvey and boarded a train for home.

1951 Fall—A fresh run of salmon arrived in the morning and settled down in the current at the tail of the pool below the mouth of the Sabbies River. Seabury rolled 10 fish, but they weren't taking well.

Wendell Allen shot a small buck in the woods in back of Camp Stanton.

The fall's catch for three weeks was 15 grilse and 29 salmon for an average of a little more than two rods. That's about a fish a day per rod. Seabury himself had 30 of those fish, so he averaged one and a half per day.

1953 Spring—George Allen died of a heart attack on his way to the Boston sportsmen's show the previous winter. He had no will, and despite promising to leave the business to Wendell and Doris, there was no legal provision for that, and Wendell got nothing, which created some issues. Seabury, however, held a mortgage on the property and intervened, getting a better deal for Wendell and Doris in return for his re-mortgaging the property to the new majority owner, George's son Neil. Wendell got a 20-year lease to operate the late George Allen's lodge on the main river, and Seabury also transferred to Wendell and Doris the Popples camps on the Cains. The negotiations weren't final until the fall. Everyone seemed reasonably satisfied with the arrangements.

1953 Fall—Meanwhile, in between all these negotiations, Seabury landed 13 grilse and 18 salmon, including a

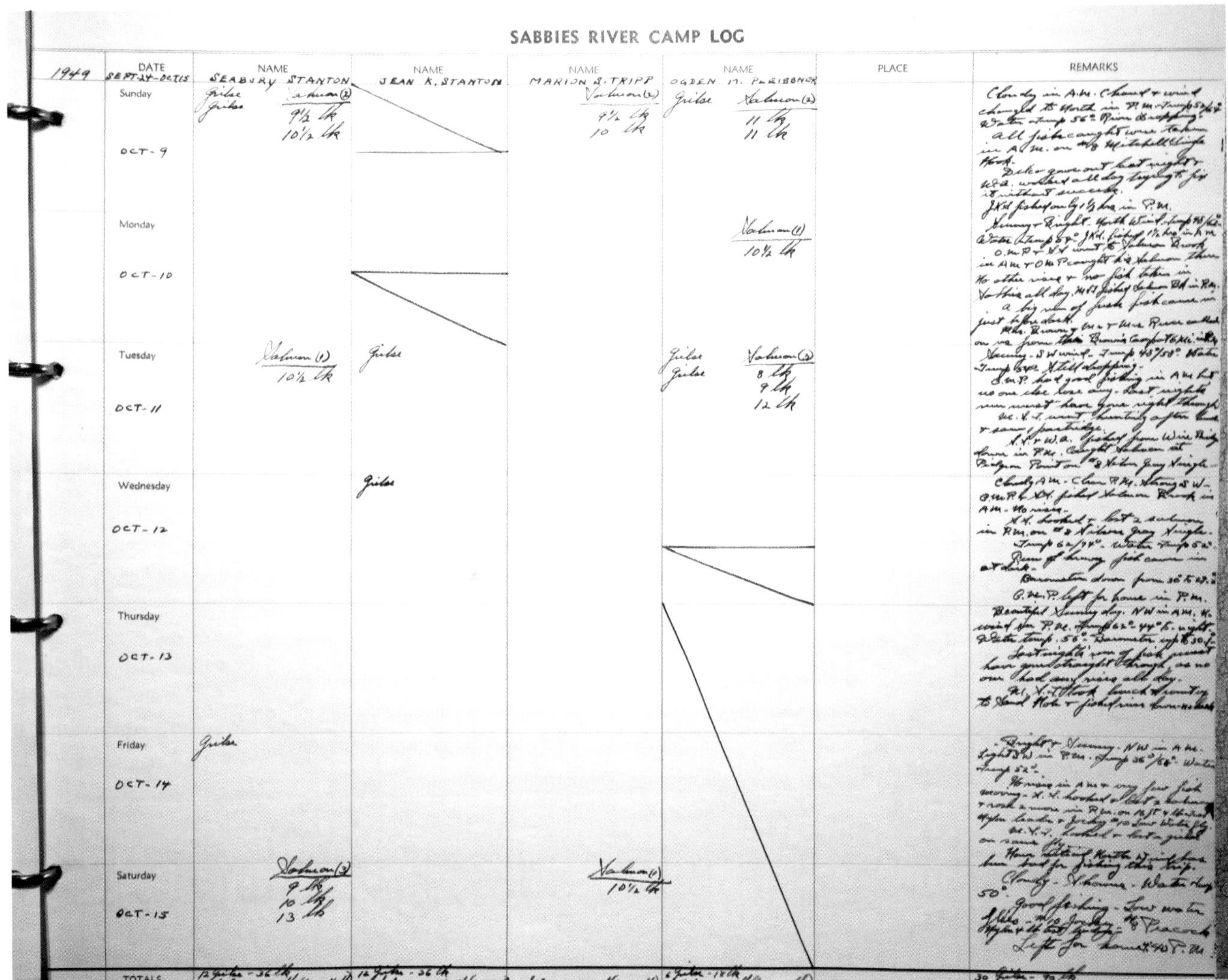

SABBIES RIVER CAMP LOG

DATE	NAME	NAME	NAME	NAME	PLACE	REMARKS
1949 Sept 24–Oct 15	Seabury Stanton	Jean K. Stanton	Marion S. Tripp	Ogden M. Pleissner		
Sunday Oct-9	Grilse, Grilse; Salmon (2) 9½ lb, 10½ lb		Salmon (2) 9½ lb, 10 lb	Grilse; Salmon (2) 11 lb, 11 lb		[illegible]
Monday Oct-10				Salmon (1) 10½ lb		[illegible]
Tuesday Oct-11	Salmon (1) 10½ lb	Grilse		Grilse, Grilse; Salmon (3) 8 lb, 9 lb, 12 lb		[illegible]
Wednesday Oct-12		Grilse				[illegible]
Thursday Oct-13						[illegible]
Friday Oct-14	Grilse					[illegible]
Saturday Oct-15	Salmon (3) 9 lb, 10 lb, 13 lb		Salmon (1) 10½ lb			[illegible]
TOTALS	[illegible]	[illegible]	[illegible]	[illegible]		[illegible]

These entries in the Camp Stanton log show that Ogden Pleissner was top salmon rod during his stay on the Cains.

28-pounder, for only nine days of fishing, so about three and a half fish per day. Year after year, this total is consistently amounting to more salmon than grilse.

1954 Spring—On April 22, Jack Stanton went up to the Arbo Pool—note that "Arbo" and "Arbeau" are used inconsistently in various writing about the Cains River to spell the name of this pool—and hooked but lost a good salmon. He reported that there were many boats out fishing the section all the way up to Trout Hole. The Arbeau Pool is about 16 miles upriver from Camp Stanton—a long run in a motorized canoe during the cold weather of April.

1955 Fall—Plenty of fish are said to be holding near the mouth of the Cains, but none are running up the river. The water is dreadfully low, and there are simply no fish in the pool. Elbridge Bolong, the regular fall tenant of the Popples Lodge who fishes at Salmon Brook every year, left early because there was no fish. Charles Colford came up to Sabbies Pool with a horse and dredge to remove the bar just below the island at the mouth of the Sabbies River that the Stantons feel is harming the fishing in the pool. Colford, Wendell Allen, and Wendell's staff of guides labored to remove the bar.

Ted Williams of the Boston Red Sox and Julian Crandall, owner of Ashway Fishing Lines from Rhode Island, showed up with a camera crew to make a movie. They left after a brief stay, though, because there was no water and no fish.

Camp Stanton's catch, which was frequently over 100 fish for three rods during the last two or three weeks of the season, was three grilse in 1955. What a difference a flow of water makes.

1956 Fall—This was a year of moderate water and good runs of fish but poor takers. On October 14, Jean Stanton reported that river was low, but the run of fish that started at 3 p.m. the previous day was still underway. The fish were moving right on through and would not take a fly. The Stantons took a canoe trip downriver to the Popples, and along the way, they saw fish rolling and jumping for the entire distance.

The Yankees beat Brooklyn 2–0 on a no-hitter by Don Larsen—first ever in a World Series game. Seabury Stanton celebrated his 64th birthday, and a big bull moose provided

SABBIES RIVER CAMP LOG

Logbook page that contains some great entries of fish caught in October 1950—the author was born two days after the close of the 1950 season. Seabury had 37 fish for the week with slightly over half being salmon rather than grilse. Two of these weighed 19 pounds each.

Left: At the end of the fishing season in 1953, the catch is good, including a 23-pound salmon as well as others of 21 and 19.5 pounds.

further entertainment by wading across the river in front of the camp.

The year's catch was a moderate 10 grilse and 16 salmon. The grilse averaged only three pounds apiece. The salmon averaged nine and a half pounds. The Stantons left on October 16 during what they described as a hot day. The water temperature was 52°F, indeed fairly warm for mid-October.

1957 Fall—This year was low water again, and the catch for three weeks was one grilse. The Stantons can see clearly to the bottom of their pool almost everywhere, and there are no fish to be seen holding there. Unsatisfied with the work

SABBIES RIVER CAMP LOG

DATE	NAME	NAME	NAME	NAME	PLACE	REMARKS
1960 Oct 4–16	Seabury Stanton	Jean K. Stanton	Marion S. Tripp			
Sunday Oct-9	A.M. DID / P.M. Birthday Party (The ???)	NOT	FISH		4th Game - New York; Pittsburgh - 3; New York - 2	[illegible]
Monday Oct-10	A.M. DID / P.M.	NOT	FISH		5th Game - New York; Pittsburgh - 5; New York - 2	[illegible]
Tuesday Oct-11	DID	NOT	FISH		No game	[illegible]
Wednesday Oct-12	DID	NOT	FISH		6th Game - Pittsburgh; New York - 12; Pittsburgh - 0	[illegible]
Thursday Oct-13	A.M. DID / P.M.	NOT	FISH		7th Game - Pittsburgh; Pittsburgh - 10; New York - 9	[illegible]
Friday Oct-14	A.M. DID / P.M.	NOT	FISH			[illegible]
Saturday Oct-15	A.M. DID / P.M.	NOT	FISH			[illegible]
TOTALS	0 - Grilse; 0 - Salmon	0 - Grilse; 0 - Salmon	0 - Grilse; 0 - Salmon	Total 0 - Grilse; 0 - Salmon		[illegible]

Very low water and again no fish at all for the 1960 fall season contrasting with very good catches in each of the two previous seasons. The difference is simply whether or not there is a good height of water.

done two years ago to remove the bar, the Stantons brought in a bulldozer this time and put the bar back on the bank. The notes say that they had gotten government permission.

1958 Fall—Camp Stanton was broken into, and clothes, blankets, and other furnishings were taken. The thieves even took the lead flashing from under the edge of the roof.

There was fair water and reasonably good fishing. The Bollong party of two rods and the Stantons of three fishing at Salmon Brook for two weeks landed 78 fish, or about one apiece each day. The angling pressure, though, was by no means relentless, and many sessions and even days were taken off.

This year the grilse were quite small, averaging about four pounds each.

1959 Fall—Bollong, who lived in Wellesley, Massachusetts, lost his wife this year and fished with the Stantons. They caught 27 grilse and 34 salmon in the last couple weeks of the season.

1960 Fall—There was very low water this fall and no fish in the pools. The catch for the Stantons and Bollong combined was zero for the whole of their fall season. Wendell Allen took them all to Quarryville, where they reported seeing great numbers of large salmon waiting for water to ascend the river.

The Pirates beat the Yankees 10–9 in Game 7 of the World Series. It is deemed the greatest game ever played.

1961 Spring—the Stantons didn't arrive until May 18 this year, but they had decent fishing despite high water until May 26. It continued to rain, however, and with the water rising, the Stantons left on May 28. On their way downriver, the water was up to the bottom of the Popples Camp and was four feet above the floor level of the Admiral Pool camp. It turned out to be the worst flood on the river since 1923.

1961 Fall—The big news is that a group of doctors from Worcester, as Jean Stanton described them, had paid Lou Butterfield $50,000 for his pool at Black Brook but allowed him a life tenancy to fish there and stay in his small camp.

SABBIES RIVER CAMP LOG

DATE	NAME	NAME	NAME	NAME	PLACE	REMARKS
1961 May 18-28	SEABURY STANTON	JEAN K. STANTON	MARION S. TRIPP			1961 - News
Sunday						
Monday						
Tuesday						
Wednesday						
Thursday MAY-18	DID	NOT	FISH			
Friday MAY-19	Salmon (1) 8 lb.		Grilse			
Saturday MAY-20	Grilse DID Salmon (1) 7 lb.	NOT Grilse	FISH A.M.			

Time changes everything, and this year Lou Butterfield sells his pool to the Black Brook Salmon Club for $50,000. That began a new dynasty in its own right, and Coleman Moore buys the Brophy Pool. The Brophy family has owned this pool and land since the original Crown grant was issued to them in 1840. Moore now owns two of the top four or five salmon pools on the river.

Coleman Moore, who owned a pool in Shinnickburn, bought the Brophy Pool for $8,000.

The Stantons again, for two years in a row, caught no fish. The low water was compared to 1957, and it was said the water at the mouth of the Cains was full of fish. It was reported that a strong run of fish went up the Cains after the season ended.

1962 Fall—The Stantons had their property surveyed by Cook and his assistant, Curtis. Cook told the Stantons that there was a strip of Crown land 64 feet deep all along the edge of the land bordering their side of Salmon Brook Pool, and that Stanton did not own private fishing there. The Stantons had been under the impression that they had owned this ever since their purchase in 1944.

1963 Fall—On October 7, during a heavy run of grilse up the river, a fish hits the bow of Seabury's canoe and almost comes into the boat. The next day, another one leaps from the water so close to Jack Stanton's canoe that it throws water all over him.

1965 Spring—As a consequence of the Warren Buffet takeover, Seabury Stanton resigns all positions and retires on May 10 at 73 years old after 50 years at Berkshire Hathaway. The Stantons decide to try for the early summer sea-run trout and come up on May 30, staying until June 12. They fished all up and down their section of the Cains River from the Whirlpool down to Salmon Brook and caught plenty of trout, but the largest was only one pound.

1965 Fall—The catch this year was 19 grilse and seven salmon.

1966 Fall—On October 6, Wendell Allen reports his two guides working at Salmon Brook threatened to quit unless they get a raise from their current level of $7 a day plus meals. This is Allen's standard pay plan. Allen told them to go ahead and quit and supplied Bollong with another guide. On October 16, Allen discovered that the locks on the freezer at his lodge had been pried open and all the food inside had been stolen. The

Mounties came and fingerprinted the place, but no more is ever written about the outcome.

The catch this year was 31 grilse and 11 salmon. The ratio of grilse to salmon appears to have made a flip-flop in recent years with more grilse now than salmon.

1967 Fall—The big news is that the new daily bag limit is only four salmon.

The Red Sox lost at home to Saint Louis in Game 7 of the World Series.

The catch for 51 rod days is 85 grilse and 21 salmon. That is better than two per rod day and is quite good. Seabury himself had 40 grilse and 14 salmon for 21 days of fishing. Two and a half fish per day over a 21-day period is an excellent catch almost anywhere. The grilse averaged five pounds each, and it appears that they were all weighed. This is the year that DFO biologist Bill Hooper called the last really great run on the Miramichi, estimating that nearly 600,000 fish entered the Miramichi system in this year. There was clearly a pile of grilse, and they were quite well-fed as five pounds each is the largest average size I saw for 30 years in the Camp Stanton logs.

1968 Fall—Neil Allen offers to sell his Black Brook lodge and Howard's bank fishings to Wendell for $25,000, and Wendell accepts. Seabury doesn't like the 10 percent interest deal that the bank offers Wendell and finances it to him for 6 percent canceling out the mortgage that he already has on the property to Neil. Wendell thinks this is a good investment since he feels he can get much more than this from what Jean records as "Cities Service"—actually Atlantic Richfield—who had recently bought Wade's Fishing Lodge, which Herb Wade later bought back at a reduced price.

The Stantons saw Warden Bastarache in Blackville. He has a black eye from a fight with poachers. Also saw Ted Williams in town with his dark-haired wife number three.

There has been no rain, and despite good daily catches down on Wendell's side of the Black Brook Pool, no fish are being

On successive days of a heavy grilse run, two fish hit the Stantons canoes while jumping up the river and almost landed in the boats. Runs during these years were massive, and it is certainly possible that 30,000 grilse or more ran through the pool that year.

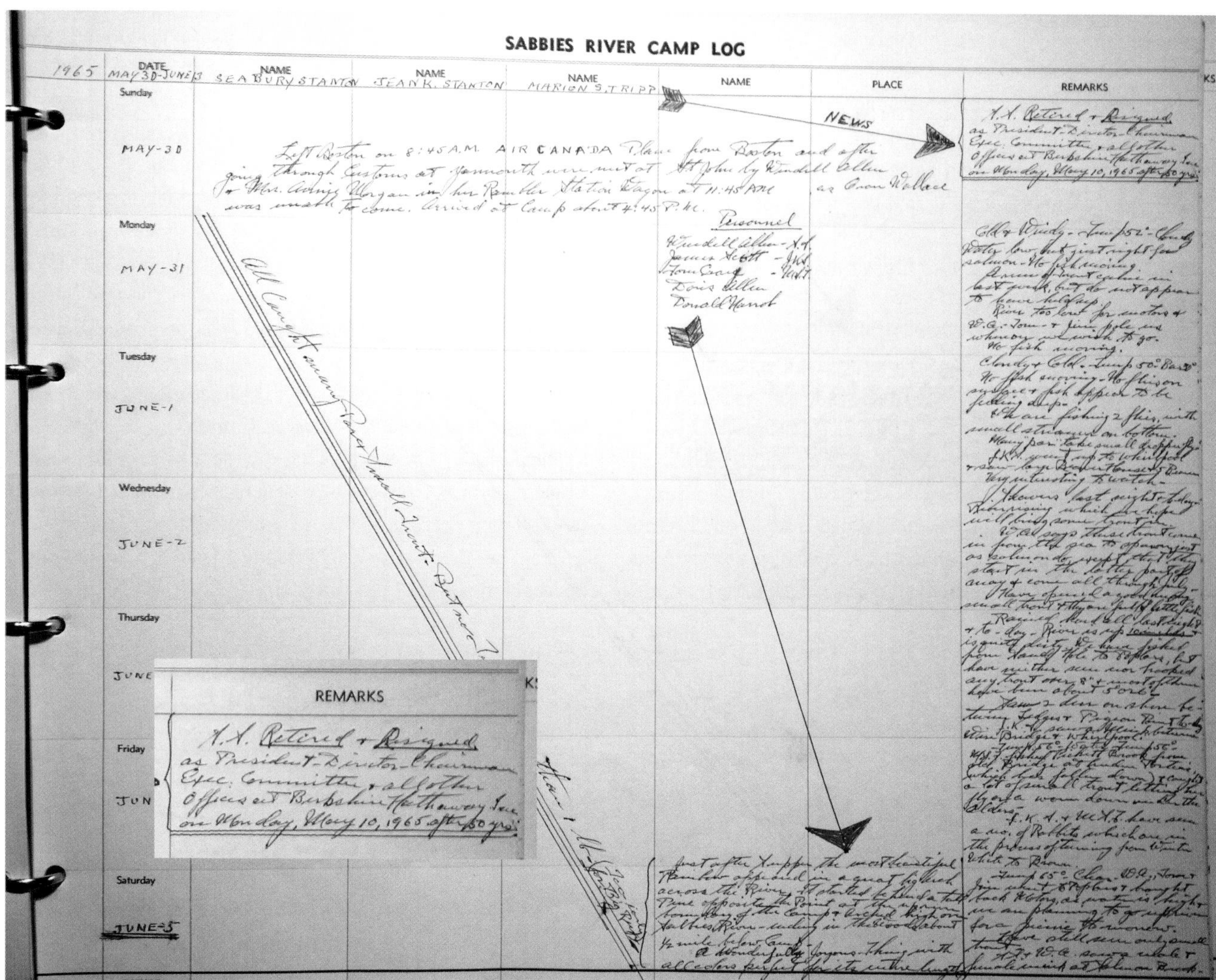

Stanton resigns all positions at Berkshire Hathaway after 50 years with the company. There is no mention of the Warren Buffet takeover in Jean's notes.

caught at Salmon Brook or the mouth of the Sabbies River Pool. Wendell says there are many Cains River salmon waiting for water to come up. Jean reports that three grilse and one salmon are holding in the slack water at the top of the pool but will touch nothing. The rain doesn't come, and the season ends with one grilse and one salmon caught. Seabury caught these with a 12-foot-long leader ending in a six-pound test tippet and armed with a number 10 brown bomber wet fly. What a difference can exist between consecutive seasons!

A.A. caught salmon in slack
water just below old upper end
of island across from Camp pool
#10 Brown Bomber + 12 ft, 6 lbs
leader.

Seabury Stanton was a sophisticated and persistent fisherman. Often, he fished quite small flies such as the #10 wet fly on a very long and light leader mentioned in the log. Because of the light tippets, some of the larger fish that they landed at Camp Stanton required a comparatively long time to bring to the net.

1969 Spring—On January 8, Wendell Allen suffered a heart attack but lived to make it to the hospital in Fredericton, where he expired on January 24. On January 12, the Stantons arrived at the hospital and tried to see Wendell but were not allowed to. The Stantons returned to Dartmouth, Massachusetts, with Seabury himself suffering from congestive heart failure and pneumonia. After convalescing in the hospital for two weeks, he returned home with a nurse. It was never quite the same in the last couple of years at Camp Stanton.

1969 Fall—Quite a good height of water this fall but fishing is just so-so in spite of it.

One day during Seabury's after-lunch nap, the guides saw a man walk down along the Sabbies River, cast into the pool, and hook a salmon. The wardens drove the man away. Seabury never owned that land, so he must have had a lease from the paper company. The poachers were two sports from Atlantic Richfield—previously Wade's Fishing Lodge—with a guide who must have known that Stanton had an exclusive lease on the water from the lumber company.

Jean notes that Seabury had a very nice 77th birthday with friends, receiving presents, cake, and ice cream. Jean said that it was a great time except for missing Wendell.

The catch for the fall season was 20 grilse and six salmon. Grilse have now dominated the catch for about a decade.

1970 Fall—On September 23, Seabury and son Jack flew from Boston to Saint John, New Brunswick, and met up with Doris Allen and Gram Wallace for a late lunch. Doris then flew back to Boston to meet up with Jean K. Stanton to drive up to camp via Houlton.

The Stantons arrived in camp after being driven over from Brophy's and were happy to find the camp "back on its foundations." There was an epic flood during the spring of 1970—which is probably why the Stantons didn't come up then fishing—that swept away bridges and flooded land and streets with water and ice all up and down the river. Apparently, Camp Stanton was moved on its foundations. The Popples too was moved off its foundation and was then moved back farther up the hill. Jean Stanton writes that looking up the river from the house many big trees along the river were simply snapped off. Bill Boyd of Mountain Channel stopped in, and later in the week, Millet Underhill also came by to introduce himself.

Jean never added up the catch this fall, but it was 17 grilse and nine salmon. The largest salmon was only nine pounds.

1971 Spring—The Stantons came into camp on May 1 by driving to Shinnickburn and coming in by canoe. The road from Brophy must have been impassable. The canoe ride down was cold, according to Jean.

The log was all chitchat this spring. Jean remarked that Doris washed and set her hair one day, someone picked May flowers, the guides chased a bear away from the meat house with an axe, they had picnic upriver, and took a ride to visit up at Six Mile. But no one fished much at all, an hour or two here or there, and if there were any fish caught, they were not recorded.

At 9:30 a.m. on May 17, the Stantons shut the door for what turned out to be the last time and left the Cains via canoe. From Blackville, they drove to the Lincoln, Maine, airport, where they took off for home at 2:30 p.m.

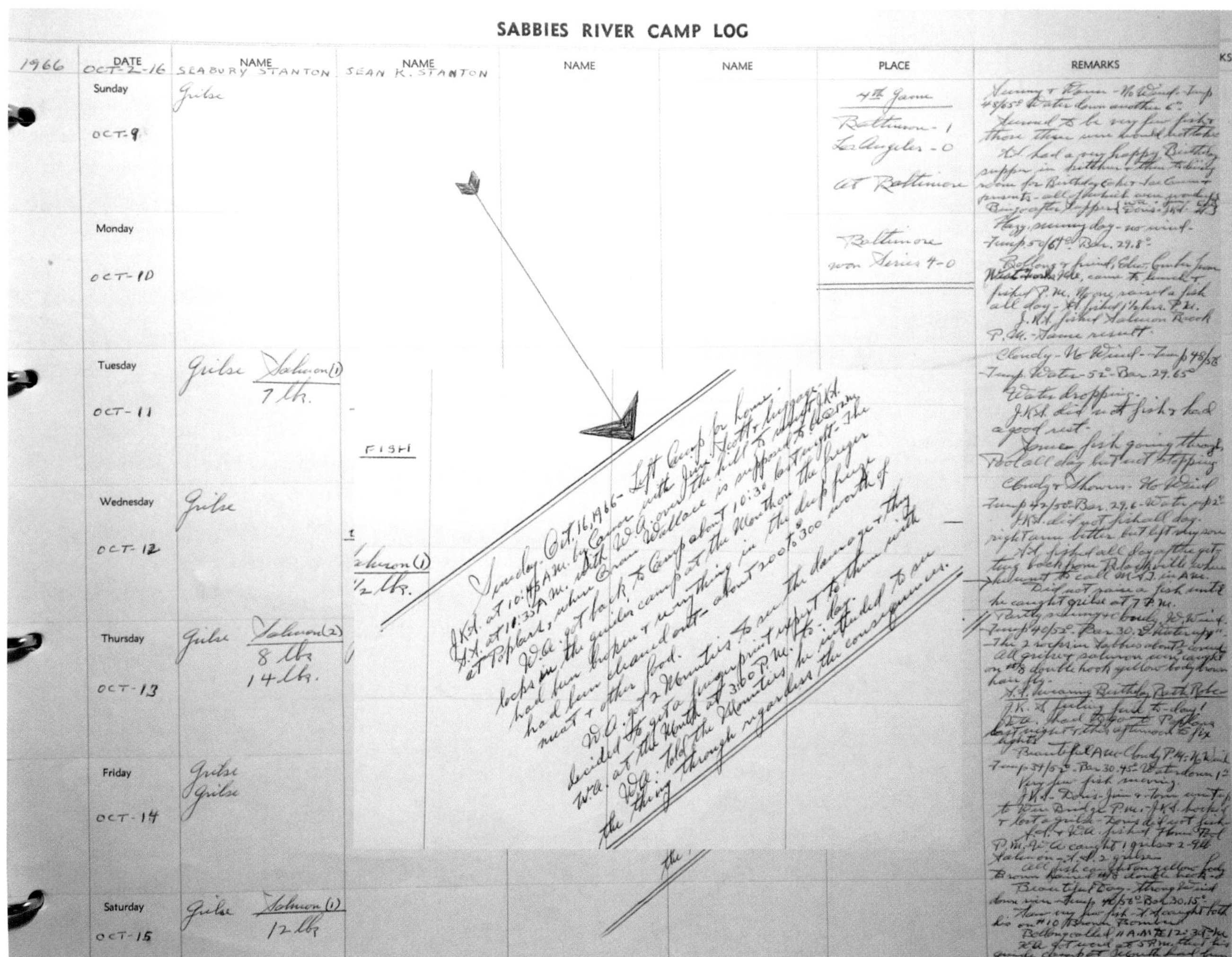
SABBIES RIVER CAMP LOG

1966 DATE	NAME Seabury Stanton	NAME Jean K. Stanton	NAME	NAME	PLACE	REMARKS
Oct-2-16 Sunday Oct-9	Grilse				4th Game Baltimore - 1 Los Angeles - 0 At Baltimore	[illegible]
Monday Oct-10					Baltimore won Series 4-0	[illegible]
Tuesday Oct-11	Grilse Salmon (1) 7 lb.	Fish				[illegible]
Wednesday Oct-12	Grilse	Salmon (1) ½ lb.				[illegible]
Thursday Oct-13	Grilse Salmon (2) 8 lb. 14 lb.					[illegible]
Friday Oct-14	Grilse Grilse					[illegible]
Saturday Oct-15	Grilse Salmon (1) 12 lb.					[illegible]

Wendell Allen has a dispute with a couple of his guides over wages, and the day after the season ends, the locks are cut, and several hundred dollars' worth of food in the lodge freezer is stolen. If anyone was apprehended, it is never mentioned.

SABBIES RIVER CAMP LOG

1971 DATE	NAME	NAME	NAME	NAME	PLACE	REMARKS
Sunday MAY 16	SEABURY STANTON	JEAN K. STANTON	MARION S. TRIPP			38°–65° — hazy sun, wind SSE. Salmon Brook. Wet-fished for trout at Pickard Brook. Cloudy afternoon – hockey game Montreal 4 – Chicago 3
Monday MAY 17						LEFT CAMP 9:30 AM for Shinnickburn, Oran Wallace there – cold – rain + fog. Drove to Fredericton after stopping at Nashwaak Restaurant, saw Muriel, drove to Lincoln Airport. Pilot David Frawley + Chris Norwood. Took off 2:30 PM – customs at Bangor – New Bedford at 5 PM.
Tuesday						
Wednesday						
Thursday						
Friday						

REMARKS

38°–65° — hazy sun, wind SSE. Salmon Brook. Wet-fished for trout at Pickard Brook. Cloudy afternoon – hockey game Montreal 4 – Chicago 3

LEFT CAMP 9:30 AM for Shinnickburn, Oran Wallace there – cold – rain + fog. Drove to Fredericton after stopping at Nashwaak Restaurant, saw Muriel, drove to Lincoln Airport. Pilot David Frawley + Chris Norwood. Took off 2:30 PM – customs at Bangor – New Bedford at 5 PM.

The final trip was quite unremarkable, other than it was high water and poor fishing, and one gets the impression that there was no question about whether or not they would be back in the fall. After all, the Stantons had been coming for 33 years. Their last trip home was like many with lunch in a restaurant along the Nashwaak and a private flight from Lincoln, Maine, down to Dartmouth, Massachusetts. Seabury died that fall, ending one of the most remarkable runs that anyone, especially anyone from outside of the province, ever had on the river.

Jan. 8, 1969 Wendell Allen had a Coronary and went into the Hospital in Fredericton, where he died Jan 24th. S.S. went to Fredericton Jan 12th with Jean but was not allowed to see Wendell + came home on Jan. 15th with pneumonia + congestive heart failure. Went into Hospital – Intensive Care Unit night of the 15th + returned home 1/31/70 with Mrs. Aurore Chace (wife of Capt. Robert M. Chace 666 Elm St. So. Dartmouth) Registered Nurse – Under care of Dr. Radcliffe + limited in activity since that time.

This is the saddest possible news for all concerned. Wendell is gone, and it almost kills Seabury himself. Things will never be the same for the Stantons, and Wendell will never come into his own as the outfitter on the river that he might otherwise have been.

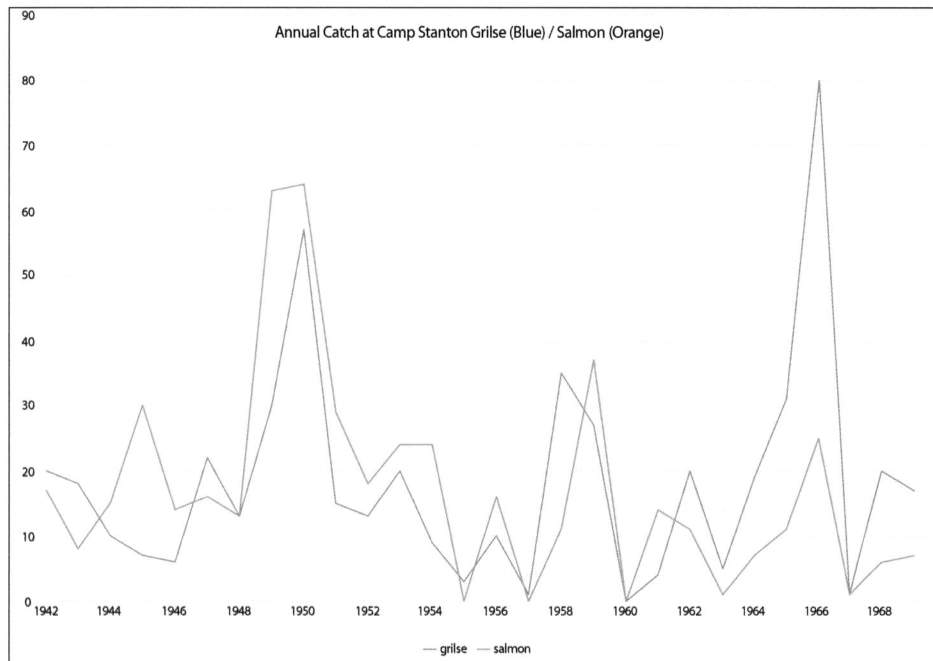

The orange graph line shows the multi sea winter salmon catch every year at Camp Stanton. It runs from a low of zero to a high of 64. The grilse catch is the blue line, and it runs from zero to 80. It is very clear that in all but a very few years between 1942 and 1962 that salmon catches surpassed grilse. In fact, during that period, the total salmon catch was 412 compared to 320 grilse, so about four salmon to every three grilse. *The trend reversed in 1963, and from that point onward, grilse dominated the catch.* There were no years between 1962 and 1970 when more salmon were caught than grilse, and the totals for those nine years were 193 grilse to 69 salmon, or 2.8 grilse for every salmon. This trend has continued to the current day.

ANNUAL CATCH AT CAMP STANTON GRILSE—BLUE LINE—COMPARED TO SALMON—ORANGE LINE		
1942 through 1970		
year	grilse	salmon
1942	20	17
1943	18	8
1944	10	15
1945	7	30
1946	6	14
1947	22	16
1948	13	13
1949	30	63
1950	57	64
1951	15	29
1952	13	18
1953	20	24
1954	9	24
1955	3	0
1956	10	16
1957	1	0
1958	35	11
1959	27	37
1960	0	0
1962	4	14
1963	20	11
1964	5	1
1965	19	7
1966	31	11
1967	80	25
1968	1	1
1969	20	6
1970	17	7

Seabury passed away that fall on October 19, and doubtless, his failing health kept them from returning for the fall fishing. Jean lived on until 1976, but since the camp was sold to Charlie Valentine during early 1972, it seems clear that she never returned to the camp without Seabury. I didn't research it, but I would guess that Seabury's health was deteriorating and that is why he hardly fished that spring. They probably had the sale of the camp in the works or maybe even finalized before Seabury's death in October. In any case, it was quite a chapter in Cains River salmon-fishing history. It is remarkable for its 33-year length, the passion that both Stantons clearly had for the place and the fishing, the fact that it almost all took place back in the Miramichi's glory years. The Stantons were very wealthy, even aristocratic people of their day, yet were capable of being happily immersed in the simple, backwoods culture of the Cains River. They clearly loved it enough to invest a month and a half to two months each year at the camp. On top of this, Jean Kellog Stanton's clear pen and detailed notations preserved the flavor of their times on the river better than any set of camp records that I have seen. I certainly feel very lucky to have been able to pore through all the pages.

Another interesting legacy of the Camp Stanton logbooks is the record of its catches. It is clear by looking at the catches every year that there were a lot more fish around in the 1940s, 1950s, and 1960s than there are today. They had their good and bad years, but in the good years, Seabury himself regularly had five-, six-, or seven-salmon days. You have to legally stop at four now—even though they are all released—but the days in recent years when you could exceed that if you wanted to are few and far between on any pool on the river. The decline in the numbers of fish isn't really news to most of us anymore, but what is additionally clearly defined in the logs is the changing ratio of grilse and salmon. I'm not sure exactly what it means regarding the health of the salmon stocks—if anything—but it is nonetheless very interesting. Have a look at the table and graph on this page.

Only theories exist to explain these statistics, but it seems logical that the salmon population in the earlier years was much closer to the river's natural run. During the last few seasons, grilse numbers are much lower relative to salmon than at any time since the 1960s. Are we for some reason looking at a return to the original relationship?

The author plays a very active Cains River grilse in the Wood's Pool during hight water in the last week of September 2019. Consistently high water brought the run upriver a little early that fall. PHOTO COURTESY OF DENNY DENHAM.

CHAPTER 8

Cains River Brook Trout

All sections of the Cains River provide excellent brook trout habitat. There are stretches with good bottom for spawning in many places, not only in the main stem of the Cains itself but also in the many streams that feed it. Keith Wilson talks about walking through stretches of the river near his Wildcat camp that have small gravel and sandy riverbeds. In places, he said that one can see the spring water puffing up through the bottom sediments and watch the brook trout spawning.

The Cains has a great forage base for the brookies, with many species of aquatic and terrestrial insects, fish eggs, and various prey species of small fish. During cooler weather, the Cains River has numerous brook trout living in every mile of it from the huge network of small brooks and beaver ponds that make up the headwaters to the mouth of the river at Black Brook. The Achilles heel of almost the entire Miramichi River system, though, is that it can get much warmer in summer than brook trout can tolerate, and they must have a source of cool water to pass this period. In river systems that contain large ponds or lakes, the fish can retreat into these places that also offer the safety of depth. In the Cains, these thermal refugees are created by springs and brooks, but pools must also be deep enough to provide protection from various birds of prey. The headwaters area above the Grand Lake Road, including the stretch known as the Cains River Daily Crown Reserve Sector, has the river's greatest concentration of habitat that meets all the requirements for large brook trout to survive the summer season.

SEA-RUN BROOKIES

The large brook trout that the Cains River is really famous for are sea-run brook trout. These are brook trout that, according to many biologists, just occur randomly in the population with some choosing after spawning in October to drop down the river to tidewater, while their brethren remain within the freshwater stretches of the river and its feeder streams. While most of the Cains River brook trout live their lives moving between the main stems of the rivers and the many cool, shade-providing streams that flow into it, a certain percentage of the fish drop down into the main stem of the Miramichi and from there on down to the estuary and finally into Miramichi Bay.

Brookies like this 18-inch male are caught in many locations within the upper stretches of the Cains River during the fall salmon-fishing season. This one was caught and released by the author at his Mahoney Brook camp a mile or so above Six Mile Brook on the Cains River in the fall of 2018. The brookie took a three-inch, #2 October Killer streamer fly that was being fished for salmon.

The MSA's Mark Hambrook theorizes that the downstream migration may in part be a function of growing larger. As the trout grow, they drop down the river looking for larger pools and impoundments, and eventually, they end up in the estuary.

The Bay and the estuary provide large quantities of nutritious feed for the brook trout, which, by reputation, are very versatile feeders. I found a study of winter sea-run brook trout feeding habits done in 2014 by a collaboration of Nova Scotia Universities. This was done in Antigonish Harbor, Nova Scotia, which is about 80 miles south of Miramichi Bay, but it is also on Northumberland Strait. The available feed would be very much the same at the two locations. The prey was divided between saltwater and freshwater habitat as the fish ranged between the two as they do in the Miramichi system. The brook trout ate just about everything small enough to go down their gullets, including many things I would never have thought of, like spiders and honeybees. In the marine environment, the most common prey by far, though, were small fish. Eels, killfish (mummichogs), smelt, Atlantic spearing, sand shrimp, fish eggs, and marine worms were all found commonly in the stomachs of the brook trout. In the freshwater areas, several various aquatic and terrestrial insects were found. The food eaten was also quite dependent on the season. For example, a number of species of fish eggs were found in the springtime. All in all, it amounted to a very diverse forage base.

Tabusintac Club guide and manager Donny Robertson holds a five-pound-plus sea-run brookie caught and released by the author on a Green Machine fly in August 2014. Brook trout from the Tabusintac and Miramichi River systems have been recorded large enough to be of near world record status. A few minutes before this moment, I caught a mid-teen-sized salmon that was laying in the same small but deep, cold pool.

Historically, the "sea-run" strategy has been used by brook trout in streams connected to the ocean from New Jersey to Labrador. Populations of sea-run brook trout that exist in good numbers, and that attain large sizes, are essentially nonexistent today south of the Canadian border. The farther north you go, the more prolific they become. I've found them in great abundance in northern Labrador and in rivers running into Ungava Bay. Sea-run brookies don't grow any larger, however, than those found along the Northumberland shore of New Brunswick. All the rivers that make up the Miramichi area system—including not only the Cains but the Southwest Miramichi, Renous, Northwest Miramichi, and all its tributaries plus the Bartibog and Tabusintac, and the several rivers on the south side of Miramichi Bay—all host sea-run brookies that can potentially reach great sizes.

Keith Wilson told me that his finest big trout moment on the Cains came when on back-to-back casts he personally landed two 24-inch brook trout from a pool near Wildcat Brook. According to one chart that I looked at, Keith's fish would have weighed five pounds, five ounces—darn near six pounds—each. That is the kind of fish people have historically flown to Labrador to try and catch. Barrie Duffield, who guided brook trout trips on the Cains for years, says that the largest one that he ever actually landed measured 27 inches. Such a fish would have weighed more than seven pounds. Numerous examples such as this exist. One day, Barrie was telling a Cains River warden that he knew about his 27-inch fish, and the warden said, "Well, Barrie, I got you beat there." The warden said that he had released one that was 30 inches long a short time before Barry caught his. A documented brook trout of 14.5 pounds from the Nipigon River in Ontario, taken in 1915, was 31.5 inches long, so the warden's fish would certainly have weighed upward of 10 pounds, perhaps 12, depending on condition, a tremendous brook trout for anywhere at any time. Darrell Warren, who guides a lot of spring kelt fishing on the Miramichi, tells me that he knows that brook trout in the vicinity of 10 pounds were historically taken in the Gaspereau nets near the mouth of the river. Perhaps most remarkable about these catches is that they were not necessarily from 50 years ago. Wilson's, Duffield's, and the warden's big fishes were all caught and released during the early 2000s.

Not all the fishing for sea-run trout is while they are summering in the headwaters. As soon as the ice goes out in April, fishing begins for salmon kelts. A great deal of this fishing is done in the lower stretches of the Miramichi River called the Rapids located a few miles either way from the head of the tide. Clearly, the sea-run brook trout regard this as part of their winter feeding grounds because it is not at all unusual for anglers fishing for kelts with large streamer flies on heavy, sink-tip fly lines, to catch the occasional large brook trout in

Guide Karl Wilson is fishing the Crown reserve section of the Cains River in front of Wildcat Camp. In the first photo, Karl has a small brookie on the line. Wildcat Camp is visible in the background. At times, this pristine habitat has offered world-class fishing for brook trout of six pounds or more.

this part of the river. I've spent hundreds of hours kelt fishing myself a dozen or more miles up the river from the Rapids where brookies are also commonly taken, and though not all that far from the Rapids, during that early spring fishing, I have never caught or seen caught any larger than the occasional eight- to 15-inch brook trout that we believe to be resident trout and not sea-runs.

Once the heavy spring freshet is over in the middle of May, the river starts to drop down toward more summer-like heights, and the pools begin to take on definition. At that time the sea-run trout begin to migrate up the river heading for their summer grounds. Sea-run brookies are taken in many of the pools along the lower Cains River and especially near the mouths of the major brooks such as Black Brook, Otter Brook, Salmon Brook, Sabbies River, Muzzeroll, Six Mile, and Mahoney Brook, just to name a few. This run usually continues from the last week in May until the second week in June, and an angler fishing early in the morning or late in the evening during that time stands a pretty good chance of intercepting a large sea-run brookie at almost any brook mouth along the Cains River. As this upriver sea-run trout migration reaches farther up into the Cains, the velocity with which the fish pass by seems to slow down. It is not unusual at some of the fall salmon pools located in the lower 25 miles of the Cains to have decent sea-run trout fishing for a period of up to a week or more sometime between the last week in May and the first two in June. The exact timing, though, can be very hard to pin down, and some years, the trout seem simply to run by without stopping.

Early-season salmon anglers also catch the large sea-run brookies from time to time on the big, early-season Atlantic salmon wet flies. I have caught these fish myself down in Campbell's Pool in Blackville while fishing for early-run salmon in late May and early June. The fish look pretty much like any other brook trout, except that when you catch them on their way up the river, they have very glossy, almost silvery sides, and the color of their spots is somewhat subdued. Also, except in the case of the really large ones, they tend to be longer for their girth than still-water resident brook trout would be—assumedly from their life of swimming against the tides in the estuary. The large brookies also seem especially fond of Green Machines. Many consider it the very best brook trout wet fly. I have always thought that in the water the Green Machine has a very buggy, nymph-like appearance.

During much of the June Miramichi bright salmon fishery, it is not at all unusual to catch brook trout. These are largely

Kevin Sabean's Chestnut canoe beached at the point in front of the author's Mahoney Brook Camp. Kevin is an expert canoe man and "sails" the Cains every year in late May or early June for a crack at sea-run brookies. The canoe is fully loaded for camping. Note the pole and traditional stern anchor pulley. PHOTO COURTESY OF KEVIN SABEAN.

six- to 14-inch resident trout that are thought to summer in the brooks around the area we are fishing. Almost always by the last week in June, the lower stretches of the Southwest Miramichi are too warm to function as brook trout habitat. Insect hatches are nearly constant during early June, and one can frequently see small trout rising in the shallows along the shorelines. Every now and then a larger trout is caught, but the silvery, sea-run fish are very seldom encountered once the run of the headwaters fish described in the last paragraph has passed up the river. According to Mark Hambrook, this is also true of the other Miramichi branches and tributaries. The headwaters are the areas that have a large, dependable, and sufficiently deep inventory of cold-water holding pools to house the sea-run brookies during the warm period.

But not all of the large trout summer all the way up in the headwaters. Some cold-water sources throughout the Cains River have brook trout in residence all summer long. During the fall salmon migration, we see and catch a few more of these large brookies lower down in the river. A fair number of 10- to 16-inch brookies, and even occasionally a substantially larger one, are taken while salmon fishing some of the same pools—in fact, the same lies—that we fish for Atlantic salmon. At times, the action can be quite good, even though—since we are fishing for aggressive fall salmon—we often use flies that are probably larger than ideal for the trout.

While most of the large brook trout in the Cains River are sea-runs, it is not necessarily 100 percent so. Ernest Long of Wilson's said that in the 1950s and 1960s, it was not unusual early in the springtime, before the sea-runs had made it back upriver, to catch three- and four-pound brook trout in the Cains River headwaters. He said that not only by the time of year but by the coloration it was clear that these fish had never been to sea. With the clearing of the forest and increased fishing pressure of modern times, there are less of these fish, but occasionally, a really large resident trout is still taken.

Keith Wilson with good sea-run brookie taken on a dry fly from a Crown reserve section pool. You can see that Keith's hat is full of bombers. Generations of the Wilson family have guided and outfitted on the Cains River headwaters. PHOTO COURTESY OF KEITH WILSON.

BROOK TROUT FISHING ON THE CAINS RIVER

Because of the relatively shallow and fast-flowing nature of its upper reaches, the Cains River provides fishermen with some classic brook trout fly water. The Cains, especially in the stretches above the Grand Lake Road, is a succession of relatively deep pools that tail into aerating rapids. The dark, waters of the Cains are fed by many brooks and springs with a moderate year-round temperature. While many brookies are taken with streamers and wet flies, many more, including some of the largest, are taken on dry flies. There are some prolific insect hatches during the summer months, but as is the way with brook trout, there is usually no need to match the hatch exactly. The brookies respond very well to attractor-type flies such as the Royal Wulff, Rat Faced McDougal, or even the bombers commonly used for salmon. It can be helpful, though, to offer patterns that somewhat resemble the size and coloration of the current hatch.

Barrie Duffield, who guided in the headwaters for years, said that the large, sea-run brookies really love big and bushy dry flies. Barrie has developed several flies such as his Burdock, based loosely on the salmon bomber, but with the long, thin tail of a mayfly, that he and his sports caught many of their largest brookies on. While salmon are famous for liking large bombers, brook trout, by Barrie's experience, often want them even larger. I guess that shouldn't be a big surprise. I remember from my days of Labrador brook trout fishing that we caught many of them on huge, shaggy-headed, Muddler Minnows that we thought imitated swimming lemmings. That the big brookies would eat lemmings we knew for sure since on one Labrador trip we trapped some in a plastic bucket that we had baited and planted at ground level. We took those onto a fast-running narrows on Crook's Lake and tossed them into the flow. They never got far before a big brook trout emerged from a dark hole among the boulders and ate them. The Miramichi system is host to some very large insects too. Foremost in my mind are a species of giant dark stonefly or salmonfly that we see a lot of in late June and early July. These stoneflies can be nearly three inches long.

Summer brook trout fishing in most places that I have done it, including the ponds of Maine and lakes of Labrador, is mostly a morning and evening sport. On cloudy or rainy

Barrie Duffield's "Burdock" dry fly does look like those prickly, dried things that embed themselves in any article of soft clothing that brushes up against them. This fly won't win any beauty contests, but it has caught a great many large Cains River brookies for Barrie and the sports that he guided. I think of it as a bomber variant. The fly is highly floatable, has the wings of a mayfly, and a long tail that could suggest either a mayfly or even one of the large stoneflies that the Cains and Miramichi have lots of.

days, the fish can be taken readily during the day, but generally speaking, aquatic insect life is more active in the low light of morning and evening, and that is true of the upper Cains. The brook trout tend not to range too far from their cold-water refuges and will often start to feed on the very edge of dusk. While brook trout may lack the horsepower of Atlantic salmon, the large ones especially are excellent fighters, and contacting one on light equipment in such a beautiful place as the upper Cains River is as good an experience as fly fishing offers.

The Wilsons do a lot of guiding on the upper Cains River, and Karl's equipment is very much the same as one would see on any northern Maine trout lake. A four or five-weight, nine-foot rod, with a floating line and a nine-foot, six-pound test leader is pretty much standard issue. A sink tip is normally unnecessary, since, by the time the sea-runs make it up to the headwaters area beginning at the end of May, the water is typically low enough, and warmed up enough, so that a full floating line will do the job. It could be, though, that in higher-than-normal early- or late-season water a sink tip for fishing streamers would be helpful. Weighted flies of all types are illegal to use on the Cains River—for trout or salmon—so a sink tip would be the only way to provide a little extra depth to work a deep, cold pool.

Just how nicely sea-run brook trout fishing can dovetail with salmon fishing on the Miramichi system is well-illustrated by this episode related to me by Kris LeBlanc of Moncton. Kris began the morning of July 7, 2011, by wading into the Buttermilk Pool on the Cains. There were a good number of salmon already in the Cains that year despite the early date, and Kris could see salmon rising here there around the pool. In spite of their relative freshness to the river, they weren't easy to catch, but eventually, one grabbed a #8 black-bear green butt that Kris had tied just the night before. Happy with his salmon, Kris also had a permit that day for the Crown reserve water and decided to try his luck up in the headwaters. This meant driving back down the south side of the Cains to Blackville, driving west on Route 8 to near Boiestown, and then heading into the backcountry to reach his favorite stretch of the river.

As he passed through town, Kris decided to fish a private salmon pool owned by a friend, and on the first pass through, he succeeded in adding two grilse to his total for the day. It was now early afternoon, and he had already released three salmon, just one short of a limit. By any standards, the day was already complete. Variety, though, is the spice of life, and it was a good fishing day featuring a solid cloud cover.

Late in the afternoon, Kris started working his way through an unnamed pool near Wildcat Brook. He was using a standard-issue attractor dry fly on the end of a 14-foot leader that ended in a five-pound-test tippet. A few hundred feet farther downriver Kris saw a big trout rise to take an insect off the surface. A few minutes later, the big sea-run brookie surfaced again in essentially the same spot. After seeing this trout rise twice more in 10 minutes, Kris had now worked into casting range, but after covering the area of the last rise several times, he failed to receive a look.

Kris decided to rest the fish for a few minutes. The evening was getting late, and there was no real hatch underway. Things had become very quiet, and in keeping with the mood of the evening, he switched to a #14 Black Nat, which barely dimpled the surface as it landed gently at the end of the long leader. The big brookie instantly took the fly. This brook trout was 23.5 inches and probably weighed in the vicinity of five pounds.

Kris LeBlanc of Moncton with a monster Cains River brookie from the Crown reserve section of the Cains River that took a #14 Black Gnat fished dry. PHOTO COURTESY OF KRIS LEBLANC.

EVOLUTION OF THE CAINS RIVER BROOK TROUT FISHERY

As we discussed in the chapter on early outfitters, the original Cains River leases covered the entire river and all branches. This continued on until Harry Allen's death in 1932, and the river was split into several leases that weren't always easy to sell. Beginning in the early 1950s, the government offered just one angling lease on the Cains River, and that was for a single 14-mile section in the upper part of the river officially described as follows: Cains River, not including the branches, from the ford approximately a half mile above Hopewell Lodge, to, but not including, the pool at the mouth of Lower Otter Brook. This section became the Cains River Daily Crown Reserve sector. The rest of the Cains River just became Crown open water available to the public for fishing. For many years, Wilsons held this lease and outfitted for the summer brook trout fishery that they based around their camp at Wildcat. This is the lease that Keith Wilson said they gave up in 1987 due to the poor fishing, making it unviable for the outfitting business. Nonresidents of the province such as myself cannot fish in this Crown reserve section during the special catch-and-release trout season, which runs from June 1 to September 15, though it can be fished earlier and later than those dates.

Here's how Keith Wilson, the current generation clan chieftain of the Wilson clan, sums up the progression of the sea-run brook trout fishery during his lifetime: "My earlier recollection as a kid was watching Dad and his friends catch numerous large trout (16 to 22 inches) on flies while us kids could easily catch a mess of trout (eight to 12 inches) for supper with worm and hook. As the forest roads opened up on both sides of the Cains through the 1970s, there was an immediate increase in anglers doing the annual spring run on the entire river retaining hundreds of trout by bait or fly. And, of course, our success diminished until in 1987 we gave up the lease. At this time, DNR scheduled (fly fishing only) the entire river and turned the old angling lease into the Cains River Daily Crown Reserve sector and began stocking. We saw an immediate improvement in angling and a greater number of large trout." Keith also said that in his 50 years of fishing the Cains,

The Daily Crown Reserve sections of the Cains River headwaters are accessible by old lumbering roads that honeycomb the area. The province has set up signs such as these that point the way to the many fine brook trout and salmon pools.

The author didn't catch any 20-inch brookies on his morning at the Hopewell Pool with guide Karl Wilson, but I did catch several smaller resident fish like this pretty specimen.

the very best trout fishing that he has seen came between the years of 2005 and 2010, only a very short while ago. During those years, it was not unusual for an evening session under decent conditions in the Crown Reserve Section to produce a half-dozen brookies in the high teen to low 20-inch range.

CURRENT STATE OF THE FISHERY

According to all sources, the fishing in 2018 was down, and this marked the latest in a five- or six-year decline from what had been very good trout fishing with a relative abundance of large, sea-run brookies. The brookies face considerable obstacles from several sources. First, there is fairly energetic fishery all through the lower stretches of the Miramichi that allows five brook trout per day to be retained with two of these allowed to be larger than 30 centimeters, or 12 inches. The fish are believed to go back down the estuary after spawning and feed under the ice in the estuary and out in Miramichi Bay. We know they are there because some are caught annually in the winter smelt fishery.

The brook trout also have the same enemy that the Atlantic salmon smolts do, and that is an outsized population of striped bass. Striped bass are a historic spawning species in the Miramichi system. For a variety of possible reasons, the population had become very low, and the government put a complete moratorium in place on catching them—or even attempting to catch them. There is no ocean net fishery for the coast-hugging bass; most of their original ocean feeding competitors such as cod have been severely depleted, and so the open niche combined with the highly protective regulation gave the bass a terrific break. The result has been an explosion from what was believed to be a few thousand adult fish to current estimates in the vicinity of one million individuals. The bass gather to spawn near and in the mouth of the Northwest branch of the Miramichi in late May and take a terrible toll on every other fish that tries to utilize that section of the river during that period. Smelts, gaspereau, shad, sea-run brook trout, and Atlantic salmon numbers are all severely depleted, and most fingers are being pointed at the out-of-proportion striped bass population.

CHAPTER 9

The Modern Cains River Sport Fishery

The Atlantic salmon population of the Miramichi River and tributaries, and for that matter in almost all the salmon producing rivers of North America, has declined materially since the 1970s, and more so since the early 2000s. There has been plenty written about it by many people, but there is no single explanation that even the majority of people close to the issue can agree on. Regardless, the populations almost everywhere have declined. There have still been some very good catches made, including during the last few years, but good action is much harder to anticipate.

There is also no question that our average summer temperatures are warmer than they were. This is especially tough in the Miramichi fishery because it has always struggled with high summer temperatures that can cause the fishing to grind to a halt. It has become persistent enough in recent years to make July and early August fishing dates quite undependable.

This great henfish was caught in the Shinnickburn area by Marc Cabot on the last day, in the next-to-last hour, of the 2018 season. Marc has been fishing the Miramichi and Cains Rivers since the 1960s. The fish was only out of the water a second and was never weighed, but certainly it was well over 30 pounds. This goes to show that the Cains still has some salmon as large as ever. Note also the extremely dark color of this fish. Due to its tannic waters, the salmon that run up the Cains take on a really dark camouflage coloring. PHOTO COURTESY OF CLARENCE CURTIS.

In addition to the smaller number of returning salmon, the outfitters must face other issues too. Alex Mills, a New Brunswick lawyer who had a lot to do with getting commercial fishing for Atlantic salmon banned in the Miramichi, and the onetime proprietor of Old River Lodge in Blissfield, once wrote that the rise of Caribbean bonefishing had greatly hurt the Atlantic salmon outfitting industry. That is probably true also. People can only afford a certain amount for travel fishing vacations. The gentle warmth of the Caribbean probably has more appeal for modern generations of anglers than does the raw weather of New Brunswick. However, the reality is that the Atlantic salmon outfitting business along the Miramichi has declined along with the runs of fish.

That isn't to say that Atlantic salmon outfitting along the Miramichi is dead. That is certainly not true, and outfitters with a modern, adaptive approach like Country Haven, Upper Oxbow Outfitters, The Ledges, and Wilson's, just to name a few, are doing just fine. Atlantic salmon angling definitely has a very devoted following, and there are new anglers discovering the king of game fish all of the time. For many fishermen, when Atlantic salmon are there to be angled, whether you are catching two a day or two a week, there is no other quarry nearly as rewarding as Atlantic salmon. There are also none that live in more appealing surroundings than the Miramichi or Cains River Valleys. There would never be enough autumn days in a long lifetime to wade along the shores of the Cains, casting for salmon, as many times as I would like to do it. The Miramichi and Cains Rivers have always been well-known for their autumn, or as they say in Scotland, "back end" run. Autumn is still the single most dependable combination of suitable weather and fish availability, and it can still be difficult to book dates on the Miramichi at the lodge of your choice in September and October.

The successful outfitters, though, must offer better solutions than were available in years past. Access to a cold-water buffered pool is critical to summer fishing, as is the ability to catch fish in both low- and high-water conditions. Also, as the lodges in Scotland have needed to adapt to, less of the business is going to come from the same group booking the

Autumn is the best time on the Cains River, and nothing is more iconic there than a male salmon "Cains River cockfish" dressed in its spawning colors. You hear fishermen talk about them every day during the fall. The author made this weathervane for his Mahoney Brook camp that reflects the passion that anglers feel for these great salmon.

whole lodge for the same week every summer until they are all too old go anymore. Today, with the Miramichi only 11 hours of easy driving by car from New York City, and eight from Boston, people are using the internet to monitor the latest in weather conditions and making last-minute commitments to break away for a few days if things look good.

Another adaption is the increase in angling clubs and personally owned properties. There can never be an increase in the total number of privately-owned pools since they all stem from the Crown grants made over 150 years ago, but the number of the pools that are actively fished and maintained seems to have increased. These approaches both make a lot of sense, depending on one's preferences and pocketbook, and with over a million people living in New Brunswick alone, there is no shortage of people to buy the few pieces of private water that come up occasionally for sale. The Miramichi and Cains River fisheries live on, but they are changing, and so is our approach to fishing them.

This chapter is about salmon fishing on the Cains River as it exists today. We're going to talk about the timing and logistics of the run and about some of the tactics that I have found to work for catching Atlantic salmon on the Cains River.

The season begins with spring fishing, which is fishing for kelts—the salmon that spawned the fall before and have been existing under the ice in the relative safety of fresh water. There are a few hungry otters in the river during the winter, but there are no seals and sharks to prey upon the spent spawners, and no commercial fishing draggers either. The salmon don't know that, but over the eons, Atlantic salmon evolved to choose between returning to the sea after spawning or taking their chances in the river. It is still not something that is totally understood, but some studies I have read believe that

This 55-inch kelt from the Northwest is just about as large as Miramichi salmon get. Because they are actively feeding, unusually large fish such as this are more often caught as kelts than as bright fish. PHOTO COURTESY OF COUNTRY HAVEN FISHING LODGE.

the salmon instinctively decide whether their chances are better at sea where there is food but predators, or remaining in the river where it is safe but with no food until spring. It is widely believed that most remain in the river, though the spring fishery generally includes very few large male salmon. Did these cockfish die after spawning, or did they instinctively realize that their aggressive spawning activities had so drained them that they had to have nourishment or perish? We don't know at this time, but we do know that many of the female salmon and the grilse—grilse are largely males—remain in the river for the winter.

In the outfitter W. Harry Allen's time, the salmon runs were much larger, and river conditions were different. Some number of kelts apparently hung on in pools from the present Grand Lake/Doaktown Road Bridge all the way to the mouth of the river well into May. You can see from the relatively light clothes and snowless ground in the photographs that I found of Harry Allen's trips that temperatures were much milder than the frigid weather we often endure during April fishing. Also, the fishermen are shown wading and fishing from the banks. In most modern kelt fishing, the water is up into the alders and wading is impossible. It may very well be that most of the kelts had already left the river in mid- to late May—when Allen's sports fished for kelts as if they were bright salmon—but the remaining numbers were apparently still enough to provide good fishing.

We find today that even in April, very few kelts are present in the Cains much above the bottom six or seven miles of the river. The early-season kelts don't hold in the fast water runs, but instead, they prefer the slower-moving stretches that would not interest bright fish. The lower portions of the Cains do not offer a lot of those areas during spring runoff, but there are some. Much of the fishing is done in pockets or eddies along the shorelines where the fish can get out of the heavy current, even if only in a small area. These places are also not normally very deep. It is unusual to catch a kelt in more than six feet or so of water. In summer, I see the areas all along the rivers where we caught spring salmon months before. By July, most of these areas are uncovered beach.

Jason Curtis has run a Sharpe canoe since the early 1990s and an outboard-powered Chestnut Ogilvy before that. He has fished the Cains during the spring kelt fishery for more than 30 years. In his view, the kelt fishing in the Cains normally holds up pretty well through April, but when the water starts to drop in early May, the amount of fish available declines quite quickly. During the 2017 season, we had some nice weather in early May and motored up to our Mahoney Brook camp to try a little trout fishing. To our surprise, we got a grilse kelt and lost another in the relatively quick and shallow water at the tail of the home pool in front of the camp. We ran into Keith Wilson, who was staying with friends at a camp farther down the river. In addition to some nice trout, they

Jason Curtis holds up an April kelt from the lower Cains. The fish is in good condition. Note the snow still in the woods. The air temperature was about 40°F.

had also caught a couple of kelts in the Shinnickburn area. We were pleasantly surprised because we had fished this far up the river before during spring fishing but had never caught anything but brook trout.

A few days after that outing, Jason told me that the water in the Cains had gotten low enough so that it was almost impossible to take even a jet canoe up through the shallows around the island at the Admiral Pool camp. This means that no other type of craft could make it at all.

To fish the Cains that late in the spring, you would need to do it by a downriver canoe trip as Harry Allen had organized 100 years ago. One could speculate as to how much fishermen have softened over the last century, but I think today it would be tough to find clients to take a weeklong mid-May camping trip down the Cains River to fish for kelts. Does this mean that there are a decent number of kelts still up in the Cains and that we could catch them if we put the effort in to fish for them as was done 100 years ago? It is an interesting question, and my intuitive response is to say no, it doesn't make sense considering what we know about the current status of the runs, but there may well be a few here and there as we found at Mahoney Brook last spring.

Almost as soon as the spring fishery is over, the Rocky Brook salmon start making their way up the Miramichi River. It seems as if all the Canadian Rivers have their own stock of these early

The Cains frequently gets too low for any motorized canoe to run without hitting rocks or scraping over gravel bars. In lower water, a canoe such as this 70-year-old, 20-foot Chestnut that the author restored, pushed by a pole, is still the best way to get around.

fish. Retired Rocky Brook Camp manager Manley Price told me that by the end of May they always had fish in their pools. Maine's Penobscot River sent the president of the United States the first bright salmon every year in mid-April. Every year, the Matapedia River in Quebec registers at least a few silver monsters—often the first fish are very large—during late April and May. The Miramichi is actually a somewhat later-running river than the more northerly Gaspe Rivers as tag returns from fish caught many years ago during May in the commercial net fishery off Miramichi gully proved. Fish tagged at approximately the same time, and in the same area just outside the mouth of the Miramichi, were returned from several of the Gaspe Rivers only a short while later, but it was normally well into June before the first of these fish were angled from the Miramichi River.

Early-season success is quite variable, but there are years when May fishing for bright fish can pay off. Some of those years were 2010, 2011, and 2012. Jason Curtis caught a salmon at Black Brook in late May of 2010, I caught one at our Keenan Pool on Memorial Day weekend during 2011, and Jason caught another one at the Campbell's Pool during late May in 2012. Other salmon anglers posted fish on the internet that they caught in May during those years too. There was a lot of fish in our pools that weekend in 2011, and we touched and rolled a number of salmon before hooking up. We also saw several free-jumping salmon making their way up the river.

What caused this May surprise? We'll never know for sure, but we do know that 2011 was also the best run of the last 15 years, and 2010 was right behind it, so maybe the early run is at least in part a function of the overall size of the run that year.

Were there any May salmon in the Cains during 2011? No one knows for sure, but I would doubt enough to fish for. I say that because year after year we start trying for early Cains River salmon in the Brophy Pool, which is only 2.6 miles up the Cains. This is one of the locations that fish hold in during the summer period, and the first ones always seem to show up on the lasts day or two of June, a solid two to three weeks after we have made our first contact four miles below in the Miramichi. There is, though, one interesting piece of evidence that suggests that at one time there was at least a small earlier run of salmon in the Cains River. Dorothy Noyes Arms wrote in *Fishing Memories* about the "spring run" fish that they caught while fishing for kelts: "Why some come up at that season, instead of six months earlier, I do not know, but the fact remains that almost every year we catch one or two silver-bright from the sea, and one year there were many. There is no mistaking them, for, both in color and girth, they are absolutely distinctive, and even their battle up against the bitter current beneath the ice has not affected their looks or their strength." By six months earlier, she clearly means during the fall run, which she, therefore, understood contained the spawning fish that became the kelts that were also now in the river. Assuming that she never went on a float trip for kelts any later than the third week in May—and that is really, really stretching it—catching a few bright fish every year and *many* another year is absolutely unheard of by today's experiences. Then again, if the 1920s salmon run was 25 times as large as it is today—which, by biologist Bill Hooper's estimates, it may well have been—then these few early-run fish may have been enough to have a real presence.

It is also true that from about May 10 until June 10 along the Miramichi and Cains Rivers, there is very little fishing done that is likely to result in catching a bright salmon. Beginning in late May, and running until the salmon arrive, a few people do fish for sea-run trout, but most of that fishing is done along the shorelines with relatively small flies, and taking a salmon is somewhat unlikely. You almost never hear of anyone catching a bright salmon until close to the end of this period, and

Rodney Colford, son of Hall of Fame guide Gary Colford, is the umpteenth generation of his family to be a top-notch guide and salmon fisherman. This magnificent very early June salmon was caught by Rodney in the mouth of the Cains River. The kype is already evident. This fish would be a rebuilt kelt that had spent the previous winter feeding in the ocean. PHOTO COURTESY OF RODNEY COLFORD.

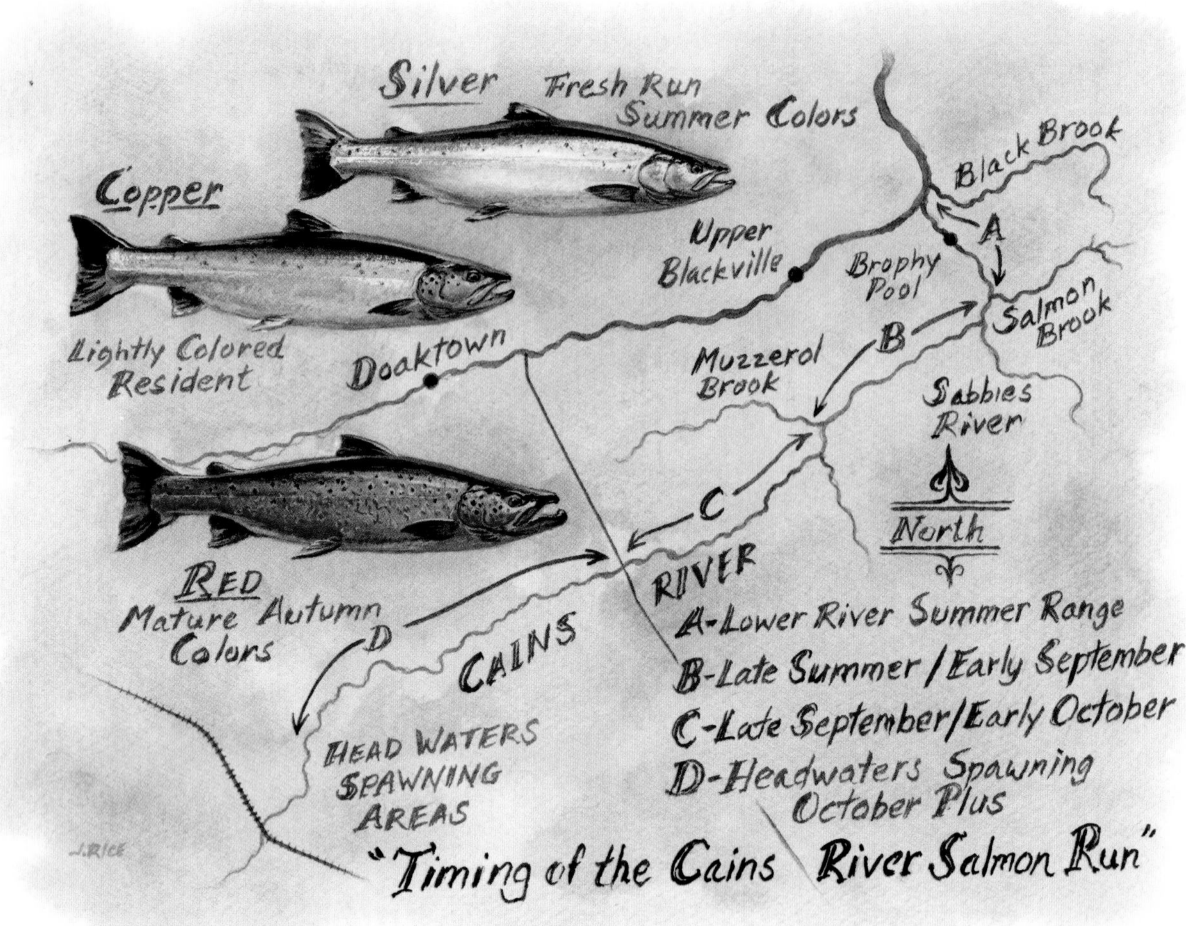

Bright salmon begin entering the Miramichi in early June. As soon as they enter the river, some of these salmon will swim quite rapidly all the way to the headwaters where they will eventually spawn, and others hold at various locations along the river moving up from time to time with raises of water, but the run normally spreads out fairly well all along the river. The Cains is quite different. Similar to some of the Northumberland Shore rivers, the run in the Cains stays in the estuary or lowest section of the river during the summer, and then, beginning in the early fall, it spreads out into the upper reaches of the river. Areas that offer quite good fishing in early October are usually totally barren in August.

that is further evidence that neither the Miramichi nor the Cains are early-run rivers.

Salmon running the river take on the camouflage colors of the riverbed, gradually losing their silver sheen—but it doesn't happen all at once. We catch darkly colored salmon in the fall many miles up the Cains River that are still carrying sea lice. Even though the Miramichi estuary is salt enough for the sea lice to live, it is also fresh enough to encourage the fish to adopt their riverine color scheme.

While there are definitely fish entering the Miramichi all through June, statistically, the first big push of salmon and grilse makes its way into the Miramichi during the second week in July. Some of those fish are destined for the Cains River. Given reasonable conditions, by the second week in July, all the Cains pools from the mouth up through Salmon Brook, some seven miles or so upriver, start to hold salmon. Conditions mean a great deal. If there is very low, warm water all summer as there was in 2017, most Cains fish won't enter the river but will instead hold back in the estuary. Of those that do enter, most will stay in the low-water pools of the main river, especially Black Brook, presumably because it is the last stop before jumping into the main stem of the Cains.

It is well-documented by tag returns that the great majority of the fall run destined for the Miramichi and its tributaries is in the estuary by late July or August. Whatever the exact time, the biologists tell us that the fish running the river as late as the end of October are not just coming in straight out of the ocean. Many of them still hold sea lice, but they have been biding their time in the estuary waiting for just the right conditions. Tag returns showed that a nice, mid-teen-sized cockfish that I caught up at Mahoney Brook, 20 miles up the Cains, on October 15 of the 2016 season, sat somewhere between the Millerton trap net—a net set on poles in the estuary used to capture salmon for tagging—and where I finally caught it, for three months. We know this because Joe Sheasgren of the Department of Fisheries and Oceans reported that the tag number I took from that salmon, YY39947, was tagged in the Millerton trap as an 81.4-centimeter wild salmon on July 4, 2016. We know that these fish can cover that whole distance in a day or two. We know that because we have caught sea-liced fish at Mahoney Brook Pool, and the lice live only three days in freshwater. Still, this salmon took three months to move up this distance, obviously programmed by Mother Nature to bide his time in the lower river rather than place himself in the thin waters of the upper Cains during the warm, low-water conditions of summer or early autumn.

There are two variables that must be considered when discussing the quality of summer fishing on the Miramichi and Cains Rivers. These are first, the temperature of the water, and second, the amount of water, and during the summer, the two go hand in hand. Some years are warmer than others, but looking back through my records and my memory, I find that there have been no years with both strong water flows and overly hot temperatures. The reality is that deep water is harder to heat up than shallow water. Also, the velocity of the water when the river has more water is faster than when

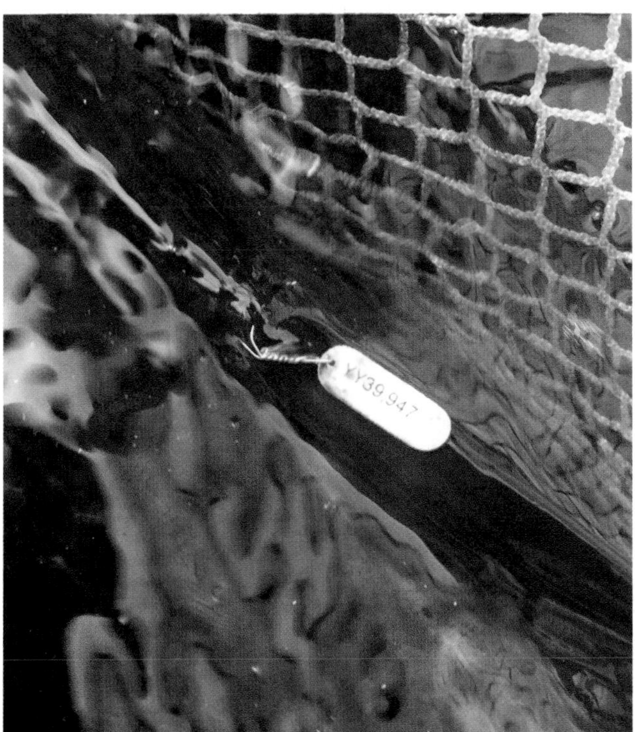

This cock salmon with plainly visible tag number was caught on the last day of the 2016 season 20 miles up the Cains River from Black Brook. The salmon had been tagged at the government fish trap in Millerton on the Fourth of July and had been waiting somewhere in the lower Miramichi or Cains for more than three months before heading up the Cains to spawn.

it is slow. This means that the water in the broad river being heated up by the sun is on its way downstream and out of the river faster, and it is being replaced by water flowing at greater volume from springs and streams. This all keeps the water from heating up as much as it would if the river were flowing slowly and was shallower.

Even on warm days, rain is much cooler than the river water. A great deal of rain, even in summer, starts high in the atmosphere as snow. The act of falling through the air keeps the rain cool, and when it is raining, the sun is not shining, and it is the sun that really heats up our rivers.

Let's look at the Campbell's Pool catch log for the high-water summer of 2008. On July 14, Willy Bacso was fishing alone at Campbell's. The water height was nine-tenths of a meter on the Blackville gauge. It is important to understand how this gauge works. The height given is the height of the water in this exact spot at any given time. When the gauge is working, which is most of the time, it updates constantly. The nine-tenths of a meter measurement doesn't mean that any other particular spot is nine-tenths of a meter, but whatever the depth is at any reasonably nearby spot, it can be related to the Blackville gauge. For instance, there is a rock just off the bank at our Campbell's Pool near where we land our canoes. When the Blackville gauge registers one meter in height, we can glide right over the rock on our way onto the shore. If the water in Blackville is lower than that, we will hit the rock, and at about 0.85 meters, the tip of the rock starts to come out of the water. There are other little nuances to the relationship of height in different sections of the river, but what I've described is a good start to getting some benefit out of the information.

When the water is at nine-tenths in Blackville, it is also a wonderful fishing height four miles upriver at Campbell's Pool. I think of nine-tenths of a meter as a medium water height. It was, however, mid-July, and Willy's note says it was cloudy and hot. The river water was at 70°F and would likely have been much warmer but for the clouds. We had a little rain, and the river started to rise; the next day, it reached a height of one meter. The water temperature then dropped to 68°F.

In early August that same year, the water got up to two meters. Two meters on the Blackville gauge signals high water. It stayed in that area through most of August. Water temperatures ranged from 59°F up to a high of 65°F. The records show that there were a ton of fish in the river and that they took the fly well. The logbook shows several grilse and an 18-pound salmon released by Kal Kotkas and me on August 8 and 9. I remember that very well. We had just spent three days at the Gaspe's Camp Bonaventure—an excellent lodge—where we had good fishing. When we got back to the Miramichi, though, I was just stunned by how many more fish were present than we had seen on the Gaspe. We had seen the occasional salmon roll on the surface of the Bonaventure, and in the clear waters, we could see pods of fish as we drifted

Captain Steve Bellefleur with an August cock salmon that ran back and forth through every inch of the Brophy Pool several times. The fish was caught on a bomber dry fly early on a dark, drizzly day. August can be very good if we get some damp, cool weather.

over the pools. But on the Miramichi, there were many fish rolling and jumping clear as they worked their way along the edges of the river swollen from rain to two meters on the Blackville gauge. That's what a good flow of water will do for the fishing, and that's the Miramichi when times are good.

In the beginning of the book, I talked about the incredible difference in the salmon catches on the Cains—and for that matter, the Miramichi, but more so the Cains—between the seasons of 1967 and 1968. Now, while we are talking about the value of rain to the Miramichi and Cains River salmon fisheries, is the appropriate place to discuss this further. In 1967, the rod catch of Atlantic salmon was as follows:

MAIN SOUTHWEST MIRAMICHI 34,280 BRIGHT SALMON	
Little Southwest Miramichi	3,675
Northwest Miramichi	2,320
Renous/Dungarvon	1,009
Cains River	**6,480**
Total for system	47,764
The Cains River percentage of the total equals 13.6 percent. Note it a good reality check, because this is essentially the same percentage of all Miramichi system salmon habitat that the Cains itself has to offer.	

For 1968, here are the rod catch statistics:

MAIN SOUTHWEST MIRAMICHI 11,356 BRIGHT SALMON	
Little Southwest Miramichi	4,282
Northwest Miramichi	1,168
Renous/Dungarvon	1,942
Cains River	**284**
Total for system	19,032
Cains River percentage of total 1.49 percent	

What are some of the implications of these figures? Assuming biologist Bill Hooper's estimate that the run in 1967 was 500,000 or more fish, the Cains percentage—based on the rod catch—amounts to 65,000 salmon and grilse! That is a stunning total by all standards.

In 1968, the 1.49 percent of 19,000 fish would be 932—estimate of Cains River run based on its share of the total catch! It simply isn't plausible that the run went from 65,000 one year to 932 the next.

To look for an explanation for these widely varying statistics, let's review the historical rain totals from the Provincial Climate Archives. Between July 1 and the end of the 1967 salmon-fishing season on October 15, Fredericton—not far from the headwaters of the Cains—received 312 mm (millimeters) of rain. That is a period of about 15 weeks, and so the average was approximately 21 mm—or just under an inch—per week.

For the same period in 1968, Fredericton received just 127 mm, or about 40 percent as much. What is worse between these two comparisons is that during 1967, in the all-important Cains fall-run period of September 1 to October 15, the Cains received 197 mm or two-thirds of the rain for the entire fishing season. In 1968, though, the rain total for the same fall period was an arid 40 mm, or only about 20 percent as much as the previous year. Only eels could have run up the Cains in the height of water that must have existed! These conditions and the state of the run are verified by a look at Seabury Stanton's records for that fall. The Stantons were moaning about the lack of water and not seeing any fish. Wendell Allen was reassuring them that there were many salmon waiting below Black Brook in the slack water in front of his camps on the Miramichi to come up the Cains. I'm sure that he was right.

Here's what happened next in 1968 right after the season closed. A total of 106 mm of rain, or approximately four inches, fell during the second two weeks of October. Without a doubt, the fish poured up the Cains at that time. Maybe there weren't as many salmon in the Cains during 1968 as in 1967, but clearly, the rod catch of 284 fish is not representative of the river's real stock of fish that spawned later that fall.

By the end of the second week in July, the Miramichi is experiencing the height of its summer run, historically bolstered by a high percentage of grilse. This run is very well known by anglers, and its timing can easily be demonstrated statistically. Fish do start entering the Cains in early to mid-July too, but raises of water are very important. Here are a couple of examples.

On July 21, 2015, a couple of my regular fishing friends, Kal Kotkas and Tim Politis, and I arrived at my camp in Blackville. We had a rainy forecast after what had been a couple of weeks of typical warm, sunny July weather. We hadn't fished in two weeks, but the catch report was very slow. The water height at the beginning of our first day was 0.62 meters on the Blackville gauge—low water—but it was raining and overcast, and the water was only 63°F—a very good temperature for summer on the Miramichi. We managed only one grilse on the Miramichi at Campbell's, but my notes say that we raised five fish and touched three but with no other hookups. Clearly, we had raising water and moving fish that weren't taking well. That continued the next day as the raise finally topped out.

On July 23, conditions settled down, and we went up to the Brophy Pool that morning. The water height in the river had

The author and guide Darrell Warren fighting a large salmon at the Brophy Pool that was caught during a short-notice trip to the Cains after a good August rain. PHOTO COURTESY OF HARVEY WHEELER.

risen to one meter on the Blackville gauge. There was a lot of activity with fish rolling on many of the lies. We landed a 12-pound salmon and three grilse.

In 2016, the warm weather again set in during late July and early August. Our last entry in the book was July 11, and I know we hadn't been up during the last month. On August 12, water hit a low of half a meter—very low water—but a week of rainy weather was forecast. I called Jim Graul, who is often good for leaving on the spur of the moment, and on August 14, we drove up through the rain. The Blackville gauge reported a water height of 1.2 meters the following day. This was a significant raise of water. One of our guides, Darrell Warren, said that he had run into one of the guides from the Black Brook Salmon Club that morning at the Irving in Blackville, and they had absolutely killed them the evening before. All the fish, he said, were caught right at the mouth of the Cains.

We really lucked out and had drizzly, cool, rainy weather from our start on August 15, running right through our last day on August 18. This kept the water between 63 and 65 degrees. The height gradually increased to 1.3 meters. Jim and I put 22 in the net fishing just mornings. Country Haven had the pool in the afternoons, and doubtless, they also did well. They were mostly grilse, but there were salmon of 18 and 17 pounds in our catch. I later heard that folks did quite well up at Buttermilk and Salmon Brook as well. We watched salmon rolling on the surface from all the way down to the corner by Hoopers to as far as we could see up the river toward Herman Campbell's. Clearly, a large percentage of this group of fish had been holding at Black Brook and were just waiting for a good flow of cool water to head into the Cains. We were in the right place at the right time, but it wasn't entirely by luck.

There is an old saying that salmon run up the Miramichi but crawl up the Cains. We will see time after time how that is often true. It may, as much as anything, be a characteristic of small rivers. I remember Wayne Curtis telling me about a summer that he spent guiding for the late Andre Godin over on the Northwest Miramichi. There was a bridge over a pool that they regularly fished. Wayne said that in July a fish arrived in that pool with a peculiar mark on its back that was clearly visible as it lay beneath the bridge. When Wayne was wrapping up his guiding season there in September, the fish was still holding by the same rock. There is no place on the Cains to provide such a view—unless perhaps you crawled out onto a big pine limb hanging out over a pool—and if there is such a limb, the river is normally so dark that you can't see down into it any distance anyway, but I am confident that salmon and grilse regularly take up fairly long-term residence in the pools of the lower sections of the Cains River.

One does not often see fish jumping and rolling as they come up the Cains River unless there is a substantial raise or flow of water in the late fall. Even then, it is still quite uncommon. By comparison, almost every day on the Miramichi finds at least a trickle of fish making their way up through the river. If one has their eyes open for it, you can see a splash here, a fin break through surface here, and a roll beside a rock, all in places that an experienced person knows will be moving as opposed to holding fish. This has long been one of the Miramichi's strong suits compared to most salmon rivers. That is if conditions are at all reasonable, and you are covering some good water, the chances are good that even if there are no takers holding within the arc of your fly, that at some point before too terribly long, a fresh one will come along that may take your fly. On the Cains, it is much more likely that the fish laying in the pool when you get there will be the ones that you

While a good amount of fish enter the Cains River during the summer and early fall, a great many of them don't leave the estuary and taste fresh water until the end of the season draws near. Here, I am pointing to the sea lice on this dark, fall salmon. This fish is freshly in from water salt enough for the lice to live in. They will drop off in about three days from the time that they enter pure fresh water. Notice the large October Killer fly lying on the bottom of the net to the left of the fish. Fresh, late-running fish such as this can be aggressive, and this is attributed both to having recently been saltwater predators and also to becoming territorial as spawning time approaches. They will often attack a large fly that they would have avoided a month earlier.

have to work with. You are not likely to get a constant supply of newly arriving fish that you often have in the Southwest Miramichi. This is something that a smart angler will make allowances for in his/her strategy. The most important of these would be not to overwade the water or do other things—like make a lot of noise and splash around—that would be likely to drive the fish off their close lies. Many of the fish I have caught on the Cains have been lying very close to shore in water no greater than knee-deep. The Cains, though, also offers some advantages that help to make up for this comparative lack of moving fish.

First, the Cains generally runs a degree or two cooler than the Miramichi. In July and August, it can be the difference between 69°F and 71°F, and it can make the difference between taking and ignoring a fly. Second, the Cains, especially the lower Cains from Salmon Brook down, is heavily treed and steep-walled. The river spends a longer part of each day in the shade, and to me, shaded water provides much better salmon fishing than water with bright light shining into it. Third, except under the lowest of water conditions—in which case there just isn't much fishing in the Cains River anyway—the Cains runs a dark tannic color. This dark color seems to make the fish more comfortable and secure on their lies, and thus, they are more ready to act aggressively when a fly swings by them. I guess I can't prove that, but it makes sense, and many things in fishing are hard to prove.

Due to high, cool water conditions, we usually start the June fishing out on the Miramichi with #2 size flies. When fishing for these early fish in the Miramichi, I've had good luck on the Silver Rat, on the theory that it is bright and light-colored similar to the sand eels or capelin the salmon may have eaten recently at sea. We also use similar-sized blackish patterns, such as the Black Bears, Same Thing Murray, and Black Ghost. We even have Green Machines with bodies tied of woven flash—like flash chenille—on these same large hook sizes. By the time, though, that we are seeing fish regularly in the Cains, say early to mid-July, the water temperature and height call for smaller flies. If we do have a strong rise of water, we usually adjust upwards in size a bit, since it is likely that a moving fish, or one that is freshly arrived on its lie, will be more motivated to take a larger fly that more readily catches its attention. I'd be careful not to overdo that, though. Raises on the Cains are not usually of the magnitude that they are on the Miramichi, and I have found that, in general, somewhat smaller flies are more productive on the Cains than the main river.

The size of a rise of water—along with water temperature and the general weather forecast, which will predict the degree of sun or cloud cover—is one of the most important factors to consider in deciding whether to go to the Cains or stay in the Miramichi, or if you have limited time whether to go fishing at all. Let me say here that I always go fishing if I can, because you just never know what will happen with the weather and exactly how the fish will react. Still, if you are looking to play the odds, these are important pieces of information.

As I write this, I'm aware that the sources I give you may not have the same internet addresses in the future, so maybe the reader 30 years from now will roll his eyes at my old websites, but these are the places I usually go to currently to formulate my fishing plans.

Water height and whether it is raising or falling

https://wateroffice.ec.gc.ca/report/real_time_e.html?stn=01BO001—This site is run by the Canadian Government. The address takes you to a gauge in Blackville that gives you a graph of water height and a week's worth of history. You can also select "table" at the top right and get a very detailed look at the exact height for every hour.

Water height and water temperature

http://mreac.org/project/real-time-monitoring/—The river sites go offline for the winter, but what you see at this web page is quite self-explanatory. In Doaktown, you will see Miramichi water temperature and also water height. The second water height source is very helpful because a raise of water coming down the Miramichi is like a long wave. It will begin and end earlier in Doaktown than it will downriver, so to a degree, you can learn to predict how long before, and in which direction, your own water height will change.

Weather forecast

https://weather.gc.ca/forecast/canada/index_e.html?id=NB—I have found this Environment Canada site to provide the most accurate weather forecasts available. Select Chipman for the headwaters of the Cains.

Rainfall history

http://www2.gnb.ca/content/gnb/en/departments/erd/natural_resources/content/ForestsCrownLands/content/FireManagement/FireWeatherLatestObservations.html

This government site shows you the amount of rainfall that has taken place at various locations around the province. Some of the sites are automated, and they stop functioning from time to time, but when they work, it is a very handy tool. There are two sites important to the Cains, and they are Bantalor and Meadowbrook. Meadowbrook is slightly to the south of the Cains and at about the halfway point between the headwaters and the mouth. This means that a big rain in Meadowbrook can bring the lower Cains up a bit but do nothing for areas upriver farther than 25 miles from the mouth. Bantalor, on the other hand, represents the headwaters, and rain there flows the whole length of the Cains. It is important to note a few things about Cains water versus Miramichi. A raise in the Cains will benefit the Miramichi but only from Black Brook on down to the mouth. A raise in the Miramichi will in itself do nothing to affect the height of water in the Cains. It does happen that rain sometimes misses the Cains but hits the Miramichi and vice versa.

Radar

http://www.intellicast.com/National/Radar/Current.aspx?animate=true&location=USNH0020—This website is for Intellicast radar, and I have it set for the Berlin, New Hampshire, zone, which is the farthest northeast available. It gives you a great look at where the rain is in and around the province. The site also features predictive and past animation so you can see where rain has fallen and is supposed to fall.

What do you look for from these sources—individually, and more often in combination—to determine your chances of good fishing?

During the summer, temperatures that are cool enough are the first consideration. If the water hasn't been below 70°F for a couple days, you probably aren't going to catch anything, and for the sake of the fish, you shouldn't be fishing. Anything lower than that, or even if it is only getting to 72°F in the afternoon, you may still do OK in the morning, especially if there is a decent flow of water. The cooler the better.

The radar will help you know how much longer conditions will remain as they are, or when they may change concerning rain or cloud cover. It will also tell you if rain is or isn't falling, how heavily, and where rain fell from a storm that was supposed to just skirt the area. All this can help you decide whether or not to jump in the car and make that trip.

I love dark, drizzly, or rainy weather. I have seen great fishing until almost the middle of the day just shut off like a light switch when the sun comes out. Most bites don't last very long anyway. If you have good conditions for the morning, and you can only stay that long anyway, don't worry about the afternoon; just go fish the morning and do something else with the rest of your day. On the flip side, a day that was hot and sunny and had the water up over 70°F was not likely to magically improve very much at dusk. Again, if you are in camp, then, by all means, give it a shot and keep at it until late, especially if fish are starting to show. Overnight, though, big changes can occur. The fish move at night, especially in a smaller river such as the Cains where daytime movement between pools is very limited except in high water.

While the water gauge at Blackville can mean nothing to the Cains, usually there is quite a strong relationship in height between the two rivers, especially if recent rains have taken place in Bantalor, where headwaters of the Cains and tributaries of the Miramichi are interlaced. Meadow Brook is well off to the south and east, and storms that skirt us to the south may hit Meadow Brook but still not provide much of a raise on the Cains. Generally speaking, low water on the Miramichi

The Cains is very beautiful on a bluebird day such as this, but outside of the early morning and late evening hours, the fishing is usually just casting practice, unless there has been a recent raise of water to liven things up.

Niels Jensen caught this nice, late September cockfish in a slow, deep section of the Brophy Pool in low water. The fish was destined for spawning in the Miramichi Salmon Association hatchery. PHOTO COURTESY OF HARVEY WHEELER.

also means low water on the Cains. If you are looking at water heights on the Miramichi of lower than seven-tenths of a meter or so, it will normally be quite low on the Cains. If the Miramichi is reading six-tenths of a meter, you would rarely have decent fishing on the Cains. Even though the Cains has some decent low-water-holding pools, the flow in the Cains slows down much more so than it does in the larger Miramichi pools when water is low.

Another great thing about the Cains, though, is its ability to absorb a good raise of water and still offer good fishing. In the Miramichi, especially the part that lies downstream of the Cains, fishing during raising water is often tough. There is a lot of watershed upstream, and the gradient in the Miramichi downstream of the Cains is quite low. The result is that raises tend to magnify there. Just look at the size of the bank in Blackville. It takes a raise of nearly 20 feet to go over the bank. In Doaktown, the Miramichi bank is less than six feet high, and up on the Cains, it is about the same. While a large raise on the Miramichi can put you out of business for several days, it is rare when you can't fish the next day on the Cains. Also, while it is an old but accurate saying that fish don't take on rising water, it applies much more to the Miramichi than it does the Cains. I suspect that is because Cains raises are usually smaller and gentler than on the Miramichi.

Even if you have a good raise on the first of August, the fish aren't going to all leave the lower Cains River pools and go up 15 miles to Shinnickburn. From my experience, none, or next to none, of them do that—because we just don't see fish up there until well into September even if you have several good raises. Evolution must have bred into them that to run up the Cains too early is to risk being caught in warm pools with no flow where they may not survive until spawning time. A few pages back, we discussed some extraordinarily good fishing that Jim Graul and I had in early August. On that trip, the water on the Cains made a double-topped raise that took about three days of slowly raising water to achieve. We caught fish in the same pool throughout the period. It didn't seem to matter a bit that the water was rising. Perhaps that is because the fish were just staying put and did not intend to run the river anyway.

CAINS RIVER FLY SELECTION

A lot of material has been written about Cains River flies, but for the most part, it pertains to autumn patterns. We'll talk more about autumn flies in a few pages, but there are definitely some patterns and sizes that I have found particularly effective in the normal Cains River summer conditions of moderately low, warm water.

Summer Flies

Chenille Green Machines—Green Machines are definitely one of, or possibly the most successful, family of flies to have ever been fished for Atlantic salmon, and they work awfully well for brook trout too. The standard recipe fly is tied with a body of spun deer hair, clipped as close as reasonably possible, and then a feather is wound through it four or five times. Most of the older ones I have seen had no tail, and often, they had two or three butt colors wound on with red and green floss then a silver tinsel tip being the most popular. They work just fine, but some people believe that the fly is enhanced by a tail of either bucktail or krystal flash. Both tail materials are very popular.

Rising to the surface and waking is a problem for many small Green Machines, so we started tying Green Machines in the early 2000s using artificial body materials that were less buoyant than spun deer hair. Some may feel that a waking fly is good. It may be on some salmon rivers, but I have personally never had much luck with skated flies of any kind on the Miramichi or Cains. I know that will leave me open to hear from some folks who have had luck with skated or hitched flies, but I went into it with an open mind and tried it quite a lot, including when there were many fish in the pool. I have also caught salmon on skated flies in Iceland and Newfoundland. I've caught one or two on skated flies—usually a fouled wet fly, or a bomber picking up speed late in the swing—but I believe that in our tannic waters the far better wet fly presentation is subsurface.

Even if you prefer traditional, spun-hair bodies to other materials, you will have to admit that traditional Green Machines are very hard to clip in sizes smaller than #8 or so, and that is just too large in a lot of summer fishing conditions. I often want to fish with #10 and #12 wet flies, though I don't usually go smaller than that. If I need smaller, I just tie low-water style and leave some of the hook shank bare. It seems to work just fine. There are three materials that I have found that make very satisfactory Green Machine bodies in those smaller sizes. The first is peacock herl. I really love the fishiness of peacock herl

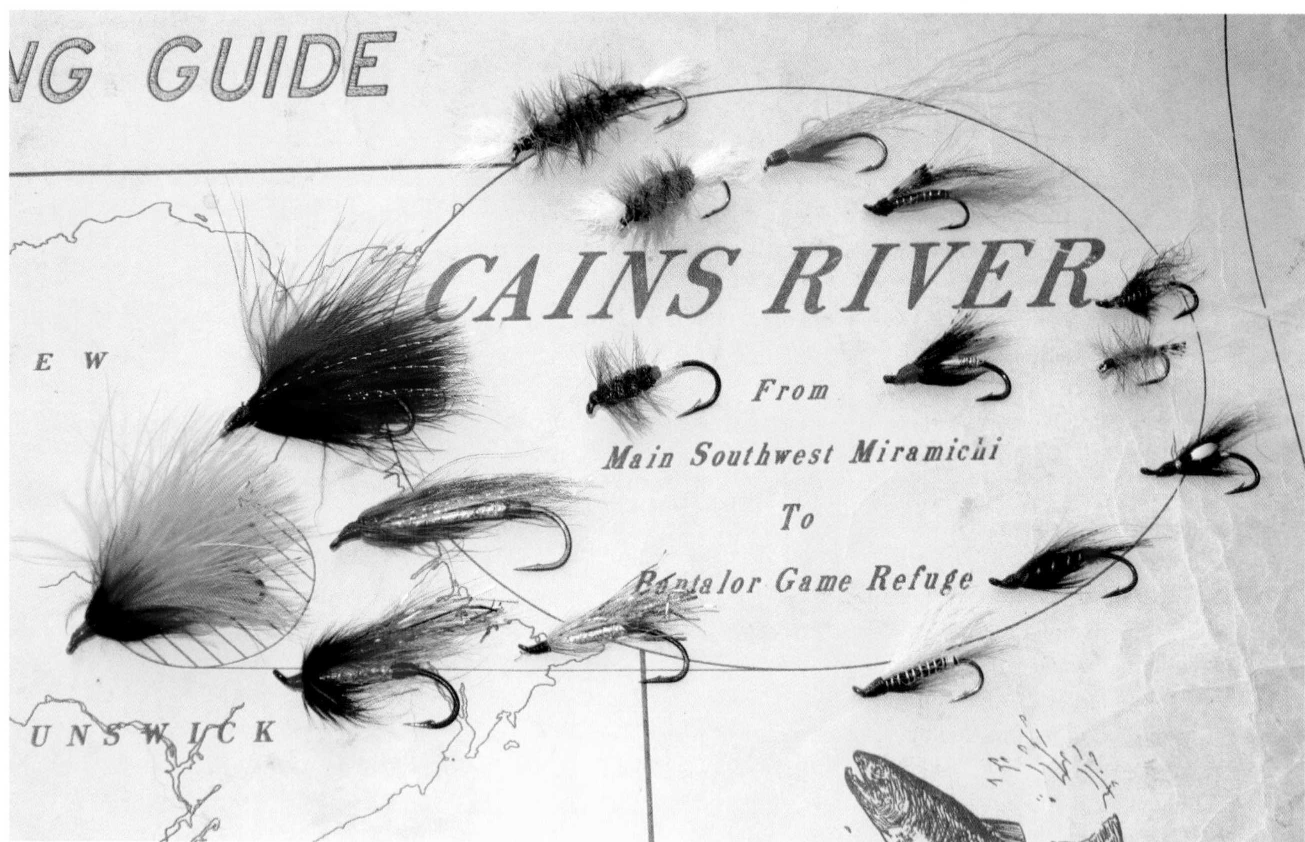

This selection of mostly wet flies provides an example of every fly type that is necessary for fishing on the Cains River any day of the season. Starting at the left side of the top are a pair of bombers, small and large. Going clockwise from the bombers, we reach a Sneaky and an Ally's Shrimp. Next are a group of black wet flies. I honestly think that one is more or less as good as the other, but some days, the salmon seem to have a preference, so you need a selection. In the middle of those flies is my favorite warm and low-water fly, a micro chenille Green Machine with a tiny flash tail. I fish this on a 15-foot, 6-pound-test leader. On the left-hand side are two marabou streamers for slow-water pools, and to the right of those are three October Killers in different sizes. The smaller one is called an October Killer Junior, and that particular fly is being saved to copy because it has caught several large cock salmon. Note the ragged red tag on the back of the fly from being chewed by the spawning teeth of the cockfish.

flies, but the stuff is terribly delicate. A caught tooth from even a small grilse can total the fly. The second material is variegated chenille. This comes in different sizes, and when wound around the hook, it creates a nice-looking, flashy body that is much slimmer than can be accomplished with deer hair. The third material, and my favorite for #10 and #12 flies, is ultra-chenille. Chenille has a nice segmented look when wet, and the ultra is small-diameter stuff. You can use some tiny hackle with ultra-chenille and make a very buggy small fly.

I have tried different tail materials, and I like these flies with a fairly short, sparse krystal flash tail. Even on the small flies, I like to cut the chenille into relatively short pieces and tie each on separately by its middle. I find that six or eight of these strands are plenty. If you tie them in by the middle of each piece, they form a little v, and you end up with a tail that stays open and lets the water flow between the pieces. It works very well. I've done well with bodies tied in olive, chartreuse, and black.

Black wet flies—You will need a few different black flies. Over the years, I have used the Black Ghost, the Black Bears—both green and red—Black Rats, Undertakers, and, in recent years, the Same Thing Murray. They will all catch fish, and really, I don't have a big favorite among them. Which one of these flies you actually catch a fish on is probably the proverbial self-fulfilling prophecy based around which one that you tie on the end of your leader. If I was forced to choose one, though, I'd probably tie on an Undertaker. The reason is simply that peacock herl might be the fishiest material for fly bodies that the Lord ever made. The Black Rat also has a herl body, and I've done very well on that fly over the years. I guess that I just prefer a black bear wing instead of the gray squirrel tail, though in reality, the fish may not care one bit either way. Ray Best, the longtime head guide at Cooper's Minipi Lake Lodge in Labrador, said to me one time that all flies tied with peacock herl catch fish. It is hard to argue with.

Long Flies—The Ally's Shrimp this is not really thought of as a summer fly, at least not in New Brunswick. In Scotland, where Ally Gowan and this fly are from, they fish long-tailed orange flies from the beginning of their season, which is February in many rivers. I mention orange because we use it too on the Cains and Miramichi Rivers, but we think of it as a fall color. I'm sure that this is just in our own minds, and it will work on early salmon over here just as it does in Scotland. One of the Scottish authorities on salmon fishing wrote a few years ago that 53°F was the magic temperature at which point he went away from the long-tailed fly designs to the more compact and conventional wet fly structures. I have seen, though, the long-tailed flies be effective even in warmer summer waters if the fly is small. A few years back, we were fishing the Brophy Pool in August. We had caught a little cool, wet weather break that ended what had been a warm stretch of midsummer weather. Tim Politis began fishing our early morning session with a #8 Ally's shrimp on the end of his line. He landed a nice salmon and a grilse fairly quickly. A look in the book tells me that the water that day was 65°F and that the height of water in the main river was 0.95 on the Blackville gauge. That reflects a good height of water for the middle of August—traditionally a low-water time—and an average, or slightly below average, morning temperature. If the water had been lower, 65°F would normally be a temperature at which we would fish a Green Machine or standard wet fly pattern in the #8 to #10 size. The Ally's Shrimp was right in that size range, but with the tail, it was much longer than a regular #8 or #10 wet fly. The increased flow of water that morning excited the fish and made them more aggressive takers, so they didn't hesitate to take the slightly larger flies.

Bombers—During the summer and early September, the Cains is also a great place for a bomber. I have often begun my morning by working carefully down through the pool with a confidence wet fly and take mental note of where I saw fish rise, or where I worked a fish without getting it to take finally. Then, I work down through the same water again, this time dropping a bomber over what appear to be the most likely spots. Very frequently, the result is to hook one of the fish that had refused the wet fly and raise other fish that hadn't shown at all on the first pass. A fair question might be that if I have such faith in the bomber, why didn't I just start with it to begin with? If conditions are right, I often do start with a bomber. If I have low-light, moderately warm water, and I can see fish showing in moderately close range, I may start with a bomber. Both my old guide Willy Bacso and Jason Curtis schooled me when I began salmon fishing on the Miramichi to always start with a wet fly. Their reasons were that you are more likely to get a solid hook up if the fish will take the wet fly, that you usually beat the pool up less with a wet fly swing than when casting large dry flies such as bombers, and you cover the water more efficiently. I'd say that I buy all these arguments. I like the methodical covering of a pool that takes place by the old cast-and-swing, take-a-step-and-repeat concept of locating salmon. You can also cast a wet fly a lot farther, and a lot more easily, so you are covering more water, and the fly is fishing a much higher percentage of the time.

Nonetheless, there are times when salmon will take a bomber when they will not touch a wet fly. I know that salmon have been caught the last day of the season on dry flies, but my experience has been that once the water drops below the high 50s, salmon don't rise as readily to dry flies. My own catch on bombers after the middle of September is a much smaller percentage of my total than it is back in the summertime. In that persistently 65°F to 72°F water of July, August, and early September, the bomber is very effective. Don't be too inflexible, though, to give bombers a try in the late season if you are working over some reluctant fish. On September 24, 2018, I was casting over fish under very low-water conditions. Many of these fish had been in the pool since August, and it

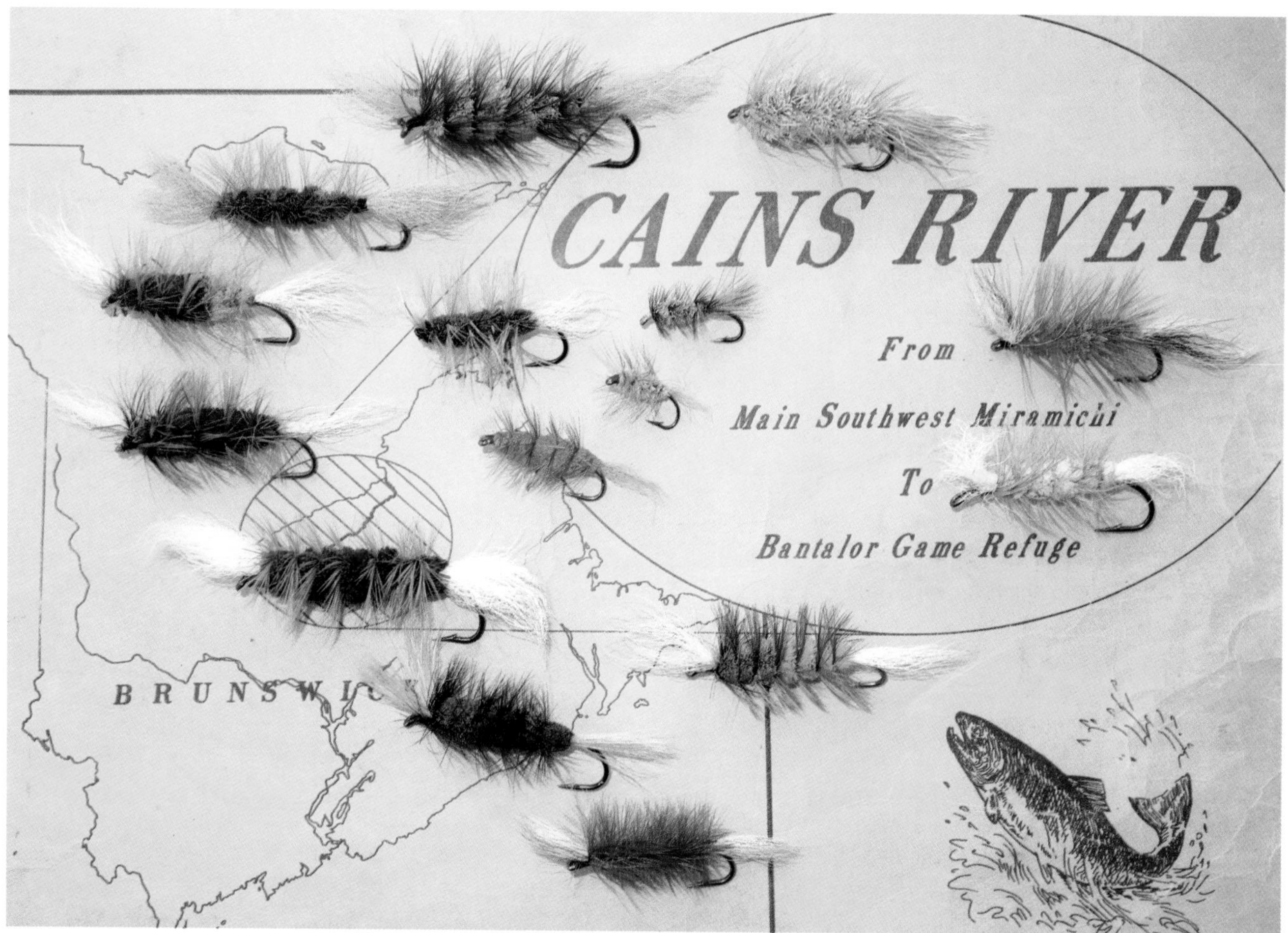

Here is a selection of bombers and bomber-like dry flies—such as the wingless Carter Bug, one-o-clock position—that will all work on the Cains. The smaller sizes like the ones in the center of the photo come into their own in late summer and early fall low water when there are lots of grilse about. Even then, though, I usually do better on the larger bombers. Colors are much more important with dry flies than with wet ones. I have seen days when you can't raise a fish on a natural-colored deer hair bomber—usually very effective—but a green one with orange hackles will work wonders. Who knows why. If you find a salmon that will look at a bomber, just keep casting and trying different colors. When and exactly what they will take is totally unpredictable, but very frequently, after lots of casting, a salmon will for no apparent reason just take the fly.

was very difficult to get them to take anything. Near dusk, as it often does, the activity in the pool started to increase and dead-drifting a #10 Sneaky on a six-pound test leader, I connected with a 12-pound salmon. I released this fish and had just clipped off my bedraggled Sneaky when another salmon made a beautiful head and tail rise just 25 feet out and slightly downstream of me. I had a small green bomber with orange hackle on my fly patch, and almost without thinking, I tied it on and dropped it over the spot where the salmon had risen. It was instantly taken, and we estimated 13 pounds for the entry in the logbook that evening. The water was very low, and the temperature was just 55°F.

I like large bombers. As a general rule, I have found that salmon that would not take a large #4 or so bomber won't usually take a smaller one well either. There are lots of body shapes and designs, but for me, a moderately slim cigar shape with a split white wing and tail is the way to go. I've had good luck with body colors of natural brown, brown with a yellow thorax, green, and blue. I like either some sort of brown hackle or brown and orange.

If I do search with a bomber, I like to be fishing a stretch of water that I'm quite sure is holding some fish. Here is the technique that I generally use to search for salmon with a bomber:

- Enter the water near the top of the stretch you want to fish. Wade out not quite to the farthest point where I am completely comfortable that I will not be spooking any fish. If in doubt, be conservative.
- Pull out a small amount of line and cast out and as far upstream as that length of line allows. We are eventually going to wade downstream because it is easier and creates less commotion than pushing against the current.
- Let the fly drift only about four feet, definitely no longer than six feet, then pick it up and put it back down exactly where it came off the water to start your next drift.

- Repeat this without moving your position until your fly is drifting as far downstream as you started upstream. For each cast to land where the one before it came off, you will need to shorten your amount of line as the casts are closer to you and then lengthen it as you need a longer cast to reach downstream. Don't push it, though. The dry fly cast should be very controlled and accurate so that it can be easily and exactly duplicated if you raise a salmon.
- After you have covered this line of water from top to bottom, pull off a little more line and repeat the pattern a little farther out. How much farther? That depends on how thoroughly you want to cover the area. If you are confident there are fish there, go very slowly and maybe make the next line of casts just a couple of feet beyond the one before. It is remarkable how close you sometimes have to land the fly to a salmon to get it to take. For that matter, some will watch it go by without showing any interest and then take it on the next cast even though it seemingly landed in the exact same spot. I believe, though, that most salmon that are willing to take a fly at all with make some move for it the first time it gets close. This may be just a bulge under the fly or a flash underwater as they turn on their side. You must be observant and catch this sign that a salmon has looked at your fly, then you can work the fish.

WORKING A SALMON THAT YOU HAVE ROLLED

How to work a salmon has been covered thousands of times in various books and magazine articles, but I have a twist or two on the subject that may be helpful. Working a salmon isn't all that different with a wet fly or a dry fly. What we have is a salmon on a lie in the pool within casting range. We saw this salmon come after our fly either very aggressively or very tentatively, but we saw it, so we came very close to getting a strike. Why didn't the salmon take the fly? It could be that the fish isn't going to take anything, but on the other hand, your odds that sticking with this fish for a while will pay off are much better than trying to find another—at least most of the time. It could be that taking your fly required him to move farther than he wanted, or that the fly was too big, too small, or something about the pattern didn't suit him. Those are probably the variables at play.

Let's start with a wet fly. My first attempt is just to remake exactly the same cast and in the same way. If the fish is going to take eventually, my experience is that half the time it will take right then on that follow-up cast. If the fish does not take, then I immediately again make the same cast, with the same fly, but this time as the fly begins to approach the fish, I pump the rod. This technique that I learned as the Gaspe Pump is made with your rod arm hanging down at your side with the line dead to the reel. Swing your arm to pull the rod a foot or so backwards and then let it swing forward again; repeat rhythmically, depending on water speed, until the fly is well past the fish. I have seen it work wonders many times.

If the above-mentioned techniques don't work, then I may do one of three things depending upon my sense of how hot a fish this is. If it is early in the season, and I think this is a fish that is very likely to take, then being very cognizant of exactly where I am standing—usually by noting my position next to a prominent rock on the bottom—I walk back upstream, counting the steps to perhaps six or about 10 or 12 feet. I then make identical casts regarding my original angle out into the river—my first cast should land 10 or 12 feet above where my cast that rolled the fish had landed—and take one step down toward the fish with each cast. This brings the fly a foot or two closer to the fish with each cast.

If this fails to work by the time I get to my original position, I will change flies to the same or similar pattern except one or two sizes smaller. If I now roll the fish but it doesn't take, I may try again but with the pumping action this time. If I still don't have a strike, I will go smaller still and/or try a completely different fly pattern.

Willy Bacso used to tell me to never give up on a fish without casting again the exact same fly that had originally raised the fish. For whatever reason, it frequently does work.

Another technique favored by Jason Curtis is to take a couple of steps straight downstream—bringing you closer to the fish—and a step or two inshore, away from the fish. This has the effect of the fly reaching the fish while the line is still more perpendicular to the current. The fly will come across the fish with more speed through the water, and that, too, often works.

To see Jason do this while guiding from his canoe is to witness a well-practiced routine. Jason turns the outboard—not running—all the way to steer away from the fish, then quickly lifts the anchor and plants his pole in the bottom, holding the canoe in position while the current swings the bow away from the fish. Then he drops the anchor, neatly positioning the boat almost a full canoe length away from the salmon's lie and a little farther downstream. All these things could be tried, though I would only put this much time and effort into a fish if I suspected that there were very few others around. Salmon fishing is all about playing the best odds. When you raise a salmon on the Miramichi or Cains, it often means a couple of things: one, the fish are in a taking mood; and two, there are likely several fish holding in the pool. You do not want to give up on a taking fish too early, but you also do not want to waste valuable, productive time on a fish that is only interested enough occasionally to make a half-hearted move toward the fly.

If I have rolled a fish on a wet fly and it will not take, I will very frequently wade out nearer the fish's lie and put a bomber over it. Wet fly lovers find it hard to believe, but many times, a salmon that has refused all wet fly offerings will aggressively take a bomber the second it gets near it.

Lee Wulff said that a salmon is as likely to take a dry fly on the hundredth pass over it as on the first—or words very close to that. I think that is a bit of a stretch, but it is absolutely true that you can cast the same fly, to the same spot, for the same fish on a given lie, and after many casts where the fish showed no interest at all, it will take. Is it angered into taking as some suggest? Who knows what goes on in the pea brain of a salmon? Not me, that's for sure, but with a dry fly, persistence can pay off. You do often have the advantage of knowing the fish is there, either because you see it laying on the bottom, or because you have seen it roll or "show" in some fashion at various times in the process. You can try different colors, maybe different sizes, cast farther above the fish for a longer drift, or cast right on top of it. You can leave it, and depending on how you are sharing the pool, you can come back to it in a half hour and try again. One thing about most dry-fly fishing is that the casts are relatively short and easy. You can often put yourself in the position where the next cast can be made by just quickly lifting the rod into the backcast position and then coming forward. You should never be so far away that it takes more than a couple of strips to recast the fly.

AUTUMN FISHING

As warm as it can be, the New Brunswick summer doesn't last all that long, and soon, the dog days of summer start to fade into cooler evenings and earlier sunsets. By the third week of August, being on the Miramichi and lower Cains is quite a bit different than it was in early July. The average daily temperature is several degrees cooler, the sun's angle is lower, and the days are very perceptibly shorter. Statistically, the counting trap at Millerton shows its smallest daily catches from around the first of August to the end of the first week in September. Statistically, the trap counts are similar throughout this period of time, though of course, it varies greatly from year to year depending on rain and the weather. If there are both a decent rain and rise of water, the salmon fishing can be terrific in August and early September. I've seen it many times. My wife and I used to come up every year for Labor Day weekend with Captain Steve Bellefleur and his wife, Susan. Some years, it was warm and very low water, and we just canceled the trip; other years, it was cool and rained, and we had terrific fishing. One year, between Campbell's Pool and the Half Bar on the Miramichi, Jason Curtis guided Steve to a limit of salmon every day for four days in a row. But still, statistically speaking, it is the second week of September before we see the first solid increase in salmon numbers, and they build every week from then until the end of the first week in October, which is the peak. They drop down in the second week of October, but statistically, that week is still the second highest of the fall run. In five weeks, we go from almost summery weather to a season that often ends in bare trees and snow squalls. This changeable and robust weather is part of the incredible allure

Darrell Warren holds a fish I nicknamed "The Champ." This is very likely a rebuilt grilse kelt that spent two full years feeding in the sea before returning to spawn. Pound for pound, this teen-sized cockfish was an excellent contender for the title of the toughest fighter among all the Atlantic salmon I have ever hooked.

of fall fishing in New Brunswick, and it is the time when the Cains River really shines.

Gone now are the silver bullets of June and July. Even the rosy-sided, lightly colored salmon of August have been replaced by fish that look like huge brown trout. Some fish have vivid red and black spots that combine with intricate wavy patterns, making a lovely contrast with relatively drab olive and dark brown skin. Still other Cains River salmon, especially during the last couple of weeks, are as black as coal. All this somber coloration is designed to make these fish invisible in the tea-colored water against the dark, gravelly bottom. This is also the time for the famous Cains River hookbills. Dorothy Noyes Arms wrote about these by name back in the 1930s. They make an impression on fishermen. In a paper written by biologists Atkinson and Moore called the "Case for Releasing Grilse," they talk about what happens to the majority of male grilse that survive kelthood and return to the ocean—it is a relatively small percentage because of the aggressive spawning life of the male grilse, but male grilse do make up the largest aggregation of any salmon class in the Miramichi population—so you are starting with a relatively large number. Many of these grilse kelts stay out in the ocean a full two years and return to the Miramichi system fresh from the ocean as meter-long, mid-teen-sized cockfish or hookbills. Most years, we catch a few of these in both the Miramichi and the Cains, and to say they are memorable is a great understatement. I wrote this passage in my blog from September 2015 after catching what I suspect was one of these rebuilt grilse kelts. "Early season fish are characterized by their high-speed runs while the fall fish usually don't have that kind of zip, good fighters as fish go, yes, but not the equal of June salmon. This cockfish was a stellar exception. Shortly after the fish was hooked, the line could be heard and seen zipping through the water running upstream and away from the canoe. I was immediately into my backing, and soon the fish leaped from the water 50 feet upstream of the boat and a good 150 feet away across the river from us. Next, the fish ran completely across the river where my downstream neighbor was fishing on his point of land. The fish blew off a hundred yards of backing against the tight drag of my reel, then jumped a couple of feet clear of the water landing with a huge splash about 30 feet from the startled fisherman. We ended up going ashore on the Keenan bar and followed the fish downstream. As they often do, the fish returned to roughly where it had been hooked, before again running off at least another 100 yards of backing while we stumbled down the bar in knee-deep water. I had seen this fish and knew it was no 40-pounder, but that cockfish really had heart. Darrell Warren netted the beast, and upon being released, it simply shot off into the river. Darrell, a man who in his youth could pinch steel bottle caps between his thumb and finger, said he could feel the strong muscles in the fish as he held it. If salmon like that grew to 50 pounds, regular salmon-sized fly equipment could never hold them!" The day before, Jason Curtis was fishing in the Jardine Pool across the river from his house and got one himself. He said that the fish never went any distance into the backing, but that he drifted a very long way downriver with it on the line, and that it was one of the toughest and most memorable fights from any salmon that he had ever caught.

The Progression of the Fall Run

I liken the progress of the fall run up the Cains River to an underwater game of musical chairs. While prior to early September there are normally very few fish farther up the Cains than the Mouth of Sabbies Pool, with the autumn rains and regular raises of water, fish leave the downriver pools and move farther up toward the headwaters. By the middle of September, and given decent conditions, there are salmon in the various pools all the way up to Moore's Pool in Shinnickburn, though that is typically the upper limit, and the numbers that far upriver are usually sparse. Meanwhile, new recruits come in daily from the estuary or from holding pools like Black Brook and others all the way down through the Rapids. If we get little rain, the progress is stifled, then many of the fish will hold up in the bottom Cains River pools, or stay back in the lower Miramichi and not come in at all during the open season as they clearly did in 1968 and in 2017. On the other hand, if we have storm after storm and repetitive large raises of water, the lower river can be essentially cleaned out of fish, and many fish get all the way up another 40 miles plus into the headwaters well before the end of the season. That happened in 2009, to a lesser degree in 2012, and again in 2015 when a huge raise at the end of September provided very good fishing up beyond Route 123 during the first days of October.

Most years, water conditions are somewhere in the middle, and by the first of October, there are fish strung out all the way to the headwaters, but the majority of them are found in the lower 20 miles of river. The next two weeks provided the best action from pools upstream of Muzzeroll, though there were some fish left in all of the holding pools along the river. These must largely have been the fish that were preparing to spawn locally. In 2008, when we fished the extended season the last week in October, there were salmon working on redds in several areas of the Admiral Pool waters, and at the same time, we watched a school of new fish one morning running through the pools on their way up the river. I remember closing out the fishing season some years at the Mahoney Brook pool and watching the repeat rises of salmon holding there on the last days of the season. I can't know for sure, but these fish seemed firmly committed to the pool. I had seen some in the same locations for days in a row. There was plenty of water for them to move up. I have to assume that at least some of these fish were waiting for their time to spawn and that they were holding there because their natal spawning beds were nearby.

Therefore, what does all this knowledge of the fall salmon run mean for selecting the best fishing strategy for the Cains? First, it can help point you in the right direction. Whether you choose to "sail" down the river in a canoe or hike into a public fishing pool, if it has been a very low-water fall, most of the action is going to be from the Mouth of the Sabbies River on down. The fish will either still be down low in the river or they won't have arrived yet. Prior to October 1, unless it has been a very high-water fall to that point, there isn't much point in fishing above Muzzeroll Brook. After the first of October, especially if there is some decent rain, the fish can be anywhere in the system, with the best action probably upriver of Shinnickburn.

Have a look at the Plan 1 through 5 maps of the Cains originally put out by the New Brunswick Department of Natural Resources and Energy on page 83. This will tell you the locations of public and private pools along the river. The Cains is a scheduled salmon river, and unless you are a resident of the Province of New Brunswick, you will need a guide. The guide can take nonresidents onto public open water, but they also frequently have the connections to get you on to privately owned stretches for a reasonable daily fee.

Fall Flies

When fishing the Cains after the middle of September, we are normally going to be using fall flies. If it is still mild and low water, these should still be small. You may be able to use the flies we talked about a few paragraphs back for summer as water conditions dictate. If the water is up a bit, it is getting cooler, and the fall run is on, you will do better with the tried-and-true, aggressively colored attractors such as the Chief Needahbeh, Mickey Finn, Ally's Shrimp, and the General Practitioner. Of course, there is seldom a better choice at any time of the season than an appropriately sized Green Machine. There are also some European patterns not sold locally, but they are very successful on the Cains and Miramichi Rivers and can easily be bought from the internet or ordered online. Leading among them is the venerable Willie Gunn. The namesake of this fly, Willie Gunn, was a famous Scottish ghillie. The fly is black, yellow, and orange colored bucktail, and some kind of suitable flash material, spread in a circle of the hook and tied in at the head. The body is gold-ribbed black floss, though a very popular version today calls for a gold body. This sort of long, flowing fly without a top or bottom, and with the material just spread around the hook shank, lends itself very well to tube flies or a concept called the Waddington shank—in modern times, the Intruder shanks. These are pieces of stiff metal wire bent so that a hook can go at one end and the line can be tied to the other. The fly is tied on this piece of wire. The advantage to the shank is that you can have a long fly where the hook is back by the tail, so it is likely to catch a fish coming up on the fly from behind making a short strike.

I have fished all these flies and many variations in the Cains during the fall season, and they all worked. My guess is that none are materially better than any other. The fish now are focused on spawning. The males especially can be very aggressive and will try and drive away any fish that they think will interfere with them successfully spawning. The females are also very aggressive and protective of their chosen lies. This means that long, attractor-type flies that salmon may see as intrusive are often just the ticket. It can, though, be overdone. I would typically size my offering to the conditions. If the water is up and rolling along nicely on a dark, windy day, then a three-inch offering tied on a #2 streamer hook may be just the ticket. The #2 is the largest hook size that I use. I fear that hooks larger than this can make a wound too large in the fish. There is just no need for anything bigger than a #2 XXL streamer hook. From there on down, I use many different sizes depending on conditions, with some of these patterns being tied on a regular #4 salmon irons hook as a good intermediate step.

Fall, though, does not mean that stealth is gone. In recent years, including the ultra-low-water fall of 2017, a fly called the Sneaky was productive. This skinny little fly is very, very effective on reluctant fish pooled up in low water. I will be the first to admit, though, that on many sessions I have seen lots of fish holding in a given pool but been unable to get any of them to even look at a Sneaky or for that matter any fly at all. That, as they say, is salmon fishing. There are pictures and tying information on the Sneaky in the fly chapter coming later.

I fish the Sneaky two ways. First, I simply cast it out and let it come around on its own with absolutely no action imparted by me beyond the natural swimming motion of the fly passing through the water—the standard wet fly swing. This fly is all about being very subtle. I assure you they will find it if they want it. The other way I fish this fly is in the famous slow pools of the Cains. During the summer the salmon in the Cains hold mostly in the conventional salmon pools with a decent flow, brooks entering, and so on. In the fall, though, their choices can be quite different. Adjacent to many of the faster pieces of water on the Cains are relatively deep—which is why I think they like them at this time of the year—slow-moving pools. The salmon often seem to prefer holding in these easygoing, deep, dark bodies of water instead of the traditional, lively streams normally thought of as salmon water. No one knows for sure, but it makes sense that with the cold, oxygenated water of October that these fish don't need the aerating rifles, and that with their focus on spawning they are content to sink deeply into a safe pocket near their natal beds and wait quietly for their moment.

Presentations to these fish laying in the deeper pools are often made more effectively with sink-tip lines. Not all sink tips are created equally either. We want the tip to sink quickly after the cast and then to more or less maintain this depth

Bill Utley and guide Darrell Warren with a salmon taken 12 miles up the Cains River using a sink tip line on the next-to-last day of the 2018 season.

during a slow, perhaps hand-over-hand or finger-twist retrieve. For this work, a relatively short sink tip of no more than 15 feet or so is called for, compared to something like a full sink line used to dredge the bottom of a lake with the fly eventually being retrieved almost straight up and down because the line sank continuously during the entire retrieve. This sort of line will have you snagged up in the Cains on every cast.

With both the floating and sink-tip presentations, I will often try imparting some kind of action. In the slow pools, especially with a sink tip, you may need some kind of stripping action just to keep the fly from hanging up. Sometimes, I will use a fairly long, slow strip followed by a considerable pause; other times, I will try very short jerky strips to make the fly dart around. You can never be sure what the fish will respond to.

Here is another area where double-handed rods provide a significant advantage over single hand. In Europe for Atlantic salmon, and in the Pacific Northwest for steelhead fishing, two-handed lines have gone through a lot of excellent development in recent years. There are a number of very easy-to-cast, multi-tip design lines that feature loop-to-loop, interchangeable tips ranging from floating to intermediate, then in several steps all the way down to extra-high density. An experienced caster can simply strip into the head, do one maneuver like a snap-T on the water's surface, and flick the fly out there 80 feet. Similar concept lines are made for single-handed rods, but all the ones I have used are clunky and difficult to cast smoothly.

The last fly and technique for the late season that we haven't talked about is fishing the slime fly. One of my fishing partners, Bill Utley, is committed to sinking line fishing for salmon, and his conviction really deepens in the fall. One day in late September a few years back, at the lower end of Keenan's Pool, we had seemingly good conditions and were seeing a few fish, but the catching was slow. I worked down the pool with a floating line and my dependable October killer streamer—just a Mickey Finn with a hackle collar, it will appear in the tackle and fly chapter. I neither rolled nor touched a fish. Bill came along behind me with a green slime tied to a short mono tippet, attached to a moderately quick-sinking tip. He soon caught a nice fall grilse. Some of these fall grilse are almost the size of early-run two multi-sea winter hen salmon. Perhaps 15 minutes later, Bill again hooked up, using the exact same setup, and landed the twin of the first grilse. I had just carefully worked these same waters without a touch. It would be hard for me to believe that his sink-tip-and-fly combination wasn't responsible for his results compared to mine.

The slime fly can be tied a number of ways, and one can use rabbit fur instead of marabou, but the most common version is tied on a streamer hook of the desired size and are simply marabou, wound down the shank and tied off at the end with the tip of a bushy piece hanging off an inch or two. You can add some flash if you want. I often do, though I don't know that it makes any difference. Typically, these are quite large flies, more or less equivalent in dimension to other #2 or #4 streamers, but another fishing buddy, Casey Cramton, had some good results earlier one recent fall down at the Brophy Pool using some small ones not much over an inch in length. Marabou's finest attribute is that it will wiggle incredibly at even the very slowest retrieve speeds, or no retrieve at all if held in any measurable current. A slow presentation of the marabou fly at a fair distance below the surface is very often just the ticket for fall salmon.

Harvey Wheeler, the "Maven," holds a mid-teen-sized cockfish that took a #2 Octover Killer in the Slow Pool below the author's camp at Mahoney Brook. Note the two-handed rod. Harvey is a rare, experienced Atlantic salmon handler who became very competent with a two-handed rod, even though he didn't take it up until late in his angling career. PHOTO COURTESY OF NIELS JENSEN.

CHAPTER 10

Tackle, Techniques, and Flies for the Cains River

Atlantic salmon fishing on the Miramichi and even more so for the Cains does not require heavy equipment. Even though some of the fish can be very large, they are not going to head back to the sea and take all the backing off your reel. Most salmon are very reluctant to leave the pool that they were hooked in, but even if they do, you can usually follow the fish downriver as needed with no real problem. Usually, even if they do run downstream for a hundred yards or so, they will turn around and swim back up to where they were hooked.

The reality is that many more salmon are lost by pulling too hard on them as opposed to not pulling hard enough. All you really need is to make sure that you have a reel that holds at least a couple of hundred yards of minimum 20-pound test backing. All of my salmon reels are loaded with 300 yards of 30-pound test spectra backing—which is about the same diameter as 20-pound-test Dacron. I've got a mixture of old and new design reels, largely based on nostalgia as opposed to practical considerations. A modern large arbor reel with

Bill Utley and the author are preparing to walk through the woods to a Cains River salmon pool. My rods are leaning against the trees to the left. Each of us has a light Spey rod for wet-fly fishing. I have a single-handed rod for dry flies, and Bill has a switch rod set up for the same purpose.

Captain Steve Bellefleur and guide Darrell Warren hooked to a big salmon on the lower Cains. The fish was 100 yards downriver in this photo, but it ended up being netted just a few feet from where they were standing for this photograph. Most salmon have a strong tendency to eventually return during the fight to an area of the pool near where they were originally hooked. If steady but gentle pressure is applied, salmon can often be simply walked up the river to a location that provides a good place to land the fish.

a good drag is the best equipment that you can use because salmon are famous for rapid turns of direction, and the faster reeling speed will help you keep up a tight line. I never fish with a very tight drag. I use a light tension that makes it easy to pull line out of the reel. This is because, in salmon fishing, we are frequently reeling line up to change positions and then stripping it back out to cast it. Once I am hooked to a fish, I add any additional pressure that I need with my reel hand fingertips. It doesn't take much.

The largest fly I ever use is tied on a #2 streamer hook, and a seven- or eight-weight single-handed rod is all that is really needed for casting any salmon flies that you will use on the Miramichi or the Cains.

Of your fishing, 95 percent will be done with a floating line, and some excellent anglers never use anything else. I like to use a tapered mono leader with my floating lines that is approximately equal to the length of the fly rod. I like sink-tip lines at times in the fall when the water gets really cold, but that can also be accomplished with a single-handed rod by switching from the standard nine-foot tapered mono leader to a six-foot poly leader of the appropriate sink speed and a short mono tippet.

Leader combinations with Spey lines are a bit more complex depending on the type of line you are using. The modern, Scandi-type lines are largely designed to be cast with a 10-foot poly leader as part of the line, though in warmer water, I often just use tapered mono leaders instead that are at least the length of my rod. Attach a straight tippet of four to six feet to the end of your poly leader. Also, the new, multi-tip Scandi lines are really a pleasure to cast, and with a little pouch that contains the different density tips and some tippet material, you are ready for any situation.

Tippet strength begins with 12-pound test in June or other high-water times, and I progressively decrease during the summer to ten, then eight, and finally to six in low-water conditions when we are using very small flies. This isn't so much because the fish are leader shy. I doubt that they are really leader shy at all, but heavy tippet kills the lifelike presentation of small flies. You are just asking to lose fish to use light tippet with big flies in the big water of the early season.

Personally, I greatly prefer Spey rods for wet-fly fishing, but you should be quite proficient with them, or they are better off left at home. Too many salmon fishermen want to get into Spey casting, but they don't put in the practice time required to become good with the equipment. The time to practice and learn is not while wading in a salmon river. The basic principles of "Speying out a line" can be learned on the grass and by stepping on the end of the leader to mimic a water anchor. This isn't ideal, but it will teach you what a D-loop is and the basic principles behind a cast made with a water anchor. One of my friends who lives in the Rangeley, Maine, area does a lot of brook trout fishing and comes over to the Miramichi salmon fishing with me a few times a year. He just bought a very light Spey rod to fish the streams and lakeshore near him for brookies and landlocked salmon. He will become good at using the equipment. The problem with not being good at it is that you will end up continuously making casts that don't turn over properly and the fly lands 10 feet behind the fly line—which also lands in a pile. You are halfway through the swing when the whole mess straightens out and begins to fish. Beyond that, you won't be able to fish in the wind, and you may hook yourself and your guide. Unless you are willing to make the commitment to practice with the Spey rod when you are not on the river, then you should use the equipment that you are comfortable and proficient with.

Properly used, the benefits of a Spey rod are several. Most wet-fly fishing is comprised of casting out across the current—on the Miramichi and Cains, this usually means at a high angle to the current flow. This will give your fly more speed, and you will cover more water by casting out farther into the stream. The fly swings with the current, swimming along as your line is pulled downstream. When the line is hanging straight downstream, you give the fly a small pull or two to attract any fish that may be following it. Then you strip in the fly line to the point of where you can pick it up and make another cast. Before making the next cast, you take one or two steps downstream, and thus, you progress down through the pool paying particular attention to fishy-looking spots and where your guide tells you that salmon are likely to by lying. The Miramichi is a large salmon river, and even the smaller Cains has many places over its length where a long cast is helpful. A long cast with a single-handed rod is 80 feet, 90 if you are a hero. To do this, most fly fishers must really work at it. You will need the head stripped into the rod tip to pick it out of the water. The 30-foot head and 10 feet inside the rod amount to 40 feet. That means that you will have to deal with 50 feet of running line to make a long cast. If you are wading to your waist, this all becomes much more difficult than if you are standing in a canoe or on shore. With a Spey rod, you are picking up more like 45 feet of line, and the rod with a little overhang is approximately 15 feet, so to make the same 90-foot cast, you only need to strip in and handle 30 feet of running line, not 50. That is quite a difference. Once you learn how to do it a long cast from a thigh-deep wade, it is much less tricky to accomplish with a Spey rod than with a single-handed rod. Also, because you do not have to strip in as much line, you can make the casts much more quickly, and you spend a higher percentage of your fishing time actually fishing as opposed to stripping and false casting.

There are other advantages: you can mend line and, therefore, control your presentation better, you will land more of the fish that you hook because the long bend of the Spey rod will keep some level of tension on the hooked fish even when it is jumping. Also, if a fish pulls very hard and changes direction a lot, the long rod will act as a shock absorber for your leader and tippet.

When it comes to Spey rods, I sometimes use a 15-foot 10-weight in big water, and with sink tips, but 90 percent of my Spey rod fishing—and all of it on the Cains—is done with an 8-weight Spey rod. If it is cold enough for sink tips, you can use poly leaders with this setup too, but personally, I think the modern, multi-tip Scandi lines cast and fish fabulously with Spey rods. I love the versatility of having a variety of sinking tips all held in a little pouch in my pocket.

Not everyone, though, is going to commit to Spey casting, and that is absolutely fine. A decent single-handed rod caster can efficiently fish the Miramichi and Cains with no problems.

PLAYING SALMON

My old mentor Willy Bacso, a longtime guide at Wade's Fishing Lodge, taught me to let a freshly hooked salmon run around under relatively light pressure for the first minute or two of the fight. After the initial frantic bursts, the salmon will fight more doggedly, and you can usually work into a more favorable position and apply more pressure.

The best thing that you can do to shorten up the duration of playing a salmon is to get to a position that is at least parallel with the fish and very preferably somewhat downstream. One thing that I read about in much of the old writings about salmon fishing was the extreme duration of the time it took them to land a 20- or 25-pound fish. It should not take 15 minutes for a skilled angler to land any salmon that he can work downstream of. If the fish has to swim into the current to stay away from you, and you are at the same time pulling him back, down current, he will tire very quickly. This is best for the fish as it is not as completely exhausted when you do release it. The old-timers used to think it was man against fish and pulled what they thought was hard-to-get fish back upstream to where they were. The current against the body of a fish is 75 percent of what you are fighting in that situation. A big fish played that way would be tough to land if it never moved at all. The old rods were soft, and anglers thought they were applying a lot of pressure, but it was the angler who was getting the worst of the long rod's leverage.

When the salmon jumps, there is an age-old philosophy of bowing to the fish. Some anglers take it to an extreme and instantly drop their rod flat to the water. I do reach forward a bit to relieve tension—though I am not sure it does any good—but I always try to keep the shock absorber of the bent rod. It is also one of the reasons that I love to fight a big fish on a Spey rod. The distance the rod can bend back and forth without completely unloading line tension is wonderful for keeping fish on the hook. You do want some tension on that fly at all times or it can simply fall out—especially barbless—but too much tension on a jumping fish can break tippet or rip out flies.

I'm a fan of netting salmon in a well-wetted, soft, very large, catch-and-release net. Either you or your guide holds the net at a low angle against the bottom in water that is less than two feet deep. The salmon is guided to a point in light current that is just above the upstream end of the net. The tension on the rod is released all at once, and the net is lifted. The salmon will drop down in the water column and back into the net. I shudder when I see people drag fish up onto the shore and see the fish beating itself upon the rocks or wiping away its protective slime on grass or sand. After netting, the fish should be unhooked while still in the net, and then, unless

Here is the ideal scenario for netting a salmon. The fish is being led into relatively shallow-moving water. The angler is slightly upstream of the guide with the net. The fish is led over net, the tension on the line is released by moving the rod toward the fish, the surprised and tired fish drops back with the current, and the net is simultaneously raised with a minimum of commotion. Game over!

completely exhausted, the net is simply turned inside out, and away the fish swims away. A really large, tired fish can be held, or rather cradled, facing into the current. But hold it very lightly, because while you are holding that fish it is captured and still struggling. Being free in the water to swim off into the depths and regain its strength is the best situation for the released fish.

WADING GEAR

Most of the Miramichi and Cains River bottoms are relatively easy gravel wading. If you are 30 years old, you can wear anything; when you are older, and the balance isn't what it was, some kind of spikes are indispensable. A wading staff is a matter of choice. I hate dealing with them if I don't need to use them, and I don't need them yet on the Miramichi. That may change, though.

VEST, CHEST PACKS, SLING, ETC.

Personally, I love vests, but I tend to stuff too much into them. The vest then gets heavy, and the weight can make my back

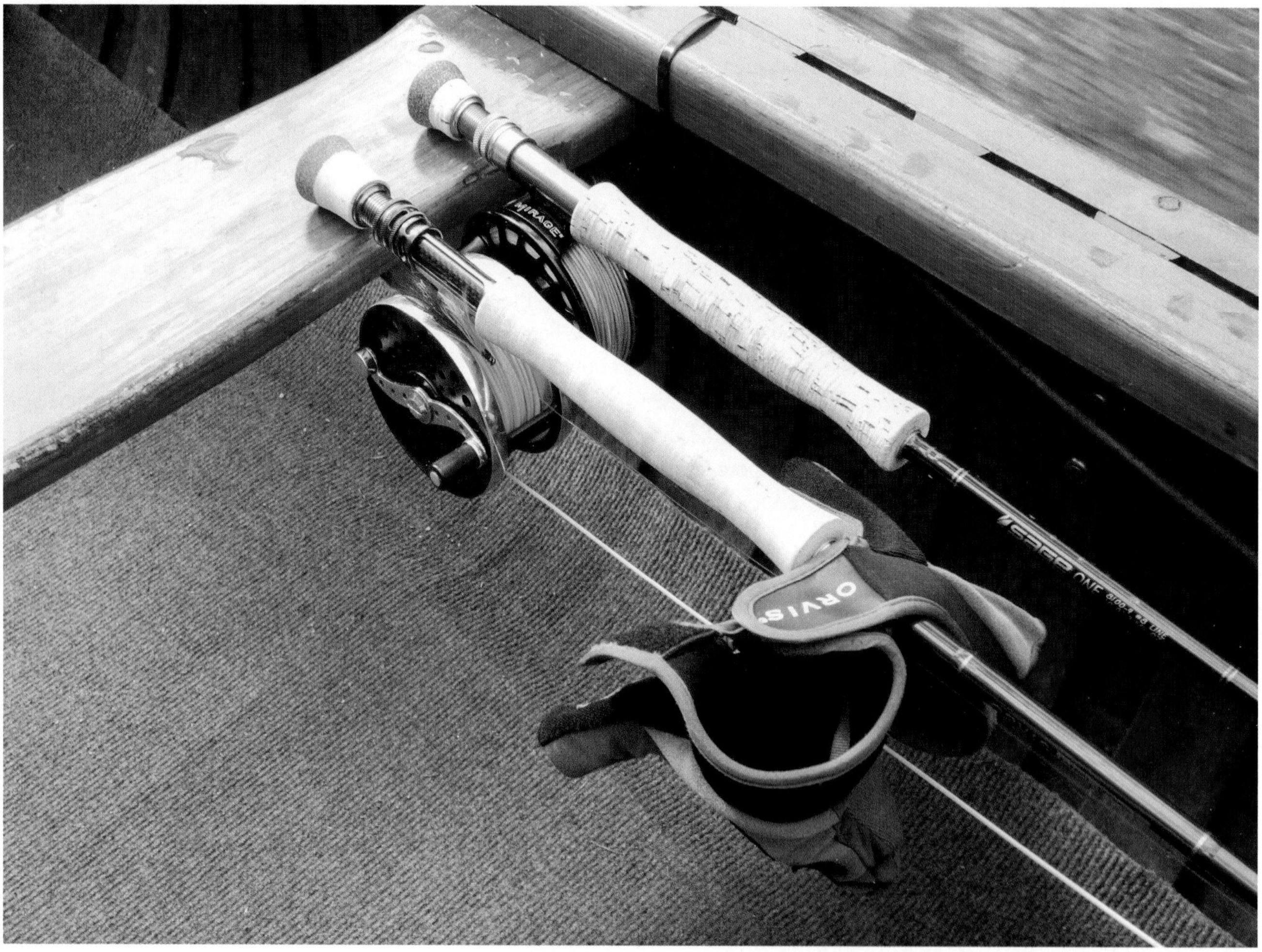

A pair of good casting gloves is a big help in stripping and in not getting blisters when casting. They also provide some sun protection and a little warmth. Note that these are a pair of eight-weight single-handed outfits, all that is needed to handle Cains and Miramichi salmon.

hurt when I do. I have a very small chest pack, and I often wear just that with a pair of nippers, one spool of Maxima tippet, a pair of forceps, and one fly box with a small hand-picked selection appropriate to the fishing at the moment. When I'm going out in the canoe, I take the vest as a sort of soft, wearable tackle bag. I hang it on the back of my canoe seat. When I'm wading, I take the chest pack.

I leave the camp every morning with a waterproof bag that has extra clothes and gear in it that I think I may need. This sets by the bench or rides in the canoe. If I'm going for an extended walk, which I really only do when it is the late season and I am at my upriver camp on the Cains, I almost always wear my foul-weather jacket and stuff an extra fly box and maybe more tippet into the pockets. Try to travel light; otherwise, you are a slave to your gear. I can count on one hand the times I've really needed something that I didn't have, but I have often wasted time and energy carrying along a lot of gear that I just didn't need.

WET FLIES

The earliest flies for fishing the Miramichi and Cains Rivers were standard English salmon-fishing flies. Harry Allen sent Lee Sturges to the hardware store in Fredericton to pick up Silver Doctors, Wilkinsons, Parmachene Belles, and Durham Rangers for his trip in 1915. The Parmachene Belle was originated by an American tyer and named after a famous Maine brook trout lake, but the rest are English patterns from the 1840s and 1850s. It was inevitable that the Miramichi system would develop its own styles. The complicated arrays of exotic feathers, French silk floss, and the tinsels that went into making traditional feather-wing salmon flies probably weren't available in early twentieth-century New Brunswick, and very few people living in the province in the early 1900s would have had any idea how to tie such flies anyway. However, the local fishermen were better off without them. The more practical and lifelike substitutes made with the feather, hair, and fur of local birds and animals were excellent fish catchers, plus they were far easier and less expensive to tie than classic patterns.

The first flies of locally inspired design that I see any record of were the Cains River Streamer series. In the Early Outfitters chapter, we discussed these streamers being inspired by seeing a salmon nail a fly that had snagged a long piece of riverbank grass on a low backcast. Harry Allen reportedly bound a few long chicken feathers to a hook, and the Cains River streamer was born. From there, a man named Fred Peet, in 1924, was said to have created what is officially known as the Cains River Streamer—both the design concept and a particular fly in the series by that exact name. Peet was a fisherman and tournament distance caster of considerable reputation, and he was from Chicago, as was Lee Sturges. While I have found no writings that directly link Peet to Sturges, I would bet money that they knew one another. We do know that Peet journeyed to New Brunswick and fished the Cains River with Harry Allen. In his book *Fly-Tying*, William Bayard Sturgis wrote that: "This particular type of fly first made its appearance in 1924, when Mr. Fred Peet and his party of friends from Chicago visited the Cains River in New Brunswick. Using these and stout, single-handed tournament rods, they succeeded in taking salmon up to twenty pounds."

All the Cains River Streamers have a long tail of barred wood duck and a body of double-wound tinsel—either silver or gold. The Cains River streamers were feather wings, though hair wing versions were also tied. There were two pairs of feathers for a wing, often of two different colors, and the feathers extended to almost twice the length of the hook shank. There was no topping. Long jungle cock eyes were then added that extended back to the hook point, then two hackles, usually of different colors, are wound one in front of the other as a collar at the head of the fly. These brightly colored feather wing flies are examples of the transition that wet flies also went through from the days of gaudy English salmon flies to modern salmon flies—largely hair wing—in which most patterns are designed to mimic the actions of prey species, be they aquatic insects or marine baitfish.

That these flies worked well on the Cains and Miramichi was also confirmed in the writings of Dorothy Noyes Arms when she wrote that, once introduced, they became "the accepted takers" for spring or high-water conditions. She also wrote about watching a guide named Clarence—Clarence Wade, Charlie's brother—sitting in a tent during the evening tying these streamer flies from bucktail by gaslight. The bucktail versions, Arms wrote, were not universally liked by all the guides, but the Armses found them to be deadly.

A friend and fishing partner of Peet, Oscar Weber of the Weber Tackle Company in Wisconsin, then began to tie these flies commercially. Weber claimed to have developed two patterns that he named after Harry Allen: Allen's First Choice, and Allen's Last Chance. He then developed three others that he named after three of Harry's guides: Aleck's Wonder, Dunk's Special, and Wade's Choice.

These Cains River Streamers were designed originally as spring flies, but it has long been established that on both the Miramichi and the Cains River, streamers work very well during the fall, or even the late summer, if there is a sufficient height of water. I had also seen quite a few instances during the fall when fish that were not readily taking normal-sized offerings, even though the water wasn't terribly high, immediately struck a large bucktail streamer when it came their way. This can be especially true if there is a strong wind ruffling the surface of the pool.

During the summer and early fall, many fish that are part of the Cains River fall run hold up in the junction of the Cains and Southwest Miramichi at Black Brook. This big pool, holding many fish waiting for a raise of water, has made the

Bill Utley shows the Cains River Streamer tied by him but designed 100 years ago that just produced a nice late-season salmon. The 14-foot nine-weight Spey rod is the maximum casting tool one will need on the Cains. Most of the Spey rods that we use on this midsize river are in the eight-weight range, but a little extra heft is nice when casting sink tips and big flies.

Black Brook Salmon Club a breeding ground for low-water flies dreamt up to tempt these frustrated fish. Angus Curtis, a 1970s guide, is an innovative fly tier, and together with Black Brook Salmon Club member, the late Doctor Joseph Sherer, they created a pattern that at one time was used heavily at the Black Brook Salmon Club called the Almost—meaning that it is said to be almost always effective.

One time in August, I was up at Campbell's, and we had quite a few stale fish holding in our water two miles downriver from Black Brook. I was rolling an occasional salmon on the bomber, and if I fished long enough into the evening, I might get a pull on something like a black bear, Green Machine, or black ghost down in the #10- or #12-size range, but the action was poor. Misery loves company, and after lunch one day, I dropped in at Black Brook to see how everyone upriver was doing. Gayden Curtis, then the head guide, told me that they too were struggling—even though he estimated that they had more than a thousand salmon in their pool—and that of the few being caught they were taking either a blue bomber or one of the incredibly sparse little wet fly creations that Dr. Joe Sherer was tying. "Just a second," he said. "I'll get you one." Gayden returned with a couple of Dr. Sherer's creations. Each had a tiny silver butt, a black body with silver rib, no throat, and a wing comprised of about six or eight black bear hair fibers. The fly was a #12. "Fish it on long 6-pound test tippet," were Dr. Sherer's instructions.

That evening back at Campbell's, I got one fish on each of those flies, my first fish in a couple of days. Was it the flies, some new confidence, or a new fish or two in the pool? Who knows, but I was fishing the hot flies.

I'm someone who tends largely to discount the minor differences in fly patterns, but there are so many stories from incidents where subtle differences seemingly did make a real difference that one can never discount them altogether. There are certainly those days when the fish can be caught on nearly anything that you cast into the pool, but there are definitely days where getting a strike means that everything must be done just so. A 1978 article from *Field and Stream Magazine* written by the famous comic and sportsman writer Ed Zern had him fishing years earlier at the Doctor's Island Club on the Miramichi. The fishing was very good, and when he arrived, he was told that a small black fly with an orange butt was the killer. Paul O'Haire, then the owner of the lodge before it became a private club, told Zern that the fly was so popular that the fly shop in town was temporarily out, but he could lend him his last one. Zern looked the fly over and politely declined, saying that he had the exact same fly with a scarlet red instead of orange butt and that he was sure it would work. You guessed it, Zern's fly caught nothing while other anglers fishing the run repeatedly hooked up. Zern put on the hot fly clipped from a fellow angler's line and immediately started to catch fish. Zern goes on to say that the moral of the story is to carry a substantial selection of flies and keep changing them until you find the one that works. If you follow that advice, I would add not to forget to bring a few extra spools of tippet with you on every outing. My personal modification to the instructions would be to fish with a confidence fly, one that your guide suggests—unless you are very experienced on the river—and when you have reason to believe that your fly is not being taken, try something else, otherwise you will spend most of your time on the water changing flies and not fishing. Generally speaking, if you are casting to salmon you will know it, especially on the Miramichi, as they frequently show themselves. I also believe that most fish ready to take a fly will at least look at a reasonably selected fly the first time that it passes over them—as long as the size, profile, and coloration are roughly appropriate for the fishing conditions. That look, or roll, will let you know that there is a player in front of you, and you can then get down to work finding a fly, angle of cast, or some action imparting technique that will get a solid take.

DRY FLIES

Atlantic salmon fly development on the Cains River was not limited to wet flies. The Miramichi system can lay claim to being the origin of two very important dry flies. The first one, the Bomber, is easily the most popular salmon dry fly ever designed. I guess that we could add a third fly to the list, and that is the Carter Bug that has been heavily promoted by Atlantic salmon-fishing legend Bryant Freeman. I'll stick my neck out, though, and say that it is essentially a roughly clipped, Bomber variant with no wing. Freeman maintains that it is softer and when a fish closes its mouth on one, they are not as likely to quickly spit it out.

The development of the Bomber during the 1960s was credited to the late Reverend Elmer Smith. Jerry Doak doesn't completely disagree with that, but he feels that a large part of the credit should probably go to the inventor of the highly successful Ingalls Butterfly wet fly, the late Maurice Ingalls. Jerry says that the Bomber may well have been a "product of simultaneous invention" and says that it would

We have just risen a fish here on a wet fly but have not been able to get it to come back and take. Guide Jason Curtis, who has netted many hundreds of Atlantic salmon caught on dry flies, is glancing at the fish's lie while he ties on a new bomber for me to try on the fish.

not be the first fly to be created like that. Ingalls was the first person to tie the Bomber in commercial quantities for Jerry's father, Wallace Doak. Since the Bomber is so well-known, and it is not directly attributable to the Cains River, I'm not going to write a lot about it in this book beyond occasional references to it and some general instruction on fishing dry flies for salmon.

The other dry fly is the Whiskers developed at Black Brook by the late Lou Butterfield. I spoke with both Jerry Doak and Rip Cunningham—a member of Black Brook Salmon Club who fished alongside Butterfield on many occasions—regarding the timing of the Whisker's origin. No one seems to know for sure, but Doak remembers that it appeared in an Orvis catalog during the 1970s, and he thought that it probably dated to the 1960s, similar to the Bomber. There could be no higher endorsement for a fly than Butterfield's, since his catches—which ran to several hundred fish in some years—were absolutely legendary. I'd say that a small book on the life and times of Lou Butterfield on his pool above Black Brook would be warranted, but a flood in the 1970s carried away his camp, tackle, and all his record books, so there wouldn't be a lot to go on. There is a part of the Black Brook Salmon Club history written by the late member Ted Lyman that tells of watching Butterfield and two friends limiting out when the daily limit was ten salmon per angler. Butterfield was reported to have landed 15 of them to his own rod.

The Whiskers to me is essentially similar in design concept to the bi-visible dry fly. These flies depend to a large degree on the tips of their hackles resting in the surface film of the water for their flotation. Like the bomber, the Whiskers has a tail and a wing, though in both cases, these are usually shorter than on the bomber. The bomber has a body of spun and then moderately tightly clipped deer body hair. The Whiskers has a floss or yarn body—the original was said to use yellow yarn—and bucktail wings and tail. A matched pair of feathers are quite tightly palmered the length of the body, and the fly is generally tied on a streamer hook, so it is fairly long.

The two big differences between these flies are first, the longer, thinner profile of the whiskers, and second, the more cork-like way that the bomber floats compared to the more deeply, settled into the water presentation of the Whiskers—other than maybe the first couple of casts while it is still bone dry.

My original guide at Campbell's and Keenan's Pools, Willy Bacso, was a great fan of the Whiskers. Bacso really tutored me on Miramichi salmon fishing, and he gave the Whiskers nearly as much billing as he did the Bomber. The whiskers is also the favorite fly of Ralph Campbell, who has fished his whole life on the waters around Campbell's Pool camp. Ralph would come fishing with just a couple of the most bedraggled Whiskers flies you had ever seen, but he knew exactly how to fish them, and on his line, they were deadly.

I admit that I have gotten away from the Whiskers in favor of the Bomber, and that is simply a matter of my being lazy. The Bomber floats a lot more readily than the Whiskers, and if you are in that part of the summer when you are fishing dry flies a lot, you will need to change Whiskers much more frequently than you do Bombers or you will not be fishing a floating fly. The presentation of the Whiskers also needs to be more delicate or you will sink it right off the bat. That isn't all bad, because I think that all too often dry flies are not presented as delicately to salmon as they should be. A big salmon will sometimes just explode on a dry fly, but other times, its mood is much more subdued, and the tip of its snout will just break the surface and the fly disappear in a tiny swirl. The Whiskers will keep you in the practice of making delicate presentations. A good plan for using the Whiskers is to do your searching of known salmon lies with a Bomber, but if you roll a reluctant fish, give the Whiskers a try.

Rip Cunningham remembers that Lou made precise and delicate presentations to the known lies where fish would be showing. He did fish the bomber as well as the whiskers and would switch back and forth if one wasn't working. Rip also said that Butterfield never let the fly drift very far, something he also agrees with, and I would cast my vote along those lines too. Perhaps the other thing of importance about the Whiskers is that, considering that Butterfield did almost all of his salmon fishing just below the mouth of the Cains River, we can truthfully say that is the official Cains River Atlantic salmon dry fly.

The next chapter will show, grouped by basic design concept, the flies that the fishermen and guides we talked with, and that by our own experiences are productive salmon flies for the Cains River. We have also included the recipes for all of them.

CHAPTER 11

Cains River Salmon and Trout Flies

The flies appearing in all the groupings are tied by William T. Utley except for certain bombers marked as tied by Warren Duncan.

BLACK OR VERY DARK WET FLIES

All the flies pictured below share an essentially black appearance. Some like the Black Ghost have a black body but a white wing. Some of the flies just have a throat of hackle barbules while others have a full palmer-wound collar. Beyond this, there is often a fair amount of variation in the way the recipes are followed. I tend to believe that, in most cases, the small changes make very little difference, but there are senior salmon anglers who would take great exception to that, claiming that squirrel rather than bear, or a gold rather than silver rib, makes all the difference. When I look in my own fly boxes to make a choice, I see that, due to my own lack of fussiness when tying, my flies of the same pattern and size often vary quite a bit from one another. This variation could exist in any aspect of the flies' design from the shape of the hook to the density of the wing, to whether I used floss or mohair for the body, the width of the rib, the shade of green in the butt, and so on. I like these variations, though, and pick the one that seems to have the best feel for the conditions I am fishing. Frankly, plain old gut feeling goes a long way when it comes to fly selection. I am very partial to flies that are "pre-chewed" since I know that to be a stamp of approval from the only opinion that really matters.

If I had to pick a confidence fly from this lot, it would be the Same Thing Murray. First, I like the peacock herl body; second, it has a prominent green butt that seems to be a common thing in many successful salmon flies; and third, it has a palmered hackle collar. The palmered collar dams up a little water and causes the fly to swim back and forth a bit when retrieved. If the water was really low, and I wanted something very stealthy, I might make a different choice like a tiny Black Ghost or Green Butt Bear Hair—mostly because they are just a little simpler and generally come out better in small sizes—or I might tie something custom with only a very few wing fibers, no throat, no butt, no rib, a thin black floss body, and one piece of micro krystal flash.

HAIR WING JOCK SCOTT

- **Hook:** Standard or low-water salmon single or double
- **Tag:** Silver tinsel
- **Tail:** Golden pheasant crest
- **Body:** Rear half—Yellow floss; Front half—Black floss
- **Rib:** Oval silver tinsel
- **Hackle:** Guinea fowl tied as a collar and pulled down
- **Wing:** Scarlet, yellow, and blue dyed gray squirrel
- **Head:** Black

Source: Bates, J. D. *Atlantic Salmon Flies and Fishing*. Stackpole Books: Harrisburg, PA; 1970. Page 316.

HAIR WING BLACK DOSE

- **Hook:** Standard or low-water salmon single or double
- **Tag:** Oval silver tinsel
- **Tip:** Yellow floss
- **Tail:** Golden pheasant crest and a few red hackle fibers
- **Body:** Black floss or wool
- **Rib:** Oval silver tinsel
- **Hackle:** Black palmered from the second turn of tinsel and pulled down at the head
- **Wing:** Peacock sword fibers with black bear or arctic fox over
- **Cheeks:** Jungle cock
- **Head:** Black

Source: Stewart, D., and Allen, F. *Flies for Atlantic Salmon.* Northland Press: Interval, New Hampshire; 1991. Page 27.

GREEN BUTT BEAR HAIR

- **Hook:** Standard or low-water salmon single or double
- **Tag:** Silver tinsel
- **Tip:** Green floss or wool
- **Tail:** Black hackle fibers
- **Body:** Black floss or wool
- **Rib:** Oval silver tinsel
- **Hackle:** Black tied as a collar and pulled down
- **Wing:** Fine black bear hair (black squirrel or Arctic fox also works)
- **Head:** Black

Source: Stewart, D., and Allen, F. *Flies for Atlantic Salmon.* Northland Press: Interval, New Hampshire; 1991. Page 26.

RED BUTT BEAR HAIR

- **Hook:** Standard or low-water salmon single or double
- **Tag:** Silver tinsel
- **Tip:** Red floss or wool
- **Tail:** Black hackle fibers
- **Body:** Black floss or wool
- **Rib:** Oval silver tinsel
- **Hackle:** Black tied as a collar and pulled down
- **Wing:** Fine black bear hair (black squirrel or Arctic fox also works)
- **Head:** Black

Source: Stewart, D., and Allen, F. *Flies for Atlantic Salmon.* Northland Press: Interval, New Hampshire; 1991. Page 26.

UNDERTAKER

- **Hook:** #6 to #12 standard or low-water salmon single or double
- **Tag:** Gold tinsel
- **Tip:** Fluorescent-green and fluorescent-red floss
- **Tail:** None
- **Body:** Peacock herl
- **Rib:** Oval gold tinsel or gold wire
- **Hackle:** Black tied as a collar and pulled down
- **Wing:** Fine black bear hair (black squirrel or Arctic fox also works)
- **Cheek:** Jungle cock
- **Head:** Black

Source: Stewart, D., and Allen, F. *Flies for Atlantic Salmon.* Northland Press: Interval, New Hampshire; 1991. Page 77.

ALMOST

- **Hook:** #6 to #12 standard or low-water salmon single
- **Tail:** Brown hackle fibers
- **Body:** Black wool or dubbing
- **Wing:** Fine black bear hair (black squirrel or Arctic fox also works)
- **Head:** Black

Source:: Salmon Flies, "Black Bear" Series & Dark Wing Patterns. W. W. Doak & Sons online catalog.

SAME THING MURRAY

- **Hook:** #6 or #8 low-water salmon hook
- **Tag:** Oval silver tinsel
- **Tail:** Orange hackle fibers
- **Body:** Rear two-thirds—green floss; front third—peacock herl
- **Wing:** Six strands of green krystal Flash with black hair over (moose, bear, squirrel, or Arctic fox)
- **Hackle:** Black tied as a collar and pulled back
- **Head in three parts:** A band of red floss; black ostrich herl; black thread

Source: Marriner, P. C. *Modern Atlantic Salmon Flies*. Frank Amato Publications: Portland, Oregon; 1998. Page 69.

RUTLEDGE, AKA CAINS RIVER SPECIAL

- **Hook:** Standard or low-water salmon single or double
- **Tag:** Oval silver tinsel
- **Tail:** Fluorescent-green wool
- **Body:** Rear half—fluorescent-green wool; front half—peacock herl
- **Rib:** Fine oval silver tinsel or wire
- **Hackle:** Throat hackle of several strands of peacock sword followed by black hackle fibers
- **Wing:** Black squirrel (fine black bear hair or Arctic fox also works)
- **Head:** Black

Source: Stewart, D., and Allen, F. *Flies for Atlantic Salmon*. Northland Press: Interval, New Hampshire; 1991. Page 70.

LIGHTNING BUG

- **Hook:** Standard or low-water salmon single or double
- **Tag:** Oval gold tinsel
- **Tail:** Fluorescent-red wool, cut short
- **Body:** Rear third—Fluorescent-green wool; Front two-thirds—peacock herl
- **Rib:** Oval gold tinsel
- **Hackle:** Black tied as a collar and pulled down
- **Wing:** Fine black bear hair (black squirrel or Arctic fox also works)
- **Head:** Black

Source: Bates, J. D. *Atlantic Salmon Flies and Fishing*. Stackpole Books: Harrisburg, PA; 1970. Page 243.

BLACK GHOST

- **Hook:** Standard or low-water salmon single or double
- **Tag:** Silver tinsel
- **Tail:** Golden pheasant tippet
- **Body:** Black floss or wool
- **Rib:** Oval silver tinsel
- **Hackle:** Bright yellow tied as a collar
- **Wing:** White polar bear or Arctic fox
- **Head:** Black

Source: Stewart, D., and Allen, F. *Flies for Atlantic Salmon.* Northland Press: Interval, New Hampshire; 1991. Page 27.

NIGHT HAWK

- **Hook:** Standard or low-water salmon single or double
- **Tag:** Silver tinsel
- **Tip:** Yellow floss
- **Tail:** Golden pheasant crest with kingfisher substitute over
- **Body:** Flat silver tinsel
- **Rib:** Oval silver tinsel
- **Hackle:** Black as a collar pulled down
- **Wing:** Fine black bear or squirrel with a golden pheasant crest over
- **Head:** Black or red

Source: Stewart, D., and Allen, F. *Flies for Atlantic Salmon.* Northland Press: Interval, New Hampshire; 1991. Page 59.

LIGHTER OR BRIGHTER COLORED FLIES

I don't fish these flies very often. The exception for me is that I fish a #2 Silver Rat quite a bit in the Miramichi during June when I'm hoping for a big silver bullet fresh in off the tide. The theory is that the shiny silver body and gray squirrel wing make this fly look a bit like a saltwater bait fish. I'd say over the years that this has been my best June fly for big, early salmon on the Miramichi.

A small Brown Bomber was probably Seabury Stanton's favorite Cains River wet fly. It is not to be confused with the bomber dry fly that is often tied in brown or natural deer hair color.

The Copper Killer is a very famous Cains River fly mentioned by a lot of people. The theory here is that the red colors and copper-colored body show up well against the tannic water of the Cains River. Is it true? I don't know, but many hundreds of Cains salmon have been caught on the Copper Killer.

BROWN BOMBER

- **Hook:** Standard or low-water salmon single or double
- **Tag:** Silver tinsel
- **Tip:** Yellow floss
- **Tail:** Golden pheasant crest
- **Butt:** Black ostrich herl or wool
- **Body:** Brown floss or wool
- **Rib:** Silver oval tinsel
- **Hackle:** Brown tied as a collar and pulled down
- **Wing:** Red pine squirrel with a golden pheasant crest over
- **Cheeks:** Jungle cock
- **Head:** Black

Source: Leonard, J. E. *FLIES: A Dictionary of 2,200 Patterns.* A. S. Barnes and Company: Cranbury, New Jersey; 1950. Page 271.

YELLOW FAIRY

- **Hook:** Standard or low-water salmon single or double
- **Tag:** Silver tinsel
- **Tail:** Golden pheasant crest
- **Body:** Yellow wool or dubbing
- **Rib:** Oval silver tinsel
- **Hackle:** Yellow palmered over the front half of the body
- **Wing:** Bronze mallard in strips
- **Head:** Black

Source: Bates, J. D. *Atlantic Salmon Flies and Fishing*. Stackpole Books: Harrisburg, PA; 1970. Page 305.

COSSEBOOM

- **Hook:** Standard or low-water salmon single or double
- **Tag:** Oval silver tinsel
- **Tail:** Olive-green floss (Pearsall's #82)
- **Body:** Olive-green floss (Pearsall's #82)
- **Rib:** Flat silver tinsel
- **Wing:** Gray squirrel extending to the end of the tail
- **Hackle:** Lemon-yellow tied as a collar
- **Head:** Red

Source: Bates, J. D. *Atlantic Salmon Flies and Fishing*. Stackpole Books: Harrisburg, PA; 1970. Page 237.

MIRAMICHI COSSEBOOM

- **Hook:** Standard or low-water salmon single or double
- **Tag:** Oval gold tinsel
- **Tail:** Kelly-green hackle fibers
- **Body:** Kelly-green floss or wool
- **Rib:** Gold flat tinsel
- **Hackle:** Yellow tied as a collar
- **Wing:** Gray squirrel
- **Head:** Black

Source: Stewart, D., and Allen, F. *Flies for Atlantic Salmon*. Northland Press: Interval, New Hampshire; 1991. Page 38.

SILVER RAT

- **Hook:** Standard or low-water salmon single or double
- **Tag:** Fine oval gold tinsel or wire
- **Tail:** Golden pheasant crest
- **Body:** Flat silver tinsel
- **Rib:** Oval gold tinsel
- **Hackle:** Soft grizzly tied as a collar
- **Wing:** Gray fox guard hairs
- **Head:** Red

Source: Stewart, D., and Allen, F. *Flies for Atlantic Salmon*. Northland Press: Interval, New Hampshire; 1991. Page 67.

RUSTY RAT

- **Hook:** Standard or low-water salmon single or double
- **Tag:** Oval gold tinsel
- **Tail:** Peacock sword fibers
- **Body:** Rear half—orange-yellow floss vailed on top with several strands of the floss; front half—peacock herl
- **Rib:** Oval gold tinsel
- **Hackle:** Soft grizzly tied as a collar
- **Wing:** Gray fox guard hairs
- **Head:** Red

Source: Stewart, D., and Allen, F. *Flies for Atlantic Salmon.* Northland Press: Interval, New Hampshire; 1991. Page 67.

CAINS COPPER

- **Hook:** Standard or low-water salmon single or double
- **Tag:** Copper wire
- **Tail:** Red hackle fibers
- **Body:** Flat copper tinsel
- **Rib:** Copper wire
- **Hackle:** Black tied as a collar
- **Wing:** A few hairs of orange tied squirrel over which is gray squirrel
- **Head:** Black

Source: Stewart, D., and Allen, F. *Flies for Atlantic Salmon.* Northland Press: Interval, New Hampshire; 1991. Page 35.

COPPER KILLER

- **Hook:** Standard or low-water salmon single or double
- **Tag:** Copper wire
- **Tip:** Fluorescent-green floss
- **Tail:** Red ringneck pheasant body feather
- **Butt:** Red floss or wool
- **Body:** Flat copper tinsel
- **Rib:** Copper wire
- **Hackle:** Orange hackle fibers tied as a throat
- **Wing:** Red pine squirrel tail
- **Head:** Red

Source: Stewart, D., and Allen, F. *Flies for Atlantic Salmon.* Northland Press: Interval, New Hampshire; 1991. Page 37.

PROFESSOR

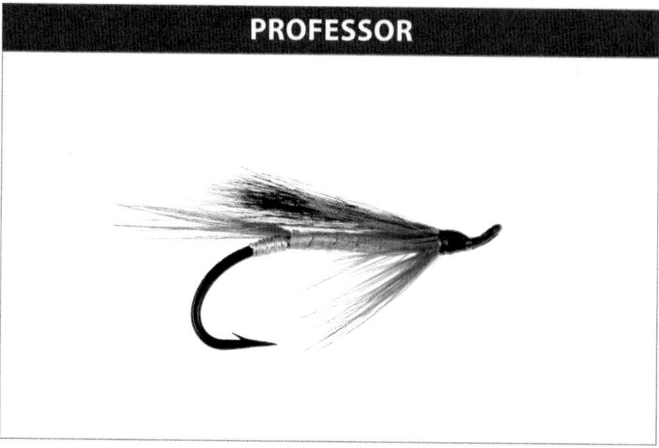

- **Hook:** Standard or low-water salmon single or double
- **Tag:** Oval silver tinsel
- **Tail:** Red hackle fibers
- **Body:** Yellow floss
- **Rib:** Oval silver tinsel
- **Hackle:** Brown hackle tied as a collar and pulled down
- **Wing:** Red pine squirrel tail
- **Head:** Black

Source: Leonard, J. E. *FLIES: A Dictionary of 2,200 Patterns.* A. S. Barnes and Company: Cranbury, New Jersey; 1950. Page 266.

FALL STREAMERS

Fall streamers touch the heart of Cains River salmon fishing. We are talking about cold-water, gray days with a little wind-blown rain and big, aggressive fall salmon determined to beat out all competitors for the opportunity to spawn with the mate of their choice.

I used to believe that salmon struck flies out of an old predatory reflex, and I still have no doubt that is the major part of it throughout most of the season. I've caught, though, big cock salmon that were laying behind individual boulders in narrow, fast runs in the upper Cains that I am convinced were simply waiting there for the hen of their dreams to swim by. These fish would outright hammer the fly when it came close and then put up an incredible struggle. The hens, too, at this time of year are often very aggressive and territorial. I now believe that the flies that they take are often seen as competitors for their spawning rights, as in a parr that might try to sneak in and fertilize the hen salmon's eggs, or a brook trout that might eat those same eggs.

The chief qualities of a successful fly for this application would be to appear lifelike and highly visible. On this side of the Atlantic, fall flies are very often red and orange colored and contain a lot of flash material. Brook trout are available in virtually all the salmon streams of North America, and they adopt red coloration in the fall. I have seen spawning salmon in the Cains River actively drive brook trout away from the redds that they are building. I'm sure the brook trout are crowding the salmon hoping for a meal of salmon eggs. I've little doubt that mimicking the fall color of the brook trout is a main reason that so many successful, large fall patterns have red and orange colors.

You won't find any detailed recipes for the Green and Red Assed Bastard flies. According to Joe Bate's in *Streamer Fly Tying and Fishing*, these were given to him by a noted fisherman and—according to one of my friends who knew him—a very colorful man from Worcester, Massachusetts, named Paul Kukonen. The fly was developed while fishing at Ted Crosby's camp at Wasson's Bar in Blissfield, New Brunswick—a few miles above the Mouth of the Cains. These flies had shaggy black wool bodies, fluorescent-green or red butts, and were tied with red squirrel wings, and according to Bate's, they were the top pattern that Crosby's camp used on the Miramichi and the Cains.

According to Byron Coughlin, owner of Country Haven Outfitters, whose guides fish the Cains more than anyone that I know, the Mickey Finn is the best fall salmon fly that there is. I have always liked it a lot too, but I wanted a version of it with a hackle collar at the head and plenty of flash material. If we have good water, it is not unusual for me to fish the last three weeks of the season using nothing but my October Killer fly. I generally tie these large on #2 streamer hooks, but I also fish the October Killer Junior with which I drop down to #4 salmon iron as my hook. The flies goes from almost three inches long down to under two. To turn a standard Mickey Finn into an October Killer, just add a piece or two of your favorite flash between each color of hair, leave a little room at the head and palmer in pair of orange or orange-and-black hackles as a collar, and add an appropriately sized pair of jungle cock eyes—though I treat the eyes as optional.

Not all streamer fishing is about sticking a huge fly in the face of a cock salmon. There are such things as sparse streamers, and in the case of a fly called the Sneaky, it is even ultra-sparse. I tie the Sneaky on #12 or #10 doubles by preference, though I do fish singles as well. The Sneaky has an orange floss body, silver tinsel for a butt and rib, two or three strands of gold krystal flash in the micro or midge size, and a wing of orange-and-black bucktail. I tie this fly so sparsely that I actually count the hairs. It is a little different every time depending on my material, but I would say maybe a dozen strands of bucktail. I like about two-thirds orange and one-third black. I put in just an equally tiny amount of orange hackle tips for the throat. There is no topping. I usually add very small jungle cock eyes, too, though I'm not sure that it matters. I've had the very best luck with this fly or an equally sparsely tied Ally's Shrimp, swinging it very slowly on six- or even four-pound test in the lowest of low-water conditions.

WILLIE GUNN

- **Hook:** One-inch to two-inch tube or Waddington shank
- **Body:** Gold tinsel or black floss
- **Rib:** Oval gold tinsel or wire
- **Wing:** Spare mix of yellow, orange, and black bucktail tied all around the tube or shank
- **Head:** Red or black

Source: Mann, C. *Hairwing & Tube Flies for Salmon & Steelhead.* Stackpole Books: Mechanicsburg, Pennsylvania; 2004. Pages 194–95.

GRAY GHOST

- **Hook:** Heavy streamer or low-water salmon
- **Tag:** Silver tinsel
- **Body:** Orange floss
- **Rib:** Flat silver tinsel
- **Hackle:** Sparse white bucktail under the hook, five or six Peacock herl longer than the bucktail, a golden pheasant crest
- **Wing:** Blue dun hackles
- **Shoulder:** Silver pheasant breast feather
- **Cheek:** Jungle cock
- **Head:** Black

Source: Leonard, J. E. *FLIES: A Dictionary of 2,200 Patterns*. A. S. Barnes and Company: Cranbury, New Jersey; 1950. Page 263.

ALLY'S SHRIMP

- **Hook:** #4 to #12 single or double salmon
- **Tag:** Fine oval gold tinsel
- **Tail:** Orange bucktail with strands of pearl krystal flash
- **Body:** Rear half—red floss; front half—black floss
- **Rib:** Oval gold tinsel
- **Underwing:** Gray squirrel tail, top and bottom, tied flat as a vale
- **Wing:** Golden pheasant tippet ending in line with the tag
- **Hackle:** Hot orange hackle tied long
- **Head:** Red

Source: Marriner, P. C. *Modern Atlantic Salmon Flies*. Frank Amato Publications: Portland, Oregon; 1998. Page 88.

GENERAL PRACTITIONER

- **Hook:** Standard or low-water salmon single or double
- **Tail/Antennae:** Sparse orange bucktail valed by a small golden pheasant red body feather
- **Body:** Rear half—orange dubbing or yarn to the middle of the hook shank
- **Rib:** Oval gold tinsel to the midpoint
- **Hackle:** Orange hackle palmered to the midpoint
- **Mid-Wing/Back:** Golden pheasant tippet cut into a "V", cemented and tied in flat at the midpoint, then covered with a golden pheasant body feather
- **Body:** Front half—same as the rear half
- **Rib:** Same as the rear half
- **Hackle:** Same as the rear half
- **Front-Wing/Back:** Golden pheasant body feather tied flat
- **Head:** Red

Source: Stewart, D., and Allen, F. *Flies for Atlantic Salmon*. Northland Press: Interval, New Hampshire; 1991. Page 22.

BRAD BURNS OCTOBER KILLER

- **Hook:** #2 to #6 strong streamer or low water salmon
- **Tag:** Red floss
- **Body:** Silver flat mylar or tinsel
- **Rib:** Oval silver tinsel
- **Wing:** Red bucktail, over orange bucktail, over yellow bucktail with plenty of flash mixed in
- **Hackle:** Three wraps of orange or red hackle followed by two wraps of black hackle as a collar
- **Head:** Black

Source: Burns, B. *Closing the Season*. Burns Fly Fishing: Falmouth, Maine; 2013. Page 95.

MICKEY FINN

- **Hook:** Standard salmon or heavy streamer hook
- **Tag:** Silver tinsel
- **Tip:** Red floss
- **Body:** Flat silver tinsel
- **Rib:** Oval silver tinsel
- **Wing:** Small bunch of yellow bucktail, followed by a similar size bunch of red bucktail, with a large bunch of yellow bucktail on top
- **Head:** Black

Source: Stewart, D., and Allen, F. *Flies for Atlantic Salmon*. Northland Press: Interval, New Hampshire; 1991. Page 56.

RED ASSED BASTARDS (RAB)

- **Hook:** Heavy streamer (Partridge CS2)
- **Tag:** Silver tinsel
- **Tail:** Brown hackle fiber
- **Butt:** Fluorescent-red yarn
- **Body:** Brown dubbing or wool
- **Rib:** Oval silver tinsel
- **Hackle:** Throat of brown hackle
- **Wing:** Red pine or fox squirrel
- **Head:** Black

Source: Bates, J. D. *Streamer Fly Tying and Fly Fishing*. Stackpole Books: Harrisburg, Pennsylvania; 1950. Page 60.

GREEN ASSED BASTARDS (GAB)

- **Hook:** Heavy streamer (Partridge CS2)
- **Tag:** Silver tinsel
- **Tail:** Black hackle fibers
- **Butt:** Fluorescent-green yarn
- **Body:** Black dubbing or wool
- **Rib:** Oval silver tinsel
- **Hackle:** Throat of black hackle
- **Wing:** Black squirrel wing
- **Head:** Black

Source: Bates, J. D. *Streamer Fly Tying and Fly Fishing*. Stackpole Books: Harrisburg, Pennsylvania; 1950. Page 60.

SNEAKY

- **Hook:** #10 or #12 Partridge Wilson dry fly salmon hook
- **Tag:** Fine oval gold tinsel or wire.
- **Tail:** Two strands of orange krystal flash, twice as long as the body
- **Body:** Orange floss
- **Rib:** Fine oval gold tinsel or wire
- **Hackle:** A few orange hackle fibers tied as a throat about half as long as the body
- **Wing:** No more than 10 fine orange bucktail hairs and three strand of orange krystal flash, extending about three times the length of the body
- **Cheeks:** Tiny jungle cock
- **Head:** Red

Source: Marriner, P. C. *Modern Atlantic Salmon Flies*. Frank Amato Publications: Portland, Oregon; 1998. Page 96.

CHIEF NEEDABAH

- **Hook:** Strong streamer or low-water salmon
- **Tag:** Flat silver tinsel
- **Tail:** Section of red duck or goose quill
- **Body:** Red floss tied in two sections with the first third broken by a throat of red saddle hackle
- **Rib:** Narrow flat silver tinsel
- **Wing:** Red saddle hackles valing two yellow saddle hackle
- **Hackle:** Red saddle hackle tied as a collar
- **Cheeks:** Jungle cock usually tied short
- **Head:** Black

Source: Bates, J. D. *Streamer Fly Tying and Fly Fishing*. Stackpole Books: Harrisburg, Pennsylvania; 1950. Page 255.

CAINS RIVER STREAMERS

These flies still work on the Cains today, too, just as they worked for the Allens and Wades 100 years ago. When Bill Utley tied the streamers for these photographs, he saved out a few for us to fish with in the fall of 2018. We landed salmon on them at the Mahoney Brook camp during the last few days of the season. It was a great bit of nostalgia. Note that the name of the pattern originator is listed after some flies.

ALECK'S WONDER

(Oscar Webber)

- **Hook:** Heavy streamer (Partridge CS42 or Mustad S82-3906B), usually a #2
- **Tag:** Flat gold tinsel
- **Tail:** Two sections of barred wood duck flank feather with a thin section of French blue goose wing of the same length
- **Body:** Flat gold tinsel
- **Wing:** Scarlet saddle hackles covered by a rich yellow saddle hackle on each side that are then covered by a French blue saddle hackle on each side
- **Cheeks:** Jungle cock usually tied long
- **Hackle:** A collar of three turns of scarlet saddle hackle followed by two turns of French blue saddle hackle.
- **Head:** Black

Source: Bates, J. D. *Streamer Fly Tying and Fly Fishing*. Stackpole Books: Harrisburg, Pennsylvania; 1950. Page 245.

WILKINSON STREAMER

(Oscar Webber)

- **Hook:** Heavy streamer (Partridge CS42 or Mustad S82-3906B), usually a #2
- **Tag:** Flat silver tinsel
- **Tail:** Two sections of barred wood duck flank feather
- **Body:** Flat silver tinsel
- **Wing:** Two medium-brown saddle hackles covered by gray Plymouth rock (grizzly) saddle hackle on each side
- **Cheeks:** Jungle cock usually tied long
- **Hackle:** Three turns of magenta saddle hackle followed by two turns of French blue saddle hackle tied as a collar
- **Head:** Black

Source: Bates, J. D. *Streamer Fly Tying and Fly Fishing*. Stackpole Books: Harrisburg, Pennsylvania; 1950. Page 249.

PEET'S MASTERPIECE STREAMER

(Fred Peet)

- **Hook:** Heavy streamer (Partridge CS42 or Mustad S82-3906B), usually a #2
- **Tag:** Flat gold tinsel
- **Tail:** Two sections of barred wood duck flank feather
- **Body:** Flat gold tinsel
- **Wing:** Two French blue saddle hackles with a cream badger saddle hackle on each side
- **Cheeks:** Jungle cock usually tied long
- **Hackle:** A collar of three turns of chocolate-brown saddle hackle followed by two turns of French blue saddle hackle
- **Head:** Black

Source: Bates, J. D. *Streamer Fly Tying and Fly Fishing*. Stackpole Books: Harrisburg, Pennsylvania; 1950. Page 247.

HIGHLANDER STREAMER

(Fred Peet)

- **Hook:** Heavy streamer (Partridge CS42 or Mustad S82-3906B), usually a #2
- **Tag:** Flat silver tinsel
- **Tail:** Two sections of barred wood duck flank feather
- **Body:** Flat silver tinsel
- **Wing:** Two emerald (Highlander) green saddle hackles with gray Plymouth rock (grizzly) saddle hackles on each side
- **Cheeks:** Jungle cock usually tied long
- **Hackle:** Three turns of emerald green saddle hackle followed with two turns of gray Plymouth rock saddle hackle as a collar
- **Head:** Black

Source: Bates, J. D. *Streamer Fly Tying and Fly Fishing*. Stackpole Books: Harrisburg, Pennsylvania; 1950. Pages 246–47.

SCOTCH LASSIE STREAMER

- **Hook:** Heavy streamer (Partridge CS42 or Mustad S82-3906B), usually a #2
- **Tag:** Flat silver tinsel
- **Tail:** Two sections of barred wood duck flank feather
- **Body:** Flat silver tinsel
- **Wing:** Two French blue saddle hackles with a rich yellow saddle hackle on each side
- **Cheeks:** Jungle cock usually tied long
- **Hackle:** A collar of three turns of magenta saddle hackle followed by two turns of French blue saddle hackle
- **Head:** Black

Source: Bates, J. D. *Streamer Fly Tying and Fly Fishing*. Stackpole Books: Harrisburg, Pennsylvania; 1950. Page 248.

RAINBOW STREAMER

- **Hook:** Heavy streamer (Partridge CS42 or Mustad S82-3906B), usually a #2
- **Tag:** Flat gold tinsel
- **Tail:** Two sections of barred wood duck flank feather
- **Body:** Flat gold tinsel
- **Wing:** Two French blue saddle hackles with a golden yellow saddle hackle on each side
- **Cheeks:** Jungle cock usually tied long
- **Hackle:** A collar of rich yellow saddle hackle mixed with a few turns of scarlet saddle hackle
- **Head:** Black

Source: Bates, J. D. *Streamer Fly Tying and Fly Fishing*. Stackpole Books: Harrisburg, Pennsylvania; 1950. Page 247.

MIRAMICHI STREAMER

(Fred Peet)

- **Hook:** Heavy streamer (Partridge CS42 or Mustad S82-3906B), usually a #2
- **Tag:** Flat gold tinsel
- **Tail:** Two sections of barred wood duck flank feather
- **Body:** Flat gold tinsel
- **Wing:** Two magenta saddle hackles with a medium-blue saddle hackle on each side
- **Cheeks:** Jungle cock usually tied long
- **Hackle:** A collar of three turns of magenta saddle hackle followed by two turns of medium-blue saddle hackle
- **Head:** Black

Source: Bates, J. D. *Streamer Fly Tying and Fly Fishing*. Stackpole Books: Harrisburg, Pennsylvania; 1950. Page 247.

ALLEN'S FIRST CHOICE STREAMER

(Oscar Webber)

- **Hook:** Heavy streamer (Partridge CS42 or Mustad S82-3906B), usually a #2
- **Tag:** Flat silver tinsel
- **Tail:** Two sections of barred wood duck flank feather
- **Body:** Flat silver tinsel
- **Wing:** Two French blue saddle hackles with a cream badge saddle hackle on each side
- **Cheeks:** Jungle cock usually tied long
- **Hackle:** A collar of three turns of scarlet saddle hackle followed by two turns of rich yellow saddle hackle
- **Head:** Black

Source: Bates, J. D. *Streamer Fly Tying and Fly Fishing*. Stackpole Books: Harrisburg, Pennsylvania; 1950. Page 245.

KIDDER STREAMER

(Fred Peet)

- **Hook:** Heavy streamer (Partridge CS42 or Mustad S82-3906B), usually a #2
- **Tag:** Flat gold tinsel
- **Tail:** Two sections of barred wood duck flank feather
- **Body:** Flat gold tinsel
- **Wing:** Two chocolate brown saddle hackles with a gray Plymouth rock (grizzly) saddle hackle on each side
- **Cheeks:** Jungle cock usually tied long
- **Hackle:** Chocolate brown saddle hackle tied as a collar
- **Head:** Black

Source: Bates, J. D. *Streamer Fly Tying and Fly Fishing*. Stackpole Books: Harrisburg, Pennsylvania; 1950. Page 247.

HERMAN'S FAVORITE STREAMER

(Raymond Herman)

- **Hook:** Heavy streamer (Partridge CS42 or Mustad S82-3906B), usually a #2
- **Tag:** Flat gold tinsel
- **Tail:** Two sections of barred wood duck flank feather
- **Body:** Flat gold tinsel
- **Wing:** Two scarlet saddle hackles with medium brown saddle hackles on each side
- **Cheeks:** Jungle cock usually tied long
- **Hackle:** A collar of medium brown saddle hackle
- **Head:** Black

Source: Bates, J. D. *Streamer Fly Tying and Fly Fishing*. Stackpole Books: Harrisburg, Pennsylvania; 1950. Page 246.

ROARING RAPIDS STREAMER

- **Hook:** Heavy streamer (Partridge CS42 or Mustad S82-3906B), usually a #2
- **Tag:** Flat silver tinsel
- **Tail:** Two sections of barred wood duck flank feather with a thin section of red goose wing in between
- **Body:** Flat silver tinsel
- **Wing:** Two scarlet saddle hackles with a rich yellow saddle hackle on each side
- **Cheeks:** Jungle cock usually tied long
- **Hackle:** A collar of French blue saddle hackle
- **Head:** Black

Source: Bates, J. D. *Streamer Fly Tying and Fly Fishing*. Stackpole Books: Harrisburg, Pennsylvania; 1950. Page 248.

SILVER DOCTOR STREAMER

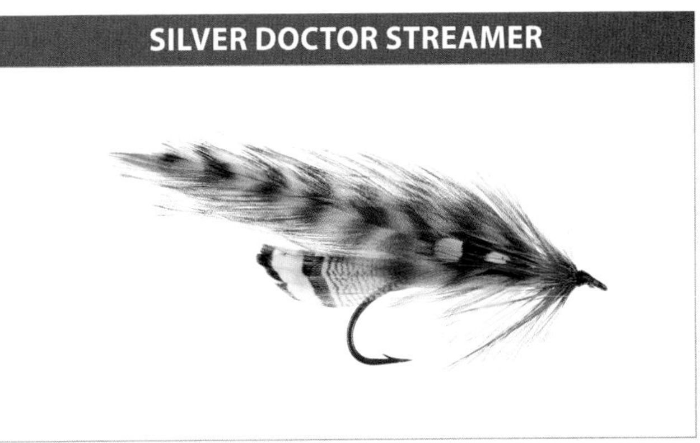

(Oscar Webber)

- **Hook:** Heavy streamer (Partridge CS42 or Mustad S82-3906B), usually a #2
- **Tag:** Flat silver tinsel
- **Tail:** Two sections of barred wood duck flank feather
- **Body:** Flat silver tinsel
- **Wing:** Two medium-brown saddle hackles with a gray Plymouth rock (grizzly) saddle hackle on each side
- **Cheeks:** Jungle cock usually tied long
- **Hackle:** A collar of three turns of French blue saddle hackle followed by two turns of gray Plymouth rock (grizzly) saddle hackle
- **Head:** Black

Source: Bates, J. D. *Streamer Fly Tying and Fly Fishing*. Stackpole Books: Harrisburg, Pennsylvania; 1950. Page 248.

SILVER GREY STREAMER

(Oscar Webber)

- **Hook:** Heavy streamer (Partridge CS42 or Mustad S82-3906B), usually a #2
- **Tag:** Flat silver tinsel
- **Tail:** Two sections of barred wood duck flank feather
- **Body:** Flat silver tinsel
- **Wing:** Two bright orange saddle hackles with a gray Plymouth rock (grizzly) saddle hackle on each side
- **Cheeks:** Jungle cock usually tied long
- **Hackle:** A collar of gray Plymouth rock (grizzly) saddle hackle
- **Head:** Black

Source: Bates, J. D. *Streamer Fly Tying and Fly Fishing*. Stackpole Books: Harrisburg, Pennsylvania; 1950. Page 248.

WADE'S CHOICE STREAMER

(Oscar Webber)

- **Hook:** Heavy streamer (Partridge CS42 or Mustad S82-3906B), usually a #2
- **Tag:** Flat silver tinsel
- **Tail:** Two sections of barred wood duck flank feather with a thin section of French blue goose wing feather in between
- **Body:** Flat silver tinsel
- **Wing:** Two gray Plymouth rock (grizzly) saddle hackles with a scarlet saddle hackle on each side and then covered by a rich yellow saddle hackle on each side
- **Cheeks:** Jungle cock usually tied long
- **Hackle:** A collar of Plymouth rock (grizzly) saddle hackle mixed with a rich yellow saddle hackle.
- **Head:** Black

Source: Bates, J. D. *Streamer Fly Tying and Fly Fishing*. Stackpole Books: Harrisburg, Pennsylvania; 1950. Pages 248–49.

CAINS RIVER STREAMER

(Fred Peet)

- **Hook:** Heavy streamer (Partridge CS42 or Mustad S82-3906B), usually a #2
- **Tag:** Flat silver tinsel
- **Tail:** Two sections of barred wood duck flank feather
- **Body:** Flat silver tinsel
- **Wing:** Two French blue saddle hackles with a beige saddle hackle on each side
- **Cheeks:** Jungle cock usually tied long
- **Hackle:** Beige saddle hackle tied as a collar
- **Head:** Black

Source: Bates, J. D. *Streamer Fly Tying and Fly Fishing*. Stackpole Books: Harrisburg, Pennsylvania; 1950. Page 246.

DUNK'S SPECIAL STREAMER

(Oscar Webber)

- **Hook:** Heavy streamer (Partridge CS42 or Mustad S82-3906B), usually a #2
- **Tag:** Flat silver tinsel
- **Tail:** Two sections of barred wood duck flank feather
- **Body:** Flat silver tinsel
- **Wing:** Two magenta saddle hackles with a French blue saddle hackle on each side
- **Cheeks:** Jungle cock usually tied long
- **Hackle:** Three turns of magenta saddle hackle followed by two turns of French blue saddle hackle
- **Head:** Black

Source: Bates, J. D. *Streamer Fly Tying and Fly Fishing*. Stackpole Books: Harrisburg, Pennsylvania; 1950. Page 246.

ALLEN'S LAST CHANCE STREAMER

(Oscar Webber)

- **Hook:** Heavy streamer (Partridge CS42 or Mustad S82-3906B), usually a #2
- **Tag:** Flat silver tinsel
- **Tail:** Two sections of barred Wood Duck flank feather
- **Body:** Flat silver tinsel
- **Wing:** Two French blue saddle hackles with a gray Plymouth rock (grizzly) saddle hackle on each side
- **Cheeks:** Jungle cock usually tied long
- **Hackle:** A collar of three turns of gray Plymouth rock (grizzly) saddle hackle followed by two turns of French blue saddle hackle
- **Head:** Black

Source: Bates, J. D. *Streamer Fly Tying and Fly Fishing*. Stackpole Books: Harrisburg, Pennsylvania; 1950. Page 245.

SPECIALTY WET FLIES AND BUGS

This category is a sort of catch-all for flies that don't fit into the standard hair-wing wet fly and streamer molds. Perhaps one of the most famous of these alternative fly designs is the very famous Muddler Minnow, designed to imitate sculpins for brook trout fishing. It isn't as popular for Atlantic salmon these days as it still is for brook trout—several folks I talked to about upper Cains River brook trout said that it was their favorite fly—but the Muddler is still a great salmon fly. For me, the common thread with all the flies in this group is their tendency either by a palmer wound feather and/or thick body as in the Green Machine, or dual splayed out wings as in the Butterfly, or shaggy, spun deer hair head of the Muddler Minnow, is for the fly to push around a bit more water than most flies. This isn't always the answer, but sometimes it is.

On any given day, at any time of the season, there are probably more people fishing on the Miramichi or the Cains Rivers with a Green Machine than all other flies combined. The reason for this is that the fly just plain works well. You can tie this "bug" with no tail at all, or you can add a tail—95 percent of mine have tails, just because it feels right—of krystal flash, bucktail (or similar), or hackle barbules. Mostly, I prefer flash cut short and with the strands tied in individually so that they don't clump together in the water.

One of the drawbacks of the Green Machine is that the standard ties of spun deer hair are quite buoyant, and the smaller sizes tend to skim along the surface. Personally, I have never caught a salmon on the Miramichi or Cains with the fly doing this. As a result, I started tying these years ago using various chenille products for the body instead of spun, hollow deer hair. The flies do sink a lot better, and they catch fish. Perhaps there can be no higher stamp of approval than the fact that the fly is very popular at the Black Brook Salmon Club, where they nicknamed it the "Yum Yum." Tying your own Yum Yum is also much easier than tying a standard Green Machine. Just follow your favorite Green Machine recipe, but instead of spinning deer hair, select a flash or variegated chenille that fits the size of the fly and wind it on in place of spinning hair. I find that the palmer-wound feather of the Green Machine disappears into cactus chenille, so I have stayed away from that material. One of my most productive, very-low-water salmon fly designs is a very small Green Machine tied using micro chenille for the body. I tie it on #12 hooks. It is very hard to spin deer hair finely enough for flies that small, plus, because the fly is so light, it will often break the surface on the swing. I have not had success on the Miramichi or the Cains with flies that plane along the surface on the swing.

Another hot fly of recent times, especially in the deep, slow fall pools of the Cains River, is the marabou streamer. Two colors in particular have found great success. One is nicknamed the Slime Fly, and it is simply lime-green marabou fibers, and the other is the Grape or Purple Slime fly, which uses a dark-purple-colored marabou. No fly that I know of has as much wiggle in slow-moving water as a marabou streamer.

The last fly on my specialty list is the Butterfly, often called the Maurice Ingalls Butterfly, after its inventor, Maurice Ingalls. The main characteristics of this fly are the dual calf tail wings that pulse backward and forward as the fly is stripped or pumped. It was designed for slow-water fishing on the Southwest Miramichi, and until the invention of the Green Machine, it was regarded as the hottest salmon fly on the river. It has fallen out of favor, and one reason I suspect is that it is really a slow-water fly, and with the water-damming feature of the twin upright wings, it would not swim well in quick water. The wings are also hard to tie well, and with easier-to-tie flies around that are also effective, most anglers just don't bother with it.

MUDDLER MINNOW

- **Hook:** Strong streamer (Partridge CS42)
- **Tail:** A pair of short mottled turkey wing sections curving down
- **Body:** Flat gold tinsel
- **Underwing:** Gray squirrel tail
- **Wing:** A pair of mottled turkey wing quill sections, fairly broad
- **Head:** Spun natural deer body hair clipped to form a head and collar

Source: Stewart, D., and Allen, F. *Flies for Atlantic Salmon.* Northland Press: Interval, New Hampshire; 1991. Page 57.

GREEN MACHINE WHITE TAIL

- **Hook:** Strong wet fly (Mustad #3399A)
- **Tail:** White calf tail
- **Body:** Green-dyed deer body hair
- **Hackle:** Brown palmered from the butt
- **Head:** Black

GREEN MACHINE FLASH TAIL

- **Hook:** Low-water salmon
- **Tail:** Eight to 10 strands of krystal flash extending slightly beyond the bend of the hook
- **Butt:** Fluorescent-green floss followed by fluorescent-red floss
- **Body:** Green-dyed deer body hair
- **Hackle:** Brown
- **Head:** Black

FLASH-BODIED GREEN MACHINE, AKA "YUM YUM"

- **Hook:** Strong wet fly (Mustad #3399A)
- **Tail:** White calf tail with krystal flash over
- **Body:** Fluorescent-green/pearl variegated tinsel chenille
- **Hackle:** Brown
- **Head:** Black

"GREEN SLIME" MARABOU

- **Hook:** Heavy streamer (Partridge CS2) or tube
- **Body:** Flat silver tinsel
- **Underwing:** Lime-green or chartreuse krystal flash
- **Collar/Wing:** Chartreuse green or lime marabou wound collar style
- **Head:** Chartreuse floss

Source: Marriner, P. C. *Modern Atlantic Salmon Flies*. Frank Amato Publications: Portland, Oregon; 1998. Page 46.

"THE GRAPE" PURPLE MARABOU

- **Hook:** Heavy streamer (Partridge CS2) or tube
- **Body:** Flat silver tinsel, but not required
- **Underwing:** Clear or purple krystal flash
- **Collar/Wing:** Marabou wound collar style; equal parts magenta first with purple over
- **Head:** Black

Source: Marriner, P. C. *Modern Atlantic Salmon Flies*. Frank Amato Publications: Portland, Oregon; 1998. Pages 84–85.

BUTTERFLY WHITE WING

- **Hook:** Strong wet fly (Mustad #3399A)
- **Tail:** Red hackle fibers
- **Butt:** Fluorescent-green yarn
- **Body:** Peacock herl
- **Wing:** White goat or calf tail divided and tied delta wing style to the sides
- **Hackle:** Brown as a collar
- **Head:** Black

Source: Stewart, D., and Allen, F. *Flies for Atlantic Salmon*. Northland Press: Interval, New Hampshire; 1991. Page 34.

BUTTERFLY ORANGE WING

- **Hook:** Strong wet fly (Mustad #3399A)
- **Tail:** Red hackle fibers
- **Body:** Peacock herl
- **Wing:** Orange goat or calf tail divided and tied delta wing style to the sides
- **Hackle:** Yellow as a collar
- **Head:** Red

DRY FLIES

There is already a lot written about fishing the Bomber and the Whiskers in chapter 9 of this book. A great deal of information exists online about how to tie the Bomber. The Whiskers is much the same except that you don't have the complications of spinning deer hair. One thing to take into account, though, is that when you palmer the hackle onto a bomber, the thread and hackle stem will sink down a fair distance into the spun hair body. This has the benefit of hiding the thread and hackle stem and keeping them safer from the teeth of salmon. This means that when you tie the whiskers you will need a slightly different hackle size relative to the hook than with the bomber so that it won't be of too skinny a profile.

The Carter Bug, championed by Bryant Freeman, is essentially a less densely packed bomber without a front wing and clipped into a much fatter shape. People get into things such as aging the fur used to tie Carter Bugs and bombers in widows over the winter to obtain a more translucent hair fiber etc. I'm not sure how important all that really is, but as with all fly tying, there are folks who think their particular style or touch makes the fly far more successful than other designs.

I carry a selection of dry flies with me during most of the season, though I think they are far less effective early and late in the season when the water is under about 55°F. Having some small ones, on #6 or #8 shorter shanked hooks that have no tail or wing, is a good idea. Stale fish holding in low-water pools will often take these less aggressive offerings when they won't look at a larger fly. Normally speaking, though, fresh Miramichi and Cains salmon love a big #2 or #4 cigar-shaped bomber.

Nearly every color scheme is deployed in Atlantic salmon dry flies, and there are many excellent guides and experienced anglers who believe in having a good selection of patterns to throw at fish that will look at a bomber and not take it. I'm very partial to a natural deer hair body with a brown or brown-and-orange wing—I almost always wind two hackles through my bombers. I've also had very good luck on green bodies with orange hackle as well as green bodies with a yellow thorax, and the Smurf or blue bomber. I don't know why, but frequently, that is the color that they seem to want.

BOMBERS

ORANGE/BROWN BOMBER

(Warren Duncan)

- **Hook:** Strong streamer (Partridge CS42)
- **Tail:** Spars natural deer body hair tied short
- **Body:** Fine natural deer body hair packed tightly
- **Hackle:** Orange saddle hackle palmered through the body
- **Wing:** None
- **Head:** Black

ORANGE/TAN BOMBER

- **Hook:** Strong streamer (Mustad R74-9671)
- **Tail:** White calf tail
- **Body:** Natural deer body hair
- **Hackle:** Orange saddle hackle palmered through the body
- **Wing:** White calf tail tied short
- **Head:** Black

TWO TONE BROWN/ORANGE BOMBER

(Warren Duncan)

- **Hook:** Strong streamer (Mustad R74-9671)
- **Tail:** Natural deer body hair tied short
- **Body:** Fine natural deer body hair from two different hides packed tightly
- **Hackle:** Orange saddle hackle palmered through the body
- **Wing:** Natural deer body hair tied short
- **Head:** Black

GRIZZLY HACKLE BOMBER

(Warren Duncan)

- **Hook:** Strong streamer (Mustad R74-9671)
- **Tail:** Natural deer body hair tied short
- **Body:** Fine natural deer body hair packed tightly
- **Hackle:** Grizzly saddle hackle palmered through the body
- **Wing:** Natural deer body hair tied short
- **Head:** Black

SUNBURST BUCK BUG

- **Hook:** Strong streamer (Partridge CS42)
- **Tail:** Natural deer body hair tied short
- **Body:** Natural deer body hair tightly packed and trimmed to thin profile
- **Hackle:** Yellow and orange saddle hackles palmered through the body
- **Wing:** None
- **Head:** Black

SMALL BOMBER/BUCK BUG

(Warren Duncan)

- **Hook:** Strong streamer (Mustad R74-9671)
- **Tail:** Natural deer body hair tied short
- **Body:** Natural deer body hair tightly packed and trimmed to thin profile
- **Hackle:** Orange saddle hackle palmered through the body
- **Wing:** None
- **Head:** Black

SMALL ORANGE/BROWN BOMBER

- **Hook:** Strong streamer (Partridge CS42)
- **Tail:** White calf tail
- **Body:** Natural deer body hair
- **Hackle:** Orange saddle hackle palmered through the body
- **Wing:** White calf tail
- **Head:** Black

ORANGE/BROWN BOMBER

- **Hook:** Strong streamer (Partridge CS42)
- **Tail:** Natural deer body hair tied short
- **Body:** Natural deer body hair
- **Hackle:** Orange saddle hackle palmered through the body
- **Wing:** Natural deer body hair tied short
- **Head:** Black

BOMBER

(Warren Duncan)

- **Hook:** Strong streamer (Partridge CS42 or Mustad R74-9671))
- **Tail:** Natural deer body hair tied short
- **Body:** Natural deer body hair tightly packed and trimmed to thin profile
- **Hackle:** Orange saddle hackle palmered through the body
- **Wing:** Natural deer body hair tied short
- **Head:** Black

BROWN/YELLOW BOMBER

- **Hook:** Strong streamer (Partridge CS42)
- **Tail:** Natural deer body hair tied short
- **Body:** Natural deer body hair
- **Hackle:** Yellow saddle hackle palmered through the body
- **Wing:** Natural deer body hair tied short
- **Head:** Black

CARTER BUG

- **Hook:** Strong streamer (Partridge CS42)
- **Tail:** A clump of deer body hair three-quarter inch to one inch long
- **Body:** Light tan deer body hair tied fairly loose
- **Hackle:** Five turns of natural red or brown hackle palmered the length of the body
- **Head:** Yellow

Source: Freeman, B. "William Earl 'Bill' Carter." http://www.flyfishingnb.com/billcarter.htm.

WHISKERS

- **Hook:** 4X long streamer hook (Mustad R74-9671)
- **Tail:** A large bunch of gray squirrel tail tied fairly long
- **Body:** Polypropylene floating yarn with a turn or two of yarn under the tail to support the tail
- **Hackle:** Brown stiff saddle hackle palmered the length of the body
- **Wing:** A bunch of deer body hair tied upright and forward.
- **Head:** Black

Source: Stewart, D., and Allen, F. *Flies for Atlantic Salmon*. Northland Press: Interval, New Hampshire; 1991. Page 12.

FEATHER WING SALMON FLIES FROM LEE STURGES'S BOOK *SALMON FISHING ON CAINS RIVER NEW BRUNSWICK*

SILVER WILKINSON

- **Hook:** Standard salmon (Partridge M2)
- **Tag:** Gold tinsel
- **Tip:** Yellow floss
- **Tail:** Golden pheasant crest long and silver pheasant crest short
- **Butt:** Red wool
- **Body:** Flat silver tinsel
- **Rib:** Oval silver tinsel
- **Hackle:** Magenta and teal at throat only
- **Wing:** Married strips yellow over blue over red on each side of golden pheasant tippet—bronze mallard over; golden pheasant crest topping
- **Head:** Black

Source: Leonard, J. E. *FLIES: A Dictionary of 2,200 Patterns*. A. S. Barnes and Company: Cranbury, New Jersey; 1950. Page 278.

DURHAM RANGER

- **Hook:** Standard salmon (Partridge M2)
- **Tag:** Silver tinsel
- **Tip:** Gold floss
- **Tail:** Golden pheasant crest and Indian crow substitute
- **Butt:** Black ostrich herl
- **Body:** Equal section of yellow floss, orange, fiery brown, and black seal fur dubbing substitute
- **Rib:** Flat silver tinsel and silver twist (round tinsel)
- **Hackle:** Yellow badger palmered over the dubbing
- **Throat:** Light blue hackle
- **Wing:** Two jungle cock feathers set back to back, veiled with two pairs of golden pheasant tippets
- **Sides:** Jungle cock
- **Cheeks:** Blue chatterer substitute
- **Topping:** Golden pheasant crest
- **Horns:** Omitted
- **Head:** Black

Source: Jorgensen, P. *Salmon Flies—Their Character, Style, and Dressing*. Stackpole Books: Harrisburg, Pennsylvania; 1978. Pages 131–32.

PARMACHENE BELLE

- **Hook:** Strong wet fly (Mustad S82-3906B) or salmon
- **Tail:** Two small sections of red-and-white swan wing feather, married with the red on top
- **Body:** Dark yellow wool or dubbing, larger toward the head
- **Rib:** Oval silver ribbing
- **Hackle:** One red and one white hackle wrapped as a collar and pulled down
- **Wing:** Pair of wings, one from right and one from left swan wing primary feathers. Each wing made up of married white, red and white sections of equal length extending beyond the tail.
- **Cheeks:** Jungle cock (optional)
- **Head:** Black

Source: Bates, J. D. *Streamer Fly Tying and Fly Fishing*. Stackpole Books: Harrisburg, Pennsylvania; 1950. Page 245.

SILVER DOCTOR

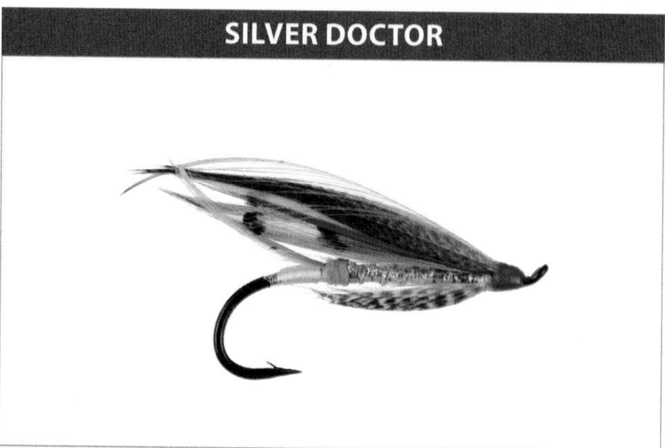

- **Hook:** Standard salmon (Partridge M2)
- **Tag:** Silver tinsel or wire
- **Tip:** Golden-yellow floss
- **Tail:** Golden pheasant crest and blue chatterer substitute
- **Body:** Flat silver tinsel
- **Rib:** Oval silver tinsel
- **Hackle:** A throat of pale blue hackle followed by widgeon
- **Wing:** Mixed golden pheasant tippet in strands with golden pheasant tail; married strands of scarlet, blue, and yellow swan, florican bustard, peacock wing, and light mottled turkey; narrow strips of teal and barred wood duck were omitted; bronze mallard over; a golden pheasant topping over all.
- **Head:** Red

Source: Stewart, D., and Allen, F. *Flies for Atlantic Salmon*. Northland Press: Interval, New Hampshire; 1991. Page 4.

Index